RESEARCH IN ORGANIZATIONAL CHANGE AND DEVELOPMENT

RESEARCH IN ORGANIZATIONAL CHANGE AND DEVELOPMENT

Series Editors: Abraham B. (Rami) Shani
Debra A. Noumair

Previous Volumes:

RESEARCH IN ORGANIZATIONAL
CHANGE AND DEVELOPMENT
VOLUME 29

RESEARCH IN ORGANIZATIONAL CHANGE AND DEVELOPMENT

EDITED BY

ABRAHAM B. (RAMI) SHANI

California Polytechnic State University, USA

And

DEBRA A. NOUMAIR

Teachers College, Columbia University, USA

United Kingdom – North America – Japan
India – Malaysia – China

Emerald Publishing Limited
Howard House, Wagon Lane, Bingley BD16 1WA, UK

First edition 2022

Reprints and permissions service
Contact: permissions@emeraldinsight.com

British Library Cataloguing in Publication Data
A catalogue record for this book is available from the British Library

ISBN: 978-1-80262-174-7 (Print)
ISBN: 978-1-80262-173-0 (Online)
ISBN: 978-1-80262-175-4 (Epub)

ISSN: 0897-3016 (Series)

Printed and bound by CPI Group (UK) Ltd, Croydon, CR0 4YY

ISOQAR certified
Management System,
awarded to Emerald
for adherence to
Environmental
standard
ISO 14001:2004.

Certificate Number 1985
ISO 14001

INVESTOR IN PEOPLE

CONTENTS

ABOUT THE CONTRIBUTORS

Oğuz N. Babüroğlu holds the ARAMA Chair of Action Research at Sabancı University, İstanbul, Turkey, and is the Founding Manager of ARAMA Participatory Management Consulting since 1995. He received his PhD in 1987 at the Wharton School of Business at the University of Pennsylvania in Social Systems Sciences. He specializes in transforming large-scale systems toward new generation models within the action research perspective and has published in the leading journals within this line of inquiry. His publications have appeared in journals such as *Journal of Action Research*, *Human Relations*, *Systems Practice and Action Research*, and *Organization Studies*, largely on topics within the Emery–Trist perspective. He has worked with organizations over 1,200 action research projects ranging from large corporations to civil society institutions, government agencies, and municipalities; has helped design three universities from ground up; and has set up about 15 corporate academies in Turkey as well as in Europe, United States, Russia, and the Middle East.

Ewa Bogacz-Wojtanowska is Professor of the Jagiellonian University and Dean of the Faculty of Management and Social Communication. She conducts research on management of NGOs and social enterprises, functioning of various organizational forms and structures in a civil society, as well as management in higher education institutions. She is an active quality researcher, using for her research in particular observations, individual and group interviews, as well as the methodology of action research.

W. Warner Burke, with a BA in Psychology from Furman University in 1957, taught a semester of high school before serving 2 years of active duty as a Lieutenant in the US Army. After an MA and PhD from the University of Texas, he was a faculty member at the University of Richmond for 3 years. He joined the National Training Laboratories for 8 years responsible for sensitivity training and OD. Returning to academia at Clark University, he served as Chair, Department of Management and the MBA program, for 3 years before joining Teachers College, Columbia University, in 1979. His scholarly work includes over 20 books and 200 articles. He has received many awards, for example, the initial distinguished scholar-practitioner award from the Academy of Management.

Mateo Cruz, is an Assistant Professor of Management at Bentley University. His primary research focuses on diversity, equity, and inclusion (DEI) in workplace contexts using an intersectional lens. His most recent studies examine the different ways women/LGBTQ+ people/BIPOC contend with systemic stereotype threat in occupations where they face chronic underrepresentation. As a scholar-practitioner, Mateo's work is guided by one central goal – to design and deliver evidence-based interventions that advance change leaders at the intersection of identities. He holds 15+ years of experience as an Organization Development (OD) Consultant specializing in inclusive leadership, group & team dynamics, and organization change.

Iben Duvald is an Anthropologist and Assistant Professor at the Department of Management, Aarhus BSS, Aarhus University. In her research, she combines organization design theory and qualitative methods in order to study organization design challenges, collaboration, and social practices within and between organizations within the Danish emergency healthcare system. She is studying organizations at both a macro level (structures) and a micro level (processes and social practices/strategies on an individual level). Since 2014, she has been affiliated with the Emergency Department at Viborg Regional Hospital, Regional Hospital Central Jutland.

Alexis Fink, PhD, has spent more than two decades leading Talent Analytics, Workforce Strategy, Talent Management, and Large-Scale Organizational Change Teams at leading global organizations, including Facebook, Microsoft, and Intel. She has done extensive work in organizational transformation, organizational culture, leadership assessment, and the application of advanced analytical methods to human capital problems. She is an author of a comprehensive book on people analytics, *Investing in People: Financial Impact of Human Resource Initiatives*, and has coedited the recent book on employee surveys, *Employee Surveys and Sensing: Driving Organizational Culture and Performance.*

Frank D. Golom, PhD, is Associate Professor of Applied Psychology at Loyola University Maryland and former founding Associate Director of Executive Education Programs in Change and Consultation at Teachers College, Columbia University. His expertise sits at the nexus of workplace diversity, group dynamics, and organization development and change. He has received several awards for his research, including two Best LGBT Research Awards from the Society for Industrial and Organizational Psychology (SIOP) and a highly commended paper award from Emerald Publishing. He regularly consults to for-profit and not-for-profit organizations on issues of diversity, equity, inclusion, and change, and currently serves as Chair of the Department of Psychology at Loyola.

Anna Góral is Assistant Professor in the Department of Cultural Management, Jagiellonian University. For many years, she has been involved in the work in the nongovernmental and public sectors. She has authored numerous academic publications on issues related to national heritage management, in particular the role of intersectoral cooperation in the development of the heritage. Her special interests include diversity management in organizations, civic activity, and cultural organizations.

Beata Jałocha is Assistant Professor in the Institute of Public Affairs, Jagiellonian University. Her research interests focus mainly on project management and projectification processes, as well as action research. She teaches and conducts research projects involving action research as a methodological approach to solving social and organizational problems.

Piotr Jedynak is Professor of Management. He works at Jagiellonian University in Cracow, Poland, where he holds the positions of Vice President for Personnel Policy and Head of the Management Systems Department. He specializes in risk management, strategic management, and management systems. He is the author of numerous publications and an auditor and consultant to many public and business organizations.

Alec Levenson, PhD, is Senior Research Scientist, Center for Effective Organizations, University of Southern California. His action research and consulting work with companies optimize job and organizational performance and HR systems through applying organization design, job design, human capital analytics, and strategic talent management. Dr Levenson's approach combines the best elements of scientific research and practical, actionable knowledge that companies can use to improve performance. He uses economics, strategy, organization behavior, and industrial–organizational psychology to tackle complex talent and organizational challenges that defy easy solutions. He has trained HR professionals globally in operating model optimization, and the integration of organization development and people analytics.

Michael R. Manning is Research Director and Professor of Leadership, Strategy, and Change at the Center for Values-Driven Leadership, Daniel L. Goodwin College of Business, Benedictine University. He is also a Doctoral Faculty in the School of Leadership Studies at Fielding Graduate University and serves as Associate Editor of *The Journal of Applied Behavioral Science*. His research focuses on occupational stress, the role of emotions in processes of change, and whole systems change. Dr Manning is past Division Chair of the Organization Development and Change Division of the Academy of Management. He has held faculty appointments at New Mexico State University, Case Western Reserve University, and the State University of New York at Binghamton.

Joe McDonagh is Associate Professor of Business (Strategy and Change) at Trinity Business School, Trinity College Dublin, Ireland. His research, teaching, and advisory work focus on the process of leading large-scale strategic, organizational, and technological change programs in civil and public service organizations. He has extensive experience working with government organizations in Ireland, the United Kingdom and Northern Ireland, the European Commission, the Commonwealth of Independent States, and the United Nations.

Grażyna Prawelska-Skrzypek is Professor of Humanities in the field of Management Sciences and Head of the Public Management Department at the Institute of Public Affairs of the Jagiellonian University. She deals with the science of public management and public policy in a humanistic context. Grażyna Prawelska-Skrzypek participated in a social project of action research and conducted classes for doctoral students developing competence in consulting based on action research.

Mathis Schulte's current research focuses on understanding the creation of social networks within organizations, and their effects on employee satisfaction, customer service, and financial performance. His research appeared in the *Journal of Occupational and Organizational Psychology*, the *Journal of Applied Psychology*, and *Organization Science*. Prior to joining HEC in 2009, Mathis was a senior fellow at the Wharton School, University of Pennsylvania, and lectured on Negotiations and Conflict Resolution. Mathis holds an MS in Psychology from the University of Hamburg and a PhD in Social–Organizational Psychology from Columbia University, New York.

Brenda A. Barker Scott is an Organizational Consultant and Educator dedicated to the design and cultivation of impactful, healthy, and collaborative workplaces. As a consultant, she has led ambitious transformation efforts with governments, agencies, and private firms. As an educator, Brenda is an Instructor of OD for the Queen's University Industrial Relations Centre and has taught at the graduate level in the Schools of Industrial Relations and Public Administration. Brenda is coauthor of *Building Smart Teams: A Roadmap to High Performance* and is a frequent contributor to the IRC press. Brenda holds a PhD in Human and Organizational Systems from Fielding Graduate University.

John W. Selsky is a Consulting Fellow at the Institute for Washington's Future, a public-policy center in Seattle, Washington. He studied under the late Eric Trist in the Social Systems Sciences Department at Wharton and has held academic positions in New Zealand, Australia, Turkey, and the United States. He has published in major and minor organization studies journals on systems theory, strategy making in turbulent environments, cross-sector partnerships, and natural resource management. He is retired from university-based educational labor, having managed to evade the worst excesses of the digital academic workplace.

Baruch Shimoni is a Professor of Sociology and Organization Development at the Department of Sociology and Anthropology at Bar-Ilan University, Israel. In his most recent research project, Professor Shimoni links the Bourdieuan concept of habitus to the field of ROCD in order to incorporate the individual and the social in the field. Professor Shimoni published his theoretical and practical ideas in leading journals such as *The Journal of Applied Behavioral Science, Organizational Dynamics*, and *Academy of Management Perspectives,* and in a book *Organization Development and Society: Theory and Practice of Organization Development Consulting* (Routledge, 2019).

Maura Stevenson, PhD, joined MedVet as Chief Human Resources Officer in 2017. Maura oversees all aspects of the Employee Experience, including talent management, compensation and benefits, leadership and employee development, and organizational development. Prior to joining MedVet, Maura served as Vice President of Talent Management at The Wendy's Company, Vice President of Human Resources at Starbucks, and held positions of increasing complexity with Merrill Lynch and The Hartford. She holds a BA from Amherst College, and an MA and PhD from The Ohio State University in Organizational Psychology.

Marc Thompson, BA (Hons), MA (Oxon), MSc (Econ), DSc, is a Governing Body Fellow at Green Templeton College, Oxford, and Coacademic Director of the HEC-Oxford's joint program on Change Leadership. Marc's research interests have focused on workplace and organizational change. He recently coedited *The Oxford University Handbook on Meaningful Work* and has published in the *Journal of Management Studies*, *Human Resource Management*, and the *International Journal of Human Resource Management*, among others. He teaches in a range of degree, open and custom programs at Oxford.

PREFACE

The foreword for ROCD 28, which was written in early February 2020, ended with the invitation to consider contributions to ROCD 29 that reflect new insights and practice stemming from the global COVID-19 pandemic. As we were writing the foreword, no one anticipated the magnitude and unprecedented devastation of the pandemic and its impact on humanity, society, continents, regions, communities, organizations, and families. One of the discoveries across all spheres of life was the phenomenon of individual and system resilience and agility. Becoming agile became a necessity in most aspects of life, work life and organizational life.

Most of the published academic and practitioner work during the past year and in increasing pace during the last few months seems to capture the monumental shifts in mindsets, mental models, nature of work, essence of management, the meaning of participating in emerging change, as well as designing and managing change and development. Some of the road maps of change and planned change that we have had seem to have worked while others did not. Some of the theories and models of change and development that we have had were found to be relevant while others were not. Similar experience can be found around the essence and practice of research and discovery orientations and practice.

This volume, while not addressing head on the pandemic and its impact, includes 10 contributions from colleagues around the globe with powerful insights and potentially relevant impact for researching and practicing organization change and development during and post the pandemic. The emerging people analytics subfield and organization development perspectives are brought together to present an integrated framework that can guide future theoretical development and practice. Bourdieu's concept of social position in the form of "habitus-oriented approach" is advanced to advocate for a new theory that focuses on habitus and social position in order to expand our understanding of human behavior. Kurt Lewin's original view of political labs is advanced to examine the emerging phenomenon of labs as mechanisms for organization change and development. The alignment challenges of strategy and digital technology in government organizations are examined via the use of collaborative inquiry. The essence and context of collaboration in teams is investigated in the emerging new workplace. The current state of organizational DEI practice, including the mixed and limited effectiveness of many individual-level DEI interventions and the lack of clear guidance on how to frame DEI issues from a systems perspective, is examined, and the context-level culture (CLC) framework for diagnosing and addressing diversity-related challenges in the workplace is introduced. While focusing on digital transformation, a new class of socio-technical system, called the Platform STS (P-STS), with new guiding design principle is advanced. The establishment of a small-scale collaborative community and utilization of an action research process generated new insights into the challenges faced by healthcare organizations. The role of action research orientation as a tool that supports new cooperation and partnership between universities and external organizations is examined. Last, in the new ROCD section "Reflection," the author compares organization development (OD) and change management (CM) across eight concepts that are relevant to both OD and CM. The argument is made that OD stresses development of people and change regarding the organization, whereas CM emphasizes facilitation and expanding their business with the client organization. A concluding statement for the comparison of OD and CM is that OD has a rich underpinning of *theory* and a clear set of *values* that provide guidelines for the work with clients, and CM has neither.

These contributions represent a commitment to the future of organization development and change viability and continuous impact on organizational agility. The field continues to evolve, and as the manuscripts in this volume demonstrate, so is the ability to generate a new level of understanding of the emerging complex nature of organizations. If some of the recent views of the emerging work systems that advocate that due to the impact of the pandemic, future workplaces are likely to be hybrid-based, with more hybrid ways of organizing, hybrid ways of managing, hybrid ways of engaging organizational members, hybrid ways of communication, hybrid ways of manufacturing, and hybrid ways of interfacing with suppliers and customers, the field of OD is in a position to be an important player in this transformation.

As can be seen, this volume includes chapters from colleagues across nine countries that explore organization change and development themes in Canada, Denmark, France, Ireland, Israel, Poland, Turkey, United Kingdom, and United States. Collectively, the volume represents rich diversity: multiple generations of authors including senior scholars and practitioners, one of the field's founders, well-established thought leaders and colleagues at various stages of career including newly minted OCD researchers and practitioners, wide variety of topics, ranging from a contribution that is an extension of Kurt Lewin's work to a new conceptual framework that is based on Bourdieu's concept of social position, to the exploration of a new design principle for sociotechnical system theory that meets the reality of digital transformation, to the exploration of "labs" as the engine or learning mechanism for OCD efforts, to the utilization and advancement of our thinking and practice about action research initiatives, to deep level of exploration of collaboration in team development to a new framework for consulting to DEI in organizations from a systems perspective to attempting to differentiate between the field of organization development and change management. Collectively, these chapters and the collaborative inquiry they represent contribute to a sustainable trajectory of research and practice that will enhance our ability to be a relevant player as the world is moving through the pandemic and to deepen the role that the field can play globally.

This volume also introduces a new component to the series. As the field continues to evolve, we felt that asking a member of the community to reflect on an issue or a theme or trace the evolutionary trajectory of a key concept or theory based on their work and bring it to our current digital context for the future would be of added value, as we are approaching volume 30 of ROCD. In this volume, ROCD 29, we are introducing this idea with a manuscript by W. Warner Burke that examines the evolution of OD and CM and draws some distinct boundaries that can be helpful for both future inquiry and practice.

From our editorial perspective, one of the best parts of our work on this series is that our collaboration with the authors always brings new learning, whether in the form of making history accessible and relevant, challenging assumptions, extending the theoretical pillars of our theory in creative ways, or integrating perspectives that heretofore have remained separate. The series has been around long enough to substantiate the claim that we have published some true classics in the field of organization change and development. We have provided scholar-practitioners across career stage, sector, and geography with a platform to share their work and for colleagues to learn from each other in order to inform future collaborations. Moreover, the ROCD series has provided reliable sources for contributing to the ongoing development of organization change and development theory, research, and practice. It is our hope, that as you read through the volume, you will consider your own thoughts and practice and possible contributions to the field and the community and you will contact us to suggest topics or themes for future volumes.

Abraham B. (Rami) Shani
Debra A. Noumair
Editors

ARE OD AND ANALYTICS TWINS SEPARATED AT BIRTH? TOWARD AN INTEGRATED FRAMEWORK

Alec Levenson, Maura Stevenson and Alexis Fink

ABSTRACT

Organization development (OD) and people analytics (PA) have developed and are typically practiced as entirely separate and nonoverlapping disciplines in organizations. We review the principles underlying each of the two disciplines and show much greater overlap and similarities than commonly believed. An integrated framework is provided, along with examples of OD tools that should be part of the PA toolkit for any practitioner. Case studies of what the integrated framework looks like when applied in practice are discussed.

Keywords: Organization development; people analytics; HR analytics; workforce analytics; talent analytics; talent management; organization change; team performance; organization performance

And if I say to you tomorrow

Take my hand, child come with me

It's to a castle I will take you

Where what's to be, they say will be.

But the wind won't blow

You really shouldn't go

It only goes to show …

What is and what should never be. –Led Zeppelin

This chapter is about the intersection of organization development (OD) and people analytics (PA). On the one hand, OD and PA are closely related, with action research forming a core of OD practice as described by the researchers

Research in Organizational Change and Development, Volume 29, 1–31
ISSN: 0897-3016/doi:10.1108/S0897-301620210000029002

who write about and study the phenomena (Coghlan, 2011; Cummings & Worley, 2009; Greenwood & Levin, 2006; Reason & Bradbury, 2001; Shani & Coghlan, 2018). On the other hand, as practiced in organizations, the fields of OD and PA are often viewed as almost polar opposites, invoking metaphors such as left brain vs right brain, head vs heart, etc.

The common perception is that OD is the domain of people who like to work on people issues and change directly in the organization, rolling up their sleeves and diving into the interpersonal and team dynamics. In contrast, PA is viewed as the domain of people who only like to work with data and statistics and try to stay above the fray of the messy reality and ambiguity of working with real people in real time. While all stereotypes are overly simplistic, in this case, the reality is not far removed from the characterization: the overwhelming majority of OD people would never identify themselves as doing PA, and vice versa.

Since analytics is at the core of action research, and action research is a foundation of OD, we find the current state of affairs to be a bit puzzling. Moreover, both OD and PA seek to use information about the organization to improve its functioning, so they share common principles, even though the methods can differ greatly. In this chapter, we explore the intersection of OD and PA: where they overlap in principle and how they might be better integrated in practice. While published research has a place in academic discussions of OD and PA, for the discussion here we draw primarily from the collective experiences we ourselves have had working with organizations along with our colleagues who work in both areas.

In the first part of the article, we start with a discussion of the domains of OD and PA, defining the foundations and boundaries both perceived and actual. A key issue is the deviation of OD practice from the ideals set down by the leading teachers and researchers in the field: when working in organizations, practitioners rarely have the time, resources, and support to do OD process the "right way." The parallel issue in PA theory versus practice is the biases frontline practitioners have toward "hard" data analysis and away from qualitative methods, even though proper social science training encompasses both. The conclusion we reach is that there are opportunities for each domain to be improved by the other.

The second part of the article addresses the intersection of OD and PA in practice. We start with a discussion of specific examples of techniques that can be used dually for diagnosis and change instruments, as well as for data collection and measurement. We end with discussion of case study examples that satisfy the features of Cummings and Worley's comprehensive approach, including data collection and analysis as a core element – demonstrating how an integrated OD and analytics approach can be realized in practice.

DEFINING THE FOUNDATIONS AND BOUNDARIES OF OD AND ANALYTICS

The origins of OD and analytics are quite distinct. OD is grounded in the aspirational and human-centered ideals of the time it emerged, around the 1960s, and focused on how the organizational system can be improved in the interest of both the shareholders and the humans who work in it. In contrast, PA focuses on measuring and improving the efficiency, effectiveness, and impact of human resource (HR) programs, policies, and systems. PA also tries to link people data to business outcomes but often struggles to make a direct connection.

The foundations and boundaries of OD: Cummings and Worley (2009) comprehensively define OD as:

> Organization development is a systemwide application and transfer of behavioral science knowledge to the planned development, improvement, and reinforcement of the strategies, structures, and processes that lead to organization effectiveness.

Specifically,

- OD focuses on "the system," where system can be the entire organization, a business unit, a department, a single site/location, a work group or team, or individual role (job). Transformation of the entire organization or a subsystem is often a primary objective.
- It applies systems diagnostics and bespoke design, using behavioral science research knowledge and insights derived from practice, such as leadership, group dynamics, work design, strategy, organization design, and international relations.
- It is concerned with managing planned change to accomplish the system-level objectives, through an adaptive process for planning and implementing change, not a blueprint for how things should be done.
- It also involves reinforcement of change beyond the initial efforts to implement a change program to a longer-term concern for appropriately institutionalizing new activities within the organization.
- It is oriented to improving organizational effectiveness, which includes (1) building the capability for organizational members to solve their own problems, (2) achieving the desired financial and technical performance needed to execute the strategy, (3) enabling its workforce to be engaged, satisfied and learning, and (4) satisfying external shareholders and stakeholders.

The comprehensiveness of Cummings and Worley's definition also highlights the challenges of taking such an approach in practice. In the real world, there are numerous factors and complexities that get in the way of achieving true organizational effectiveness. Most important are time and resources needed to support OD work and the attention of leadership. The world of business (and nonprofits) moves fast and rarely is there enough time and commitment to engage in such a rigorous process. The lament typically voiced among those on the frontlines is that the world has already changed by the time you finish the rigorous OD process.

A related issue for OD practice is reducing scope to what can be dealt with reasonably, given the available time, energy, and resources. There may be clear organization-wide or larger scope challenges that need to be addressed ultimately. Yet doing so often is not practical because of the complexity: it would require engaging too many stakeholders, dealing with too many interdependencies, etc., rendering it impractical or even impossible to make meaningful progress on the biggest picture challenges in a reasonable amount of time. Instead, the OD practitioner identifies a smaller-scope challenge to address, fully recognizing that addressing the biggest systemic issues will require expanding the scope for diagnostics and solution solving further down the line. The objective is to achieve progress, not perfection, so tangible gains can be made to further a broader agenda.

Because of the challenges of scope, time, and resource availability, rather than engage in the full end-to-end OD process as defined by Cummings and Worley, in the overwhelming majority of cases only a "lite" approach can be applied. The lite approach emphasizes managing planned change as the primary objective, focusing on one part of the system, and applying at least some behavioral science knowledge and practice to the intervention to identify the most important primary driver(s), recognizing that secondary drivers, while important, may have to be addressed in subsequent work. In addition, reinforcement of the change is often addressed later in the process, if there is time.

In practice, the lite approach means (1) getting key decision-makers to focus more broadly on systems issues than they would have otherwise, (2) ensuring a more thorough diagnosis and development of solutions than can happen quickly, (3) introducing different ways of interpreting the data and information to describe the problems at hand, based on behavioral science knowledge, and (4) making sure both the business operating model and needs of the people who work within the operating model are addressed.

Though the lite approach often falls short of Cummings and Worley's ideal in a number of ways, most expert OD practitioners – as well as expert HR business partners and PA practitioners – work hard to ensure that both sides of the perceived trade-off between "what's good for the business" and "what's good for the humans/people" are addressed in their work. The business benefits are measured in terms of the financial and technical performance metrics, and/or measures of strategic success as defined by external stakeholders, such as introducing new products, entering new markets, developing better relationships with government regulators, etc. The people benefits can be any one of the many examples of employee engagement, satisfaction, learning, career advancement, and building bench strength for succession planning or talent pipeline objectives.

In practice, a lot of OD practitioners' time is spent developing and maintaining trusted relationships with senior leaders and key stakeholders throughout the organization. A good case in point is the video the OD Network put together highlighting "What is organization development?" (https://youtu.be/X9NE-_G4AJM). The vignettes address critical challenges such as developing and maintaining trust with key stakeholders, working through complex diagnosis and change challenges, focusing on the system, and relying on scientific knowledge. Yet the specific acts of measurement and analysis are never mentioned.

The reasons for this can be seen by examining the OD competency model developed by the OD Network (https://www.odnetwork.org/page/global-framework). The main competencies of the model are the following:

- Systems change expert: systems change leader; culture builder; innovator
- Efficient designer: efficient designer; process consultant; data synthesizer
- Business advisor: strategic catalyst; results-oriented leader; trusted advisor
- Credible strategist: credible influencer; collaborative communicator; cross-cultural navigator
- Informed consultant: self-aware leader; equity advocate; life-long learner and practitioner

The data synthesizer role, under the efficient designer competency, includes the following:

- Understands and applies basic data gathering methodologies, including both qualitative and quantitative techniques (e.g., surveys, interviews/focus groups, etc.)
- Analyzes performance, identifies the root causes of a system's current level of effectiveness, and proposes tailored solutions at all levels of the system
- Notices similarities between different and apparently unrelated information and quickly identifies the central or underlying issues
- Integrates and translates salient information into simple insights that create clarity and commitment

So the data synthesizer role clearly includes the domain of analytics, yet in practice, analytics – especially advanced statistical analysis – is often the least-employed skill of the OD toolkit. Viewed this way, one could say that, in principle, analytics competencies are just a subset of OD competencies, yet in practice, virtually no one would say that's the case.

Consider the weight given to data analysis itself in this global OD competency model: it is only one of 14 elements listed under the efficient designer competency, and that competency is only one of five main competencies, each of which have 15–16 elements within them, for a total of 75 total elements across the five main competencies. So data analysis accounts for a single, solitary element and represents only 1/75th (1.3%) of the knowledge, skills, and abilities needed for successful OD.

The reality is that most OD practitioners spend the overwhelming majority of their time focusing on activities that are in the other 74 elements that do not cover data collection and statistical analysis; and when they do focus on data collection, it's just as likely to be qualitative data as quantitative data and often directional at best. PA professionals, in contrast, are mostly quite happy to only focus on databases that lend themselves to quantitative analyses and ideally to advanced statistical analysis and often feel like they are operating way outside their comfort zone when presented with situations that require qualitative data collection and analysis; and when they engage "non-hard data" analytic techniques, their approaches typically fall far short of robust and nuanced qualitative analysis.

The foundations and boundaries of people analytics: According to van den Heuvel and Bondarouk (2017), HR (or people) analytics is "the systematic identification and quantification of the people drivers of business outcomes, with the purpose of making better decisions." Another common framing is that PA provides a data-driven approach toward HR management (Lawler, Levenson, & Boudreau, 2004). The following description of an executive education program at MIT nicely summarizes the expectations for PA (https://executive.mit.edu/openenrollment/program/leading-people-at-work/): The course

...illustrate[s] how leading companies are using cutting-edge techniques to analyze data about their employees to make their organizations and their individual employees more successful. Participants will gain a deeper understanding of how and when people analytics can be applied to improve critical issues such as recruiting and hiring, performance evaluation, promotion and training, compensation, and organizational change.

These definitions highlight the emphasis of PA on data and statistical methods, and that PA is designed for scale from the very beginning. PA is designed to address large-scale data analysis from the outset, from data intake through analysis and results distribution. In contrast, OD is designed for very hands-on, bespoke work and solutions. In keeping with that difference, PA draws from research on how to apply social science methodologies to the statistical analysis of people issues in organizations. The approaches often include a role for qualitative work, but usually only as a follow-up to the quantitative analysis, where organizational stakeholders are engaged in sensemaking of the study results to determine potential courses of action to be taken and to validate, even if only in a rudimentary way, the statistical analysis results. Very few PA practitioners would consider conducting qualitative analysis that starts or solely includes interviews of key stakeholders and applies techniques such as case study analysis and informed storytelling without including a statistical analysis to drive the storytelling.

The two main priorities for PA traditionally are (1) data that already exist in various computer systems (compensation; performance management; time keeping/scheduling; job assignments; competency ratings; etc.) and (b) data that are collected through systematic methods like surveys and peer ratings (such as 360-degree feedback). These are the main sources of data used to estimate models of employee engagement and performance. More recently, advances in computer software and in collaborative applications such as Slack, and applying techniques such as natural language processing, have enabled the systematic coding of large volumes of text data which previously had to be coded manually, which had made them too cumbersome to include in the models.

On the one hand, the rapid development of PA capabilities within companies has been very impressive, especially in large organizations with the resources to afford the investment. In many cases the groups are well staffed with deep technical expertise in statistics, surveys, and data science and complement those capabilities with one or more people with more of a general HR and business background. Yet for every group that is blessed with an abundance of such resources and expertise, there are many more organizations where the headcount and levels of expertise are much more limited.

As a consequence, many dedicated PA groups often struggle to move beyond basic data management and reporting, let alone rudimentary statistical analysis, because of a lack of expertise, resources, and/or both. In smaller organizations and/or those with few dedicated PA resources, the basic issue of getting data into a state where it can be used effectively is often a huge challenge: before any advanced analysis can be considered, basic tasks like standardizing messy data and reliably calculating turnover first have to be effectively addressed, and that fundamental work can consume all available people and resources. In fact, the specific example of turnover and its counterpart – headcount – alone consume more PA time and resources than most other metrics combined: they are foundational to leaders understanding who is working for the organization and who is leaving and yet are fiendishly hard to calculate accurately and consistently given often rapid and unpredictable changes in personnel flows, the myriad of different types of employment arrangements that are commonplace these days (temps, contract workers, interns, etc.), and the challenges of assigning people to specific parts of the organization when there are complex matrix reporting relationships and team-based assignments.

Even in the more advanced groups, the focus tends to remain first and foremost on what can be addressed using data that can be analyzed statistically. This leads to the classic challenge articulated as "not everything that can be counted counts, and not everything that counts can be counted." (Note: Most Internet searches attribute this quote to Albert Einstein, though with no reference to any printed citation. Perhaps the first printed citation for the quote is from Cameron, (1963), according to quoteinvestigator.com (https://quoteinvestigator.com/2010/05/26/everything-counts-einstein/)). The counterpart is "you treasure what you measure," meaning once you count or measure something, you pay too much attention to it. This tendency has been memorialized by the classic joke about the person looking for their keys in a dark parking lot, but only under a solitary lamp, even though it's obvious the keys are not there, "because that's where the light is."

This PA emphasis on "hard" data typically leads to a bias toward analyses that are statistically rigorous but which may provide only incremental improvements in understanding the drivers of motivation and behavior: the analyses and insights are overwhelmingly at the individual level because that's the source of the vast majority of reliable data available for statistically rigorous analysis (Levenson, 2015, 2018). In a positive development, the recent proliferation of newfangled ways of analyzing unstructured text in PA has generated a lot more data that can be analyzed statistically; yet at the same time it has created an unfortunate dichotomy. On the one hand, techniques such as natural language processing have meant that rich information buried in open-ended comments in surveys and the like can now be systematically processed to identify broad themes in employee sentiment. On the other hand, even with the recent advances, such techniques cannot be fully automated and require time-consuming human intervention to ensure the right analyses are conducted and proper sense is made of the results. And adding more data at the individual level does not address the challenge of how to conduct analyses at higher levels of aggregation (team, business unit, enterprise) where interdependencies in the work either enable or block successful strategy execution.

Even more of a challenge is that the potential false sense of security engaging in such techniques can provide for PA experts, who may incorrectly assume that such analysis is the only type of qualitative approach they need to employ. In reality, there are many situations where qualitative analysis is the only or primary option including (1) analysis of the drivers of overall organizational performance or performance of individual business units, (2) identifying the sources of cross-functional and cross-business unit collaboration and conflict that arise from the organization design, (3) comparing the performance of teams that are structured very differently and have different objectives, (4) analyzing culture, (5) identifying and comparing the drivers of managerial performance, and many more.

The unifying characteristic of all these examples is that they lack the basic requirement for statistical analysis: a large number of observations drawn from a homogeneous sample. In the case of the enterprise or a business unit, the sample size is only one observation. In the case of dissimilar teams, there is too much heterogeneity to allow for classical statistical techniques. Statistical analysis is possible only when there are data on many instances of "the same thing" such as hundreds of people in a role or tens upon tens of different teams doing the exact same type of work. While the toolkit of the typical PA practitioner may fall short for doing analysis at the enterprise, business unit, and dissimilar team levels, the good news is that the OD toolkit is perfectly suited for such work and provides a strong foundation for collaboration and cross-pollination.

WHERE OD AND PA ARE MORE LIKELY TO INTERSECT IN PRACTICE TODAY

If we were to end our discussion here, it would be quite reasonable to conclude that, like the Led Zeppelin lyrics quoted at the beginning of the piece, OD and PA resemble two star-crossed lovers who are destined to travel on very different paths that never meet up. Yet the reality is much more positive. There are current examples where the practice and processes of OD and PA already intersect in meaningful ways, whether that means using both approaches in an iterative fashion or deploying them simultaneously.

One example of an area where OD methods and PA methods are complimentary might be devising a strategy around managers for an organization. An organization might begin with the quantitative (PA) insight that some meaningful proportion of those exiting the company cite difficulties with their manager as one of the reasons for their exit. That might be complemented by employee engagement survey results that show a lot of variability in satisfaction with core manager behaviors and predictive research showing that managers with more than a year of experience are more effective. Natural language processing of survey comments might further clarify that role clarity and support for developing skills and growing careers seem to be important to effective management. However, those empirical findings do not help the organization know how to select or develop for the behaviors they have now determined to be effective. Further, the organization might not necessarily even be sure that investment in managers is the best way to spend their resources.

An OD process that helps the organization deeply examine its strategic positioning is better suited to help answer the "should we even do this" question. A deep diagnostic process that explores how role clarity is created and shared and what career coaching from excellent managers actually looks like and how that fits into the overall set of managerial expectations and organization structure and design is more closely aligned to an OD approach than to a traditional PA one. Further, a systems approach within an OD project might further discover the important role of performance evaluations and realistic job previews as part of setting an organization up for successful performance. PA processes could then be developed to test and evaluate various strategies. This overly simplified example demonstrates that PA and OD can be very complimentary as skill sets and approaches to enhancing organizational performance.

A second area is organizational network analysis (ONA) which is becoming a common tool for using analytics to model the informal organization. ONA is an interesting case study because the analyses are fairly technical – the domain of PA experts – yet the results need to be interpreted from the perspective of how work is performed interdependently across people, teams, and units within the organization – the domain of OD experts. Thus ONA can only be effectively applied to drive decision-making and change when there is close partnering between OD and PA.

A different type of application is forecasting and modeling evolving workforce trends and future competencies, which help inform strategic planning decisions. Advances in software and technical sophistication of PA experts allow for more and more sophisticated approaches which can increase the accuracy of such models. Yet at the same time, each new type of data that can be considered and different ways of approaching the modeling increase the complexity of the decisions to be made regarding what to include in the models, how to interpret them, and what actions should be taken – all of which require the perspective of the OD expert to help guide the right decision-making.

Since there clearly are instances where OD and PA intersect in current practice, while the common perception is the two disciplines rarely overlap, it may be helpful to consider the way OD and PA work are carried out. Taking a process-based approach, let us explore what typical processes look like for applying PA vs OD in practice. If you do an Internet search for OD processes, a typical result is something like the following seven steps:

(1) Organizational diagnosis
(2) Identification of alternative strategies
(3) Development of the change strategy
(4) Implementation of the change strategy
(5) Measurement
(6) Evaluation
(7) Feedback

Note that, like the OD Network's competency model, there is not a strong emphasis on analytics, though data clearly are part of the measurement step.

Another key point is that only the first four steps form the core of what most people would consider standard OD practice as applied by most practitioners: they do a great job of going from diagnosis to implementation of the change strategy, yet are challenged to do the final three steps of measurement, evaluation, and feedback. There simply is not enough time and resources for after-action review, so the OD practitioner quickly moves on to the next fire to be put out.

The OD process above is just one of the many ways to follow the principles of OD as defined by Cummings and Worley. For comparison, consider the following example of a different OD process, laid out side by side with the analytics process one of us often uses in doing their work within organizations (Fink, 2016), which we have labeled "OD process #2" (see Table 1). We have also included the first OD process from above, labeled "OD process #1."

OD process #2 is similar to OD process #1, while more specifically emphasizing the role of data – which more closely aligns with the analytics process. OD process #2 still adheres to the principles defined by Cummings and Worley while serving as a type of bridge between the more common OD process (#1) and the analytics process. OD process #2 also shows more explicitly how there can be a lot of overlap between PA and OD when done thoroughly. In practice, though, there tends to be less overlap because most PA professionals skip the last two steps of taking action based on the insights and measuring results – same as most OD professionals skip the last three steps of process #1.

This leads us to recommend an integrated approach that combines key elements from both (see Fig. 1).

In the process outlined above, classic techniques from both OD and PA integrate and complement each other, capitalizing on the specificity of OD and the scale of PA to build insights and solutions that practitioners of either approach could not do alone. There are four main types of activity: org diagnosis, analysis, action, and evaluation.

While the diagram in Fig. 1 shows a linear progression that starts with diagnosis and ends with evaluation, nothing is ever that simple and straightforward in

Table 1. Analytics and Organization Development Processes Compared.

Analytics Process	OD Process #2	OD Process #1
1. Ask the right questions	1. Initial diagnosis	1. Organizational diagnosis
2. Identify right method to answer the questions	2. Data collection	2. Identification of alternative strategies
3. Locate or generate the data to answer the questions	3. Data feedback	3. Development of the change strategy
4. Effectively and appropriately analyze the data	4. Planning strategy	4. Implementation of the change strategy
5. Develop insights based on the analysis	5. Intervention	5. Measurement
6. Take action based on the insights	6. Team building	6. Evaluation
7. Measure results to determine if the action was effective	7. Evaluation	7. Feedback

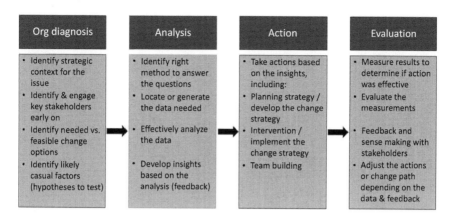

Fig. 1.   Integrated OD + Analytics Process.

practice, as indicated in part by the actions listed under each activity. For example, the last action under evaluation is "adjust the actions or change path depending on the data and feedback," which includes both the "action" activity of taking actions based on the insights and the "org diagnosis" activity of engaging key stakeholders. For that matter, the "analysis" action of effectively analyzing the data for all intents and purposes is the same as the "evaluation" action of evaluating the measurements. Similarly, the "action" activity of "taking actions based on the insights" requires engaging the stakeholders who are identified in the org diagnosis part of the work. And these are just some of the many interdependencies and overlaps among the activities. So, a mapping of the four activities in practice would show a child's art-type drawing with lines going all over the place – which is a sign of effectiveness rather than disorder or lack of discipline.

We will return to the discussion of the integrated approach in practice in the case study examples later in this chapter. To set up that discussion, we first highlight key aspects of the integrated approach in terms of merit, added value, and measurement challenges.

The merit of the integrated OD-PA framework: Through our work over the years combining OD and PA, and the similar work we see by our colleagues, we believe that the merit of the integrated approach in large part lies in how both the processes and the tools of OD and PA are brought together in each step. In practice, HR business partners and OD practitioners often do their work separately, and asynchronously, from PA professionals. To achieve better integration and seamless collaboration between the two groups, it's important to highlight how both OD and PA need to "have a seat at the table" for each step of the journey.

For example, combining stakeholder engagement with identifying likely causal factors in the org diagnosis step requires that the OD and PA perspectives work closely to ensure both happen at the beginning of an engagement, rather than waiting for hypothesis development to take place only after stakeholders have already been engaged. Similarly, hypothesis development cannot happen through PA analysis alone absent stakeholder engagement. The two parts – stakeholder engagement and hypothesis development – which ordinarily often happen asynchronously and separately, instead are combined into one integrated, synchronous step in our proposed integrated approach. Similar points can be made about the elements in the other three buckets of analysis, action, and evaluation.

Added value of the analysis phase in the integrated approach: If we were to exclude the analysis phase from the integrated approach, we would be left with org diagnosis, action, and evaluation – which are very similar to the classic OD methodology that de-emphasizes analytics and data and analysis. Explicitly including analysis as a core step helps ensure that people used to the traditional OD approach will need to consider how to integrate things that are more classically viewed as the domain of PA into their strategies and work flow.

For example, identifying the right data and methods to answer the questions is a core part of analysis, and that part is often left up to the PA professionals to carry out, often on their own when the work is done asynchronously as a handoff from OD to PA. However, under the integrated approach, both OD and PA need to be directly involved in this step, which, it turns out, also should help increase the value of the analysis conducted and insights derived. The reason is because it is the OD or HR professionals who work most closely with the business leaders and stakeholders and who best understand what needs to be addressed and why.

If these same OD/HR people are not directly involved in identifying the data and methods, the analysis that is designed and conducted often will fall short of the mark in terms of providing the best and most actionable insights. We have seen less-than-ideal scenarios play out many times in practice, where the PA group will come up with something that seems reasonable, but falls short in terms of the approach taken to doing the analysis and/or the data secured to analyze. By forcing real-time, synchronous collaboration, those risks can be minimized or even eliminated entirely.

The measurement challenge: One of the biggest issues underlying shortcomings of traditional PA approaches which are not integrated closely with OD is the relevance of what is measured. As noted earlier, the tendency to "treasure what you measure" means that there is substantial pressure on PA professionals to rely only on the data at hand when doing exploratory analysis, and oftentimes all the analysis, not just the exploratory phase. The integrated approach helps to relieve a lot of that pressure, by bringing the OD professionals directly into the process of deciding what to measure and analyze.

In practice, this takes the form of ensuring that qualitative techniques and information (data) are included whenever and wherever appropriate to make up for the gaps in understanding that would occur if only archival data (the data on hand) were relied on for doing the analysis. In our integrated approach, this means having OD directly involved in identifying the right methods to answer the questions (both qualitative and quantitative) and locating or generating the data needed (conducting interviews, focus groups, etc.). The OD value added on the measurement front also appears in the org diagnosis step, ensuring that the right people are engaged in the qualitative data processes, and in the evaluation step, since qualitative evaluation techniques often are needed to validate insights derived and acted on from qualitative data.

TAKING AN INTEGRATED OD AND PA APPROACH

Creating true integration between OD and PA is similar to the challenge of building cross-functional capability discussed by Levenson (2012). In principle, both quantitative and qualitative competencies should be in the toolkit of all HR professionals. Yet in practice, they are often like oil and water: they do not mix well together unless forced to. Levenson's (2012) examples include classics such as engineering and design competencies: one can argue that Apple has been almost singularly successful in many of the product markets where they compete because organizations usually are dominated by an engineering mindset or by a design mindset, but not both. A key part of the problem is that, left to their own devices, engineers and designers do not socialize with each other and have fundamentally different worldviews.

Since people tend to be either expert at the qualitative + systems approach of OD or the "hard" data statistical approach of PA, but rarely both, few people working on the frontlines have a deep mastery of how to apply both approaches. Yet cross-functional mastery is not a prerequisite for success. Effective integration requires that the people working on the frontlines be literate in both, recognize the need for both, and accept the influence of the other in service of a better end result. Rather than trying to force integration through mastery of both approaches at the individual level, an organization can build an effective cross-functional OD and PA team with complementary skill sets – so long as they work in a tightly integrated way, just as the engineering and design teams at Apple have done successfully for years.

In the collective 70 plus years of experience we (the authors) have had doing work with organizations, we have had ample opportunities to apply the full spectrum OD approach as defined by Cummings and Worley. We also have seen how challenging it is for people working on the frontlines in PA and in HR business partner roles to follow that same path, echoing the challenges we discussed above with integrating OD and PA in practice.

For the remainder of this chapter, we will provide examples of how to take an integrated approach of OD and PA, drawing on two main types of application. The first are examples of OD tools that can double as both measurement devices and as devices for doing what appears to be more qualitative, interpersonal work with a team or set of stakeholders, but which could be adapted to collect systematic data that can be statistically analyzed. The second are examples of how to integrate rigorous statistical approaches into an OD-type process.

Before proceeding, it is worth noting the time immemorial challenge for both OD and PA of making sure the inquiry is focused on asking the right questions. There is a long history within both psychology and economics of "dustbowl empiricism" where researchers examined the relationships between biodata (demographic data) and behavioral and employment outcomes without necessarily relying on a strong theoretical framework to guide the empirical inquiry. A common methodology is using survey or other measurements to identify factors with strong empirical relationships without proving causation; Likert (1932) was a pioneer in this area.

That tendency is playing out yet again – in a modern version of the movie Groundhogs Day – within many corners of PA where analysts do what amounts to sophisticated data mining, building strictly empirical models that are not grounded in any reason or theory, and which can throw in anything short of the kitchen sink (with some models including even that household fixture as well). Data mining can play an important role at the beginning of an inquiry when basic relationships between potential variables of interest need to be understood; but beyond that, it's essential that all model building be rooted in theory and evidence about human and organizational behavior. The alternative path can lead to highly suspect conclusions, which taken to the extreme can be quite absurd; for humorous examples, see the excellent collection of spurious correlations in Vigen (2015).

OD tools that can also be measurement devices: There are many examples of OD tools that can simultaneously be used as measurement devices. We briefly discuss four here: card sort, process mapping, stakeholder interviews, and team-based diagnoses such as the team performance model.

Card sort: This describes a family of techniques where a set of "cards" – typically physical items that participants can pick up and move around – are used as prompts as part of an interview or focus group. Typical tasks might include sorting into categories or rank orders. Facilitators can note the final (and, if relevant, the initial) sorts to provide quantitative assessment, but often more important is the narrative from participants during the sorting exercise. Where traditional surveys often capture only a rating, the conversation during a card sort adds valuable context and nuance. Skilled facilitators will offer probes to uncover meaning and participants' thinking during the exercise, asking for behavioral examples or noting seeming contradictions among the ratings.

Additionally, card sort exercises can be an important alternative method for getting to meaning in different groups. For example, it's long been acknowledged that one consequence of an effective OD intervention is that participants' understanding of a phenomenon itself might change, thus rendering comparisons between time one and time two difficult if not impossible (Golembiewski, Billingsley, & Yeager, 1976). A classic case is an organization in the middle of a shift from an authoritarian, command-and-control approach to a more team-based approach to decision-making; in these cases, the concept of "collaboration" can change fairly radically, such that a traditional agree-disagree scale on a survey might not capture the evolution in behaviors and practices. The opportunity for deep narrative as part of a card sort exercise can help detect that sort of important change in a way that extends both traditional interview methods and traditional survey-based or quantitative methods.

The principles behind card sort exercises can be integrated into online surveys through conjoint analysis, which is becoming more and more common in the

PA world. Conjoint analysis has been used in organizations for decades in product development to push consumers to choose which product attributes they most preferred. Within HR, the same technique has been used to get employees to rank their preference for different aspects of work, starting initially with compensation and benefits and more recently expanding to other aspects of the employment "deal." We have not seen online conjoint analysis used widely to address differences in management style/behavior, organization culture choices, and other more "OD-type" topics, but with the widespread adoption of such tools by many survey vendors, the only limitation is one's imagination. Expanding the scope of such programming to include more of an OD focus would bring the current practice of PA in closer alignment to a truly integrated approach.

The other benefit of an integrated strategy is potentially greater validity in the conjoint analysis approach currently being deployed within PA. Best practice in survey design includes doing stakeholder interviews and pretesting to define the scope of a survey, hone in on specific constructs to measure for inclusion in multivariate models, and refine the constructs to be included in the survey. There is a similar best practice approach that should be used when developing the items to include in a conjoint analysis, with card sort exercises being the analog to stakeholder interviews and construct refinement.

Process mapping: Many OD practitioners excel due to their ability to think in systems. For much of the general public, this approach to understanding the world is difficult. This includes PA practitioners, who often are incented to reduce a problem to its most limited and elemental components. An important tool to bridge this gap is the creation of a process map.

A process map can take many forms, but the essence of the tool is to create a shared understanding of the flows and interconnectivity through a business process or family of business processes. For example, through a mapping exercise, it may become clear that the reason that increased efficiency in step 3 did not yield improved overall outcomes was due not to a failure in step 3, but rather to a bottleneck in step 6. These maps can be important diagnostic tools, as well as important tools of communication, making previously hidden dependencies plain.

When done well, these maps can inform improved work design. With the help of a skilled analyst, optimization models or other analytical techniques can explore options for system-level improvement and prescribe efficient system-level design changes. For example, a process mapping exercise combined with an optimization modeling approach could help an organization build a strategy for increasing diverse representation or to load balance jobs and skills within a changing industry.

While process mapping can be conducted in sophisticated ways, one of the most powerful advantages is that it can be a simple and straightforward approach that easily engages the participants. All one needs is some markers, sticky notes, and large pieces of paper attached to a wall. Other approaches such as Six Sigma are very similar, are already familiar to many audiences, and use the same basic set of tools, making it relatively easy to implement process mapping in practice.

Stakeholder interviews: Stakeholder interviews are a staple of the OD toolkit, the main vehicle for collecting the qualitative information needed for most system-level organizational diagnostics. Yet they can serve a dual quantitative data measurement purpose – a much more rarely used application.

Collecting quantitative data via interviews is straightforward, by setting the flow to include a small number of coded quantitative questions among the open-ended questions. The interviewer provides the anchors for the coded questions verbally and records the answers for the interviewees, rather than the interviewees filling out the items themselves as they would in a survey.

There are many advantages to combining quantitative items in a stakeholder interview. Most important is avoiding two different interactions, an interview and a survey; asking stakeholders to do both can lead to low response rates. Well-placed coded questions in the middle of an interview can break up the monotony of a series of open-ended questions. And the conversational nature of the interview allows the interviewer to supplement the data collected by coded questions with open-ended responses where additional context is useful.

Team performance models: The research evidence on team performance is among the most comprehensive ever conducted in the field of organization behavior. Consequently, there are an almost endless number of constructs available to measure and improve team alignment and performance. Just as stakeholder interviews can be used to both gather data and drive change, any set of team diagnostics can be implemented for both measurement and intervention purposes.

A good example is the Drexler/Sibbet Team Performance Model (Forrester & Drexler, 1999) which is popular among practitioners. In our view, the main benefit of that particular model is not necessarily the specific constructs that underpin it – which are fairly standard across research and practice – but rather the value the model and the accompanying tools provide which are equally good when used for measurement purposes, intervention purposes, or both. In the hands of a skilled practitioner, the model can be used to diagnose the challenges facing a team using a rigorous set of constructs, and feedback the results to the team using statistical analysis that is sound and useful in highlighting where there are differences that matter. Simultaneously, those same diagnostics can be used directly for team interventions, driving dialogue and problem-solving focused on the team's internal challenges that are real and which, if overcome, should produce demonstrable improvements in performance.

The Drexler/Sibbet Model by no means is the only viable option out there; it's just among the more popular. Other models work equally well for both measurement and intervention. The important insight is that any validated team alignment or performance construct can serve that dual purpose, including measures of shared understanding, trust, commitment, alignment, leadership support, appropriately defined roles, conflict, feedback, recognition, and more. Moreover, any effective model will include a set of constructs to ensure the team as a system is appropriately diagnosed; one construct is never enough.

The OD tools discussed here are some of the more common types we have seen and used in practice. Their ubiquity derives from their usefulness: most OD interventions require some level of group-level diagnostics and engagement with key stakeholders for sensemaking. Team performance models are a prominent example of group-level diagnostics, for which stakeholder interviews can also be used. Similarly, card sort and process mapping can help identify and rank viable options for improving strategy execution and organizational performance. These and related tools are essential for designing and carrying out successful OD + PA interventions, to which we next turn our discussion.

Integrating measurement, data, and statistical approaches into OD-type processes: Complete end-to-end OD + PA interventions combine the best elements of both approaches and include the four main activities from the integrated process we described above: org diagnosis, analysis, action, and evaluation. While not simple to design and execute, they also are not impossible either: we each have led multiple such initiatives in our careers working with companies. We close out our discussion with some case study examples. Following each case below, we call out the actions taken in each one that align with the four main activities of diagnosis, analysis, action, and evaluation.

The concept of analytics can be overwhelming to many business leaders; it feels like you need to get the entire infrastructure set up correctly before you can begin to gain insights about the organization, much less drive action. The key here is that you do not have to wait for things to be perfect for metrics or analytics to add value. There are benefits in looking at the data you already have creatively (but still appropriately!) or using quantitative and qualitative data collection and analysis techniques in an iterative fashion to move the needle along.

Case study #1: *Organization Assessment/Design Criteria*: Organization-level assessment and design can feel very "fluffy" and for good reason: it is not uncommon for a senior leader to create an organization chart on a scrap of paper and decide that structure will be the future of the company. While an organization chart is one likely output of a robust design process, the complexity of the work, assessment of key leaders, and dependencies are often not visible in the "final" design. Organization design can appear deceptively simple, creating a dynamic where there is limited patience for a full organization design process. In some cases, the business is simply moving too quickly, especially during transformations or challenging times like COVID-19. One solution for practitioners is to blend some OD tools with analysis to help drive better decision-making and outcomes. The following case study provides an example.

A fast-growing service-based organization (nonmanufacturing) had a structure which had not scaled with the business growth, which consistently had been over 30% per year for the previous five years (the share price quadrupled in three years); the financial models projected continued growth at that pace for another five years. The leadership team saw the need for some changes to structure, but was not sure how to go about making those changes given all the different opinions and options. There were a number of problems that the leadership team hoped a new structure would solve for and they were ready to dive into solutions.

Organizational design initiatives can go astray because it's so tempting to skip the analysis step completely. In order to resist that temptation, we recommend focusing on identifying available data, the members of your "design team," and building design criteria. Often, information already available within the organization will provide much of what you need from an analysis perspective; employee data like turnover and hires, employee survey data, data on talent, financial data, and strategy documents can serve as your foundation to understand the current business context. In this case study, the following data were collected:

- Regional leadership spans, including number of team members, number of departments, number of units, amount of geographic spread, and complexity (e.g., new vs established units)
- Projected growth within each unit and for each region, which was helpful for thinking about scaling both the organization design and the capabilities of the people working in the system
- Current cost in salary dollars of regional leadership
- High-level talent assessment of leaders, including how experienced they were at their current role/level, who had potential for senior leadership, and who would need to transition out of the organization over time; who you put where depends on both the needs of the organization from a work design perspective and the needs of the individual from a career development/progression perspective

Then the CHRO convened a design team, which should be a working team of leaders who have essential knowledge about the business model, influence about how work is done, and who will be in key roles in the new organization. The design team helps the process by taking a step back and thinking through broader issues before moving to solutions and by driving ownership of the new organizational form and processes. The design team should be big enough to have a broad-based perspective, but no bigger than that. Four or five leaders is usually ideal; in addition, including several OD and HR experts to drive the process also is important. Typically, the role of the design team is to move through the organization design process and make recommendations to their peers or other senior leaders.

After the design team reviews available assessment data, talking through key findings, a next step is to have them build *design criteria*, which provide a way to frame key questions and desired outcomes instead of just jumping in and creating names with boxes in them.

Design criteria, if done well, provide guideposts to test the organization design against and gauge progress as the work proceeds. They should be mutually exclusive and collectively exhaustive, such as the classic trio of better, faster, and cheaper. They often are in conflict with one another because of competing strategic priorities: the evidence of conflict often is a good thing because it means the underlying tensions in the strategic priorities have been identified and brought to the surface to be addressed directly. Although the senior leaders may feel slowed down a bit at the beginning, getting alignment on these criteria is an essential step.

Examples of design criteria from this case study, which can be applied more generally, are listed as follows:

(1) Reasonable spans
   - Rationalize spans for leaders ("doable" size jobs)
   - Have business unit (BU) leaders who are not also regional leaders
(2) Simplified/aligned decision rights and structure of support functions (HR, finance, IT, etc.), including consistent leaders across a region
(3) Scalable structure for future growth (e.g., can the structure handle adding new units in the locations where they are planned?)
(4) Encourage efficient and effective flow of communication (not too many layers, build in processes for communication rather than rely on ad hoc)
(5) Financially responsible

After aligning on design criteria, the design team looked at over a dozen design options.

The process was highly iterative: organization design options were evaluated against the design criteria and socialized with the CEO along the way. Progress was shared with the full leadership team and walked through the different pros/cons of the different designs that were considered using the criteria as well as the data gathered in the assessment (e.g., spans, geographies). Each design was also costed out. This evaluation process was not anything complicated; it simply involved making a grid of all the different design options and scoring them on each of the criteria.

The process yielded a four-region structure that allowed the company to scale for at least the next few years without adding additional regions. It took two years, but eventually the criteria of having site leaders who were not also regional leaders and getting the support services (HR, IT, etc.) aligned to the model were realized. The process had identified a need to increase capabilities at the director and above level; a significant number of unit leaders were replaced over time to ensure there were strong local leaders, which allowed the regional leaders to elevate and focus on more enterprise-wide issues.

The new organizational design required a financial investment, but with the anticipated growth, the additional spending was something the leadership felt they could not afford to skimp on. Two years after the changes were made, the results were the following:

- Employee engagement scores focused on manager capability continued to increase across sites
- No turnover of high-performing local or regional leaders
- Financial performance improved, especially profit margin
- Multiple acquisitions were absorbed into the existing organization design without changing the structure, validating the design criteria that emphasized room for growth
- Support services alignment with the operations leadership team enabled stronger collaboration

Data as well as the OD "design criteria" shaped ultimate organization design. Success was evaluated with a mix of "hard" and softer measures, acknowledging that the design alone was not responsible for positive changes in the metrics (Table 2).

Case study #2: *Measuring and improving "culture"*: A large retail organization had brought in a new CEO and was undergoing a brand transformation; the brand was underperforming relative to the competition. Key to that transformation was the need to strengthen leadership at the VP and above level. The company needed a more consistent cadre of executives who could develop their teams, drive results, and win in the marketplace.

The head of talent worked with the CHRO and CEO to develop a set of leadership competencies. It was important to use a foundation of validated competencies while framing the specific behaviors under those competencies using words that resonated within the company. After developing the competencies, which included multiple iterations and input from a wide range of leaders, the company wanted to assess how effectively executives were demonstrating those behaviors. The company also wanted to understand collective

Table 2. How Case Study #1 Relates to the Integrated Framework.

How This Case Study Relates to the Integrated Framework:	
Org diagnosis	• *Identify the strategy context*: What the leadership team did when they realized the current organization design could not support future growth • *Identify and engage key stakeholders early on*: The design team members were identified and convened • *Identify needed vs feasible change options:* Selected design criteria • *Identify likely causal factors*: Identified that org design could not support future growth trajectory
Analysis	• *Identify right method to answer the questions*: Convened design team with the charter to evaluate and come up with best options for new org design, and defined the design criteria they would use • *Locate or generate the data needed*: Collected existing data necessary to show challenges with current org design and evaluate potential alternative designs • *Effectively analyze the data*: Compared different org design options against the design criteria • *Develop insights based on the analysis (feedback)*: Evaluated the different org design choices with input from broader set of decision makers (beyond the design team)
Action	• *Take actions based on the insights*: Chose org design option to implement • *Planning strategy/develop the change strategy*: Developed plan for implementing the new org design • *Intervention/implement the change strategy*: Implemented the plan to roll out the new org design • *Team building*: Developed alignment and teamwork within the new org design
Evaluation	• *Measure results to determine if action was effective*: Monitored the results for two years after implementation • *Evaluate the measurements*: Compared operational and talent outcomes against expected outcomes • *Feedback and sensemaking with stakeholders*: Made sure all key stakeholders' needs were being addressed by the new design • *Adjust the actions or change path depending on the data and feedback*: Minor adjustments in the design were made as needed to improve alignment and buy in from organizational members

leadership culture and where talent upgrades were needed as part of the overall transformation.

Using the new company model, the CHRO and head of talent

- Developed a custom 360-degree feedback survey with less than 30 behavioral statements
- Launched 360-degree feedback survey to all executives, including the CEO and leadership team
- Had virtual sessions where leaders were given a framework to process their results, after which individual reports were shared
- Brought all leaders together for a development session that focused on the 360-degree feedback, providing data on how the group performed collectively and reinforced where changes were needed

Likert-scale data that come from 360-degree assessments and surveys often are challenging to work with because of a lack of variability in the data, especially when aggregated to the rater level. This is especially the case at "nice" companies where the culture is to not rate people harshly. Yet the drawbacks of the data do not have to limit how the narrative is crafted to help drive change; for example, a 0.3 difference on a 1–5 Likert scale is meaningful but hard for nonscientists to conceptualize. So rather than talking about numerical differences and statistical significance, the narrative should focus on themes versus specific differences between groups. Moreover, forced choice methods such as conjoint analysis can be used to force differentiation in the distribution.

In this organization, 360-degree feedback historically were used only as part of coaching engagements where a particular executive needed to be "fixed." Using this type of tool broadly and making sure that the right messages were sent was essential to the success of the process and required socialization over time to overcome the historical stigma associated with using 360-degree feedback.

Culture is difficult to quantify, but the 360-degree data provided a good narrative to talk about the collective executive culture. Here's how the company shared that story:

- Showed aggregate data at the leadership competency level, calling out the highest and lowest areas.
- Showed aggregate data for the top five and bottom five rated items, which reflected the overall competency level themes.
- For those top five and bottom five rated items, shared where self-rating was elevated, equal to, or lower than ratings from the other. This helped leaders to understand their collective blind spots.
- Using icons instead of specific statistics, highlighted where there were significant gaps.
- Created a 2 × 2 of cultural implications looking at place versus performance and strengths versus areas of opportunity.

Interestingly, the results of the 2 × 2 were quite similar to a 2 × 2 that the head of talent had done at the beginning of their tenure that was based on a set of interviews with a cross section of people across the company. Having the data from the 360-degree feedback made it easier to get buy in than the original work done by the head of talent based solely on interviews. This integrated approach created alignment on what behaviors were needed from current leaders as well as providing the framework for the qualities needed in newly hired or promoted executives. At this particular organization, profit per leader increased by over 80% over four years following the introduction of the new model (Table 3).

Case study #3: *Integrating rigorous measurement into a diagnostic and change process*: Among the most common challenges in organizational life are the quickly designed solutions that are not based on enough data and thoughtful analysis. The first case study described this phenomenon when it comes to organization design and transformation decisions. Even more common are the

Table 3. How Case Study #2 Relates to the Integrated Framework.

	How This Case Study Relates to the Integrated Framework:
Org diagnosis	• *Identify the strategy context*: Brand underperforming the competition; brand transformation initiated • *Identify and engage key stakeholders early on*: Head of talent, CHRO, CEO • *Identify needed vs feasible change options:* Strengthen leadership at the VP and above level • *Identify likely causal factors*: Gaps in competencies among current leadership contributed to the company's underperformance and challenged future growth
Analysis	• *Identify right method to answer the questions*: Developed custom 360-degree feedback that was short and focused • *Locate or generate the data needed*: Implemented the 360-degree feedback • *Effectively analyze the data*: Individual feedback sessions for each leader + group developmental session • *Develop insights based on the analysis (feedback)*: Narrative focused on themes across the organization rather than specific differences between individuals
Action	• *Take actions based on the insights*: Got buy in from all leaders on the importance of the new competency model • *Planning strategy/develop the change strategy*: Needed alignment on what behaviors were needed from current leaders, and the framework for the qualities needed in newly hired or promoted executives • *Intervention/implement the change strategy*: Got the alignment on behavior from current leaders, and framework for new hires and promoted executives • *Team building*: Group developmental session + alignment among leaders across the org
Evaluation	• *Measure results to determine if action was effective*: Leaders were held accountable for the new competencies • *Evaluate the measurements*: Subsequent 360-degree feedback rounds, 9-block distribution change, and increased profit per leader over following four years • *Feedback and sensemaking with stakeholders*: Subsequent feedback sessions with each individual leader + improved business performance • *Adjust the actions or change path depending on the data and feedback*: Talent priorities (new capabilities needed, under-performing areas) were aligned on each year and linked to the company's talent and financial outcomes

myriad ways HR programs and strategies are called upon to solve organizational challenges without undergoing sufficient vetting to determine if they are the best or even correct option to pursue. The end result more often than not are solutions that are too narrowly targeted because of a failure to consider a broader set of factors that could be driving behavior and performance (Levenson, 2015).

The too-narrowly-targeted solutions are typically arrived at when a leader in the business or HR quickly diagnoses a challenge as requiring one part of HR toolkit without considering alternative scenarios and hypotheses. Changing compensation and running a training program are two of the most common such approaches, which are often recommended and implemented before other options are considered. One source for such quick action is the business pressures to act quickly, but that is only one part of the problem. Just as important are gaps in understanding about what organization behavior, psychology, and economics have to say about, for example, the drivers of employee motivation and behavior, and the role of skills gaps in impacting performance. These premature diagnoses are prime opportunities to apply an integrated OD and PA approach to diagnosis, solution identification, and change.

One such case study is documented in Levenson, Fenlon, and Benson (2010): a professional services firm that wanted to reduce turnover and initially diagnosed the solution as deferred compensation. The logic seemed straightforward: if the professional services staff were offered money to stay longer at the firm, then their turnover should go down. And that is where the work started: evaluating if that was the best route to take.

The first stage was a rigorous assessment of the factors that drove staff turnover in the firm, using a multimethod approach of interviews of people in leadership, middle management, and the staff themselves, followed by surveys of both current and former staff. The interviews identified not only a number of challenges with both staff engagement and turnover but also structural elements in the work design and the culture that also likely played a role. For example, the workload, especially at certain times of the year, was extremely high, and everyone knew that many people leave the firm and the industry because they prefer to work in less stressful settings. What's more is that the complex nature of the work made it virtually impossible to be done effectively on a very short-term basis, so the option of bringing in short-term on-demand help similar to temp workers in retail during the holiday season was not a viable strategy.

Thus many drivers of turnover were viewed culturally as part of the cost of doing business, and the leadership was more receptive to considering solutions that addressed factors that were easier to control, such as compensation. But there also was a cultural element among the partners in the firm. Because they had advanced their careers under the same conditions as the staff, dealing with the workload was also viewed as a type of rite of passage which truly dedicated staff should want to deal with; they wanted staff who were as dedicated to the firm's success as they were, even if that meant sacrificing personal work-life balance. Since the firm's leadership had made those same kinds of sacrifices in their careers, many had challenges identifying with hardworking staff who wanted to stay and work for the firm, but who felt the workload was more than they could deal with, given what they received in return from staying at the firm. Hence, the high turnover threatened the firm's ability to successfully execute its strategy.

The other cultural element was a deep belief among many partners that money could solve more problems than it should have been given credit for. This bias is fairly prevalent among business leaders who are more inclined to think like economists than psychologists – a common challenge across industries. What is typically missing is the understanding that comes from behavioral science research that money is an important factor in attracting and retaining people, but it is a blunt tool, and if people are paid sufficiently well, throwing additional money at them may not address what is bothering them at the margins, which was the case for the staff in the firm. While pay satisfaction almost always ranks lower than other items in employee surveys, at this firm the leadership had done a good job of ensuring everyone was paid well relative to the external market opportunities. People might have complained about how their compensation was not enough for everything they had to deal with, but the misinterpretation was that paying more in the future via deferred compensation would be the best way to get them to stay longer; rather, the issue was that "not getting paid enough" was more of a metaphor for the benefits staff received from working at the firm and putting up with the work demands.

After conducting all the interviews and a rigorous survey and set of analyses, the firm's leadership were presented the results that changing compensation would almost certainly not bring down turnover and that the workload and overall "deal" for working at the firm needed to be addressed instead. What ensued was a series of deep conversations and sensemaking around what the results meant, why compensation alone would not solve the problem, and how the leadership might address the needs of the staff.

While this case study stands out for the level of rigor taken in applying both measurement and statistical analysis to the data, the change efforts relied on expert change management leaders within the firm who deeply understood the culture and how the analyses would be received. Presenting the analysis results alone would never have ensured that the firm's leadership would have embraced the findings and leveraged them to come up with the right solutions.

As it turned out, the solution lay with not one thing but with many different things. The challenge of reducing turnover was addressed through a range of different approaches, all couched in terms of making working at the firm more attractive to those at risk of leaving. For some this meant better career opportunities; for others it was about mentoring and development; and for others it was about the workload which the firm was able to address somewhat at the margins, by shifting some work that normally occurred during the busiest time of year to the adjacent months. What was critical to enabling the change was (1) directly addressing the misperception that deferred compensation was not a magic bullet that would solve all the turnover problems, (2) doing measurement and analysis to show the role of compensation versus other factors in driving turnover, and (3) getting the leadership to understand that a one-size-fits-all solution might not be the most effective, because retention ultimately was about each person having the right mix of positive benefits from working at the firm and each person's needs varying from each other – including addressing the much harder to solve issue of reducing the workload at the margins, despite the structural challenges of doing so successfully.

This type of integrated approach is one that we and others we know have led within organizations successfully many times, combining rigorous measurement and sensemaking with more traditional change management tactics, and it represents the best of OD + PA applied in practice. The key is taking a multipronged approach that recognizes the role and importance of measurement and analysis on the one hand, along with the interpersonal and group-level challenges of making sense of the analysis results, including how the analysis should be structured in the first place to be of greatest use for the sensemaking and decision-making (Table 4).

DISCUSSION AND DIRECTION FOR FUTURE RESEARCH AND PRACTICE

Successfully integrating OD + PA requires most people to take a broader view and approach to diagnosing and solving the barriers to improved organizational performance. This usually means taking more of a systems view and approach.

The case study examples provided here show how such an integrated systems approach can work in practice. The first case study by definition was a systems approach because it addressed the design of the entire organization and the data and information needed to determine a redesign. The data collected for the design criteria used qualitative methods primarily to identify reasonable spans of control, aligned decision rights, scalable structures for future growth, communication flows, and financial soundness. Quantitative measures such as employee engagement scores, turnover, and financial performance were integrated with more qualitative measures of effective absorption of acquisitions and alignment of support services to paint holistic pictures for the key stakeholders (leaders of the firm, and the design team project group) – the essence of a systems approach.

The second case study similarly addressed the systems-level (organization-wide) issue of culture. It combined the use of a classic tool – leadership competencies – which blends measurement rigor at the level of individual leaders with part-qualitative (verbatim feedback), part-quantitative (Likert-scale data) features of 360-degree feedback coupled with individual feedback sessions. Such feedback sessions are a classic OD approach to intervention and sensemaking at the intersection of the individual (the leader/manager) and their relationship to the larger system (their role with their team and as part of the larger org structure). The subsequent sessions for groups of leaders in the organization blended aggregate ("hard") competency data, along with the storytelling enabled by creating a 2×2 with cultural implications.

The third case study addressed systems issues from more of a bottom-up perspective, starting with turnover for a specific role. The storytelling in that case directly tied turnover in that one role to the firm's overall business model and the direct links between staffing in that role and the ability of the firm to execute

Table 4. How Case Study #3 Relates to the Integrated Framework.

	How This Case Study Relates to the Integrated Framework:
Org diagnosis	• *Identify the strategy context*: Staff turnover could not be too high or too low, for the firm's partnership talent model to work • *Identify and engage key stakeholders early on*: Senior leadership • *Identify needed vs feasible change options*: Deferred compensation was proposed as the initial solution; got alignment around considering other possible solutions • *Identify likely causal factors*: Needed to understand all the main factors that drove too-high turnover
Analysis	• *Identify right method to answer the questions*: Interviews and surveys of current and former client service staff • *Locate or generate the data needed*: Conducted interviews and surveys with both populations • *Effectively analyze the data*: Qualitative analysis of interviews + quantitative analysis of surveys • *Develop insights based on the analysis (feedback)*: Worked with leadership iteratively to do sensemaking with initial results, interim results, and then final results; added analyses in response to queries from leadership
Action	• *Take actions based on the insights*: Addressed many different causes of turnover with multipronged strategy • *Planning strategy/develop the change strategy*: Worked iteratively with leadership to identify interventions (solutions) that could address the different leading causes of turnover identified by the analysis • *Intervention/implement the change strategy*: Interventions were rolled out sequentially to fit into the rhythm of the business, individual development planning cycles, and performance/feedback cycles; sequential rollout minimized the extent of change at any one point in time • *Team building*: Teams of leaders responsible for different parts of the employee value proposition, performance management and feedback processes, compensation, etc., were engaged separately and together in the sensemaking and decisions
Evaluation	• *Measure results to determine if action was effective*: Turnover was reduced to desired levels • *Evaluate the measurements*: Beyond reduced turnover, there was a greater sense of engagement and appreciation among the staff from all the interventions, as measured in the annual employee survey and through informal feedback with staff and managers • *Feedback and sensemaking with stakeholders*: Leadership owned the changes and new ways of thinking about how best to address turnover and engagement; importance of the changes taken, rather than going with the initial proposal of deferred compensation, was reinforced each year as progress was made • *Adjust the actions or change path depending on the data and feedback*: The mix of interventions was assessed and adjusted each year to ensure sustained improvements in turnover and engagement

its strategy and meet the clients' needs. Extensive quantitative data collected through (relatively long) surveys were analyzed using advanced statistics and then summarized using storytelling that tied the results directly back to the business model. The reporting included key anecdotes and examples drawn from interviews, which made the results of the quantitative analysis "come to life" in ways that connected directly with the senior leadership responsible for deciding what to do about the turnover.

Systems thinking as a concept has been around for a very long time and is the foundation for a lot of rich research and approaches to practice, including the lifelong work of Deming. Deming's work in particular has been the foundation for many changes in the diagnosis and design of work over the past seven decades. Yet in our view, there is a bit of a disconnect between the potential for systems approaches to improve outcomes in organizations and the reality of what happens on the frontlines.

In the remainder of this last section, we will share our thoughts on how both research and practice might better approach and use systems principles to increase our understanding about how things work in organizations, how they might be better assessed, and how to get better traction and impact.

One of the challenges we see is that there is a difference between the use of the term "systems thinking" by researchers and authors versus the practice in organizations. With the exception of Deming, most authors who use the term "systems" in framing their work have had large challenges getting people within organizations to pay attention and adopt their approaches. Among the more prominent academic contributors to systems thinking over the years are Burke and Litwin (1992), Harrison (1987), Katz and Kahn (1978), Lewin (1951), Leavitt (1965), Nadler and Tushman (1980), Senge (1990), and Tichy (1983). On the other hand, there are quite a few systems-type approaches that have become standard practice in organizations yet which never are called out specifically with the label "system(s)," including design thinking, Six Sigma, business process re-engineering, and agile.

More importantly for our discussion here, systems thinking is at the foundation of many organization-wide and organizational-level OD diagnoses and interventions, such as sociotechnical systems (Cummings & Srivasta, 1977; Trist, Higgin, Murray, & Pollock, 1963), strategic fitness profiling (Beer, 2013), and more. Yet while these frameworks are well known within the OD community and are part of required curricula in many university-based programs, there often is a gap between understanding of the theoretical approaches and practice in organizations.

This especially is the case for sociotechnical systems, which defined a premier engagement model for a generation of action researchers working in partnership with practitioners in organizations, yet which seems to live on mostly in the form of historical case studies rather than widespread current practice in organizations among OD practitioners and most HR business partners. In the specific case of sociotechnical systems, one potential reason may be because the most popular application is arguably self-managing work teams (Cummings, 1981; Cummings & Worley, 2009), which was a new innovation decades ago and is now part of the fabric of how work is done in a myriad of industries around the world.

In our own work, and that of our colleagues who take similar systems-type approaches, we see the direct connections and overlaps between the more theoretical frameworks of the researchers and authors, with the practice-oriented approaches that are commonly used. Yet in general in practice, few people see those connections and call them out, leading to underexploration of the benefits and trade-offs of using the different approaches. For example, one can find many practitioners who were "raised" as OD practitioners in the heyday of sociotechnical systems and who apply the principles regularly in their work today.

However, this group represents an older generation whose careers started in the 1980s and 1990s (and earlier), and there appears to be very little intergenerational transfer of the knowledge of how to make the sociotechnical systems approach work in practice among the more recent generations of practitioners who have been educated in OD since the 1990s.

From a research perspective, we would encourage a deeper exploration of why the formal systems thinking models and approaches have failed to get the traction in practice that they deserve. One avenue might involve comparing and contrasting the language and tools that come from the more academic writings with what takes hold in practice. Are there meaningful differences in the substance of what is addressed by the two different schools, the thought-leader-led school versus the practice-led school? Is it more an issue of framing and distilling down hard-to-grasp (for most people) concepts into action steps that are more practical and action-oriented? These are important questions for future research.

To help inform future research, we find it interesting to note that there are some prominent voices that have found receptive audiences in the business community which argue from a systems perspective while avoiding the use of the term "system" like the plague. One example is Bossidy and Charan in their book *Execution* (2011), which has been a bestseller in the business community. The authors make a compelling argument that leaders need to take a systems approach to diagnosing business performance and strategy execution challenges without ever invoking the specific terminology of systems. The same applies to the business process re-engineering community, which rather than talking about systems focus on end-to-end business processes and concepts such as "order to cash" (Hammer & Hershman, 2010). Such framing and language may be important for helping non–systems thinkers on the frontlines in organizations better grasp what it means to take more of a systems approach.

Another prominent contribution to consider comes from Charles Munger, Warren Buffett's lifelong partner in Berkshire Hathaway, and his book *Poor Charlie's Almanack* (2008). The book is a series of essays based on speeches he gave over many decades time, which focus on his obsession with systems approaches. Munger similarly does not use the term "system" but does embrace something analogous, focusing repeatedly on the absolute importance of taking a multidisciplinary approach to diagnosing and solving business challenges, including incorporating key insights from such disparate fields as history, psychology, chemistry, statistics, economics, biology, and more. He spent much of his career speaking to business audiences about how such multidisciplinary approaches are the only way, in his view, to determine what drives behaviors and performance in large complex businesses and applied the principles by largely teaching himself and relying on the insights without ever having any graduate training in those disciplines. Perhaps Munger's way of framing the importance of systems thinking is compelling to business audiences solely because of his outsized success as a business leader. It would be important for future research to determine whether that's the case, or whether Munger's framing helped solve conceptual challenges that other more theoretically oriented authors such as Burke and Senge failed to grasp fully.

From a practice perspective, we similarly see much room for improvement. The good news, as already noted here, is that there already are a good size number of different systems-based approaches that are common in organizations today, including design thinking, agile, and Six Sigma. Yet we see much room for improvement in how those approaches are introduced, applied, and taught. They are almost never presented as part of a common, overarching way of addressing issues systemically in organizations. Instead, practitioners are introduced to them randomly depending on where they work and the people they encounter who are trained in different approaches. What is needed are synthesis, systematic comparisons, and rigorous training in the pros and cons of the different approaches.

For example, many organizations are "Six Sigma houses," meaning everyone is taught the Six Sigma tools, which are then applied almost religiously to any systems issue in need of solutions. Yet the expert practitioners in such systems usually do not have the training to understand that Six Sigma originated in manufacturing environments where the outcomes can be measured with high precision and little ambiguity. These expert practitioners will then try to apply Six Sigma to other types of work in the organization, such as office work which is knowledge-based and where there are few to none of the objective measurements available in manufacturing. And as a consequence, the efforts usually fall short of providing meaningful, accurate insights into process improvement. More rigorous training in the multiple different types of methodologies would equip practitioners with a rich set of tools and the knowledge of which ones are best to apply in different settings.

CONCLUSION

At the start of this chapter, we proposed that there are more similarities than differences in the principles of "good" OD and PA practice and that a more rewarding approach would integrate the two disciplines as applied in organizations. We have spent considerable line space here hopefully successfully demonstrating that point.

We have proposed an integrated approach that combines OD and PA together so that they are practiced simultaneously by professionals from both communities working in real time to diagnose and solve complex organizational behavior and performance challenges. Our approach is drawn from years of practice, and we have applied it successfully in many cases. Yet the approach should be viewed as more of a general set of guideposts rather than a strict blueprint: we find that every time we are called to address issues of behavior and performance in an organization, there is no "one right way" to combine OD and PA. What parts of the approach get applied where and how is always context-specific and full of nuance. Taking the integrated approach often can feel more like art than science, or at least a healthy blend of both.

It's also important to note that ours is only one of many potential routes for combining OD and PA to achieve better insights and actionable information to improve organizational performance and outcomes for the humans in the system.

Just as systems thinking has demonstrated that there are many ways to describe and address the barriers and enablers of system-level success, so too is the case for strategies to integrate OD and PA. We look forward to many future conversations and debates, with contributions coming equally from the research and practice communities.

REFERENCES

Beer, M. (2013). The strategic fitness process; A collaborative action research method for developing organizational prototypes and dynamic capabilities. *Journal of Organization Design, 2*(1), 27–33.
Bossidy, L., & Charan, R. (2011). *Execution: The discipline of getting things done.* New York, NY: Random House Business Books.
Burke, W. W., & Litwin, G. H. (1992). A causal model of organizational performance and change. *Journal of Management, 18*(3), 523–545.
Cameron, W. B. (1963). *Informal sociology: A casual introduction to sociological thinking.* New York, NY: Random House.
Coghlan, D. (2011). Action research: Exploring perspectives on a philosophy of practical knowledge. *Academy of Management Annals, 5*(1), 53–87.
Cummings, T. G. (1981). Designing effective work groups. In P. C. Nystrom & W. H. Starbuck (Eds.), *Handbook of organizational design: Remodeling organizations and their environments* (Vol. 2, pp. 250–271) London: Oxford University Press.
Cummings, T. G., & Srivasta, S. (1977). *Management of work: A socio-technical systems approach.* San Diego, CA: University Associates.
Cummings, T. G., & Worley, C. (2009). *Organization development and change* (9th ed.). Mason, OH: Cengage.
Fink, A. A. (2016). From optimism to impact: Getting results with talent analytics. Presentation at the Twelfth Annual SIOP Leading Edge Consortium, Atlanta, GA.
Forrester, R., & Drexler, A. B. (1999). A model for team-based organization performance. *Academy of Management Executive, 13*(3), 36–49.
Golembiewski, R. T., Billingsley, K., & Yeager, S. (1976). Measuring change and persistence in human affairs types of change generated by OD designs. *Journal of Applied Behavioral Science, 12,* 133–157.
Greenwood, D., & Levin, M. (2006). *Introduction to action research: Social research for social change* (2nd ed.). Thousand Oaks, CA: Sage.
Hammer, M., & Hershman, L. W. (2010). *Faster, cheaper, better: The 9 levers for transforming how work gets done.* New York, NY: Crown Business (Random House).
Harrison, M. I. (1987). *Diagnosing organizations: Methods, models, and processes.* Newbury Park, CA: Sage.
van den Heuvel, S., & Bondarouk, T. (2017). The rise (and fall?) of HR analytics. *Journal of Organizational Effectiveness: People and Performance, 4*(2), 157–178.
Katz, D., & Kahn, R. L. (1978). *The social psychology of organizations* (2nd ed.). New York, NY: Wiley.
Lawler, E. E., Levenson, A., & Boudreau, J. (2004). HR metrics and analytics: Use and impact. *Human Resource Planning, 27*(4), 27–35.
Leavitt, H. J. (1965). Applied organizational change in industry. In J. G. March (Ed.), *Handbook of organizations* (pp. 1144–1170). New York, NY: Rand McNally.
Levenson, A. (2012). Talent management: Challenges of building cross-functional capability in high-performance work systems environments. *Asia Pacific Journal of Human Resources, 50,* 187–204.
Levenson, A. (2015). *Strategic analytics: Advancing strategy execution and organizational effectiveness.* San Francisco, CA: Berrett Koehler.
Levenson, A. (2018). Using workforce analytics to improve strategy execution. *Human Resource Management, 57,* 685–700.

Levenson, A., Fenlon, M. J., & Benson, G. (2010). Rethinking retention strategies: Work-life versus deferred compensation in a total rewards strategy. *WorldatWork Journal, 19*(4), 41–52. Fourth Quarter.

Lewin, K. (1951). *Field theory in social science.* New York, NY: Harper.

Likert, R. (1932). A technique for the measurement of attitudes. *Archives of Psychology, 22,* 1–55.

Munger, C. T. (2008). *Poor Charlie's Almanack: The wit and wisdom of Charles T. Munger.* Expanded 3rd ed. (sixteenth printing 2019). Marceline, MO: Walsworth Publishing Company.

Nadler, D. A., & Tushman, M. L. (1980). A model for diagnosing organizational behavior. *Organizational Dynamics, 9*(2), 35–51. Autumn.

Reason, P., & Bradbury, H. (2001). *Handbook of action research.* London: Sage.

Senge, P. (1990). *The fifth discipline.* New York, NY: Doubleday.

Shani, A. B., & Coghlan, D. (2018). Enhancing action, research and collaboration in organization development. *Organization Development Journal, 36*(3), 37–43.

Tichy, N. M. (1983). *Managing strategic change: Technical, political, and cultural dynamics.* New York, NY: John Wiley & Sons.

Trist, E., Higgin, B., Murray, H., & Pollock, A. (1963). *Organizational choice.* London: Tavistock.

Vigen, T. (2015). *Spurious correlations.* New York, NY: Hachette Books.

THE LABORATIZATION OF CHANGE: WHAT IS IT WITH LABS AND CHANGE THESE DAYS?

Marc Thompson and Mathis Schulte

ABSTRACT

Laboratories or "labs" outside science and technology have become increasingly popular in recent years. Their proliferation raises questions about what they have in common and the extent to which "lab" as a metaphor is still pertinent. We develop six criteria to assess these types of labs: (1) theoretical foundations; (2) experimentation; (3) collaboration; (4) boundaries; (5) governance; and (6) temporality. We identify a number of paradoxes in the operation of labs and explore their implications for research and practice.

Keywords: Labs; social change; innovation; organizational change; living labs; transition labs; social labs; boundaries

INTRODUCTION

Over the last decade or more, there has been a growing proliferation of "labs" outside of the natural science domain. We see "Innovation Labs," "Living Labs," "Urban Transition Labs," "Change Labs," "Real World Labs," "Policy Labs," "Challenge Labs," "Social Labs," and "Public Innovation Labs," among others, and the term "Lab" is increasingly appended to nonscientific activities. The lab metaphor stretches from private organizations testing products and services with customers to NGO-led activities to address social change issues.

Labs promise to help tackle the challenges we have with change in modern organizations. Their response to organizational inertia, risk aversion, and bureaucratic hurdles is a refreshing "let's do it" attitude with a strong focus on action and instant experimentation. An entrepreneurial and playful work environment with flat hierarchies promises a free flow of ideas and collaborations. Outsourcing change to labs has the advantage of a low-risk exploration of the

Research in Organizational Change and Development, Volume 29, 33–61
Copyright © 2022 Emerald Publishing Limited
ISSN: 0897-3016/doi:10.1108/S0897-301620210000029003

future. Failures can be attributed to the experimental nature of the lab, and successes can be harvested and implemented by the parent organization.

Labs are also sites for addressing complex social change problems such as inequality, the climate crisis, unemployment, affordable housing, access to healthcare, education, and so on. As governments' perceived field of action becomes constrained both in terms of resources and capabilities, labs provide a means for bringing together a range of actors from both public, private, and third sector spheres to generate collective action on these problems. These labs promise fresh insights, new policy advances, and the integration of end users into service design. They signal hope and the possibility of joined-up thinking and future action where previous initiatives taken by single actors have failed to deliver. Labs in this context become social imaginaries where new futures can be crafted and experiments launched.

We have looked at the growing but scattered literature on labs and we have visited many labs in Europe's metropoles. We have seen some labs that were highly successful in triggering change. But we have also seen many labs where the organization's lab idea remained an ideal instead of becoming reality. We noticed that many labs were designed based on a set of best practices and not tailored to the particular context and needs of the organization. This raised questions for us on the assumptions shaping labs' functioning and how they might be assessed, or *should* be assessed.

In this chapter, we are by stepping back and shedding light on the general phenomenon of labs. The scattered literature on labs tends to focus on specific types of labs and their outcomes and not on the lab phenomenon per se. Given the numerous manifestations of labs, it is seductive to start documenting and classifying them for the sake of gaining an overview of the field. This would be a Sisyphean challenge as organizations and consultancies constantly create new forms of labs that they coin with new labels to let them stand out in a crowded field. It would also not address the question of what is actually behind the general phenomenon and why the metaphor of a lab is so appealing to many organiza-tions at this juncture. Instead, we seek to understand the assumptions and expectations that underlie the creation, design, and management of labs, in the hope of gaining a better understanding of what contributes to their effectiveness and what could help lab creators make more reflective choices and assessments.

We do this by, first, taking the image of the lab quite literally and comparing labs in the social domain to its origins in natural science throughout the chapter. There is a body of mostly sociological research that looks at science-based lab-oratories (Knorr-Cetina, 1981; Latour & Woolgar, 1986) seeking to understand how knowledge is produced and legitimated. This work challenged many of the assumptions about laboratory work and provided rich insights into the contested and provisional nature of experimental activities. Second, we position labs within a historical context and explore their development and changing role since the early days of the National Training Laboratory (NTL) in Maine, founded by Kurt Lewin. And third, drawing on the emergent literature on labs and our own exploration of labs in Europe, we develop six criteria on which labs can be wevaluated and that, we hope, inspire creators to reflect on the design and organization of labs and not just their areas of action and desired outcomes.

REVISITING THE SCIENTIFIC LAB

What is a lab? The Oxford English Dictionary (Oxford University Press, 2018) gives us this definition: "A building set apart for conducting practical investigations in natural science, originally and especially in chemistry, and for the elaboration or manufacture of chemical, medicinal and like products."

The traditional idea of a laboratory is one rooted in scientific activity, and the terms raise images of a room or possibly several rooms with locked doors, populated by people in white coats who perform rigorous experiments, supported by specific measuring and testing equipment, who seek to develop generalizable knowledge to address specific problems. An important defining feature of a lab is that there is a world inside the laboratory with a controlled environment. It is carved out of the world outside where such control is not possible. Knorr-Cetina (1981) described laboratories as places where

> ... laboratory scientists operate upon (and within) a highly preconstructed artifactual reality. (...) 'Raw' materials which enter the laboratory are carefully selected and 'prepared' before they are subjected to 'scientific' tests. In short, nowhere in the laboratory do we find the 'nature' or 'reality' which is so crucial to the descriptivist interpretation of inquiry. To the observer from the outside world, the laboratory displays itself as a site of action from which 'nature' is as much as possible excluded rather than included. (p. 119)

Labs are spatial, material, and social but also procedural in that the knowledge generated is managed through the application of protocols and systematic methods that are replicable in another laboratory or space. The quest is for generalizable, non–context-specific knowledge. Kohler (2008) argues that a laboratory is decontextualized (or "placeless" in his terms) and this is because of two factors. Firstly, a lab is stable in that the environment is controlled (temperature, ambience, light, equipment, procedure etc.) and, secondly, the object of inquiry is unstable (i.e., a rat).

Labs are also sites for "consequence-free research" (Krohn and Weyer, quoted in Guggenheim, 2012). A lab offers the possibility of containment of an experiment – it will not have real-world consequences and is reversible. If the experiment goes wrong, it will not endanger the world. A lab is therefore a site of provisional, contested, and emergent knowledge. This traditional view of scientific labs implies that one knowledge domain is engaged in the lab activity (physics, biology, chemistry etc.). The idea of multiple domains of knowledge collaborating to address a specific problem is less common. However, this is increasingly the mode of working of many of the social labs that we explore in this chapter. They are sites where multiple knowledge domains and epistemologies coalesce and explore the same problem. The challenge here is one of collective action and innovation, not the application of a rigorous and controlled experimental methodology anchored in a specific, scientific discipline.

Guggenheim stresses that the inconsequential dimension of labs is really their defining feature: "a lab has to be created by scientists and that containment needs work to render actions inconsequential" (p. 4). This inconsequential dimension is the product of procedures that establish boundaries between the uncontrolled outside and the controlled inside worlds. When ideas or knowledge travel from the inside to the outside worlds, their success or failure can be accounted for by these containment procedures or procedures for generalizability.

Modern social labs adopt the metaphor of the lab as they are distinct places of experimentation. The separation from the real world exists in that they aim to separate themselves from the norms and routines of the parent organization or system. Yet, many social labs are anchored in the "real" world, be it at a neighborhood, a street, a local community, or a workplace. In Kohler's language, they are not "placeless" but rather privilege place. Their aim is to effect change and innovation, albeit in a small segment of the "real" world. The methodological principles of scientific study are applied to a small or large extent (depending on the actors involved), and the objective is to bring about direct change and, in many cases, hope that this change will have consequences and will encourage replication and scaling up. Their aim is to have immediate impact on the world, unlike scientific labs which are designed to protect the world from the consequences of experimentation until the safety of the innovation is established.

REVISITING KURT LEWIN'S SOCIAL BEHAVIOR LABS

The application of the lab idea to the social realm can be traced back to Kurt Lewin, one of the founders of social psychology. Lewin used the lab approach to apply the rigorous research method of experimentation to study social behavior. In line with natural science labs, his aim was to test theory-driven hypotheses and establish causality through the randomized experimental design. Yet, he adopted his lab approach increasingly to the social nature of his research questions. While the laboratory as initially operationalized by Lewin in the Iowa children's studies in the 1940s was far from our current views of a social lab, it already was quite distinct from the natural science lab. Lewin experimented together with his student Ron Lippitt on "political atmospheres" (Lewin & Lippitt, 1938) with different leadership styles. They took 10-year-old school children into an attic above the school to create different social contexts. This attic (or laboratory) was far from the antiseptic, white, highly controlled environment we associate with a scientific lab. In Lewin's experiment the boundaries of the lab were much more porous (Lezaun & Calvillo, 2014); the burlap sheets in the rough and ready, pragmatic attic space separated groups from the central resources of tools and material equipment which all groups and facilitators could access. Indeed, each group was aware of the others' presence in that attic. The isolation from the real world was much more provisional and uncertain. It was proximate.

In many ways the Lewinian lab in Iowa reflects the more recent variant of social labs. In the lab, Lewin created social atmospheres to study their effects on collaborative performance. Creators of modern labs also seek to create social atmospheres that are conducive to collaborative performance, but their aim is instrumental. They employ a set of techniques or organizing principles, materials, practices, and processes that shape interaction among multiple agents, fields, or organizational actors with the aim to tackle "grand challenges." The lab becomes a place of hope, a place where the necessary innovations and change processes take shape that seem impossible within the parent organizations or wider society.

The goal is to create facilitated contexts in which more participative and democratic dynamics can be curated. It can lead to better solutions than more traditional top-down models of social change. This type of laboratory is more closely aligned with the values and ambition of Lewin in terms of collective action and social change. Lewin left Germany the year the Nazis seized power to escape persecution as a Jew and immigrated to the United States. His deep interest in participative leadership as a bulwark against authoritarian regimes was born of experience. It was to a large extent normative and his interest in social change was imbued with these values. There was a strong connection between means and ends in his approach to social change. In his work, he went beyond researching autocratic and participatory leadership and developed a range of intervention methods, most notably group dynamics. He brought the notion of a lab as a protected space, in which social interactions can be studied, to his interventions. His idea of a training lab at a remote place, where participants can learn about group dynamics by the unfolding dynamics in the lab was the foundation of the National Training Laboratories for Group Development in Maine. The purpose of the lab moved from theory testing to exploration and learning in a safe space. But for Lewin research and intervention were interdependent and closely linked. "No action without research, no research without action," he concluded. For him, action research "gives credence to the development of powers of reflective thought, discussion, decision, and action by ordinary people participating in collective research on private troubles that they have in common" (Adelman, 1993, p. 8).

The modern social labs can be seen as following in the lineage of Lewin but they err too much on the side of improvisation and process-driven collaboration while failing to develop more rigorous theoretical and empirical knowledge. They are spaces where collaboration is done, not necessarily where actionable knowledge is produced. In short, the research side of action research is increasingly lost.

Modern labs are more like temporary projects with process steps, organizational and managerial technologies with deliverables, and impact metrics to achieve or be assessed against. A lab fails not because of its inability to produce new knowledge but in its ability to achieve outcome measures (reduce carbon footprint by x%, improve women's access to education by x%, provide access to low-cost energy to x% of the underserved, etc.). If there is knowledge, it is instrumental in character and deployed to achieve specific ends.

Alongside these impact measures there is also a regime of practices that are common across social labs, ranging from codesign, coproduction approaches to minimum viable product guidelines and commands to "break things" and "fail often, fail fast." Means and ends can consequently become disconnected and opportunities for learning and new knowledge generation lost.

The lab metaphor is increasingly used in organizations/sectors seeking to develop more customized product and service offerings. For example, the finance sector is seeing a proliferation of labs among large incumbent banks and finance houses, seeking to innovate as digital technologies open up more competition from challenger banks but also from other sectors which have not seen finance as a natural area to play in (tech companies, telecoms, retail organizations, etc.). In these contexts, the objective of the lab is much more tightly managed, the processes more scripted, and the facilitation more systematic. Here we have the language of agile, scrum, minimum viable product, and internal rates of return. The driving force is to produce as many ideas as possible, at lowest cost, and kill those that can't scale. Once again means and ends can become disconnected and anxiety is reduced by applying what are regarded as best practices. Furthermore, action and learning risk being separated.

The pioneering work by Lewin on lab approaches to social psychology and change inspired us to take a more systematic look at the modern lab phenomenon. We now turn to outline the six criteria we developed.

SIX CRITERIA TO ASSESS MODERN LABS

The proliferation of labs and different lab types makes it difficult to capture the field. Broadly, we observe four categories of labs involved in organizational and social change that are to some extent overlapping: (1) Living or Real-World Labs, (2) Innovation Labs, (3) Change labs, and (4) Design Labs (see Table 1 for an overview). Yet, there are many more manifestations of labs and they seem to change and evolve over time. Many of them push the boundaries of what a lab is and raise questions about why they are coined "labs" other than that it is fashionable to have a "lab." Thus, we decided against capturing an ever-changing field with very loose boundaries and instead focus on a normative rather than descriptive approach. We believe that it is a lost opportunity if organizations adopt a "we-too" strategy in creating labs. Many organizations blindly imitate labs from other organizations in the field or from what is considered standard in lab design without a more thoughtful reflection of what the lab should look like in order to fulfill its particular purpose and what alternative manifestations could provide. We developed key criteria on which labs can be assessed and that help creators reflect more on their choices in designing and managing labs. They focus on characteristics that we see at the core of what defines a lab (e.g., experimentation) and that we think can stimulate the most debate and reflections on setting up and running labs. The six criteria were inspired by first contrasting current manifestations of labs with their origins in scientific labs and Lewin's social labs.

We do not propose that modern social labs should look like natural science labs or social labs 80 years ago. But revisiting them helped us see opportunities for enriching current lab designs. Second, the criteria are also based on our interpretation of the current literature on labs, which ranges across a number of disciplinary areas including urban studies, international development, social change, management, innovation, and public policy. We looked at articles that

Table 1. Lab Types against the Six Evaluative Criteria.

	Rationale	Experimentation	Governance	Boundaries	Collaboration	Temporality
Living Lab	Product/service codesign and evaluation	Cocreation, Formalized learning from experience, Translation, Co-decision-making power, Feedback and iteration	Mostly private sector organized with limited public and third sector involvement. Monocentric. (e.g., European Network of Living Labs – ENOLLs)	Interorganizational – citizens, public, private, consultancy	Thin – tends to be one way and instrumental. User as data. Simple to medium mode of facilitation skills	Short term (1 day to 3 months) sometimes medium term (3–12 months)
Urban Living Lab	Addressing global sustainability problems – climate change, water, energy transition	Cocreation, human-centered design	Polycentric models emerging; city government as primary mover (e.g. Maastricht-LAB, Future City glasgow)	City or area in city, multistakeholder. High level of participation	Thicker – more joint working. Greater levels of conflict and need for high level of facilitation skills	Medium to long term
Transition Lab	Sustainable cities	Cocreation, systems analysis, envisioning futures, experimentation (all embraced by concept of "transition science")	Polycentric with universities central. Focus on sustainability	Multistakeholder. Niche technologies in enclaves, social change more tightly bounded. High level of participation	Thicker – actors codeveloping concepts and experiments. High level of facilitation skills	Medium to long term
Policy Lab	Public policy innovation	Design thinking Behavioral economics	Central government coordinated – monocentric	Can be government staff only, can be multistakeholder, participation is low	Thin – swift collaboration focusing on specific topic. Medium level of facilitation skills	Short term (often 1–3 days)
Social Lab	Social change/wicked problems	Open space, Design thinking Behavioral economics	Government (e.g., New Horizzon programme, EU – more polycentric NGO or consultancy run (e.g, **Rapid Results Institute, REOS** partners – more monocentric models predominate)	Multistakeholder and participation can be low to medium and also high	Thin to thick – temporary collaboration on specific topics. Medium level of facilitation skills. Longer term programs require high-level facilitation	Short term, occasionally medium to long term

Table 1. (*Continued*)

	Rationale	Experimentation	Governance	Boundaries	Collaboration	Temporality
Change Lab	Transformation of work	Activity theory, rigorous workshop methodology	University located but also increasingly adopted by agencies (e.g., Helsinki, SITRA)	Within organization or collaboration between organizations in an activity system. Participation is high	Thick – complex multistakeholder context with high level of facilitation skills	Medium to long term
Design Lab	Product/process innovation	Design thinking, human-centered design	Corporate (e.g., IBM studio, IDEO) or quasi-state (i.e., Danish Design Centre). Monocentric	Multistakeholder but engagement is low	Thin – driven by method with medium level of facilitation skills	Short to medium term

reported on lab experiments, those that sought to take a more theoretical approach, and also a growing number of review articles on specific types of labs (e.g., urban transition labs or policy labs). The multidisciplinary nature of the literature does not allow for adopting one theoretical perspective on the lab phenomenon. But we discovered a number of common themes and issues across different disciplines that influenced the creation of our six criteria. And finally, we explored various labs in Europe. Our experiences in the lab spaces and our conversations with their founders and actors gave us a deeper insight into the reality of working in a social lab. Their reflections on the good and the bad, the ideal and the feasible, enriched our understanding and made our criteria more relevant to them.

The six criteria fall into three broad categories: First, in terms of the structure and setup of a lab, we'll focus on (1) its rationale/theoretical foundation and (2) governance as they drive important design choices. We then focus on the processes within labs by taking a closer look at the core processes in social labs: (3) experimentation and (4) collaboration. We finally focus on two criteria that, based on an open-systems perspective, define the relationship of the lab to the external environment (e.g., parent organization, community, society): the lab's (5) boundaries and its (6) temporality.

Rationale and Theoretical Foundation

We found in our visits to innovation labs in Berlin, London, and Paris a surprising conformity in these spaces and it was difficult sometimes to know what city we were in. You know when you enter that you think this is a space where a different type of work takes place – or should take place. It is embedded in the design and also the wide availability of free drinks and snacks, areas for relaxation, social activities like foosball and billiard, and the ubiquitous green Vitra high-back sofa. The design artifacts signal certain assumptions and theories about what a workplace should look like that encourages collaboration and innovation. But the design choices seem rarely driven by reflecting on these assumptions and theories but are generally based on best practices of what a lab should look like or what the neighboring labs look like. Does an open space without many opportunities to retreat really trigger collaboration? Does the access to board games make lab workers playful and creative in their approach to work? Similarly, most labs adopt techniques of agile or design thinking that may be helpful but seem to be adopted without much thought about the underlying assumptions and theories about what sparks innovation.

As we reflected on the material artifacts observable in innovation labs and the implicit theories they embodied, we also began to think about the practices enacted in labs more widely and the assumptions underpinning these practices. Consequently, we identified two main dimensions along which the rationale for modern labs varied.

The first is the espoused rationale which often relates to *desired outcomes* (such as addressing health and employment challenges for a specific group or area). There appear to be two assumptions related to this aspect. The first is that collaboration is the vehicle to achieve these outcomes. The objective is to mirror the field in which the social problem is embedded and enroll the multiple actors from within this system to participate in collective experimentation. The motivation for collaboration is mutual interest among parties in achieving a desired outcome (social inclusion, poverty reduction, and skills enhancement, for example). The nature of the challenge is rarely questioned. The second dimension relates to the organization of problem-solving/innovation. The underlying assumption is that this work takes place in spaces that are separate from the real world, providing safety for actors to connect and explore new ideas which is not seen as possible in the real world where daily demands drive out the potential for cooperation across boundaries. The theoretical assumption is that affording a space can overcome the boundaries actors in a system experience in their day-to-day work.

The second dimension relates to *theories of change*. We observed in our visits to labs, not only choices in the physical characteristics and arrangements of labs but also choices made on the practices to enact. The choice of practice reveals an underlying theory of how change happens. Here, we noted both *explicit* and *implicit* theories of change at play. In terms of explicit theories, the case of labs in the international economic and social development sphere are of interest. Here, funders (either international governmental organizations or philanthropic organizations) require grant recipients to articulate their "theory of change" for use in the lab prior to receiving funding. This "theory of change" is used mainly for funders to be able to evaluate whether the agencies have delivered the impact they proposed.

It is important to stress theory in the singular, as funders, social enterprises, and philanthropic organizations have developed a consensus that in order to have real impact on the world's wicked problems, organizational actors need to subscribe to their own specific theory of change. While such a bold demand may seem sensible to funders seeking to manage impact of their investments (and maybe even to development organizations themselves who need to mirror the language of funders) it is problematic. There is an implicit expectation that the lab has an a priori knowledge of all the contextual factors, system dynamics, and values and preferences of multiple actors and how these can be deployed to have impact. This is a linear, top-down way of approaching social change.

The diversity is smoothed out to conform to the theory of change imposed by the lab, rather than worked with as a powerful resource and thereby risks minimizing the scope for innovation. To what extent do participants in a lab discuss and agree on the theory of change? Is the model seen as plausible and does it take account of the capabilities needed to sustain the intervention? As Mayne (2017) observed in a review of "Theories of Change":

> Too often, a theory of change is developed on the basis of the ideas and beliefs of those involved without much challenge and analysis. Without structured analysis and challenge, it is unlikely that a robust theory of change and the implications for intervention design would emerge. (p. 165)

While labs in the international development world must demonstrate a theory of change to trigger funding and provide an evaluative framework, these rarely if ever lead to theory development. Other labs take this work more seriously. For example, the Design Lab at the Centre for Management Science at Mine-Tech Paris applies the C-K model of knowledge generation (Hatchuel & Weil, 2003) to the innovation process within labs. This posits a space of knowledge, and a space of concepts and innovation happens when new concepts are developed and not when existing knowledge is applied to solve a problem. This idea of generativity and learning also characterizes the Change Lab method developed by Engestrom and his team at Helsinki University (Engestrom, 1987). Their approach encourages the development of new concepts to work on complex problems. In both these cases, lab work serves the dual purpose of addressing a real-world problem but also developing the theoretical model used within the lab. Actionable knowledge is the desired outcome.

While explicit and singular theories of change may frame activity in certain types of lab, *implicit theories* are also in play. Let's take Living Labs as another example. Two implicit theories of change are present. The main distinction is between living labs as a means of sourcing ideas and/or capabilities (Westerlund & Leminen, 2011) and living labs as a means of collaboration among stakeholders at a more formative stage of the innovation process (Leminen, Westerlund, & Nyström, 2014; Leminen, Nyström, Westerlund, & Kortelainen, 2016). While both may use the term "cocreation," the motives of the prime movers may differ. For some, such labs are part of a business-to-business, open innovation model, whereas for others they are core to business-to-consumer models of innovation (Bergvall-Kåreborn, Eriksson, Ståhlbröst, & Svensson, 2009).

The question arises as to whether these types of labs can produce better outcomes if implicit theories are given more consideration and rendered discussable. While labs in the international development field are often required to have a theory of change to trigger funding, the same is rarely required of the different types of Living Lab, or Design lab. However, labs often fail to have open discussions about the plausibility and robustness of their theories of change. This is a significant weakness undermining the development of actionable knowledge.

Making explicit and discussable the theories of change implicit in labs of all different types is one important priority for the future. While some labs are working with and seeking to develop actionable knowledge, others are anchored in a specific method where there is less of commitment to develop such theory. Another priority, is to take much greater account of the dynamics within labs and how this shapes their design, process, and outcomes. For example, the focus on specific outcomes (impact or collaboration) may partly blind lab designers to what is really going on in the lab. It is for this reason that we argue strongly for anthropologists and social scientists (particularly those interested in group dynamics) to take a greater interest in the phenomenon of social labs of all types.

In summary, theories and rationales underpinning social labs are often implicit, rarely discussed, or subject to critical scrutiny. As a result, the processes and outcomes of lab work can often be highly diffuse, nonactionable, and generate paradoxes and tensions which are not discussed, or at least not within the context of the lab process. As a consequence, modern social labs should become more reflexive and aware of the implicit theories and assumptions that shape their activities.

Governance and Funding

In considering the lab phenomenon, we need to take account of both their governance and funding. While many labs have an implicit or sometimes explicit rationale for their operation and impact (see Section "Introduction" above), the governance arrangements that support such labs are often underexplored. Governance is the way that rules, norms, and actions are structured, regulated, sustained, and held accountable. When labs bring together actors from across different institutional boundaries where norms may differ, the ground rules for collaboration and productive work need to be established. Institutional theorists describe these dynamics as competing institutional logics (see Thornton, Ocasio, & Lounsbury, 2012, for overview). Typically, this body of research has focused on social enterprises or similar entities which are attempting to reconcile the twin objectives of doing good while also making a profit. These values are seen to be in conflict, and theory is being developed to understand how these conflicts can be managed, if at all.

In the world of social labs, the multiplicity of actors involved from government to business to social enterprises to civil society actors significantly increases the "logics" at play and the likelihood of competing values emerging. If these are not considered, conflicts both overt and covert may develop, misunderstandings grow, and there is a risk that if not dealt with these may undermine the effectiveness of the lab.

Social labs, because they are sites where many actors connect but also belong to other power centers (government, civil society, business), raise complex governance challenges. These may be best subject to polycentric governance (Polanyi, 1951). Polyani developed this concept when thinking about how to preserve free speech and the rule of law at times of uncertainty. His insight was that the social organization of science was a model that could be extended and applied to a range of complex problems where there is no central authority imposing their view of an outcome. Indeed, he argued that any attempt to impose progress to an abstract ideal on a community that by definition is seeking to explore such ideals is likely to lead to failure. Authority drives out innovation in polycentric contexts. What enables labs to maintain their energy, commitment, and innovativeness is a governance structure that prevents the imposition of an abstract goal by the authority structure. The role of authority is to allow a multitude of ideas to emerge as well as be implemented into practice as experiments or activities. Governance becomes key to sustaining innovation in these complex, multiagency contexts where there are multiple commitments and identities at play. A monocentric power arrangement is likely to constrain labs, and an important implication is how to design governance to promote the emergence of innovation in a polycentric context. As far as we are aware, this issue is rarely discussed in practice and requires much more research to understand how labs govern these dynamics.

Social labs are fragile entities in a heavily institutionalized context and nurturing them and sustaining them is a delicate task and designing the best governance arrangements is an ongoing challenge. These charismatic organizations, in the Weberian sense, promise much but can also create anxiety and defensive behaviors by established entities which can shorten their lives immeasurably.

If we consider ownership/control as an important dimension of governance, labs can take on a number of forms. A common approach is a state-owned/controlled mode where the government identifies innovation themes and establishes labs to focus activity on these themes. In Sweden, the public sector innovation agency, Vinnova has developed a new type of lab, called "reality lab" which aims to "build labs at the very point of value creation" (quoted in Morgan, 2018). The core idea is that the labs can conduct experiments in the core business, establish proof of concept, and then scale up with the support of the host organization. It is hoped that the time between innovation and adoption can be closed but that this will not be at the cost of more radical proposals. There is, as yet, little empirical evidence to confirm or dispute this ambition.

SITRA, the Finnish government innovation agency, takes a different approach and funding model. They have established a lab to work on wicked societal problems. These activities are funded by an endowment from the Finnish government which generates an income of around €30m per year. However, the activities of SITRA Lab are not subject to direct government control. The organization reports to the Finnish parliament as a whole. This ensures that it has greater autonomy and independence with more opportunity to challenge existing norms and ways of doing things. The SITRA model is mirrored in a broadly similar UK organization, NESTA, which has endowment funding, originally from the UK's national lottery. It is now an independent charity. Labs are an integral model of how NESTA works across sectors on societal challenges, and the organization has been working in this way for over 10 years. It, too, takes on more of an intellectual leadership role, challenging existing practices, developing insights, and piloting new approaches. Its status also allows it to work across a range of organizational boundaries. This is not always the case. For example, MindLab in Denmark which was established by the Department of Business and Growth under one political party was subsequently axed when the government changed and a new Minister took over. An OECD study of labs in 2016 also noted that many policy labs had a short life cycle of between 1 and 3 years with many terminating due to budget cuts and changes in political priorities.

Governance is also critical when dealing with more limited organizational change phenomenon where questions of accountability, responsibility, consultation, and communication are key in understanding how the lab interfaces with power and decision-making centers within and between organizational entities. Who has authority to invest in experimental activities? How are the ethical issues handled? Who can make decisions on resource commitments? What rules are used to terminate lab activities or extend them? What happens when people leave the lab, how are they to be replaced, and what if new knowledge and capabilities are required to develop activities further – how are these decisions made and resources allocated? We have come across few, if any, studies that take account of these issues in the context of social labs, as opposed to the more traditional R&D lab.

Labs can also be part of a franchise model and one example is the "impact lab" which supports social enterprises in urban centers. The activities in this lab are far from experimental, with most of the activity linked to training, hosting events, and network building. This is lab as community rather than lab as innovation and experimentation. The focus is primarily on entrepreneurial support.

The evidence suggests that labs which have independent funding either through a trust/endowment or charitable giving are likely to have a higher chance of survival but more importantly have much more impact on societal problems and much higher influence with power interests at national, regional, and local levels. Consequently, those developing labs need to consider what funding and governance model are most suitable given the stated objectives.

Experimentation

Experimentation is one of the key elements of labs. Experimentation means to try out new ideas, methods, or activities and observe their effects in order to learn and generate knowledge. Experimentation is not hypothetical ("what would happen when…") but actual ("what do we observe when…"). It is a trial-and-error process that is uncertain in its effects. In scientific experiments researchers manipulate the conditions in the lab (the independent variables) in order to observe their effects on the phenomena of interest (the dependent variables). The conditions are then compared to each other. By demonstrating that the observed effects only occur under certain conditions but not others, the lab experiment is the only scientific method that can establish causality beyond correlation. Experimentation in Lewin's political labs followed this scientific process. Small groups of school children interacted and worked under different leadership conditions, enacted by the experimenters. Observers then documented differences in children's group life and interactions (e.g., aggressive behaviors) depending on whether they were under democratic, autocratic, or laissez-faire leadership (Lewin, 1948).

Experimentation in the scientific sense has been the exception rather than the rule in modern manifestations of labs. Here, experimentation is used less in the sense of testing ideas within the confines of the controlled lab and more in the sense of generating ideas and solutions in the first place. Experimentation refers less to a process of testing theory and establishing causality and more to an experimental mindset based on curiosity and playfulness that fosters the generation of creative ideas and solutions within a group of actors. The actual experimentation takes place outside of the lab – if at all. For example, experimentation in Engstrom's change lab method takes place between the lab sessions. Actors agree on activities that they implement and test in their organization. The results of the test are then presented and discussed during the next lab session (Engeström, Virkkunen, Helle, Pihlaja, & Poikela, 1996). Similarly, experimentation in Living Labs takes place outside of the lab and often involves testing ideas and planting seeds of change in cities, neighborhoods, or communities in the hope of profound shifts in human sociotechnical practices (Dell'Era & Landoni, 2014).

In these two cases, the role of the lab shifts toward that of a planning and control center that guides innovative activities that take place elsewhere. In these approaches, concepts are not fully formed but tentative. They are the products of iterative cycles of experimentation, adaptation, and further concept development. This is a generative approach to concept development wherein there are feedback loops from each intervention which modifies subsequent actions. While it seems natural to bring the ideas and solutions generated in the lab out into the field, the conclusions that can be drawn are often limited. First, they usually do not allow for comparisons of different conditions. The power of experiments lies in the contrast of carefully crafted conditions (e.g., control versus treatment conditions). If two interventions have different effects on a phenomenon of interest, the difference may be due to what sets the interventions apart. Most labs do not conduct actual field experiments in which several interventions are implemented in different groups, organizations, or communities but just implement one set of interventions without comparison. This leaves plenty of ambiguity to what any observable change can be attributed. Second, only few labs have sufficient criteria for evaluating the effects of their experimentation (Schaffers & Turkama, 2012). In other words, they cannot clearly determine when a trial was successful or not. Experimentation without clear criteria of success renders the trial-and-error process ambiguous and thus inhibits the learning from the experimentation. However, understanding cause–effect relationships is often not the purpose of these labs. They are based more on probing a problem and learning through feedback and further refinement of subsequent interventions. The hope is that this iterative process will eventually produce the impact required.

For many social innovation labs, experimentation means rapid prototyping. Largely influenced by design thinking (Bason & Austin, 2019), the idea is to generate minimal viable policy or innovation ideas and then test them quickly in the real world to learn about their potential impact. From this perspective, the lab is an incubator of ideas and solutions to pressing social problems and the drive for quick impact, often shaped by stakeholders' priorities and timelines. The benefit of this approach is that ideas are directly implemented, and results are generated quickly. The focus is on large numbers of experiments and seeing what works. However, this raises the question as to what can be learned from the results regarding its underlying mechanisms and effects and also to what extent they are scalable (Bason & Austin, 2019).

Experiments have been implemented more rigorously in the lab approach of development economists. A leading example is the Abdul Latif Jameel Poverty Action Lab at MIT, established by Duflo and Bannerjee in the late 1990s, which has relied heavily on random control trials (RCTs) to understand a range of development issues in emerging economies. This lab model is highly controlled with training being provided to economists to undertake studies all around the world. As such, the experimental approach can be seen as a method not only of understanding the world but also a method of controlling and institutionalizing disciplinary norms. But the application of RCTs also raises the question of what can be learned about the mechanisms and underlying processes that lead to the documented treatment effects. If interventions are not carefully designed based on a theoretical understanding of the change processes, their effectiveness contributes little to explaining change (Bédécarrats, Guérin, & Roubaud, 2019). In other words, through the experiment we know for sure that a treatment worked but we do not necessarily know how and why it worked, which limits its scalability.

It is not our aim to propagate a scientific understanding of experimentation for all forms of labs. They differ widely in their underlying philosophy and purpose; testing theory and establishing causality might not be a priority. But we encourage actors and designers of labs to reflect carefully on the role that experimentation plays in their labs. What is the level of experimentation and where does it take place? Given that experimentation is a way of gaining data-driven and action-based knowledge with limited risk, are there opportunities to increase the level of experimentation in the lab? But also: What conclusions can be drawn from the experimentation and how can the validity of those conclusions be strengthened? This may include contrasting two or more experimental conditions and rethinking the success criteria of the experimentation. But it also means gaining clarity about the theoretical assumptions on which the experiments are based. Is it to generate as many potential solutions and see what works? Is it to establish cause and effect? Or is it to continually refine an intervention through cycles of feedback to help make it work in context?

Collaboration

Modern labs differ greatly in purpose and design. But they are all based on the fundamental assumption that change and innovation are the result of human interaction and collaboration. While lab designers emphasize the importance of collaboration, they rarely specify what they mean by it. This is partly because collaboration has become such a widely accepted, and largely unchallenged, means for fostering innovation and tackling complex and wicked problems that no further explanation seems necessary. But a closer look at why and how collaboration helps achieve lab outcomes is warranted.

Collaboration in labs becomes important in the pursuit of (1) innovation and (2) collective action. While the traditional view of labs may suggest that one knowledge domain is engaged in the lab activities (physicists, biologists, chemists, etc.), the focus on idea generation and creative solutions requires a diversity of knowledge domains, experiences, and perspectives in the lab as it sparks divergent thought processes and the connection of otherwise unrelated elements.

Collaboration in labs can take on a number of different dimensions. There is the collaboration required within the lab itself between the various actors, some of whom may be permanent members and others with more temporary connections. These lab members bring different disciplinary knowledge and professional expertise to the work such as anthropology, ethnography, social geography, political science, sociology, design thinking, and skills such as facilitation. One of the initial challenges can be establishing common knowledge on the problem being addressed given that there may be different epistemologies in play with different interpretations of the challenge. While this diversity is important for generating a more complex and richer understanding, it requires processes for knowledge integration. Our review of the literature suggests that while there is some diversity in expertise in labs, it is much less than one may think and tends to be anchored around one or perhaps two dominant methods. For example, MindLab in Denmark predominantly deployed design thinking methods as does the Leadin' Lab at the Politecnico di Milano, whereas the Waterloo lab model (Westley et al., 2015) advocates for combining systems thinking and design thinking. The Urban Living Lab approach is anchored in a human-centered design methods and a focus on cocreation and coproduction. Our sense is that there could be more diversity in these labs' approaches and they may need to build in other modes of expertise (political science, social psychology, economic sociology, for example) when dealing with the complex issues of institutional change. We need to understand more about why certain expertise is drawn upon and others is not and what are the consequences for lab functioning, survival, and legitimacy.

In other lab contexts, designers who stack labs with actors of "the creative type" can ironically reduce diversity and falsely locate creativity entirely in individuals rather than in the interactions among diverse actors. The diversity of perspectives is not synonymous with demographic diversity. Bringing together actors with surface-level differences (e.g., nationality, gender) does not necessarily assure deep-level (or cognitive) differences in attitudes, perspectives, personalities, etc. that are essential for the creative process. But the interactions of diverse actors are prone to misunderstandings, confusions, and quarrels. As social network research suggests, group cohesion in the form of positive, affect-based relationships is more likely to develop among similar actors than diverse actors. A high level of cohesion among group members has positive effects on the group's functioning and effectiveness as well as members' satisfaction. But strong cohesion can also foster tendencies toward groupthink, the suppression of minority opinions, and the avoidance of task-related conflict for the sake of harmony which ultimately stifles creativity.

Thus, harnessing creativity from diverse lab participants means keeping the tension between cohesion and diverse perspectives. Lab participants need to be able to contend without clashing and collaborate without colluding. This balancing act requires well-calibrated interactions and high levels of social competence. Indeed, a study of 35 innovation labs in the public sector found that "the self-reported characteristics of i-labs are concentration of activities on building trust, individual, relational aspects, cooperation and empathy" (Tonurist, Kattel, & Lember, 2015). Leaders' ability to foster a climate of psychological safety (Edmondson, 1999) in which lab participants feel safe to take interpersonal risks, voice ideas, opinions, and critical comments, even if they challenge others, is of particular pertinence in this context.

Collaboration in labs also plays an important role in moving stakeholders and conflicting parties toward common objectives and collective action. Change labs, for example, bring together various stakeholders to work collaboratively on organizational, interorganizational, and broader societal problems. A dialectical change model is at the heart of this approach, and the methodology focuses on the contradictions in the system that are preventing work on the problem space. By making these tensions and contradictions discussable, the lab approach inhibits participants from getting entangled in fundamental debates and locking into opposing positions as it focuses on experimentation to resolve these contradictions and builds joint appreciation and understanding through experimentation.

Yet, lab designers need to be aware that participants may come with clashing positions and history of tension into the lab. The idea of conflict as a mechanism for organizational change has long-term historical roots going back to the original development of an early lab phenomenon, the T-Group. Golembiewski (1967) developed an organizational intervention based on the T-Group approach but one that sought to overcome the limitations of the approach by locating a lab method in the organization and engaging multiple groups in building better relationships to support more productive interdepartmental work. He called this "confrontation design" and believed it could lead to considerable innovation in internal organizational practices and processes.

Being able to bring differing parties into the lab in the first place is an important milestone and outcome in itself – whatever the final results of the collaboration would be. Close attention needs to be paid to the contracting phase and questions such as who to invite to participate, and with what expectations and level of commitment participants come to the lab, including the expectations of the groups or organizations that they represent. We encourage lab designers to think carefully about the role collaboration plays in their lab, what outcomes are expected because of collaboration, and what may foster that form of collaboration. This also means to reflect critically on simple recipes for collaboration that on the surface seem to have a lot of face validity but that could not affect or even inhibit collaboration, such as "divers people have diverse ideas" or "an open space generates an open mind."

Boundaries

The boundaries around the lab and its separation from the outside world are one of the most crucial characteristics of labs. The original idea of boundaries in the scientific lab was to prevent treatment conditions from being contaminated through uncontrollable influences. Only if conditions are shielded from all outside disturbances can differences between treatment conditions be attributed to their intended manipulations. Because of the boundaries to the outside world, labs have gained the reputation of being sterile and detached from the "real world" with a prevalent stereotype of people in white coats engaged in obscure activities.

Some labs in the social domain have adopted the notion of protection from the outside world – protection from outcome-oriented work environments and strong organizational routines and processes that threaten to crush creativity and innovation, or protection from social structures and hierarchies that limit actors to role-based behaviors and interactions, reinforcing the existing power dynamics. The boundaries around the lab promise to give new impulses that foster change and innovation and protect them from being scotched. High boundaries, for example, exist around T-group laboratories (Dunette & Campbell, 1968) as they tend to be held at remote locations, being detached from actors' workplace context, and have a strong emphasis upon the here and now. This allows actors to engage and study the unfolding group dynamics without disturbances of the preoccupations of the daily life.

Boundaries around labs can be physical, social, psychological, or political. This is best illustrated by corporate innovation labs: For example, many European corporations have innovation labs in Berlin as the city attracts a young, highly educated, and entrepreneurial-minded workforce. These labs are often distant from the headquarters, and their often strikingly different architecture and design create high physical boundaries, sending a clear signal that these places are meant to be special and that business-as-usual is not welcome here. Strong social boundaries exist as actors' characteristics often differ from those of average employees. They are younger, technology savvy, internationally diverse, cosmopolitan in outlook, and work in English as the main language. Dense social networks emerge among actors within labs as well as across labs in Berlin, creating a vibrant ecosystem, while ties to other employees in the parent company remain weak. As a result, psychological distance increases and actors may identify more with the lab and the community in the ecosystem than the organization. The typical young professional working in a Berlin lab is more likely to transition to a job in another lab in the same building or area than to another unit of his or her employing company.

While the boundaries allow something new to emerge, it can also be difficult to bridge those boundaries and bring back the lab's fruits into the main organization. Ideas and solutions from a well-protected lab space can be dismissed as being unrealistic and its actors accused of suffering from an ivory-tower mentality. Thus, strong boundaries can protect the lab and the innovative process, but they can also protect the organization from the influence of the lab – ultimately stifling the change that the lab was supposed to bring back. Here, we see the interplay of power, anxiety, and defensive routines that can stifle change.

However, the protection from the lab can be beneficial if the lab's influence is highly disruptive to the organization. Research into the Spanish flu virus and Bubonic plague happens in tightly controlled labs to protect the wider human species from infection. However, if the lab produces something beneficial such as a vaccine, this can have significant consequences for the world. Similarly, organizations may need to shield themselves from the consequences of immaturely implementing highly beneficial but underdeveloped and risky solutions from the lab.

Labs often seek to manage the boundaries and, in many cases, break them down. For example, change labs can mainly be found on the grounds of an organization (e.g., a break room dedicated to the change lab) or a space between organizations involved in cocreation of new services. In Engestrom's Change Lab approach, actors further decrease the boundaries by directly implementing their ideas into the work routines after each lab session. In social change labs (e.g., Hassan, 2014; Westley et al., 2015) the goal is to find solutions and move to "rapid prototyping" as a means of establishing proof of concept.

Boundaries also raise important issues for actors within labs and their ambitions for change. As Mulgan (2004, p. 2) has argued, people working in these labs face the radicals' dilemma: "if they stand too much inside the system, they risk losing their radical edge; if they stand too far outside, they risk having little impact." This raises important questions about not only the design of labs' interaction with other entities but also the attitudes and mindsets of actors in the lab and how the design of boundaries can enable or constrain their impact.

In summary, boundaries around the lab are crucial and can protect it from being absorbed by the larger system. But they can also become too remote and lose their influence on the larger system. Mechanisms of boundary management need to be well balanced. Boundaries are not just physical but can be of social, psychological, or political nature. They are also often implicit, rather than explicit, pointing to the need for much closer analysis of the dynamics within labs. Actors should ask themselves what boundaries exists around and how these play into the dynamics of the lab (i.e., physical, social, psychological) and what advantages and drawbacks they entail, as well as how these can be worked with productively.

Temporality

Time plays an important role in labs in that most labs are temporary – in the way they are set up and in the methods and interventions they use. The life cycle of a lab depends on its goals, budget, and political cycle. Many labs may not survive more than three years (Leminen & Westerlund, 2012). Setting them up is relatively cost-efficient in that they require modest material artifacts (e.g., flip charts, videos, whiteboards) compared to labs in natural sciences. But they can be closed down much more easily as well. Indeed, many labs are characterized by their transient nature. The uncertainty about their survival often looms large.

The literature gives some insight into living labs on this dimension. For example, Leminen, Westerlund, and Nyström (2012) suggest that user-driven living labs often have a short-term focus on organizational needs. Key participants may leave living lab activities, and there will be a need to replace such players (Leminen & Westerlund, 2012). The long-term value of living labs is also often difficult to demonstrate to businesses, user communities, and society (Guzmán, J. G., del Carpio, A. F., Colomo-Palacios, R., & de Diego, 2013). Careers cannot be made under such conditions, but labs become rather a space to renew or change careers, learn new skills, and develop networks. Consequently, sustaining commitment to an imagined future world becomes more fragile and challenging.

Therein lies the paradox of many labs: They are of transient nature but have a mission to discover the next revolutionary innovation, be the architect of new social practices, shape a new organization, if not a new world. There are expectations of real impact on large, complex issues, but often with limited resources or sustained commitment by funders and sometimes even lab members themselves. Change must happen fast, proof of concept established at speed, and impact quantified rapidly. Timeliness is critical across a number of dimensions. The focus on small-scale experimentation and direct implementation suggests that labs are based on a model of adaptive change, where little interventions lead to a gradual adjustment of the organization to its changing environment. Yet, such a model requires a continuous and long-term responsiveness to environmental changes. But the short-term, ad hoc nature of many labs is rather aligned with a model of a punctuated equilibrium, where a short period of crucial interventions leads to radical changes in the overall system (Gersick, 1991). It remains questionable if most labs are prepared for this task.

Temporality plays an important role at the micro level, regarding the methods and interventions that are employed in the lab. The lab's nature – and its beauty – is its action orientation and fast pacing, and focus on direct implementation and rapid prototyping. Lab projects have something to show for in a short period of time. Lab members feel a sense of momentum and energy that is hard to find in many conventional organizations. But it also raises the question whether there is enough time for critical reflection on the activities and processes in the lab. A fast cycle of implementations narrows the focus on small modifications in goals and processes. Opportunities to reflect on and change mental frameworks and problem definitions in the lab and thus engage in a double loop learning (Argyris & Schon, 1974) are missed consequently. Lab designers need to carefully calibrate the rhythm of action and transition in the lab as the transition phase allows for feedback, analysis, and planning between phases of action, and is crucial for the learning that takes place (Marks, Mathieu, & Zaccaro, 2001).

Temporality also plays a role in the sequencing of labs events. Some types of labs do not exist continuously but take place on a weekly or monthly basis. For example, Change Labs exist in the form of regular meetings of the various stakeholders who plan their next activities that then take place outside of the lab. Here, the challenge is to keep up the momentum and engagement of its members over time. Routines become important (e.g., meetings every Wednesday evening) so that members form habits around the lab activities.

In summary, we suggest that the temporality of labs is an important dimension in understanding its effectiveness. We often observe a mismatch between the transient nature of the lab and expectations about its role in stimulating and enabling large-scale change. The transition from experimental space to implementation space or scaling space has not been adequately researched or theorized. There is promising work in the new area of transition science linked to wider economic transition to a carbon-neutral environment. However, at this stage these models tend to be at a more macro level. These need to be complemented by more micro and meso level theorizing. Without a clear understanding of the underlying change model transitions are going to be more difficult to achieve. We also encourage to carefully consider the pace, rhythm, and sequence of lab activities in order to balance action and reflection, momentum and learning. In many lab contexts, the method is king and this often leads to lack of reflection on the method itself. We see this as a recurrent problem in most change programs, not only labs, and may point to deeper issues around human behavior and learning which need to be addressed.

PARADOXES OF THE SIX CRITERIA: IMPLICATIONS FOR RESEARCH AND PRACTICE

Our review and development of the six criteria allowed us to identify a number of paradoxes that need to be taken into account by practitioners (Table 2) but can also be a fruitful source for future research. We discuss each of these in turn.

Theory

One of the core paradoxes is that labs often need to develop a theoretical model to guide their experimental practices and generate robust knowledge. However, the theory needed to act on the problem being addressed is often quite different from the theory required to understand the problem. This is the challenge of moving from diagnosis or understanding to action and may require not only new models but also new skills and capabilities. We saw how in the labs in the international development field, there is a requirement to state your *theory of change* in relation to a specific problem (such as hunger, women's development, unemployment, etc.). These are linear models which assume a causal effect pathway to desired outcomes. However, our analysis shows that the object being acted upon is usually complex, unbounded, and emergent, morphing as context changes. This requires different theories to understand the nature of the problems and the interventions possible. Lewin addressed these dynamic issues by building

Table 2. Paradoxes in Labs.

Dimension Paradoxes in Labs		
Rationale/ Theory	Theory of change to act on an object	Theories of change to understand an object
	Concrete knowledge and solutions	Abstract knowledge and theory
	Change as adaptation	Change as revolution/reform
Experimentation	Stability of experimental context	Instability of problem/object
	Situated context of solution	Generalizability of solution
Boundaries	Enabling innovation	Frustrating innovation
	Inclusive	Exclusive
Collaboration	Sourcing ideas (top-down model)	Enabling collaboration for new ideas (bottom-up model)
	Suppressing emotions	Working with emotions
Governance	Unitarist values (often implicit)	Pluralist values (rarely explicit)
	Monocentric	Polycentric
Temporality	Short-term, temporary experiments	Long-term solutions

participative models of change which engaged multiple actors in the system developing a joint understanding of the "totality of facts" which enabled joint action on problems. Participative models of change have long been unfashionable in the corporate world and while there is a greater willingness to adopt these models in the social change arena, we note that there is less tolerance of these approaches particularly in philanthropic funded areas which draw heavily on practices and mindsets imported from the corporate world. Furthermore, the erosion of cooperation at the international institutional level and a growing retreat to national self-interest is casting a shadow over these efforts. This is being further exacerbated by growing anxiety over the speed and timeliness of transitions to a more sustainable world. We need more action but will this be at the expense of democratic institutions and processes? Future research could focus on the tension between "theory" of change and "theories" of change in lab-based modes of intervention. What theories are drawn upon and why? How much contestation is there and to what extent is there growing convergence? What role do the funders of labs have in shaping theoretical approaches?

Theoretical considerations also open up questions on the types of knowledge that are being generated and seen as valuable. A further theme is the tension between observing and categorizing practices (design thinking, cocreation, etc) within labs that are believed to generate solutions to problem spaces and more abstract knowledge which seeks to understand the more deeply embedded drivers of these problems and open up new possibilities for action. The latter approach may imply that labs adopt a more diverse set of theoretical anchors and use theories as tools to reveal and develop a greater understanding of wicked problems. Future research could identify labs which are bundling together theoretical approaches and interventions in new ways. Our own experience suggests that adapting interventions to context often requires this form of work and can reveal the limitations of adhering to one theoretical model. This raises the paradox of how to develop more abstract and generalizable or scalable knowledge when concrete solutions are situated and embedded in context. Future research could explore how labs can develop more abstract knowledge and what support needs to be put in place to enable this. For example, should labs seek partnerships with university researchers who can study developments and generate this mode of knowledge? The lab phenomenon certainly opens up considerable opportunities for collaborative research.

Finally, social labs are continually navigating the tension between developing innovations that are acceptable to incumbents and institutionalized interests (change as adaptation) and innovations that challenge vested interests and current power configurations (change as reform/revolution). In the learning and innovation literature, March (1991) identified this as the paradoxical tension between "exploiting" today's knowledge and capabilities while "exploring" new knowledge and capabilities that will inevitably replace the old model. This paradox creates considerable tension, shapes behavior in labs, and may also lead to the suppression of more radical ideas if there are not governance mechanisms in place that can manage such paradoxes (see later). Future research could explore how ideas in social labs are developed, nurtured, taken into practice,

marginalized, and/or killed. There is a helpful literature in the corporate innovation field which seeks to understand innovation processes which can be drawn
upon to explore further these issues in new contexts (e.g., Van de Ven, Polley,
Garud, & Venkatraman, 1999). The lab phenomenon also raises issues of legitimacy and institutionalization. To what extent are we seeing the emergence of
archetypes? If we conceive of labs as an institutional field, what factors account
for its institutionalization? If there is divergence, how is this sustained?

Experimentation

When it comes to experimentation, a central paradox is whether this is seen as
located in scientific method with the core objective of developing concepts that
are validated or whether experimentation is seen as a mindset or even set of
behaviors. In many social labs, we noted a focus on experimentation as mindset/
behaviors with the intention of disturbing a system within which a problem is
embedded. In this way, the lab can be seen as more of an intervention to generate
ideas rather than one to establish the rigor of the idea and its application (either
locally or globally). A further paradox is that the social problems upon which
labs work are multidimensional and often unstable, whereas the lab method seeks
to design out instability and uncertainty or control for it through practices such as
RCTs.

These paradoxes generate a range of important questions. If labs are organizational imaginaries, sites of new possibilities, spaces for invention, and locations for developing new mindsets and motives, what is required of lab designers
and participants? Research could explore the social practices, mentalities, and
political and emotional skills required to hold these spaces and maintain their
productive qualities. How can international organizations such as the UN which
is increasing its use of labs develop these capabilities and what resources need to
be put in place to sustain them? If labs are sites of knowledge generation, focused
on understanding what works and why, what skills and capabilities are needed
and how can they be sourced and maintained? Do lab designers differentiate labs
in this way and to what extent are labs for ideation linked to or separate from labs
for implementation? Of course, even how we frame these questions point to more
profound ontological and epistemological questions which need to be addressed.

Boundaries

Turning to boundaries, we find that decisions on which organizational interests
and entities are represented within the lab can by implication design in or design
out the potential for radical innovation. These choices on the boundaries of the
lab are inevitably shaped by power interests either implicitly or explicitly, and we
noted that labs that are more loosely coupled to dominant actors on the problem
area might well come up with more radical ideas but that these may be rejected by
these same actors. Paradoxically, labs that are more tightly coupled may come up
with more "acceptable" ideas but these rarely lead to significant change. Social
lab designers need to be aware of the context in which they are operating and how

boundaries either enable or frustrate innovation. This raises a number of important questions. For example, research could look at the formation and emergence of labs to understand which actors are enrolled, when and why, and with what consequences. In this context, Actor Network Theory (Latour, 2005) may be a helpful approach. Labs are also enacted in differing institutional contexts which can provide different supports. Here, researchers may want to explore the sociopolitical context and how it shapes the lab phenomenon. For example, urban transition labs are enacted in quite different city contexts. What does being an urban transition lab in Copenhagen mean compared to one in Manchester, Rome, Jakarta, Seattle or Helsinki? A comparative institutional perspective could explore the explicit and implicit norms and rules which shape labs in practice. Further research could also explore how lab designers take account of these institutional factors.

Collaboration

When it comes to collaboration, we noted that this can be designed to achieve different purposes. On the one hand, collaboration can be designed in a top-down way so as to source ideas (here decisions on boundaries and modes of experimentation are implicitly linked). The prime mover, or key actor in the lab context, be it a philanthropic funder, government, or local agency, may have set ideas about the nature of collaboration they are willing to tolerate. Collaboration in this mode is driven by the interests of the prime mover and alignment with their innovation priorities is critical. However, collaboration can also be conceived of as creating a more open context for diverse actors to engage. Here the focus is on a bottom-up mechanism for ideation and mobilization of actors for change. There is a much greater tolerance for diversity and conflict with innovation priorities less fixed. A linked paradox is how labs then deal with the emotional aspects of collaborative work in these different contexts. In the top-down model, resistance or disengagement may not be valued or worked with as a resource to question priorities. Indeed, these emotions may even be suppressed or ignored. In the bottom-up model, there is a similar risk that the emotions generated by conflicting mindsets and behaviors may be seen as derailing the search for new ideas. However, these emotions can also be used productively to explore difficult topics and generate new insights on complex problems, if facilitators have the social skills to work with them effectively (Fligstein & McAdam, 2012). Future research on labs from this perspective could follow the group dynamic processes within labs over time. Given the nature and complexity of the social issues being tackled there is likely to be powerful unconscious forces at play which can derail efforts. Collaboration also raises the potential for conflict and misunderstanding between different epistemic cultures and identities. Research could explore how such conflicts emerge, are managed or not, and with what consequences for the effectiveness of labs. Given that some labs are remaking identities around citizenship, consumption, and production, this raises important questions around how new identities can emerge, how they are grounded, and how they are taken beyond the lab into different communities.

Governance

The governance of labs is one of the less researched dimensions of social labs but is core to emerging work in Urban Transition Labs which are increasingly tasked with exploring societal transitions to net zero carbon emission city environments. In these contexts, we find the emergence of polycentric governance modes novel, and often these labs are working simultaneously on not only low or net zero carbon solutions but also the governance arrangements to support such initiatives. This approach is underpinned by a commitment to pluralistic values and their contribution to addressing wicked problems. However, there are also examples of more traditional monocentric governance modes underpinned by unitarist values and a focus on alignment to these values. The question for lab designers is what governance arrangements make most sense for their problem space. It is more likely that complex social problems are going to be enabled by a polycentric mode but this opens up important questions about how such modes are developed, variance in these models, and the skills and capabilities required to support them. Future research could track a range of labs with different governance arrangements working in similar problem spaces to understand their effectiveness.

Temporality

Lastly, we turn to temporality and the tensions between commitments to finding solutions in a fixed period of time when the lab is in operation (sometimes as short as one day in policy lab sprints) and the length of time required to institutionalize change in different contexts. The metaphor of a marathon may be more helpful to understand the challenges of change implementation when contrasted with the metaphor of sprint for ideation.

The temporal theme opens up a broad range of research questions. For example, future research could explore the temporal mindsets of funders, lab designers, and lab participants. We know from work on project management that project drift is a common issue which is often related to optimism bias in the project formation period or political game playing to win funding. Research could take a broad collection of lab projects and evaluate them from a temporal perspective. Did they meet their goals within the time frame? If not, what is the typical temporal drift and what factors are most often used to explain such drift? What are the consequences?

INTERCONNECTIONS BETWEEN THE SIX CRITERIA

The distinction between the six criteria can be a starting point for researchers to shed light on the lab phenomenon as well as for practitioners to assess and reflect on the choices in designing and operating labs. But the criteria should not be considered in isolation. Interconnections exist among them that need to be taken into account. For example, the temporality of labs can define their boundaries. A lab as a temporary intervention that exists as a series of meetings (i.e., change labs) creates low boundaries between lab and organization, whereas a lab that becomes a permanent organizational entity with long-term objectives is more likely to create a culture on its own which increases the boundaries to the organization. Similarly, collaboration and experimentation affect each other. A focus on collective action that brings together clashing stakeholders needs to secure small successes in their collaboration which can limit the level of experimentation and risk-taking involved in their activities. Implicit theories shape the governance of the lab. For example, democratic assumptions about change argue for the importance of involving all stakeholders and favor pluralistic governance models.

Future research needs to closely look at these interconnections. We could also imagine configurations across the criteria that would capture the interconnections and may lead to a typology of labs, derived either conceptually or empirically. Such a typology would cut across the current classifications of labs that are mainly based on certain procedures and outcomes and could stimulate synergies across the different domains of labs.

CONCLUDING REMARKS

Our aim in this chapter was to shed light on the contemporary lab phenomenon by taking a closer look at its historical context, the contrast to labs in the scientific domain, and by understanding labs on the basis of six criteria that reveal the underlying principles and paradoxes of modern labs. From an academic perspective, we noticed how scattered the literature is, focusing on specific manifestations of labs without much work on seeking to capture the phenomenon of labs overall. We encourage researchers to step back and take a more holistic perspective on the phenomenon and not getting lost in the details of specific applications as there is a need to understand the underlying norms, assumptions, and expectations that drive the creation of labs across different domains. There is great potential learning to be had from understanding labs operating in different contexts and knowledge domains. Our hope is that the six criteria presented in this chapter can be a starting point to capture the underlying principles of labs and also open up important questions to stimulate further research but also encourage more reflexivity by those working in social labs.

More conceptual and empirical work on these criteria is needed. A configurational approach could illuminate the interconnections among them and lead to a meaningful typology of labs across their domains and outcomes. This can help those setting up labs to take account of specific design dimensions which otherwise might be ignored and potentially undermine the effectiveness of the lab. From a practitioner perspective, we noticed how much lab creators rely on common practices and ready-made models which lead to a staggering uniformity of labs across locations and domains. These spaces, as we argued at the beginning of the chapter, can take on multiple meanings and purposes (transitional spaces, social imaginaries, spaces for control, meaning making, etc.). The common practice approach limits important choices and inhibits reflections on the underlying mechanisms and purposes. The six criteria we propose can serve as a starting point of assessing the setup and operations of labs in a systematic fashion and may lead to rethinking the way we take these design choices for granted. The six criteria could be further developed into an assessment tool of labs to systematically capture and evaluate the underlying principles and therefore a means for organizational learning and development in the labs. This, of course, requires lab members to be willing to reflect critically on the practices which they inhabit. Here, we see great potential to develop learning programs for lab designers and facilitators and also establish collaborative learning networks. In the spirit of engaged scholarship, university researchers can serve society well by seeking to lead the development of such activities.

We see a high potential in labs to trigger and advance some of the desperately needed changes and innovations that are so difficult to achieve within our established organizations and systems. We thus call for taking the lab idea seriously, to go beyond metaphor and fashion, and work toward understanding them better and make them effective and successful. Our futures increasingly depend upon them.

REFERENCES

Adelman, C. (1993). Kurt Lewin and the origins of action research. *Educational Action Research*, *1*(1), 7–24.

Argyris, C., & Schon, D. A. (1974). *Theory in practice: Increasing professional effectiveness*. San Francisco, CA: Jossey-Bass.

Bason, C., & Austin, R. D. (2019). The right way to lead design thinking. *Harvard Business Review*, *97*(2), 82–91.

Bédécarrats, F., Guérin, I., & Roubaud, F. (2019). All that glitters is not gold. The political economy of randomized evaluations in development. *Development and Change*, *50*(3), 735–762.

Bergvall-Kåreborn, B., Eriksson, C. I., Ståhlbröst, A., & Svensson, J. (2009). A milieu for innovation: Defining living labs. In ISPIM innovation symposium, New York, NY, 6–9 December 2009.

Dell'Era, C., & Landoni, P. (2014). Living lab: A methodology between user-centred design and participatory design. *Creativity and Innovation Management*, *23*(2), 137–154.

Dunette, M. D., & Campbell, J. P. (1968). Laboratory education: Impact on people and organizations. *Industrial Relations*, *8*(1), 1–27.

Edmondson, A. (1999). Psychological safety and learning behavior in work teams. *Administrative Science Quarterly*, *44*(2), 350–383.

Engestrom, Y. (1987). *Learning by expanding*. Helsinki: Orienta-Konsultit Oy.

Engeström, Y., Virkkunen, J., Helle, M., Pihlaja, J., & Poikela, R. (1996). The change laboratory as a tool for transforming work. *Lifelong Learning in Europe*, *1*(2), 10–17.

Fligstein, N., & McAdam, D. (2012). *A theory of fields*. Oxford: Oxford University Press.

Gersick, C. J. (1991). Revolutionary change theories: A multilevel exploration of the punctuated equilibrium paradigm. *Academy of Management Review*, *16*(1), 10–36.

Golembiewski, R. T. (1967). The "laboratory approach" to organization change: Schema of a method. *Public Administration Review*, *27*(3), 211–221.

Guggenheim, M. (2012). Laboratizing and de-laboratizing the world: Changing sociological concepts for places of knowledge production. *History of the Human Sciences*, *25*(1), 99–118.

Guzmán, J. G., del Carpio, A. F., Colomo-Palacios, R., & de Diego, M. V. (2013). Living labs for user-driven innovation: A process reference model. *Research-Technology Management*, *56*(3), 29–39.

Hassan, Z. (2014). *The social labs revolution: A new approach to solving our most complex challenges*. San Francisco, CA: Berrett-Koehler Publishers.

Hatchuel, A., & Weil, B. (2003). A new approach of innovative design: An introduction to CK theory. In DS 31: Proceedings of ICED 03, the 14th International Conference on Engineering Design, Stockholm.

Knorr-Cetina, K. D. (1981). Social and scientific method or what do we make of the distinction between the natural and the social sciences? *Philosophy of the Social Sciences, 11*(3), 335–359.

Kohler, R. E. (2008). Lab history: Reflections. *Isis, 99*(4), 761–768.

Latour, B. (2005). *Reassembling the social: An introduction to actor-network-theory*. Oxford: Oxford University Press.

Latour, B., & Woolgar, S. (1986). *Laboratory life: The construction of scientific facts*. Princeton: Princeton University Press.

Latour, B., & Woolgar, S. (2013). *Laboratory life: The construction of scientific facts*. Princeton, NJ: Princeton University Press.

Leminen, S., Nyström, A. G., Westerlund, M., & Kortelainen, M. J. (2016). The effect of network structure on radical innovation in living labs. *Journal of Business & Industrial Marketing, 31*(6), 743–757.

Leminen, S., & Westerlund, M. (2012). Towards innovation in living labs networks. *International Journal of Product Development, 17*(1–2), 43–59.

Leminen, S., Westerlund, M., & Nyström, A. G. (2012, September). Living Labs as open-innovation networks. *Technology Innovation Management Review, 2*(9), 6–11.

Leminen, S., Westerlund, M., & Nyström, A. G. (2014). On becoming creative consumers–user roles in living labs networks. *International Journal of Technology Marketing, 9*(1), 33–52.

Lewin, K. (1948). *Resolving social conflicts; selected papers on group dynamics*. New York, NY: Harper.

Lewin, K., & Lippitt, R. (1938). An experimental approach to the study of autocracy and democracy: A preliminary note. *Sociometry, 1*(3/4), 292–300.

Lezaun, J., & Calvillo, N. (2014). In the political laboratory: Kurt Lewin's atmospheres. *Journal of Cultural Economy, 7*(4), 434–457.

March, J. G. (1991). Exploration and exploitation in organizational learning. *Organization Science, 2*(1), 71–87.

Marks, M. A., Mathieu, J. E., & Zaccaro, S. J. (2001). A temporally based framework and taxonomy of team processes. *Academy of Management Review, 26*(3), 356–376.

Mayne, J. (2017). Theory of change analysis: Building robust theories of change. *Canadian Journal of Program Evaluation, 32*(2), 155–173.

Morgan, K. (2018). *Experimental governance and territorial development (OECD Report)*. Paris: OECD Report.

Mulgan, G. (2004). Connexity revisited. *Demos Collection, 20*, 49–62.

Oxford University Press. (2018). *Oxford english dictionary*. Oxford: Oxford University Press.

Polanyi, M. (1951). *The logic of liberty: Reflections and rejoinders*. Princeton: Princeton University Press.

Schaffers, H., & Turkama, P. (2012). Living labs for cross-border systemic innovation. *Technology Innovation Management Review, 2*(9), 25–30.

Thornton, P. H., Ocasio, W., & Lounsbury, M. (2012). *The institutional logics perspective: A new approach to culture, structure, and process*. Oxford: Oxford University Press.

Tonurist, P., Kattel, R., & Lember, V. (2015). *Discovering innovation labs in the public sector*. The Other Canon, Foundation and Tallinn University of Technology Working Papers in Technology Governance and Economic Dynamics, TUT Ragnar Nurkse School of Innovation and Governance.

Van de Ven, A. H., Polley, D., Garud, R., & Venkatraman, S. (1999). *The innovation journey*. New York, NY: Oxford University Press.

Westerlund, M., & Leminen, S. (2011). Managing the challenges of becoming an open innovation company: Experiences from living labs. *Technology Innovation Management Review, 1*(1), 19–25.

Westley, F., Laban, S., Rose, C., McGowan, K., Robinson, K., Tjornbo, O., & Tovey, M. (2015). *Social innovation lab guide*. Waterloo, ON: Waterloo Institute for Social Innovation and Resilience.

TOWARD RECONFIGURING SOCIOTECHNICAL SYSTEMS DESIGN: DIGITALLY INFUSED WORK SYSTEMS AND THE "PLATFORM-STS"

Oğuz N. Babüroğlu and John W. Selsky

ABSTRACT

The digital transformation calls for new thinking about sociotechnical systems design (STSD) because it has enabled new kinds of work systems to proliferate. We identify a new class of sociotechnical system, called the Platform-STS (P-STS), which complements the existing Industrial- and Knowledge-STSs. The P-STS has distinctive characteristics compared to the other classes because it reaches directly into ecosystems and is, therefore, "distributed," and because it is governed through market mechanisms rather than hierarchy or clan mechanisms. We introduce a new design principle, redundancy of connectivity, to ground design thinking about the P-STS. We demonstrate why fundamental STSD principles need to be reconfigured, suggest how they might do so, and conclude that socioecological designs and interventions may need to supplant sociotechnical ones.

Keywords: Sociotechnical systems; socioecological; STS design; digital transformation; platform organizations; digital platforms; systems thinking

INTRODUCTION

The current reality of companies in many industries is characterized by multiple change initiatives, very porous boundaries with their environments, and nearly continuous disruption. An important consideration in all these factors is

Research in Organizational Change and Development, Volume 29, 63–87
ISSN: 0897-3016/doi:10.1108/S0897-301620210000029004

technology advances, especially digital. The digital transformation has had an important impact on how organizations and their work systems are managed, led, designed, changed, and developed. It has disrupted many industries, affected the strategies, operations, and personnel mix of many companies, created new sites and means of innovation, sparked societal controversies over privacy and surveillance, and ushered in the emergence of new entrants. Well-known examples include Amazon and Uber, the arrival of which initially disrupted brick-and-mortar book sales and taxi services, respectively, then spread to other industries and sectors, including Web services, private and public transportation services, brick-and-mortar retail, etc. These new work systems and the enterprises that manage them are part of a broader shift in the economy and society toward what has been called the "gig economy" (Istrate & Harris, 2017), "platform economy" (Gerwe & Silva, 2020), and "platform capitalism" (Srnicek, 2017).

How can we make sense of the wide-ranging and equivocal impacts of the digital transformation? Sociotechnical systems design (STSD) offers a broad guiding framework, but it needs to be modified because work systems infused with digital technologies, especially those based upon digital platforms, challenge the foundations of STSD (Claussen, Haga, & Ravn, 2019). Given the recent proliferation of such work systems, we ask: how is the digital transformation changing the nature of work systems, and how can STSD continue to provide a viable basis for understanding and improving digital platform work systems? These questions mirror those posed by the original Tavistock researchers confronted with seemingly new work practices in the Yorkshire coal mines 70 years ago. The essential question remains the same, but the answers are vastly different because the technical aspect, the social aspect, and the environmental context of many work systems have all changed dramatically.

The question also recapitulates a long-standing debate in the sociotechnical systems (STS) field about technology. Some scholars assert that

> ...technology [is] an actual system of physical, social, and cognitive elements that are built, used, and rebuilt by people in everyday practice. We can observe, manipulate, change, and make sense of technology... and its relationships to the social setting. (Griffith & Dougherty, 2002, p. 206)

Other scholars assert that STSD "subordinat[es]... human-centered criteria to the dictates of efficiency" (Moldaschl & Weber, 1998, p. 361) and contributes to what in effect is a technological determinism. Critics believe that STSD, by largely accepting the advance of new technologies in work systems and then adapting the social relations to those technologies, has undermined the joint optimization aspiration of the STS founders (Selsky & Baburoglu, 2021).

To date, the STS literature has not said enough about the recent explosion of digitally enhanced work systems because, adhering to its intellectual heritage, it has concentrated its analyses on industrial work settings, and to some extent, on professional office work settings. Thus, in this chapter, we are interested in the profound effects that the digital transformation have had on the social and technical components that comprise the work system(s) of many enterprises and in how the reach of STS analysis and design might be extended to understand such systems.

The purpose of this chapter is to explore how a sociotechnical understanding of the digitally infused workplace calls for a reworking of STS design principles and analytic categories. After painting a picture of the social context of contemporary work systems, focusing on the rise of digital platform organizations, we lay out four developments in STS design thinking that brought the field to where we see it today. We then identify and distinguish three "classes" of STSs, including a new one characterized by the digital platform. Next, we discuss important implications of classifying STSs, in terms of system regulation, a new design principle, and strategic adaptation. Finally, we argue why basic STS principles for digital platform work systems need to be reconfigured and suggest how this might be done. The main implication of this argument is that STSD must become *socioecological* systems design in order to remain relevant going forward.

DIGITAL TRANSFORMATION AND DISRUPTION

The spread of digital technologies in workplaces over the past 20 years has been pervasive. In manufacturing facilities, this began with CAD (computer-aided design)-CAM (computer-aided manufacturing) in the 1970s–1980s and has progressed to advanced computer-controlled robotics and nearly immersive 3D design. In professional offices, from financial services firms to hospital medical records departments, computerized management information systems have evolved into integrated enterprise management/resource systems, of which SAP and Oracle are the best known.

Within workplaces the digital transformation has altered many communications, conflict handling, and decision-making patterns (see Silverman, 2019). Tasks have shrunk or enlarged in scope, discretion, autonomy, and information richness. The human interfaces with information-rich and "smart" computer apps have become more complex and intimate. In professional office applications, these changed interfaces began with introductions of new digital-control systems, such as Epic in the hospital example later in this chapter, bringing remote surveillance of the performance of highly skilled workers. They have continued through wearable technologies attached to knowledge workers to increase their productivity, decision-making capabilities, and even learning abilities (Ayaz et al., 2012). And they proceed to unknown and possibly frightening futures populated by cyborgs and fraught with power and control asymmetries (Claussen et al., 2019). Such uses of digital technologies have vast ethical implications (Lanier, 2013; Onaral, 2019).

The impact of the introduction of computerized information technology on organizational structure and communication flows has been recognized in the STS literature for some time (see Shani & Sena, 1994). However, STS scholars are only now beginning to come to terms with the "platform" organization (Ciborra, 1996; Cennamo, 2021; Cusumano, 2020). This iconic new entrant in the business landscape produced by the digital transformation has emerged and spread in many industries over the past two decades. Scholarly interest in platform organizations arguably began with the notion of business ecosystems (Moore, 1993) and the "keystone" companies that cohere and drive them (Iansiti & Levien, 2004). Keystones create "'platforms' – services, tools and/or technologies – that other members of the ecosystem can use to enhance their own performance" (Iansiti & Levien, 2004, p. 68).

In the past decade, entrepreneurial companies have created *digital* platforms – ground-level, operational business information systems grounded in sophisticated machine learning and software-based decision-making algorithms. These enterprises include well-known consumer brands, such as Airbnb and Uber. Some have enjoyed great success as they have disrupted traditional industries. They follow in the path of older such companies, such as 23-year-old Expedia and 19-year-old Wikipedia.

Advanced software is vital for the very operation of platform-based enterprises, enabling them to manage their core workforces and match their far-flung gig workers with local customers. Such digital innovations have disrupted older methods for accomplishing certain functions on which many conventional companies were built, and enabled new functions to be performed, upending some conventional business models. For example, the arrival of blockchain has created an expanding array of applications for distributed monitoring, decision-making, and authentication (McAfee & Brynjolfsson, 2017), including new ways of monitoring and enforcing ecologically sustainable practices in supply chains (Bai & Sarkis, 2019) and new modes of personal vehicle ownership and access (Gösele & Sandner, 2019). Moreover, digitally enabled activities like crowd-sourcing have democratized decision-making to some extent; vast databases of information on customers have enabled companies to personalize their offerings; and databases of sharable products and services have created a blossoming sharing economy (Gerwe & Silva, 2020).

SOCIOTECHNICAL SYSTEMS DESIGN[1]

STSD is an applied template for workplace effectiveness developed in the 1950–1960s initially to understand and improve mass-production work settings. As work technologies have changed over the years, the configurations of workplaces and the worker technology interface have changed significantly. As a result, researchers have developed new analytic concepts, principles, and management tools for STSD. New contexts, particularly professional office work, and, more recently, digitally infused work, have drawn STSD into larger units of analysis, namely, total enterprises and business ecosystems (Selsky & Baburoglu, 2021).

The STS field has provided a durable set of concepts, values, and design principles for understanding the human-technology interface at workplaces for over 60 years. Its central principle is the mutual adaptation of the social and technical components of a work system aiming for "joint optimization." Its other foundational principles are that of design choice, that is, a STS may be designed in different ways, and the intimate, "coimplicative" relation between system and environment (Emery, 1999).

However, from its beginnings the fundamental concepts underpinning STSD extended beyond those technical considerations:

> Sociotechnical systems theory... was a technical, moral and political discipline. Morally, it was based upon the idea that workers are entitled to working conditions that supported their all around competence and their relationships with work mates, politically it was grounded in the movement for industrial democracy, and technically it offered methods for designing work to minimize the errors or "variances." (Hirschhorn, Noble, & Rankin, 2001, p. 241).

Thus, STSD has represented a "liberation from the domination of the machine and mechanization [and] ... liberation from single and meaningless tasks and external control" (Baburoglu, 1992). In application, STSD has been driven by "...the need to humanize work through the redesign of jobs and democracy at work" (Mumford, 2000, p. 34). Action research traditionally has been the preferred approach, with "investigators working with management and labor to introduce change into a work setting and then attempt to learn from its results..." (Scott & Davis, 2007, p. 144; see also Eden & Huxham, 2006).

BUILDING UPON THE ORIGINAL STSD CONCEPTS

Four major developments mark the evolution of STSD from its origins in industrial work settings to its current state (Selsky & Baburoglu, 2021): (1) the introduction of high-level design principles to guide the assessment and (re)design of the STS; (2) reworking STSD for professional knowledge work; (3) conceptually situating the role of the environment; and (4) the recognition of technology choice.

Design Principles

In the mid-1960s, Fred Emery reasoned that organizations can choose to design work systems in two fundamentally different ways:

> In DP1 [Design Principle 1 organizations, called *redundancy of parts*], responsibility for control and coordination is vested at least one level above those who are doing the work, learning or planning. By fragmenting tasks into the most narrow, often single skills or movements, each person in such a one person/one job unit is easily replaceable with minimal if any training... In DP2 [Design Principle 2 organizations, called *redundancy of functions*], as many skills and functions are built into each person as possible and responsibility for coordination and control is located where learning, work and planning is being done. This results in a flatter structure... [and] self-managing groups. (Emery, 1999, pp. 106, 108)

Autonomous work groups are the prime exemplification of DP2 (see Susman, 1976).

A new approach emerged from this insight which broke with classic sociotechnical methods and sought to address the power issue impeding the diffusion of STS concepts and practice. The participative design workshop (PDW), "specifically invented as a method for diffusion," needed to supplant the conventional methods of STS intervention in order to produce the "speedy and effective redesign of existing organizational structures, i.e. currently bureaucratic or DP1 structures into DP2 structures, by the people who work and live in those structures" (Emery, 1999, pp. 20–21). The intent of the PDW is to create systems deliberately designed for learning (Emery, 1999; see also Purser & Cabana, 1998).

Knowledge-work Applications

Cal Pava (1983, 1986) initiated the reworking of the industrial STS model for nonroutine, office-based knowledge work. He construed *deliberations* as the technical component of the system and *discretionary coalitions* as the social component. Pava established that the essential conversion process in such cases is the transformation of ill-defined issues and "key dilemmas" into actionable problems via deliberations among coalition members. His fundamental innovations lay in "enlarg[ing] the notion of technology to break it free of hardware constraints," "break[ing] STS theory free from the monopolizing idea of the autonomous work group," and creating new analytical methods for nonlinear work conversion processes (Trist, 1983/1993, p. 664). This extension swept much professional knowledge work, both technical and managerial, into the domain of STSD, and laid the groundwork for its future development.[2]

Building on Pava's innovations, Hirschhorn et al. (2001) sought to rework basic STS concepts to make them "more responsive to the challenges of designing learning organizations" (p. 241). In mass-customization facilities, where "machines control variances, and a small team can oversee an entire factory" (p. 243), they argued that new design principles were needed, e.g., learning from variances instead of limiting variances, dynamic complementarity between roles rather than redundancy of functions, making boundaries rather than managing boundaries, and "meaning ... replac[ing] autonomy as the primary design tool" (p. 250).

Environment

Every STS consists of a set of interdependencies: *internal*, among the members of the work system, representing the core conversion process and the attendant issues of control and coordination; *transactional*, between the work system and its environment, representing inputs and outputs, including knowledge exchanges; and *contextual*, among elements of the system's environment, shaping the context within which the system functions as it does (Emery, 1999). These three sets of interdependencies give STSs the character of open systems.

If the social and technical aspects of a work system are jointly optimized without also optimizing the environment along with them, then the redesigned work system likely will not sustain because the environment is not (designed to be) conducive to the jointly optimized parts. The environment of a work system might be the enterprise itself, a business ecosystem, an industry, or a national industrial sector. Heller (2001) coined the term "socio-oecotechnical systems" and claimed the "classical" STS model needed to be "extended" with a stronger emphasis on the environment, including the natural environment, in order to be responsive to prevailing turbulent and risk-society conditions. In such conditions, the organizational effects on the environment become important and contribute to often damaging environmental volatility or severe maladaptations. This suggests the environment needs to be included in STSD; we take up this notion later.

Technology Choice

The prevailing assumption in STSD is that technology is given, and people must adapt to its relentless advance (see McAfee & Brynjolfsson, 2017). Lisl Klein (2014, p. 138) pointed to that lacuna in STS thinking, affirming that the technology in a work system is *chosen*, either explicitly or implicitly:

> Sociotechnical theory makes explicit the fact that the technology and the people in a work system are interdependent... Technology affects the behaviour of people, and the behaviour of people affects the working of the technology... In addition, while there is much research documenting this interdependence once technology is implemented, it also exists at the stages when technology is being designed and developed. Factors that affect individuals and organisations at the output end, that is as a consequence of technology, apply with equal relevance at the input end, that is among design teams and the organisations that contain them. In other words, technology is not only an independent variable, having consequences for skills, tasks, roles, values, relationships, careers, group functioning, departments, and the organisation in which it is implemented. It is also a dependent variable.

Thus, the choices or designs of technology in a STS are not inevitable; they are affected by factors "in the designing system" such as relations between organizations, characteristics of the organization, relations between functions/departments, group functioning, careers, roles, tasks, and skills (Klein, 2014). Going further, Klein suggests that "[a]s integration of computer technology with manufacturing and other work systems advances, we need to conceptualise organisations as open socio-structural systems. Not sociotechnical; socio-structural" (p. 141). This, she claimed, is because the boundary between the shop floor work system and total organization work system is dissolving.

The four conceptual developments outlined above have had important implications. First, Emery broadened STS interventions to designing rather than simply improving work systems; opened up the possibility of applying different design principles to STSs; determined that the choice of design principle has critical implications for operations, communications, and power in work systems; and clarified that one may, and perhaps should, apply value judgments to those design principles. Second, Pava opened up the possibility of different kinds of STSs, with different dynamics, design parameters, and assessment variables and criteria. Third, situating the environment as a crucial part of a STS swept context into the analysis and problematized the boundary relations between system and environment. Fourth, Klein's emphasis on technology choice became directly relevant for the explosion of technology-infused work systems experienced in recent times.

CLASSES OF SOCIOTECHNICAL SYSTEMS

The four developments sketched above create a pathway for new STS design thinking that can be responsive to the digital transformation of contemporary workplaces, including recent attempts to apply STSD to digital platform and virtual workplaces. Griffith and Dougherty (2002, p. 207) lay some groundwork, referring to an "explosion of STS-like work in technology management, at all different levels of analysis and focused on [a wide]... variety of problems." Winby and Mohrman (2018) critique current STSD concepts in the face of an expansion of digital platform organizations. Pasmore, Winby, Mohrman, and Vanasse (2019) use a design-lab method to imagine what STSD might become in a digitally rich future. But we think more design thinking work is needed.

We start by defining a *work system* as a semipermanent assemblage of people, technologies, and processes directed toward the production of a specified good or service, or bundle of goods/services, of economic and/or social value (see Latour, 2005; De Reuver, Sørensen, & Basole, 2018).[3] It is important to view a STS in this rather protean way because our analysis below calls into question conventional categories in which scholars have understood STSs.

For our purposes, a work system has three core dimensions:

- *Directness*: *Direct* means that the work system itself produces one or more outputs for a company at a defined position(s) in a value chain or value constellation. *Indirect* means that the work system mediates, facilitates, or brokers the production of one or more such outputs.
- *Materiality*: *Material* means that the outputs of the work system are actual material goods, services, or bundles thereof. *Symbolic* means that the outputs of the work system are not material but symbolic, such as strings of information, decision rules, or authentications (as in blockchain) (see Ciborra, 2002).
- *Ambit*: A work system is *concentrated* if it is contained within an enterprise (while acknowledging its transactional interdependencies with its environment). A work system is *distributed* if it spills across enterprise boundaries and encompasses other enterprises, parts of them, and/or other elements in the ecosystem. (See Winby & Mohrman, 2018 for how external stakeholders can be brought into the work system thrugh redesign.) For example, digital technologies managed by a platform company control the behavior of employees, contractors, and customers, as we discuss below. Thus, the work system of a platform enterprise is a *distributed* STS. We recognize that this distinction may be simplistic, for many "concentrated" work systems are porous, in that they rely on knowledge and learning from important external stakeholders.

Following the analytical path of the industrial STS and the knowledge-work STS, we argue that different "classes" of STS exist and need to be interpreted, designed, and assessed in consideration of their distinctive features. We outline each below and provide examples.

Industrial Applications

The STS enables the production of goods mainly in factories and mines, using primarily long-linked technology (Thompson, 1967).[4] The character of the work system is direct, material (e.g., coal, automobiles, iPads), and concentrated. The internal interdependencies are paramount. We call this class the Industrial-STS, or I-STS.

A typical example of an I-STS is found in a case of sociotechnical analysis at a Volvo truck cab plant in Sweden in 2000–2001 (Kuipers, DeWitte, & van der Zwaan, 2004). The factory management engaged in two change processes simultaneously: redesigning the production structure (which they associated with "lean production") and inculcating team development (which they associated with "STS"). Interestingly, the company, an early proponent of redesigning production systems around STS-inspired autonomous work groups, had decided for competitive reasons to move away from that type of design and toward a lean-production design. The authors evaluated the effects in terms of several "business performance" and "quality of work life" outcome measures. They found that the design of the production structure was not *the* determining factor for performance: "Team development appears to be just as important, although it requires a favorable context" (p. 852).

This case illustrates a typical attempt by STS-minded managers and practitioners to find the most effective workable balance among workers, production structure, and equipment. The initiative was driven by productivity and worker satisfaction concerns, and informed by the recent emphasis on lean and agile teams.

Office-professional Applications

The STS enables the production of knowledge and decisions through an assemblage of deliberations, decision-relevant coalitions, and communication flows using intensive (Thompson, 1967) or "knowledge technology" (Hickson, Pugh, & Pheysey, 1969). The character of the work system is direct and symbolic (e.g., decisions, issues). In its basic form it is concentrated, but we demonstrate in the second example below how it can also be distributed. Transactional interdependencies become important, as members of the work system exchange knowledge and learning with external stakeholders. This is the sociotechnical foundation of professional office work and services. We call this class the Knowledge-STS, or K-STS.

An example of the K-STS is a one-year sociotechnical redesign at an Israeli tire manufacturer called Gamer (Mitki, Shani, & Greenbaum, 2019). With the assistance of external consultants, the company revamped operations and changed its management structure. It developed and installed a "tapestry" of about 10 learning mechanisms – cognitive, structural, and procedural – at multiple levels to guide the redesign process. The learning mechanisms were "viewed as an integral part of the STS intervention" (p. 178) and enabled the company to achieve desired productivity and employee satisfaction outcomes. Mitki et al.'s assessment of the Gamer redesign initiative identified two capabilities developed through the redesign effort: the effective utilization of internal resources, and the ability to collect, analyze, utilize, and mobilize internal and external information (p. 179). The outcomes and capabilities persisted over the nine years of their longitudinal study.

The Gamer case is a concentrated K-STS, and Mitki et al.'s assessment emphasizes the vital roles of learning and capability development in STSD. We take up those roles later in the chapter.

As Pava implied, the K-STS represents an attempt to apply STSD principles beyond the "micro" level of the shop floor, namely, at the "meso" (total organization) level and even the "macro" (societal) level, as the founders of STS envisioned. Therefore, the unique case of the "Scandinavian model" below may be viewed as a large-scale K-STS.[5]

A "Scandinavian model" of work (Gustavsen, 2007) resulted from a radical reframing of classic STSD toward a linked set of interventions for developing not only workplaces but also the wider society in several nations. Democratization – of workplaces, industries, regions – has been a dominant thrust and has been accomplished by constructing cooperative institutional mechanisms with a variety of actors in the development and innovation spheres, at both workplace and societal levels.

This model can be traced to the initial Norwegian industrial democracy program (Emery & Thorsrud, 1976), which pioneered new participative forms of management and organization in a Norsk Hydro production complex during 1966–1973 (Gustavsen, 2007). Various initiatives in Sweden followed. For example, a STS redesign initiative in two new Volvo factories showed how advanced factory design could change the production system to make it manageable by autonomous work groups, essentially shifting the basic factory design from DP1 to DP2. Even today, Norway's regional and national development agenda bear traces of those early "field experiments." Similar long-term workplace development programs involving multiple enterprises, even entire sectors and regions, can be found in Denmark and Finland.

The systemic weaving among micro, meso, and macro levels has been a remarkable accomplishment of the Scandinavian model. A flexible, programmatic approach was used, linking work-unit experimentation to firm-level initiatives to coordination among clusters of firms, all supported financially and professionally by regional- and/or national-level labor, industry, and government interests. The broad development agenda has proceeded sequentially and organically as learnings have accumulated. This iterative approach to design has enabled different actors to be pulled in to sponsor particular programs as needed and also secured continuity through learning and mutual support for clusters, networks, regions, and the hundreds of enterprises engaged in these development initiatives. "Thus, almost from the start, multiple levels were engaged simultaneously: workplace improvement (mainly classic I-STS design), firm democratization (using K-STS principles), and community and regional development" (Selsky & Baburoglu, 2021, page forthcoming). Such multilevel, nested activity signals a *socioecological* intervention approach, which we discuss later.

Platform Applications

The STS enables the production of services by mediating transactions across an ecosystem (Thompson's mediating technology). The character of the work system is indirect and symbolic, since the enterprise does not own the critical material assets. Instead, the platform company enables transactions between customers and a set of asset-owning contractors via a suite of protocols and decision rules. Those protocols and rules replace the deliberations of the K-STS as the technical component. We call this class the Platform-STS or P-STS. A subclass are those P-STSs that rely on digital-control technology, often managed by a digital platform enterprise which designs and controls the digital protocols and decision algorithms. We refer to this subclass as the digital P-STS.

In addition to internal and transactional interdependencies, the contextual interdependencies take on added importance in the P-STS, as "work systems have become complex, technologically enabled networked ecosystems" (Winby & Mohrman, 2018, p. 401). Besides contractors to and employees of the (digital) platform company, the P-STS includes the users/customers of the platform, who in the other STS classes were in the external environment. In the P-STS, they are swept into the work system and are subject to new forms of control via the platform, starting with their "clicked" consent to be subject(ed) to the platform's rules, and ending with personal data harvested from their interaction. In this way the digital platform not only liberates the user (from the taxi system or the hotel booking system) but also disciplines them to the platform's protocols and data-harvesting terms (Calo & Rosenblat, 2017). The users may be naïve customers of Uber or skilled medical records specialists and physicians using Epic in the example below. They become participants in the STS in ways that department store customers, mediated by salespersons or even self-service checkout kiosks, do not. Thus, a distributed work system is created that is unbound from traditional organizational borders.

An example of an emerging P-STS is Winby and Mohrman's (2018) case study of Satellite Healthcare, a US company that provides in-home kidney dialysis services to its customer-patients. In 2016 this company undertook a complete STSD redesign process involving multiple stakeholders. It found it needed to develop "a digital technological application to support the patients' at-home roles and their many ecosystem connections" (p. 411). After design, prototyping, and scaling, this digital platform "enable[d] work-system communication and coordination across the ecosystem" of organizations and roles centered on the dialysis patient (p. 419). In short, the app proved successful in improving the patients' experience with the company, which then overhauled its business model and fundamental way of operating.

The Satellite Healthcare case is an early stage P-STS. The digital aspect of the redesigned work system is subordinated to the overall goal of refocusing the business on the dialysis patients' needs. This use of the digital platform appears different from a company like Uber, where customers must submit to the platform's protocols and algorithms, although insufficient information about the balance between patient and company interests is provided in the case study. That is, the Satellite platform appears to be in the service of the patients, rather than the other way around. Next, we offer an example of a P-STS further down the road toward the fusion of social and technological components of a work system.

Niederer and Van Dijck's (2010) analysis of Wikipedia as a STS identifies "the intricate collaboration between large numbers of human users and sophisticated automated systems that defines Wikipedia's ultimate success as a knowledge instrument" (p. 1370).[6] The authors claim that "[t]he online encyclopaedia's success is based on sociotechnical protocol-logical control, a combination of its technical infrastructure and the collective 'wisdom' of its contributors" (p. 1373). An analysis of that control reveals that:

> ...[s]ince 2002, Wikipedia content has been maintained by both tool-assisted human editors and bots, and collaboration has been modulated by protocols and strict managerial hierarchies. Bots are systematically deployed to detect and revert vandalism, monitor certain articles and, if necessary, ban users, but they also play a substantial role in the creation and maintenance of entries. (p. 1382)

When Wikipedia is viewed as a digital P-STS, it reveals the intricate way that people, technologies, and protocols are assembled and connected in the Wikipedia work system (Latour, 2005; De Reuver et al., 2018):

> ...[W]e propose to define Wikipedia as a gradually evolving sociotechnical system that carefully orchestrates all kinds of human and non-human contributors by implementing managerial hierarchies, protocols and automated editing systems. (Niederer & Van Dijck, 2010, p. 1373)

This example illustrates how the social and technical components of an advanced digital P-STS may become much more closely fused than the human–machine interface of the assembly line worker, data analyst, or software engineer. It also illustrates the promise of STSD analysis for coming to terms with the digital transformation and its social implications.

Hybrid Forms

We recognize that the three classes of STS above are ideal types. Interviews with senior managers of several digital platform companies in Turkey during 2020 revealed that "pure" digital platform enterprises are rare. Instead, hybrid arrangements are common, a phenomenon anticipated by Pava (in Claussen et al., 2019, p. 104):

> With the concepts of deliberation and discretionary coalition, Pava (1983) offers a new model for a flexible and scalable organisational architecture based on self-regulation. It provides a layout for how to combine self-managed work teams (in production lines, with the stamp of routine work), project teams of "hybrid work" (partly routine and matrix-organised) and the discretionary coalitions of non-routine work, coexisting within a "network organization."

An example of how the introduction of digital technology in a K-STS creates a hybrid work system occurred at an urban university hospital in the United States.[7] Several years ago hospital executives decided to abandon manually handwritten patient medical records and align with the national thrust to convert from paper to electronic medical records. It purchased a new electronic health record system called Epic, one of the most widely used such systems in US hospitals. The system went live after a complicated and contentious three-year "build." This involved extensive work by numerous committees that comprised interdisciplinary hospital staff (some permanent, some ad hoc) from many occupational categories (physicians, nursing, therapies, radiology, billing, medical records, etc.), with each committee headed by an Epic staff member. Directives and changes emanating from those committees reached into nearly all aspects of the hospital's work, including clinical care. The system came with a promise of big efficiencies over the old paper system, including the accretion of a vast database of patient information useful for research and regulatory reporting purposes. One of its main features is standardized drop-down menus that physicians and other professionals click on in order to create and update the patient record. The system is semicustomizable within its designed parameters; for instance, users can create and insert "smart phrases" into the system that can be used by certain others responsible for completing the medical record.

Previously, the paper medical record was more personalized, and DH and her medical records staff exercised extraction and interpretation skills in processing physicians' notes. With the new system she believes the record has become less specific (because the drop-down menu categories reduce specificity) and that the physicians' thinking about patient diagnosis is changing *because of the new system.* In this way Epic lowers information richness in the record and restricts the application of higher-level skills on the part of the medical records specialist and other users. In addition, Epic has new capabilities to quickly aggregate and compare patterns of individual physician behavior (e.g., therapy and drug prescriptions, time-to-discharge) in its database. It regularly and automatically delivers "deficiency" and "delinquency" reports to their inboxes. DH reports that some physicians have bridled at the system's intrusiveness, seeing it as a threat to their traditional high autonomy. Negative reactions and effects on physicians using the Epic system in other hospitals have been reported (Silverman, 2019). These effects appear to be an unintended (if predictable?) consequence of the introduction of this digital technology in the hospital STS, altering the preexisting coalitional, deliberatory, and decision-making dynamics among the diverse and numerous hospital personnel involved in delivering, reporting, monitoring, and regulating patient care. DH reported that the efficiency-gain objective of introducing Epic was indeed happening (although outcome data were not available), but she also commented that in its disruptiveness, "the system created the mess."

Epic and similar systems are in widespread and expanding use in US hospitals today. They are likely to become platforms for a new medical information and reporting ecosystem that will transform many aspects of hospital work systems, well beyond the medical records function, in significant ways. Similar "smart" information and communication technology (ICT) systems are proliferating in many knowledge-driven sectors. Typically, the implications are ambiguous:

>...the same new information technology is likely to have different implications in various companies in terms of system integration, work design, and organization structure. These implications are likely to necessitate a realignment of the entire organization. (Shani & Sena, 1994, p. 247)

This example illustrates organizational changes brought about by new technology at the boundary between the K-STS and the P-STS. Epic is a digital platform built within a well-developed K-STS and growing within it, with the potential to become all-encompassing. As such, it anticipates its eventual "realignment" to a full-fledged, hospital-wide P-STS, or perhaps some fluid hybrid of K- and P-STSs.

DESIGN IMPLICATIONS OF CLASSIFYING STSs

Aligning STSs into the three classes above has important implications for effectively designing them, especially the new class of the P-STS. Below we sketch implications for the underlying design principles, strategic adaptation, and system regulation.

P-STS Requires a New Design Principle

Emery's Design Principles 1 and 2, discussed above, apply directly to the I-STS and the K-STS. That is, an I- or K-STS may be designed such that control of work functions occurs at the level of the workers themselves (DP2) or at a level "above" the workers (DP1). However, Emery's design principles provide inadequate guidance for the design of the P-STS, whether digital or nondigital. That is because in a P-STS *contractors* to the platform company are often equally as important to the functioning and effectiveness of the work system as employees are. They deploy their assets within the established protocols and algorithmic rules, and they are often widely distributed geographically, rarely colocated in a factory or office. In addition, Emery's design principles are silent regarding the role of the *user* or *customer*, who activates the work system by invoking the platform app and by providing data feedback to the enterprise's software engineers. This makes the customer much more consequential for the effectiveness of the P-STS than for the I- or K-STS. This renders traditional concepts of the control of work activity and output, based on managing the behavior of employees, inadequate. How may we account for these differences?

As noted above, in the digital P-STS the boundary between the shop floor work system and the total-organization work system dissolves (Klein, 2014; see also Pava, 1983). The *employee* part of the work system is built around agile, project-based development and production teams consisting of software engineers, data scientists, consumer experience managers, influencers, app developers, and/or other roles. Those teams are responsible for continuously improving the platform. Improvements are driven by user feedback and by analysis of the flood of data coming in from the user/customer interface. The digital platform mediates among those employee teams, the "gig" contractors, and the customers. In these ways the P-STS transmutes the "shop floor" with its cadre of workers into a trans-organizational work system, or alternatively, the enterprise's digital information and control system eclipses the shop floor work system. Thus, Klein's insights about the expanded role of workplace information technology challenge conventional understanding of STSs and call for an enlarged notion of STSD in the context of the digital transformation. Specifically, we believe her insights call for a new principle for the design of digital P-STSs.

Selsky, Ramírez, and Baburoglu (2013, p. 392) extended the Emery design principles and introduced Design Principle 3 (DP3), which they called *redundancy of potentiality*. It focuses on potential connectivity in a field of action or network: "When potential connections are activated, that part of the network becomes a working transorganizational system. One can think of DP3 as enabling an open-ended trajectory of constantly expanding potentialities." DP3 "deals with questions of 'what if' and 'what might,' that is, questions of possibility, risk and opportunity" (Selsky et al., 2013, p. 388) in imaginable and plausible futures. Thus, for our purposes, we refer to this design principle by the more descriptive *redundancy of potential connectivity*.

Digital platform enterprises, especially consumer-facing ones like Uber and Airbnb, represent a potentiality because, unlike the I- or K-STS, the potential inherent in their work systems is activated only when a customer invokes the relevant app and triggers the deployment of the contracted asset, along with monitoring, authenticating, and evaluating protocols. The platform enterprise relies on a pool of potential need for the service offered through its platform and pulls together a potential ecosystem of diverse actors.

In such a work system design must be continuous to cope with ever-changing potentialities in the ecosystem created by the platform (see Pasmore et al., 2019; Winby & Mohrman, 2018). "Pava... acknowledged that our increasingly turbulent environment requires us to look at organisational change less as an event and more as a continuous dynamic of iterative design" (Claussen et al., 2019, p. 104).

We may link the three design principles to the three classes of STS. In the *I-STS*, design choices are prescribed by reliance on redundant parts, i.e., replaceable workers for set tasks (DP1), or redundant functions, i.e., multiple capabilities instilled in workers for variable tasks (DP2). Control over work process and product output is the main consideration, and this may be accomplished in one of those two ways, or in mixed arrangements. In the *K-STS*, design choices are prescribed primarily by DP2 (as above) and by reliance on potential connectivity among workers performing set or variable nonroutine tasks (DP3), with a remnant possibility of DP1. The main considerations are coordination and communication among highly skilled, independent-minded knowledge workers to enable effective deliberations over key dilemmas. This may be accomplished via a combination of team control over issue shaping; flexible, discretionary connections among (potentially) involved actors; and ad hoc coalition formation. In the *P-STS*, design choices are prescribed primarily by DP3 (as above), with remnant possibilities of DP1 and DP2. Effective connectivity is the main consideration, linking software engineers, other highly skilled employees, gig contractors, and customers/users to the constantly updated platform.

Remnant possibilities of DP1 exist in the K- and P-STS because digital technologies increase the possibilities for tight control over human behavior – whether they are software engineers and other technically skilled professionals employed by the enterprise, or its gig contractors – through very close monitoring of task performance.

STSD Supports Strategic Adaptation

Emery's DP1 and DP2 have been critiqued as too inwardly focused (e.g., how to jointly optimize social and technical components of the work system) and too operationally focused (e.g., DP2's reliance on autonomous work groups and self-managing teams) (Selsky et al., 2013). Hence, in today's highly volatile conditions, those design principles need to be reworked to be better directed toward an organization's strategic goals or purpose. With its emphasis on potential connectivity, DP3 is relevant for the strategic future, not just the present. Thus, DP3 is geared to deal with the prevailing corporate conditions of boundary porousness, multiple change initiatives, and nearly continuous disruptions alluded to earlier in this chapter.

STSD can support strategic adaptation if learning is embedded in processes and procedures (Pasmore et al., 2019). Recall that the intent of the PDW, a key notion in Emery's design thinking for STSs, is to create work systems deliberately designed for learning (Emery, 1999; see also Purser & Cabana, 1998). This learning mandate is supported by Mitki et al.'s (2019) call for developing multilevel organizational learning "tapestries," as was done in the Gamer case. Learning enables design to be iterative, engendering a capability for continuous, iterative (re)designing. The Scandinavian case illustrates how a learning capability can become baked into a dynamic process of organizational, sectoral, and national development over many years.

STSD Affects System Regulation

The indirect character of the work system in the P-STS stretches the bounds of what a STS can be. There are often a limited number of conventional "line" employees relative to the scale of the enterprise. Instead, there is a cadre (in the case of companies like Uber and Airbnb, an army!) of "gig workers," that is, contractors who own assets (vehicles, rooms) and submit those assets to the protocols and rules of the enterprise controlling the platform. In addition, the role of the customer is radically different, drawn closer to the core operations (see strategic adaptation above). Harkening back to Williamson and Ouchi, the essential P-STS work system is more like market regulation of an assemblage of humans, technologies, and processes than the hierarchical regulation of technical and social components characteristic of the I-STS, or the clan regulation of deliberations and coalitions' characteristic of the K-STS.[8]

Table 1 summarizes the features of the three classes of STS.

REWORKING STS DESIGN FOR DIGITAL PLATFORM WORK SYSTEMS

In answering our guiding research question, we argue that the three fundamental STSD principles are still sound, but need to be reworked for the new digital platform work systems beginning with the following guideposts.

Table 1. Comparison of Classes of Sociotechnical Systems (STS).

Class	Industrial STS (I-STS)	Knowledge-STS (K-STS)	Platform-STS (P-STS)
Work system core dimensions	Direct – material	Direct – symbolic	Indirect – symbolic
Work system ambit	Concentrated	Concentrated, but porous	Distributed
Main type of technology (Thompson)	Long-linked	Intensive	Mediating
Technical component	Production machinery	Deliberations	Digital protocols, algorithms
Social component	Individual workers (employees), semiautonomous teams	Discretionary coalitions	Employees (agile teams), gig contractors, users
Main analytic category	Production variances	Key dilemmas	Ecosystem variances/ demands, potential connectivities
Predominant design principle (Emery; Selsky et al.)	DP1	DP2	DP3
Predominant governance type (Williamson; Ouchi)	Hierarchy	Clan	Market
Focus of learning	Operations	Stakeholders	Ecosystem, stakeholders; strategic level

Joint Optimization

This principle needs reworking because part of the environment becomes incorporated in the work system and because a *potential* ecosystem becomes relevant. "While in traditional organizations joint optimization is an internal goal, in the future joint optimization will concern the external network ecosystem" (Pasmore et al., 2019, p. 78; see also Winby & Mohrman, 2018). In a digital P-STS users/ customers carry feedback data crucial to the ability of the enterprise to improve its platform regime and continually offer a market-responsive service. They are not only part of the enterprise's ecosystem, but are also a crucial component in operational and strategic effectiveness. In assessing the workings of Wikipedia, Niederer and Van Dijck (2010, p. 1377) suggest that

> …[d]escribing Wikipedians in bipolar categories of humans and non-humans, however, doesn't do justice to what is, in fact, a third category: that of the many active users assisted by administrative and monitoring tools, also referred to as software-assisted human editors.

This kind of blurring and blending in the P-STS unsettles the conventional STS concept of joint optimization of social and technical components of the internal-only work system.

Design Choice

This principle needs reworking because DP3 concepts are required, including orienting the Emery design principles to be strategic, not just operational, and making them future responsive (Selsky et al., 2013). As an example of refocusing design thinking in this way, platform companies commonly start with customer needs and go back to test all the iterative design increments to the platform design, then continually revise the design in the familiar "version" updates. This process is intimately linked to the company's strategy. In this way variances handling, a fundamental category in STS analysis, is reconfigured in the digital P-STS as the iterative redesign of the platform. The digital platform continually generates user cases and adjusts the software to fit the real-time demands of users/ customers – and depending on the acuity of the company's predictive analytics, *future* demands as well. This is qualitatively a very different kind of joint optimization, calling for a very different kind of design choice.

Technology choice needs to be considered as part of design choice, as we have argued above. Technology design and redesign have been largely neglected in STSD because scholars have tended to take advancing technology for granted as it forced the social component to adapt (McAfee & Brynjolfsson, 2017). But there are other, perhaps more important, reasons. First, the spread and success of platform enterprises have shown that *all* enterprises have the possibility of shifting toward platform form by harnessing the data inherent in the social, technological, transactional, and economic systems and processes they interact with. Digital technologies such as artificial intelligence, machine learning, robotic process automation, decision algorithms, augmented and virtual reality, blockchain, etc., may be seen as "meta" technologies that provide the foundation for digital platforms throughout many industries. Second, recent ethical concerns over the use and abuse of digital technologies illustrate that unintended social consequences of technology use take time to work their way into the social fabric (at and beyond the workplace) and surface as a social issue. Examples include the dystopian possibilities inherent in wearable neuroimaging technologies (Onaral, 2019) and digital task monitoring technologies that control worker behavior.[9] Thus, it is important to build in provisions for ongoing technology choice and redesign as part of effective STSD.

Open System

This principle needs reworking because the P-STS context is turbulent and its ecosystem is labile (Ciborra, 2002). Elements in the external environment of the I- and K-STS, namely, contractors and users/customers, become part of the work (eco)system in the P-STS. Therefore, designers need to focus at the ecosystem level and not be company-centric (Winby & Mohrman, 2018). They also need to be mindful of internal, transactional, and contextual interdependencies, as discussed above. The design of the distributed work system needs to be iterative and learningful, and thereby adaptive to turbulent conditions, as Pava (1983) foresaw. The success of open operating systems like Linux, Firefox, and Wikipedia may provide useful guidance. Relatedly, it is important to imagine possible alternative *future* designs of P-STSs, so that unintended consequences as discussed above might be foreseen and designed out.

In short, STSD needs to encompass, or even become, *socioecological* systems design (see Emery, 1999) as the appropriate template for interpreting digitally infused, platform-based work systems. With more digital P-STSs emerging in today's advanced economies, the role of technology has to be recognized and dealt with deliberately because it influences overall work systems in more impactful ways compared to the ways that technology affects the conventional production task systems of the I-STS or the professional deliberation systems of the K-STS. DP3 creates a bridge between sociotechnical and socioecological modes of analysis and design. The notion of including the environment of a STS in a STS analysis and design (Heller, 2001) anticipates the shift to the socio-ecological level. The Scandinavian case above appears to embody best these three key principles and the socioecological orientation.

Table 2 summarizes the differences in fundamental STSD principles among the three classes.

CONCLUSION

In this chapter, we have argued that the digital transformation now sweeping through the economies of many societies compel STS scholars to explore new kinds of work systems and their distinctive features. Recent research (e.g., Griffith & Dougherty, 2002; Pasmore et al., 2019; Winby & Mohrman, 2018) has

Table 2. Fundamental Sociotechnical Systems Design (STSD) Principles: Comparison among Classes.

STSD Principle	Industrial STS (I-STS)	Knowledge-STS (K-STS)	Platform-STS (P-STS)	
Joint optimization	Machine(s) and worker(s); often adaptation of worker to machine	Deliberations and discretionary coalitions in key dilemmas; deliberative and reflective learning systems	Employees, contractors, and users/customers; toward fusion of social and technical components	
Design choice	Redundancy or parts (DP1) or functions (DP2)	Redundancy of functions (DP2) or connectivity (DP3)	Redundancy of connectivity (DP3); iterative redesign of platform with explicit learning	SOCIO-ECOLOGICAL SYSTEMS DESIGN
Open system	Internal interdependencies	Transactional interdependencies with environment	Transactional and contextual interdependencies	

been a good start, showing renewed attention to this major turn in the character of systems. In this study we have sought to build upon that work.

We may summarize our study as follows: first, there are different classes of STSs. We identified three, having uncovered the third class. There may be other types. It is important to distinguish them because we found that different analytic categories, mechanisms, and criteria exist for assessing each class. In the I-STS, it is production variances and autonomous work groups, and in the K-STS, it is deliberations and discretionary coalitions. In the P-STS, we suggested it is the diverse demands in the ecosystem for efficient and ethically sound mediation of transactions which require potential connectivity. We suggested that the redundancy of potential connectivity principle is the design answer for analyzing the new P-STS.

Second, the P-STS was found to be distinctive in several ways. The platform enterprise with its associated P-STS is essentially a nexus of internal and external contracts (Reve, 1990) that invoke and cohere an ecosystem of diverse elements. The P-STS is more about regulating a market than managing a hierarchical or "clan" assemblage of people, technologies, and processes. This is due to the different nature of interdependencies and connections in the market-governed P-STS. The crucial new connections are with contractors and users/customers of the digital platform, swept into the work system and disciplined to the protocols of the platform. This shift of work system roles creates a distributed STS. The P-STS challenges traditional STS concepts of the "worker" and their "job" autonomy.

Third, STSs must be deliberately designed and redesigned, not merely "improved." The locus of design must be all components of the STS (technical component, social component, environment), not merely the social component and its adaptation to the technical requirements. Pasmore et al. (2019, p. 79) include the organization itself as a "component" and envision "next generation STS" being about

> …balanced optimization… predicated on the notion that everything is in motion. As the external environment changes, the design of the four components (ecosystem, organization, technical system, social system) need to evolve and align.

This is especially true for the P-STS. Moreover, when the boundary between the work system and the organizational system dissolves, as in the P-STS, new design challenges emerge. Design choices have implications for platform capabilities, enterprise learning, and strategic adaptation.

We do not wish to overstate the novelty of the P-STS. As we argued above, hybrid arrangements of digital and nondigital components, and routine and nonroutine work, appear to be common among platform enterprises. Enterprise-wide ICT systems like Epic have existed and affected (some would say infected) the texture of work systems for nearly 30 years. Employees have adapted to them, sometimes with controversy and resistance. From this perspective, digital platforms are merely the next turn of the wheel. Nonetheless, binding users/customers to the work system of the digital platform enterprise is unprecedented and worthy of research attention.

Implications for Practice

Designs for P-STSs need to reflect the new, broadened requirements for joint optimization, design choice, and environmental relations discussed above. Our study's main implication for practice lies in how agile teams and the digital platform interact in the P-STS.[10] This reflects a new generation of joint optimization in the context of a rapidly changing competitive environment where disruptions constantly threaten operations and strategy. The customer-facing, digital platform enterprises that we have focused on, such as food delivery services, are usually very sensitive to customer needs and changes in user behavior. Because they continuously strive to provide an impeccable user experience while engaging the company's platform, the engineers responsible for the interface software need to be able to quickly respond to fix relevant aspects of the platform as issues arise, sometimes overnight, and to periodically introduce major resets of the platform. This necessitates a muscular IT function. The preferred form is agile teams (Rigby, Sutherland, & Takeuchi, 2016), perhaps reminiscent of the autonomous work teams of the STS tradition. The push for agile teams appears to start in the crucial IT function, then diffuse to other parts of the company, such as product development which is closely linked to IT.

In many of these companies it feels like a mad scramble to keep up; speed is crucial, more important than cost cutting or being "lean." There is a strong start-up spirit, with a tendency to do everything with fewer people and with the leadership and close monitoring of the founder(s). As one executive commented on the resulting tension, "Start-up spirit is in the opposite direction of strategy work. We are no longer start-ups, but we must not lose this spirit." There is an emphasis on bringing the social system closer to the way the technical system operates and vice versa. A harmonious, aligned, or better fitting social and technical systems is the talk of entrepreneurs and corporate executives alike. A simple structure built around agile teams tends to prevail regardless of the number of people reporting to each manager and giving enormous responsibilities to managers at a younger age.

The mutual adaptation of employees, contractors, users, and technology tends to be more spontaneous and organic than the slower, more deliberate change process espoused by the STS founders. Therefore, project management using off-the-shelf software is vital, with design and redesign occurring in tandem in the digital platform/interface and in the agile teams themselves. This organic adaptation appears increasingly freed from the command-and-control structures (DP1) or even the participative-management structures (DP2) of the past, and to embody the redundancy of potential connectivity principle (DP3) discussed above.

For management practice to be responsive to the realities sketched above, new systems of compensation, work life, skill sets, and assumptions regarding where and when to work need to be redesigned for the new P-STS challenges.

Future Prospects and Research

What is the future of work systems over the next decade, given the current trajectory of technology advances? What we imagine that future to be will condition the way we design – and *think about* the design of – those workplaces (Pasmore et al., 2019). Will they be like the chaotic assemblage of mismatched, misshapen objects and people of the 1980s cult movie *Brazil*, or will they be like the clean, efficient, harmonious habitat of Captain Janeway's starship in *Star Trek: Voyager*?

Or will they be hybrids? Is the urban hospital in the Epic example moving toward the human–bot fusion seen in the Wikipedia example? Is Satellite Healthcare and the ecosystem of actors arrayed around its patients moving in that direction? Are Uber, Amazon, and indeed all digitally infused companies – and their ecosystem partners – doing so? Is it possible, with advances in neuroscience, that the hybrid work systems we have discussed could evolve into synchronized groups of cyborgs, human workers implanted with wearable smart technologies, as in a Philip K. Dick novel (see Callon, 2004; Hailes, 1999)? If all work systems are already hybrids of the three ideal classes of STSs, or are moving rapidly toward becoming such, then future research on the nature, effects, and trajectories of hybrid STSs is urgently needed.

Going forward, STSD must deepen its relationship with the digitally infused technologies that lie at the heart of today's technical and social systems (Selsky & Baburoglu, 2021). STSD scholars need to continue to commit to the promise of the three original key principles as the field evolves and comes to terms with new contexts, applications, and technologies. Equally as important, STSD practitioners need to examine carefully the meanings, effects, and consequences of digital technologies as part of *socioecological* intervention plans. Only by doing so can they advance STSD's aspiration of human development in and around enterprises in turbulent times.

NOTES

1. This section draws extensively from Selsky and Baburoglu (2021).

2. See Claussen et al. (2019) for a cogent analysis of Pava's contributions to sociotechnical systems theory.

3. This rendering of the sociotechnical system is based in actor-network theory. See also Callon (2004) on hybrid communities of humans and objects, and Griffith and Dougherty (2002).

4. This refers to conventional manufacturing, not to "additive manufacturing" using computer-aided design (CAD) to create products through 3D printing.

5. Adapted from Selsky and Baburoglu (2021).

6. This example is adapted from Selsky and Baburoglu (2021).

7. The following case information is from personal interviews with DH (pseudonym), a medical records manager at the subject hospital in October 2019 and January 2021.

8. "As observed by Trist, one of the merits of the concept of discretionary coalitions in relation to deliberations is that it offers an 'operational approach to the analysis of managerial and professional work in a nonhierarchical perspective'" (Claussen et al., 2019, p. 104).

9. Beyond the workplace are the now familiar concerns about social-media companies' key role in the promulgation of socially damaging mis/disinformation, and about surveillance technologies for facial recognition of citizens in public spaces.

10. Information in this section comes from interviews with top managers at six of the largest customer-facing, platform-based companies in Turkey during 2020.

REFERENCES

Ayaz, H., Shewokis, P. A., Bunce, S., Izzetoglu, K., Willems, B., & Onaral, B. (2012). Optical brain monitoring for operator training and mental workload assessment. *NeuroImage, 59*(1), 36–47.

Babüroğlu, O. (1992). Tracking the development of the Emery-Trist systems paradigm (ETSP). *Systems Practice, 5*(3), 263–290.

Bai, C., & Sarkis, J. (2019). A supply chain transparency and sustainability technology appraisal model for blockchain technology. *Academy of Management 2019 Proceedings, 2019*(1), 16069.

Callon, M. (2004). The role of hybrid communities and socio-technical arrangements in the participatory design. *Journal of the Center for Information Studies, 5*, 3–10.

Calo, R., & Rosenblat, A. (2017). The taking economy: Uber, information, and power. *Columbia Law Review, 117*, 1623–1690.

Cennamo, C. (2021). Competing in digital markets: A platform-based perspective. *Academy of Management Perspectives, 35*(2), 265–291.

Ciborra, C. (1996). The platform organization: Recombining strategies, structures, and surprises. *Organization Science, 7*(2), 103–118.

Ciborra, C. (2002). *The labyrinths of information: Challenging the wisdom of systems.* Oxford: Oxford University Press.

Claussen, T., Haga, T., & Ravn, J. (2019). Socio-technics and beyond: An approach to organisation studies and design in the second machine age. *European Journal of Workplace Innovation, 4*(2), 99–122.

Cusumano, M. (2020). Guidepost: The evolution of research on industry platforms. *Academy of Management Discoveries.* Online first. doi:10.5465/amd.2020.0091

Eden, C., & Huxham, C. (2006). Researching organizations using action research. In S. Clegg, C. Hardy, T. Lawrence, & W. Nord (Eds.), *Sage handbook of organization studies (2nd ed.*, pp. 388–408). Thousand Oaks, CA: Sage.

Emery, M. (1999). *Searching: The theory and practice of making cultural change.* Philadelphia, PA: John Benjamins.

Emery, F., & Thorsrud, E. (1976). *Democracy at work: The report of the Norwegian industrial democracy program.* Leiden: Martinus Nijhoff.

Gerwe, O., & Silva, R. (2020). Clarifying the sharing economy: Conceptualization, typology, antecedents, and effects. *Academy of Management Perspectives, 34*(1), 65–96.

Gösele, M., & Sandner, P. (2019). Analysis of blockchain technology in the mobility sector. *Forschung im Ingenieurwesen, 83*(4), 809–816.

Griffith, T., & Dougherty, D. (2002). Beyond socio-technical systems: Introduction to the special issue. *Journal of Engineering and Technology Management, 19*, 205–216.

Gustavsen, B. (2007). Work organization and "the Scandinavian model". *Economic and Industrial Democracy, 28*(4), 650–671.

Hailes, N. K. (1999). *How we became posthuman.* Chicago, IL: University of Chicago Press.

Heller, F. (2001). Towards a socio-oecotechnology. *Journal of Engineering and Technology Management, 18*(3/4), 295–312.

Hickson, D., Pugh, D., & Pheysey, D. (1969). Operations technology and organization structure: An empirical reappraisal. *Administrative Science Quarterly, 14*, 378–397.

Hirschhorn, L., Noble, P., & Rankin, T. (2001). Sociotechnical systems in an age of mass customization. *Journal of Engineering and Technology Management, 18*(3/4), 241–252.

Iansiti, M., & Levien, R. (2004). Strategy as ecology. *Harvard Business Review, 82*(3), 68–81.

Istrate, E., & Harris, J. (2017). *The future of work: The rise of the gig economy.* Counties Futures Lab. Retrieved from https://www.naco.org/sites/default/files/documents/Gig-Economy.pdf

Klein, L. (2014). What do we actually mean by 'sociotechnical'? On values, boundaries and the problems of language. *Applied Ergonomics, 45*(2A), 137–142.

Kuipers, B., DeWitte, M., & van der Zwaan, Ad H. (2004). Design or development? Beyond the LP-STS debate; inputs from a Volvo truck case. *International Journal of Operations & Production Management, 24*(8), 840–854.

Lanier, J. (2013). *Who owns the future?* New York, NY: Simon & Schuster.

Latour, B. (2005). *Re-assembling the social: An introduction to actor-network theory.* Oxford: Oxford University Press.

McAfee, A., & Brynjolfsson, E. (2017). *Machine, platform, crowd: Harnessing our digital future.* New York, NY: Norton.

Mitki, Y., Shani, A., & Greenbaum, B. (2019). Developing new capabilities: A longitudinal study of sociotechnical system redesign. *Journal of Change Management, 19*(3), 167–182.

Moldaschl, M., & Weber, W. (1998). The "three waves" of industrial group work: Historical reflections on current research on group work. *Human Relations, 51*(3), 347–388.

Moore, J. (1993). Predators and prey: A new ecology of competition. *Harvard Business Review, 71*(3), 75–86.

Mumford, E. (2000). Socio-technical design: An unfulfilled promise or a future opportunity? In R. Baskerville, J. Stage, & J. DeGross (Eds.), *Organizational and social perspectives on information technology* (pp. 33–46). London: Springer.

Niederer, S., & Van Dijck, J. (2010). Wisdom of the crowd or technicity of content? Wikipedia as a sociotechnical system. *New Media & Society, 12*(8), 1368–1387.

Onaral, P. B. (2019, July 29). *Personal interview.* Philadelphia, PA: Drexel University Biomedical Engineering Faculty.

Pasmore, W., Winby, S., Mohrman, S., & Vanasse, R. (2019). Reflections: Sociotechnical systems design and organization change. *Journal of Change Management, 19*(2), 67–85.

Pava, C. (1983). *Managing new office technology: An organizational strategy.* New York, NY: Free Press.

Pava, C. (1986). Redesigning sociotechnical systems design: Concepts and methods for the 1990s. *Journal of Applied Behavioral Science, 22*(3), 201–221.

Purser, R., & Cabana, S. (1998). *The self managing organization.* New York, NY: Free Press.

Reve, T. (1990). The firm as a nexus of internal and external contracts. In M. Aoki, B. Gustafsson, & O. Williamson (Eds.), *The firm as a nexus of treaties* (pp. 133–161). Newbury Park, CA: Sage.

De Reuver, M., Sørensen, C., & Basole, R. C. (2018). The digital platform: A research agenda. *Journal of Information Technology, 33*(2), 124–135.

Rigby, D., Sutherland, J., & Takeuchi, H. (2016). Embracing agile: How to master the process that's transforming management. *Harvard Business Review, 94*(5), 40–50.

Scott, W. R., & Davis, G. (2007). *Organizations and organizing: Rational, natural, and open system perspectives.* Upper Saddle River, NJ: Pearson Prentice Hall.

Selsky, J., & Babüroğlu, O. (2021). Socio-technical systems thinking: Appraisal and prospects. In D. Cabrera & G. Midgley (Eds.), *The Routledge handbook of systems thinking.* London: Routledge. (Pages forthcoming).

Selsky, J., Ramírez, R., & Baburoglu, O. (2013). Collaborative capability design: Redundancy of potentialities. *Systemic Practice and Action Research, 26*(5), 377–397.

Shani, A., & Sena, J. (1994). Information technology and the integration of change: Sociotechnical system Approach. *Journal of Applied Behavioral Science, 30*(2), 247–270.

Silverman, E. (2019, November 5). A hospital's new software frets about my 'deficiencies'. *New York Times,* p. D5.

Srnicek, N. (2017). *Platform capitalism.* New York, NY: John Wiley & Sons.

Susman, G. (1976). *Autonomy at work: A sociotechnical analysis of participative management.* New York, NY: Praeger.

Thompson, J. (1967). *Organizations in action.* New York, NY: McGraw-Hill.

Trist, E. (1983). Epilogue. In C. Pava (Ed.), *Managing new office technology*. New York, NY: Free Press. Reproduced in Trist, E., & Murray, H. (Eds.). (1993). The social engagement of social science, volume 2: The socio-technical perspective (pp. 662–673). Philadelphia, PA: University of Pennsylvania Press.

Winby, S., & Mohrman, S. (2018). Digital sociotechnical system design. *Journal of Applied Behavioral Science, 54*(4), 399–423.

FROM PSYCHOLOGICAL DISPOSITIONS TO SOCIAL POSITIONS: APPLYING A HABITUS-ORIENTED APPROACH TO ORGANIZATION DEVELOPMENT AND CHANGE

Baruch Shimoni

ABSTRACT

The influence of traditional individually oriented Organization Development (OD), with its focus on psychological dispositions, on self-development and growth, is currently waning. I argue here that individually oriented OD would be well served by a new focus on habitus and social position that expand our understanding of human behavior. Using Bourdieu's concept of social position in the form of "habitus-oriented approach," as I do here using my consulting experience, allows individually oriented OD to become a scholarly and professional site that understands human behavior in terms of both the social and the personal.

Keywords: Individually oriented Organization Development; psychological dispositions; social positions; habitus; field; capital; power; relational perspective

Research in Organizational Change and Development, Volume 29, 89–109
Copyright © 2022 Emerald Publishing Limited
All rights of reproduction in any form reserved
ISSN: 0897-3016/doi:10.1108/S0897-301620210000029005

INTRODUCTION

Men and women are indeed responsible, but what they can or cannot do is largely determined by the structure in which they are placed and by the position they occupy within that structure. (Pierre Bourdieu, 1998, p. 54)

A Call for Help

In April 2019, Philip invited me to help "Sonic Group" (SG) improve its management and administrative processes.[1] Philip is the owner and chairperson of SG, a family real estate firm, located in a small town near one of the biggest cities on America's southeast coast.

According to Philip, SG cannot improve its management and achieve its desired business development ("climb to the next phase") because of Wolf's disruptive psychological dispositions and behavior. Psychological dispositions in this chapter represent people's tendency to act in a way derived from inner character or personality traits such as risk-taking or violence, and as understood by Philip and Wolf, laziness and restless. Wolf is SG's Chief Financial Officer (CFO) whom Philip coaxed to leave his previous job in a big accounting firm and join him at SG. Philip defined Wolf as a significant partner in his development initiatives and thus was very disappointed to see that Wolf was not meeting his expectations. Philip described Wolf as a "lazy" partner who does not want to invest the effort needed for SG's growth. In turn Wolf said that it is hard to work with Philip since he is "emotional, restless and often aggressive and does not show respect." Philip's and Wolf's reciprocal blame occupied the first three consulting meetings in which they discussed how the other's disruptive psychological dispositions were stunting SG's expected growth.

Assuming that changing their psychological dispositions would help SG climb to the next phase, Philip asked me to help Wolf improve his motivation and commitment to SG, and help him (Philip) be more open and flexible with Wolf and the other employees. Philip's request that I help him and Wolf to change personally did not surprise me.

I assume that many Organization Development (OD) scholars and practitioners are familiar with the phenomenon in which clients very often define organizational problems in psychological terms, asking that the consultant help to improve employees' psychological dispositions such as motivation and commitment and other personal dis/abilities and skills. Largely, OD is a conceptual and practical framework for organizational change dealing mainly with human behavior (Bradford & Burke, 2005). Writers usually define OD as a planned change practice managed from the top and focused on the organization as a whole, from the macro level down to subdivisions and individuals, to increase effectiveness (for more definitions see Church, Waclawski, & Seigel, 1996). However, as says David Coghlan (2012), although OD has always advocated working with the organization as a whole, in practice many OD projects are engaged solely in specific programs that focus on suborganizational systems and on individuals and thus enact what I define here as "individually oriented OD." The focus on individuals, as Shani Kuna (2014) shows, largely produces managers' expectations (like those held by Philip) that OD consultants work on personal development and growth.

Social Position, Field, Habitus, and Relational Perspective at SG: A First Glance

I have no doubt that Philip's and Wolf's disruptive interactions were preventing the change SG needed. However, my meetings with the two showed that understanding their interactions could not be complete by considering only the personal level or specifically, the level of psychological dispositions. I realized that to understand the interaction between Philip and Wolf I must also investigate their unequal social positions at SG as a social field. Social positions are at the juncture of the personal and the social. They are the place people occupy in the social field in relation to others, subject to their control over the field's resources and capitals (Bourdieu, 1989). Social positions, thus, are constructed structures produced through ongoing competition over a similar set of resources and capitals. Among the central types of capital are "human capital" (knowledge, skills and expertise), "symbolic capital" (prestige and reputation), "social capital" (the ability to use the capital of other people to promote one's own interests), and "cultural capital" (arbitrary attributions like accepted language) (Bourdieu, 1989).

Social field is a social space in which people play a game according to rules that are different from the rules in use elsewhere (Bourdieu, 1989). Once adopted, these rules largely direct what people can or cannot do; they become an inner structure, natural and durable dispositions, e.g., habitus that predisposes people's thinking and behavior (Friedman, 2011). Yet, although fields represent a group with common rules, with a shared interest and habitus, group members are always in competition over similar sets of resources (at SG, mainly technology) and over different types of capitals (at SG, mainly cultural).

Habitus is a set of social dispositions (worldview, schema of thinking, practical knowledge) that generates people's thoughts and behavior (Bourdieu, 1989). People adopt these social dispositions from the social structure of groups such as the family, gender group, ethnic group, and working organization through a process of socialization (Sieweke, 2014). Habitus can be primary or specific. "Primary habitus" is acquired through early socialization and "context-specific habitus" is acquired later in life from groups such as working organizations (Cornelissen, 2016, p. 501). Both represent the group's taken-for-granted structures of power and social positions that generate thoughts and behavior from within the individual. In Bourdieu's (1990, p. 53) words, habitus is "systems of durable, transposable dispositions, structured structures predisposed to function as structuring structures, that is, as principles which generate and organize practices." Habitus, then, is internal, the cognitive and bodily site of the group's worldview, schema of thinking, practical knowledge, structures of power, and social positions.

Indeed, the more I learned about Philip's and Wolf's disruptive interactions, the more I refused to see their unproductive communication as a psychological construct, as Philip claimed it was – a construct in which two people, detached from the social structure, simply could not find the needed personal skills to approach each other effectively. I claim that Philip's and Wolf's behavior dynamically formed with and against their constant competition over capitals, resources, and positions. Philip's privileged position as the owner, defined by his control over the organization's material resources (budget, buildings), financial and cultural elements (language and knowledge and techniques), and prestige, allowed him to make his habitus dominant and to exert a level of control over Wolf, the new partner.

Competitions for the field's resources and capitals are often between two groups. On the one hand are those who, like Philip, monopolize the field's capitals, power and authority, and thus privileged positions, those whose habitus is compatible with the organization's specific habitus – with the shared worldview and taken-for-granted structure of power and social positions. On the other hand are those who, like Wolf, have just entered the field, the "newcomers" who have not yet acquired the organization's specific habitus and capitals, and thus use the habitus they acquired in a previous work environment. Wolf arrived to SG, a small and nonformal family firm, from a big and established firm. He also had to adapt to a management position, which demanded skills different from those he used as an accountant in his previous firm. Newcomers like Wolf are often interested in changing the organization's specific habitus and its accepted power relations in order to improve their social position and influence (Bourdieu, 1993, p. 73).

Philip's and Wolf's behaviors, then, are the result of relations between their different habitus and relative control over SG's capitals which defines their social positions. Bourdieu (1989; Wacquant, 1989, p. 39) presents these relations using his "relational perspective" which assumes that behavior is a function of field, habitus, and social position (capitals). Indeed, in his position as owner and chairperson, Philip holds habitus dispositions that generated attempts to achieve fast development *his* way by keeping control over SG's resources such as time, job definitions, and computer technology. From the position of a junior partner and a newcomer, Wolf, on the other hand, holds habitus dispositions that generated struggle with the way Philip runs SG and defines his (Wolf's) job – mainly with the various technologies he is expected to use and with the time he is expected to give SG.

I maintain that Philip's and Wolf's contesting positions produced different types of habitus that generated conflictual thoughts and expectations and thus disruptive interactions. Thus, the more I listened to Philip and Wolf, the more I realized that Philip's "restlessness" and Wolf's "laziness" reflected not only contesting psychological dispositions but also contesting social positions.

The discussion of Bourdieu's sociological theory in organization and management studies is growing continuously (Emirbayer & Johnson, 2008; Forson, Özbilgin, Ozturk, & Ahu Tatli, 2014; Friedman, 2011; Tatli, Özbilgin, & Karatas-Ozkan, 2015). Within this literature, one can find a small number of discussions that use the concepts of social position in order to understand, for example, institutional entrepreneurship (Battilana, 2011), sensemaking and organizational change (Lockett, Currie, Finn, Martin, & Waring, 2014), and educational management (Gunter, 2002). However, Bourdieu's theory and his concepts of habitus and social position have not yet crossed the gates of the OD field (Shimoni, 2018, 2019). My goal in this chapter thus is to integrate Bourdieu's theory into OD's research and practice. Specifically, I attempt to develop a perspective that helps OD's scholars and practitioners to understand human behavior in organizations as a combination of the social and the personal as seen in social position and habitus.

In the next section, I discuss OD's individualistic orientation, one that sees consultees' psychological dispositions, personal development, and growth as a central way of changing organizations. In the third section, I describe the consulting process at SG in detail. In the fourth section, I use Bourdieu's concepts of habitus and social position to understand the consulting process at SG in particular and to reflect on human behavior in processes of organizational development and change in general. I conclude by discussing the theoretical and practical contributions of the concepts of habitus and social position to processes of development and change and by offering directions for future research.

INDIVIDUALLY ORIENTED OD

OD discourse is characterized by the following: overwhelmingly psychological focus, construction of individuals as rational and bounded, and avoidance of sociological questions. (Maxim Voronov & Warner Woodworth, 2012, p. 440)

Critics claim that by largely focusing on psychological dispositions, individually oriented OD tries to change organizations by changing individuals (Bradford & Burke, 2005; Edmondson, 1996; Fincham & Clark, 2002). One can find a description of this kind of critique in the visionary article written by Larry Greiner (1972) in which he presents the six "red flags" that OD should consider in order not to lose its power and relevance. The flag that interests me here deals with OD scholars' and practitioners' tendency to "put the individual before the organization" (see also, Greiner & Cummings, 2005, p. 93). That is, their tendency to focus on the development of personal skills such as leadership style and team development and not on the development of the organization as a whole. According to Frank Friedlander and Dave Brown (1974, p. 325), OD's individualistic orientation "tends to value human fulfillment highly and to expect improved organizational performance to follow on improved human functioning and processes."

More recently, in an interview with David Bradford, Jerry Porras (Bradford & Porras, 2005) claims that individually oriented OD consultants have always worked on creating direct change in people's thinking and behavior while neglecting the social context in which these people work (see also French & Bell, 1999). Porras attributes the individual orientation to the intensive integration of psychologists into the OD field in the 1950s and 1960s. Organizational psychologists, he says, were trained to see internal motives and personal growth as the main reason for individuals' behavior and therefore were busy developing ways to change people (Greiner & Cummings, 2005). As a result, says Porras (Bradford & Porras, 2005, p. 51), these organizational psychologists did not have "a conceptual framework to guide their work, to help them see the big picture from which they could decide what action to take."

OD scholars and practitioners, however, have always been aware of structural and systemic aspects of the organization (Lippitt & Lippitt, 1978). The most early and perhaps important example is Kurt Lewin's (1939) field theory, which, following both physics and the Gestalt school of psychology, assumes that personal behavior should be appraised in the social context (Bargal, 2011; Burnes & Bargal, 2017). In a formulation Lewin offers, behavior (B) is a function of the interaction between the person (P) and the environment (E): $B = f(p, e)$. Other examples of the systemic orientation in the OD field are Open System Theory (Katz & Kahn, 1966), the organization culture perspective (Schein, 2010), and of course Appreciative Inquiry and the Dialogic OD (Bushe & Marshak, 2009). All of the above approaches assume that effective organizational change processes entail working on the macro level of the organization, on its technology, structure, and culture.

It is also important to note that psychological discourses in general do not focus only on individuals. Organizational psychology and organization-wide planning and strategy, for example, offer macroperspectives on organizations and management (Taylor, 1992). Similarly, in their search for the effect of unconscious behavior on organizations, scholars use psychological metaphors to represent and change organizations (see Kets de Vries, 2003). Therefore, the criticism here is not directed toward organizational psychologists or the use they make of psychological terms, but toward the use individually oriented OD makes of psychological-therapeutic discourse and practices aiming to "fix" individuals as a way to transforming organizations.

The clearest example of the use of the individualistic orientation in OD projects, what David Boje (2012, p. 404) calls "overly psychological approach," is perhaps medical discourse. Like Maxim Voronov and Warner Woodworth (2012), I claim that those who offer to *cure* organizations' pathologies conceptualize the organization in a way that relates more to the individual (personal anxiety and pain) and less to the broader social contexts in which the individual operates. For example, his or her control over resources and social position, as I do in this chapter. In other words, the medicalization of organizations leaves the impact of social and structural elements such as power and position at the margins of the consulting site. As David Coghlan (2012) correctly says, and as I often see in my own practical experience, although OD in its formal definition has always encouraged working on the macro level of the organization, in practice many OD projects focus mainly on the development of suborganizational systems and individuals.

The habitus-oriented approach I present here also focuses on individuals. However, in contrast to individually oriented OD, it searches not for psychological but social dispositions (habitus) or specifically for the way social positions generate human behavior through habitus.

THE SONIC GROUP (SG) CASE

I came from a different world. I understand now that I am a self-employed person that starts from the bottom floor (Wolf, SG's Chief Financial Officer, CFO)

SG is a real estate firm founded in the 1990s in New York City by an Israeli immigrant. Philip, the founder's son, rapidly expanded SG's business activity, geographically and financially. Today, SG owns real estate assets all over the United States' southern coast.

As part of the expansion, about 5 months before the beginning of the consulting process (April 2019), Philip recruited Wolf as the CFO and defined him as the second most important figure in the firm. In his previous job, Wolf served as a payroll accountant in a big and established firm. Philip offered Wolf the opportunity to open an accounting firm of his own in his (Philip's) office while serving as SG's CFO. All this, he promised, would better Wolf's working conditions and income, depending on his (Wolf's) ability and will to initiate new business opportunities. Specifically, Wolf was SG's employee who served as the firm's CFO and the supervisor of about 30 employees who are responsible for SG's real estate maintenance and income on the East Coast. He also was the owner of his own new accounting firm, operating from SG's offices, and a business partner who gets a share in SG's future business.

Philip: I brought Wolf in to supervise everything and open his own accounting business [in my office].

Wolf: [In my previous job] Philip was my client. Six months ago, I asked for a salary raise but they did not agree. Philip said, come to work with me. We agreed that he would fund the office while I give him [accounting] services.

A few months before the arrival of Wolf, SG moved to a new office ("head-quarter"), in which five people work, including Philip and Wolf. When I first came to the office, Philip and Wolf could not stop expressing anger and frustration. I did not have to ask anything, just to listen how unsatisfied they were for not being able to move things together:

Philip: After 5 months, I realized that I could not take a cat and teach it to bark.

Wolf: The owner [Philip] runs everything...

As we proceeded, the meetings became a site of mutual blaming in which Philip and Wolf see the other's psychological dispositions as responsible for SG's stagnant state. According to Philip, SG cannot climb to the next step because Wolf is not committed and motivated. Wolf, in his turn, said that it is hard to work with Philip since he is emotional, restless, and often does not show respect:

Philip: Wolf does not care so much...

Wolf: Philip asks in a very tough way why things do not get done [in his way]. He has an obsessive personality.

I learned that because of Philip's and Wolf's disruptive interactions, reciprocal dissatisfaction, and personal blaming, SG's business development slowed. Many apartments all over the East Coast stayed unoccupied because of disagreement on the appropriate ways to manage the employees; new acquisitions of properties meant for renovation ("flipping") almost stopped; and SG almost did not find new business opportunities, and more, as Wolf says:

> Wolf: [There is] lack of synergy... Systems and workflows for tracking reservations, rental occupancies, deposit balances, etc ... leading to many errors and tenants making claims of prepayment or being owed deposits that we couldn't confirm and were paid nonetheless. Construction purchasing processes were? unregulated, allowing workers to buy building supplies and to use some of those supplies for work elsewhere. The theft directly affects the cost and bottom line. Key employees live on property, making it impossible to separate their personal lives from the business. As a result their work ethic and daily functions and work schedule were constantly challenged ... Violations were overlooked or missed, leading to the city's shutting down operations, which led to extensive costs and loss of income. Just to name a few.

Obviously, some of these problems developed before Wolf's arrival at SG. Apparently, they were the main reason for Wolf's entrance to SG. Yet, Philip and Wolf did not take care of these problems. Their disruptive communication, the "lack of synergy," as Wolf says, stopped them from effectively addressing these problems.

My role as defined by Philip was to "fix" Philip's and Wolf's professional relationship by helping Wolf be more motivated and Philip more socially flexible. Yet, the more I listened to Philip and Wolf, the more I noticed that their subjective interpersonal interaction reflected ongoing conflictual negotiations around objective issues such as working hours, technology, and management style. Philip complained that Wolf came from a different "culture of 9:00 to 5:00." Acknowledging that he indeed came from "a different world," Wolf protested that Philip does not care about his private time resources, even when it comes to weekends:

> Philip: He (Wolf) comes to the office 3 days a week at 10:00 or 11:00 a.m. because he had an appointment with his doctor... 5 p.m. arrives and he disappears.

> Wolf: Philip asks and asks [that I work] on Saturday and I am with my kids. He makes me crazy...

Philip and Wolf's debate over Wolf's time resources (working hours and days) shows, then, that their ongoing interaction reflects not only conflicting psychological dispositions but also a competition over resources between people who occupy different positions. That is, between a junior partner, who just started working at SG and has to "start from the bottom floor," as Wolf says, defending his time resources, and an owner, a rich person who materially supports Wolf while demanding control over his time resources, including his private time:

> Wolf: [Philip often says] spend time here; sleep here. I want all of you in my house. He has a very large personality... he needs to conquer, to make people his property.

Wolf's move to SG forced him also to acquire management skills that he did not have to use in his previous job as an accountant. As we can see in the quotations below, Wolf understands and admits that his management resources as an accountant are not sufficient for his new position in which he supervises about 30 employees. Philip, from his position as experienced owner, gives Wolf advice on how to manage and reminds him that management is part of his job definition:

> Wolf: managing my time is terrible ... look, I have never learned, you know... The first organization I headed was ... 90 percent volunteering ... My management career here is different.

> Philip: You hire them [workers] sometimes for a month, two, three months until the moment comes and you say thank you very much... this is part of a manager's job definition.

Another disputed issue over SG's resources was the office's computer technology, a significant resource for the management of multiple and remote real estate sites. Philip insisted that the office keep using "Moment" (pseudo, not its real name), the computer software with which he ran SG for years. Wolf claimed that the office should buy "Future" (pseudo, not its real name), a new and updated software that in his opinion is much more effective for the management of a real estate firm.

> Philip: [With "Moment"] I open folders, I share information with people... it is convenient for my business... No, listen, listen... you came into a working system and you say let us change, let us move on.

> Wolf: I think every business should work with Future, for me it is my private home ... You want to build complex, dynamic things that people can play with ... Why the obsession with imitation?

The move to his new position at SG, however, forced Wolf to do more than accept the office's working hours, management style, and technology. It required him to adapt to a new business culture, identity, and behavior, one that cherishes informality and improvisation – the extreme opposite of the firm he just left:

> Wolf: We met with a CEO of a big bank in Florida. I came well dressed. They came with suits and ties. Philip came with simple working pants... It is such a difficult transition ... [and] it is not just clothes... Every office I have ever worked in, one that respects itself, had heavy furniture [not like here] ... I hate this office... we published a job offer. [A man came] and after 5 minutes they accepted him. Two days later, he asked to change his working conditions... Philip grants everyone [the authority] to sign checks. This is a huge mistake. They sign in New York and in Orlando, people that do not have the authority...

> Philip: I would go to meetings for closing $ 10–15 million, sitting in the group of attorneys and only this (me) idiot who actually manages the whole thing; they all eat from his hand.

After carefully listening to Philip's and Wolf's disruptive interactions, in the fourth meeting I tried to make the two see each other from a different perspective. That is, to see Wolf's behavior not as a personal attack against Philip but as reflecting the position of a newcomer; a person who occupies an unfamiliar position (without control over most of SG's resources) in which he tries to keep his ways of thinking and behaving active. As Wolf said, "it is such a difficult transition." I also tried to make Philip and Wolf see Philip's behavior not as a personal attack on Wolf but as a reflection of his position as SG's owner who tries to defend the thinking and behaving that have worked for him so far. As Philip said, "I open folders, I share information with people... it is convenient for my business."

At the last part of the consulting process at SG, I recognized that my efforts to move Philip's and Wolf's focus from psychological dispositions to social positions had some success:

> Philip: Baruch helps me look at my less attractive sides as well, even though he tries to make them beautiful and he says ... it is okay [Philip's unbeautiful sides]... so this is, come on, let us start with our goals. Let us start with that, after that we might go on to [other] things ... accounting, bookkeeping.

As we can see in the previous and in the following quotations, at this point in the consulting process the language between Philip and Wolf changed from personal accusations to social negotiations and focused on the objective level of the interaction. Specifically, the language that changed from "you" and "me" to "we" and "us" focused on SG's resources such as the computer software, division of work, working hours, and management:

> Wolf: I do not have enough hours a day to finish what I have to do.

> Philip: There are not enough hours a day, I accept it, come on, OK, let us sit down and talk. How do you get more hours a day? If we have to give her (the bookkeeper) to you 90 percent or 100 percent you can have her ... Next month she is 100 percent yours, we will not drop anything on her, nothing. I think we need to sit down and solve these things in order to help Wolf grow... Put Future on the table ... build some functions that I do not have ... Come, sit for fifteen minutes and show me... Now, the neat folders I have, maybe they do not match what we are doing now... Let us take it as a model and throw away what we do not like, let us keep what we love.

> Wolf: Come on, fun – let's do it!

At this point, then, Wolf got the authority to use "Future" as SG's computer software, to decide on his working hours, including working 2 days a week from home, and to build new processes in the office. The control of these resources seemed to improve his position and thus motivation ("Come on, fun – let's do it!"). SG's situation seemed inflexible but was in fact open to change. It presented the opportunity for me to think of human behavior and OD and change in terms of habitus and social position.

APPLYING BOURDIEU'S SOCIAL POSITION AND HABITUS AT SG

Social Position

In this chapter, I say that Philip's and Wolf's disruptive interactions are the result of the position they occupy within SG. That is, their interactions largely derived from their contesting social positions: an owner of a small family firm versus a newcomer who holds the habitus he acquired as an accountant in a big and established firm.

Social positions, as noted, are personal and social. They are the locations individuals occupy in social fields in relation to others, depending on their control over the field's resources and capitals (Bourdieu, 1989). Individuals adopt their positions and develop their points of view and behavior accordingly. As the literature shows (Neilsen, 1996), for example, managers and other figures in dominant positions in organizations internalize their dominant position and develop their habitus, points of view, and behavior accordingly (Bourdieu, 1993, p. 169). They can identify each other in accordance with the way they speak and behave, build on one another's ideas, and enlist their own supporters in managerial decisions. Their control over the organization's resources and capitals enables them to enhance their leadership positions and define their points of view as the organization's specific habitus. Specific habitus, to remind the readers, is the organization's taken-for-granted worldview, structure of power, and social positions.

This is what Philip apparently tried to do. Seemingly unconsciously, his habitus as the owner who holds a powerful position that controls most of SG's capitals, the cultural (how things happen at SG), the social (his personal connections with all the employees that he himself hired), and the economic (his ownership of SG's budget, offices, and real estate assets), generated his attempts to reproduce SG's specific habitus originally produced by him. That is, to make sure that SG operates in accordance with his own traditional thinking and behavior, e.g., working hours (undefined), technology (the computer software, Moment, with which he ran SG for years), informal organizational behavior (dress code), and management style (tough and aggressive).

Contesting Social Positions

The reality in social fields, however, is much more complicated. Social fields host many social positions and thus multiple points of view. Bourdieu says (1989, pp. 327–328),

> ...there will be different or even antagonistic points of view, since points of view depend on the point from which they are taken, since the vision that every agent has of the space depends on his or her position in that space.

Thus, the fact that people in powerful positions use their control over significant types of capital to distribute and impose their points of view on others does not always create total acceptance by those with less power. Often, the efforts invested by those who monopolize the field's power and authority in order to impose their points of view create among those with less power, competition, hostility, and actual attempts to change the existing situation (Bourdieu, 1993). People, including those with less power and lower social position, have the ability to act creatively by acquiring access to capitals and resources (Sewell, 1992). As we have seen, Wolf struggled with Philip over SG's resources and specific habitus, that is, over working hours, technology, and behavior, inside (aggressive) and outside (dress code) SG. Wolf's behavior expressed the competition and hostility Bourdieu is talking about and a deep refusal to comply with Philip's point of view and demands and with the existing power relations according to which he was supposed to think and act in accordance to SG's/Philip's traditional processes and behavior.

Within this theoretical framework, therefore, it seems valuable to view Philip's and Wolf's disruptive interactions not only as attached to clashing psychological dispositions but also to contesting social positions. Philip, a powerful agent in a privileged position, controlling most of SG's resources, tried to keep control of SG's specific habitus and accepted processes and behavior (Philip [rising his voice]: "No, listen, listen... you came into a working system and you say let us change, let us move on"). Wolf, a powerless agent, tried to get control over SG's resources in order to improve his position and change SG's habitus and behavior (Wolf: "I think every business should work with Future [the computer software] ... Why the obsession with the imitation?").

Bourdieu's Relational Perspective

Using Bourdieu's conceptual tools to understand human behavior requires the adoption of a relational perspective according to which objects only get their meaning in relation to other objects. Specifically, Bourdieu's relational perspective entails seeing the concepts of habitus, field, capitals, power, and social position as interconnected. [I]n Bourdieu's analysis, according to Cynthia Forson, Mustafa Özbilgin, Mustafa Bilgehan Ozturk, and Ahu Tatli (2014, p. 64), "key concepts such as habitus, field, capitals [social positions]... work together to generate the social reality."

To clarify his relational perspective, Bourdieu invites us to look at his critique of "realism" and "substantialism." Both ideas, he says, "recognize no reality other than those that are available to direct intuition in ordinary experience" (Bourdieu, 1989, p. 15). In his critique of substantialism, Bourdieu follows Ernst Cassirer (1923, p. 9) who distinguishes between "things" and "relations." The logic of things, for Cassirer (1923, p. 291), what he defines "the naïve view," represents people's intuitive sense that the outside world is a composition of physical, natural, and constant objects perceived by the individual mind. The logic of relations, on the other hand, is that social reality and human behavior are the product of interactions between capitals, power, and social positions. In Bourdieu's words, "what exist in the social world are relations, not interactions between agents or intersubjective ties between individuals, but objective relations, which exist independently of the individual consciousness and will" (quoted by Wacquant, 1989, p. 39). Bourdieu expresses his relational perspective by the following formula (Maton, 2014, p. 50):

$$\text{Practice [behavior]} = (\text{Habitus} \times \text{Capital [social position]}) + \text{Field}$$

This formula expresses at least three beliefs that are relevant for our discussion of social position. First, a *systemic* belief according to which behavior (practice) is a function of the social context (field and positions). Second, an *objectivist* belief according to which behavior is a result of objective social and structural relations determined by capitals, power, and social position people occupy in a given social field. Third, a *relational* belief according to which behavior is a function of field, habitus, and social position (capitals). Behavior is not realistic or substantive, an entity with constant and objective meaning of itself, one that "can be touched with the finger," as Bourdieu says (quoted by Everett, 2002, p. 71), and thus defined by categories such as restlessness or laziness. Instead, behavior is relational in nature. Its meaning develops within changing and ongoing relations between field, habitus, and social position (capitals).

For the OD practitioner, the relational approach is crucial since it captures the deeply connected and interwoven nature of social and structural elements that produce participants' behavior. Indeed, what was considered *real* by Philip and Wolf was *relational* for me. That is, exchanges such as "he is lazy" or "he does not care so much" (Philip); "he has an obsessive personality" or he is "aggressive and does not show respect" (Wolf) encouraged me to make Philip and Wolf see that the behaviors they are referring to might also be a result of relations among capitals, power, and social positions. That is, I encouraged Philip and Wolf to pay attention to the possibility that their behaviors, which they defined as "restlessness" and "laziness," are not necessarily natural and substantive entities with their own intrinsic meaning and thus something I should change directly, but relational.

Based on this understanding, I put the question to Philip and Wolf this way: "Can you see your behavior in terms of not only internal motivation but also the different positions you occupy at SG and thus the different understandings [e.g., habitus] of how you should run SG?" I asked Philip: "Do you agree with my assumption that excluding Wolf from SG's main decision-making and disregarding his expertise by ignoring his knowledge, his cultural capital, contribute to the development of his 'passive' outlook [e.g., habitus] and behavior? I asked Wolf: "Do you understand that by choosing to behave passively, you participate in the production and reproduction of an understanding among other employees [e.g., context-specific habitus] that it is useless to try to help SG reach better results?"

The task of the OD practitioner, then, is to help consultees see behaviors not as constant, natural, and objective, belonging inherently to the individual only, but as entities situated in a specific time and space, representing a constructed and relational social reality. Put another way, the OD practitioner is encouraged not to work only from a substantial perspective that focuses on subjective relations and psychological dispositions, aiming to change and develop individuals' given skills and abilities. Rather, the OD practitioner is well advised to adopt a relational perspective that focuses on the ways social positions (control over capitals) in a given social field (organization) shape human behaviors through habitus – and vice versa.

CONCLUDING DISCUSSION

When Philip asked me to help SG, he expected me to change him and Wolf. For him, improving their psychological dispositions (Philip's "restlessness" and Wolf's "laziness") seemed the only way to achieve SG's desired development.

Perhaps if I had simply used my traditional individually oriented approach to answer Philip's request, worked on their psychological dispositions, and helped them communicate better, I might have satisfied both of them and created a better atmosphere in the office. However, SG's lack of success ("tracking reservations, rental occupancies, and deposit balances" (Wolf)) would have remained unresolved, since we would then have been dealing with Philip's and Wolf's interpersonal communication and not with their contesting social positions, that, as I demonstrated to them, played a significant role in delaying the achievement of SG's business goals.

In this chapter, the claim is, then, that psychological dispositions are important factors in generating human behavior (Oreg et al., 2008). However, investigating only psychological dispositions without considering that individuals are constantly engaged in power relations and competition over resources and capital and thus embedded in social positions falls into what David Bradford and Warner Burke (2005, p. 199), following Porras (Bradford & Porras, 2005), define as a "reductionist trap." Using that concept of a reductionist trap, OD consultants try to change organizations by changing individuals while ignoring the context in which they operate (Beer, Eisenstat, & Spector, 1993; Edmondson, 1996; Fincham & Clark, 2002). Specifically, a focus only on Philip's and Wolf's psychological dispositions would have missed the opportunity to understand the impact of their social positions on their behavior.

Yet, Why Social Position?

The habitus-oriented approach offers, then, at least three answers to the question of how the concept of social position can work to help OD consultants in processes of development and change. First, social positions are social constructions and thus are changeable. That is, since they are a product of struggles and competition over resources and capitals, they can be changed by shifting the distribution of those resources and capitals. At SG, this specific theoretical understanding encouraged me to engage in intensive discussions of the asymmetric power relations between Philip and Wolf, their unequal control over resources and capitals, and the different place each occupies in the organization's social structure – owner vs newcomer. As part of the discussions, Philip considered implementing structural changes that could improve Wolf's position, "help Wolf grow," to use his words, and enhance Wolf's positive involvement, though these changes would make their positions more symmetric. Furthermore, Philip granted Wolf the authority to decide which computer software ("Future" rather than "Moment") SG uses; rather than adhering to SG's traditional culture of working "around the clock," he let Wolf decide on his working hours, including working 2 days a week from home; and he gave him the authority to build new processes in the office. (Philip: "Put Future on the table ... build some functions that I do not have.")

Second, the concept of social position is important to OD and change because of the concept's natural correspondence with the macro level of the organization. That is, the focus on social position, which defines the place a person occupies in the social structure, goes beyond the individual self. It goes to the organization's social and structural level that in a hidden way generates personal thoughts and behavior and social interactions. At SG, the concept of social position allowed me to focus on the resources, capitals, and power (technology, business culture, administrative processes and positions) that shaped Philip's and Wolf's conflicting habitus and behaviors. I invited Philip and Wolf to see Philip as an owner who occupies a privileged social position who is now under threat and thus behaves in a way defined by Wolf as restless. In the same way, I invited them to see Wolf as a newcomer who refuses to adopt new ways of thinking and practicing while occupying an ill-defined, unstable, and unsafe social position, and thus defined by Philip as lazy.

Third, the focus on social positions and not on psychological dispositions has a great potential to encourage consultees to participate voluntarily and effectively in OD and change projects. In my work at SG, I noticed that Philip and Wolf respected my refusal to put their psychological dispositions at the heart of the consulting process (as they themselves did). They saw my approach as nonpersonal, one that represents a "professional" standpoint that does not put the blame for preventing the desired change on their psychological dispositions but focuses on learning what their behavior represents in terms of the organization and the development process in which we were all involved. This view puts the social and the structural, the objective, and not only the emotional and the subjective on the consulting table and thus has the potential to create participation and collaboration.

The Habitus-oriented Approach: A Theory of Social Life and Human Agency

The habitus-oriented approach, then, offers a theory of social life and human agency that is able to identify structures like social position as it shows itself in personal behavior. A concrete reflection of this theory is Philip's efforts to keep controlling SG's resources and capitals such as technology, business culture, and other administrative processes, and Wolf's efforts to gain control over these specific capitals by exchanging them for those familiar to him. Philip's and Wolf's contesting positions (social life) generated different and conflicting behaviors (human agency) that produced misunderstandings, aggressiveness, and ineffective communication that slowed SG's expected development.

As a theory of social life and human agency, how can the habitus-oriented approach help OD practitioners understand human behavior in organizations as a combination of the social and the personal, which is the goal of this chapter? Advocates of role conflict theory, for example, might claim that we do not need Bourdieu in order to understand Philip's and Wolf's disruptive interactions. The fact that their job definitions have never been clearly defined, or more importantly, that Wolf was an SG employee, an owner of his own accounting firm operating from SG's offices, and a business partner, such advocates would say, was largely responsible for those disruptive interactions. Specifically, Philip's and Wolf's lack of agreement on the boundaries of their responsibilities and authority is a good prescription for conflicts and mis-understandings. I agree with this argument. However, I assert that the focus on roles only partially represents Philip's and Wolf's disruptive interactions; role conflict theory does not consider deeply the social field in which struggles for power, capitals, and social positions happens, as does Bourdieu's relational perspective. Specifically, Bourdieu's relational perspective breaks through the boundaries of roles to offer a much more comprehensive view of behavior. It sees the organization's social field as an arena of power in which a compe-tition over capitals and positions produces habitus and behavior. Organiza-tional change, according to Mustafa Emirbayer and Victoria Johnson (2008, pp. 29–30), "might be understood to emerge from a pattern of mismatches between members' habitus and their positions in the organization-as-field."

The argument here is, then, that a reduction of Philip's and Wolf's disruptive interaction to the personal and the interpersonal levels, to psychological dispo-sitions (their inability to communicate well), and to roles would overlook the fact that their interactions were part of a competition over valuable capitals at SG as a social field. Bourdieu's relational perspective helped me to see Philip's and Wolf's contesting positions, objectively defined, as nurturing conflicting habitus and behavior. On the one hand, Philip the owner tries to maintain his control over SG's capitals, specific habitus, and behavior, and on the other hand, Wolf the newcomer strives to get control of some of SG's resources and capitals to improve his position and to redefine SG's specific habitus and accepted behavior.

For the habitus-oriented practitioner, then, the individual's inner world still matters. However, this inner world consists of not only psychological but also social dispositions (habitus), capitals, and social positions.

Future Research and Practice

Many years of work as an OD consultant have taught me that talking about the objective (structural and macro) aspects of human interactions is not a simple matter in light of the almost total conquest of organizations by individually oriented discourse and practices that tend to frame human interactions in terms of psychological dispositions (Costea, Crump, & Amiridis, 2008). Future research should develop ways in which OD scholars and practitioners can incorporate a habitus-oriented approach into OD. One available way to do that is by inte-grating Bourdieu's theoretical view, which considers not only the personal but also the social as well as the interaction between the two, into OD's research and practice. An example would be using the habitus in the practice of 360-degree feedback, an individual-based intervention within an organizational context. Allan Church, Dawson, Barden, Fleck, Rotolo, and Tuller (2018, p. 53) suggest using the 360-degree feedback results for individual development and planning, for individual or team coaching, and for leadership programs. Using habitus in the practice of 360-degree feedback can expand the intended results by seeing individual development processes (in leadership programs, for example) not only in terms of self-development, improving skills and abilities, but also in terms of habitus that reflects both the personal and the social.

The use of habitus can also serve in future research and practice as an integrating mechanism between first-, second-, and third-person practices in OD projects. David Coghlan and Abraham Shani (2020, p. 1) in their inquiry into Action Research see three uses:

> The first-person voice of individuals inquiring into their own thinking and learning, the second-person inquiry into the collaborative engagements between the actors as co-researchers and the third-person contribution to knowledge for a wider audience.

Following William Torbert (2013), Coghlan and Shani (2020, p. 5) suggest integrating the three practices (first, second, and third person) by abductive reasoning, which "yields tentative answers and produces exploratory hypotheses." Incorporating the concept of habitus, which by definition combines the personal and the social into simple and reasonable interpretation, enables OD scholars and practitioners to integrate first-, second-, and third-person practices (Forson et al., 2014). That is, it enables them to investigate individual thinking and behavior (first person), interactions between individuals (second-person inquiry), and knowledge at the organizational level and beyond (third person). As we have seen, the focus on habitus (and social position) goes beyond the individual self, to the group and the organization levels.

Another research direction would focus on resistance to change. Current research on resistance to change sees the roots of resistance in the personal (Oreg et al., 2008), the social Dent and Goldberg (1999), in the interaction between the two Ford, Ford, and D'Amelio (2008, p. 362), and in habitus (Shimoni, 2017). In general, all four approaches above focus mainly on the resistance of employees that are *not in managing positions*. Future research, in contrast, could use the concept of social position to focus on resistance among managers and other figures in dominant positions. Identifying resistance among figures in dominant positions is possible since every social position, including managers' and owners', is embodied in and thus defined by a wider social and structural context. This is why my focus on social position at SG enabled me to learn not only about Wolf's (the employee's) resistance to changing his behavior and adopting SG's specific habitus and behavior but also about Philip's (the employer's) resistance to changing his points of view on subjects such as computer technology, job definitions, and the office's working hours.

Other future research can use Bourdieu's (2003) concept of *strategy* for a better understanding of organizational problems in development and change processes. A strategy is a behavior that is both the product and the producer of the organization's social structures. Thus, research that focuses on strategy would search for the roots of organizational problems (like SG's inability to move to a more advanced phase) both in the individual's specific behavior and in the organization's social structure (for example, structures of power and social positions) and in the interaction between the two. Research of this kind at SG would search for SG's slow development *equally* in Philip's and Wolf's strategic behaviors and in the role of these contesting behaviors in the production and reproduction of SG's destructive structure of power and social positions.

Practical Applications for OD Projects

In this chapter I offer the OD consultant a way to see conflicting points of view as "more than simply [a contradictory] worldview in the classical sociological sense" (Dobbin, 2008, p. 58). I offer them a way to view misunderstandings and opposing perspectives as a result of competition over resources, capitals, power, and social positions. Specifically, I encourage the OD consultant to make explicit the positions consultees occupy in the organization's social structure and the influence of these positions on their own and others' ways of thinking and patterns of behavior.

The discourse that organizes the OD project, then, invites consultees to identify in their own and others' experience the social positions that generate behavior. This discourse says, for example, "For a while, let's not talk about behavior in terms of psychological dispositions such as internal commitment and responsibility. Instead, let's talk about behavior in terms of power relations and positions in the organization and how these positions shape people's perceptions and behaviors"; "Let's talk about how seniority influences the way people in this organization think and behave and how this specific behavior helps them achieve their senior positions." "Let's talk about the ways people's position in the organization influences their behavior, or specifically, about the different ways the owner (who controls most capitals of the organization) and the employees act in the organization. Do you see the difference?"

ACKNOWLEDGMENT

I thank my consultees and students for giving me the stage to develop the ideas I present in this chapter. Obviously, without them, I would not have written this chapter. I deeply thank Eyal Ben Ari from the Hebrew University of Jerusalem and Harriet Bergmann for their insightful comments. Special thanks to Debra A. Noumair and Abraham B. (Rami) Shani, ROCD's editors, for their helpful advice and comments through all the stages of this chapter.

NOTE

1. Names of people and organizations have been changed. All quotations have been translated from Hebrew by the author.

REFERENCES

Bargal, D. (2011). Kurt Lewin's vision of organizational and social change: The interdependence of theory, research and action/practice. In D. M. Boje, B. Burnes, & J. Hassard (Eds.), *The*

Routledge companion to organizational change (pp. 31–45). London and New York, NY: Routledge.

Battilana, J. (2011). The enabling role of social position in diverging from the institutional status quo: Evidence from the UK National Health Service. *Organization Science, 22*(4), 817–834.

Beer, M., Eisenstat, R. A., & Spector, B. (1993). Why change programs don't produce change. *Harvard Business Review, 68*(6), 2–29.

Boje, M. D. (2012). Introduction. In D. M. Boje, B. Burnes, & J. Hassard (Eds.), *The Routledge companion to organizational change* (pp. 403–405). London and New York, NY: Routledge.

Bourdieu, P. (1989). Social space and symbolic power. *Sociological Theory, 7*(1), 14–25.

Bourdieu, P. (1990). *Homo academicus*. Cambridge: Polity.

Bourdieu, P. (1993). *Sociology in question*. London: SAGE Publication.

Bourdieu, P. (1998). *On television and journalism* [P. P. Ferguson (Trans.)]. London: Pluto.

Bourdieu, P. (2003). Participant objectivation. *Journal of the Royal Anthropological Institute, 9*, 282–294.

Bradford, D. L., & Burke, W. W. (2005). The future of OD? In D. L. Bradford & W. W. Burke (Eds.), *Reinventing organization development: New approaches to change in organizations* (pp. 195–214). San Francisco, CA: Pfeiffer.

Bradford, D. L., & Porras, J. I. (2005). A historical view of the future of OD: An interview with Jerry I. Porras. In D. L. Bradford & W. W. Burke (Eds.), *Reinventing organization development: New approaches to change in organizations* (pp. 43–64). San Francisco, CA: Pfeiffer.

Burnes, B., & Bargal, D. (2017). Kurt Lewin: 70 years on. *Journal of Change Management, 17*(2), 91–100.

Bushe, G. R., & Marshak, R. J. (2009). Revisioning organization development: Diagnostic and dialogic premises and patterns of practice. *The Journal of Applied Behavioral Science, 45*(3), 348–368.

Cassirer, E. (1923). *Substance and function, and Einstein's theory of relativity*[W. C. Swabey & M. C. Swabey (Trans.)]. Chicago, IL: Open Court.

Church, A. H., Dawson, L. M., Barden, K. L., Fleck, C. R., Rotolo, C. T., & Tuller, M. (2018). Enhancing 360-degree feedback for individual assessment and organization development: Methods and lessons from the field. In D. A. Noumair & A. B. Shani (Eds.), *Research in organizational change and development* (pp. 47–97). Bingley: Emerald Publishing Limited.

Church, A. H., Waclawski, J., & Siegal, W. (1996). Will the real OD practitioner please stand up? A call for change in the field. *Organization Development Journal, 14*(2), 5–14.

Coghlan, D. (2012). Organization development and action research: Then and now. In D. M. Boje, B. Burnes, & J. Hassard (Eds.), *The Routledge companion to organizational change* (pp. 45–58). London and New York, NY: Routledge.

Coghlan, D., & Shani, A. B. R. (2020). Abductive reasoning as the integrating mechanism between first-second-and third-person practice in action research. *Systemic Practice and Action Research, 141*, 1–12.

Cornelissen, S. (2016). Turning distaste into taste: Context-specific habitus and the practical congruity of culture. *Theory and Society, 45*(6), 501–529.

Costea, B., Crump, N., & Amiridis, K. (2008). Managerialism, the therapeutic habitus and the self in contemporary organizing. *Human relation, 61*(5), 661–685.

Dent, E. B., & Goldberg, S. G. (1999). Challenging "resistance to change". *The Journal of Applied Behavioral Science, 35*(1), 25–41.

Dobbin, F. (2008). The poverty of organizational theory: Comment on "Bourdieu and organizational analysis". *Theory and Society, 37*, 53–63.

Edmondson, A. C. (1996). Three faces of Eden: The persistence of competing theories and multiple diagnoses in organizational intervention research. *Human Relations, 49*(5), 571–595.

Emirbayer, M., & Johnson, V. (2008). Bourdieu and organizational analysis. *Theory and Society, 37*(1), 1–44.

Everett, J. (2002). Organizational research and the praxeology of Pierre Bourdieu. *Organizational Research Methods, 5*(1), 56–80.

Fincham, R., & Clark, T. (2002). Introduction: The emergence of critical perspectives on consulting. In T. Clark & R. Fincham (Eds.), *Critical consulting: New perspectives on the management advice industry* (pp. 1–18). Oxford: Blackwell.

Ford, J. D., Ford, L. W., & D'Amelio, A. (2008). Resistance to change: The rest of the story. *Academy of Management Review, 33*(2), 362–377.

Forson, C., Özbilgin, M., Ozturk, M. B., & Ahu Tatli, A. (2014). Multi-level approaches to entrepreneurship and small business research-transcending dichotomies with Bourdieu. In E. Chell & M. Karatas-Ozkan (Eds.), *Handbook of research on small business and entrepreneurship* (pp. 54–69). Cheltenham: Edward Elgar Publishing.

French, W. L., & Bell, C. H., Jr (1999). *Organization development: Behavioral science interventions for organization improvement.* Upper Saddle River, NJ: Prentice-Hall.

Friedlander, F., & Brown, L. D. (1974). Organization development. *Annual Review of Psychology, 25*(1), 313–341.

Friedman, V. J. (2011). Revisiting social space: Relational thinking about organizational change. In D. A. Noumair & A. B. Shani (Eds.), *Research in organizational change and development* (pp. 233–257). Bingley: Emerald Group Publishing Limited.

Greiner, L. E. (1972). Red flags in organization development. *Business Horizons, 15*(3), 17–24.

Greiner, L. E., & Cummings, T. G. (2005). OD: Wanted more alive than dead! In D. L. Bradford & W. W. Burke (Eds.), *Reinventing organization development: New approaches to change in organizations* (pp. 87–112). San Francisco, CA: Pfeiffer.

Gunter, H. M. (2002). Purposes and positions in the field of education management: Putting Bourdieu to work. *Educational Management & Administration, 30*(1), 7–26.

Katz, D., & Kahn, R. L. (1966). *The social psychology of organizations.* New York, NY: Wiley.

Kets de Vries, M. F. R. (2003). *Organizations on the couch: A clinical perspective on organizational dynamics.* Retrieved from www.insead.edu/facultyresearch/research/doc.cfm?did=1321

Kuna, S. (2014). *Liquid professionalism: A critical view of management consulting* (In Hebrew). Tel-Aviv: Resling.

Lewin, K. (1939). Field theory and experiment in social psychology: Concepts and methods. *American Journal of Sociology, 44*(6), 868–896.

Lippitt, G., & Lippitt, R. (1978). *The consulting process in action.* San Diego, CA: University Associates.

Lockett, A., Currie, G., Finn, R., Martin, G., & Waring, J. (2014). The influence of social position on sensemaking about organizational change. *Academy of Management Journal, 57*(4), 1102–1129.

Maton, K. (2014). Habitus. In M. J. Grenfell (Ed.), *Pierre Bourdieu: Key concepts* (pp. 60–76). London and New York, NY: Routledge.

Neilsen, E. H. (1996). Modernism, postmodernism and managerial competencies: A multidiscourse reading. In D. M. Boje, R. P. Gephart Jr, & T. J. Thatchenkery (Eds.), *Postmodern management and organization theory* (pp. 266–292). Thousand Oaks, CA: Sage.

Oreg, S., Bayazit, M., Vakola, M., Arciniega, L., Armenakis, A., Barkauskiene, R., & Hřebíčková, M. (2008). Dispositional resistance to change: Measurement equivalence and the link to personal values across 17 nations. *Journal of Applied Psychology, 93*(4), 935.

Schein, E. H. (2010). *Organizational culture and leadership.* San Francisco, CA: Jossey-Bass.

Sewell, W. H., Jr (1992). A theory of structure: Duality, agency, and transformation. *American Journal of Sociology, 98*(1), 1–29.

Shimoni, B. (2017). What is resistance to change? *Academy of Management Perspectives, 31*(4), 257–270.

Shimoni, B. (2018). Bringing agency and social structure back into organization development: Toward a practice of habitus consulting. *Journal of Applied Behavioral Science, 54*(2), 208–225.

Shimoni, B. (2019). *Organization development and society: Theory and practice of organization development consulting.* New York, NY and London: Routledge.

Sieweke, J. (2014). Pierre Bourdieu in management and organization studies – A citation context analysis and discussion of contributions. *Scandinavian Journal of Management, 30*(4), 532–543.

Tatli, A., Özbilgin, M., & Karatas-Ozkan, M. (2015). Introduction: Management and organization studies meet Pierre Bourdieu. In A. Tatli, M. Özbilgin, & M. Karatas-Ozkan (Eds.), *Pierre Bourdieu, organization, and management* (pp. 1–16). London and New York, NY: Routledge.

Taylor, R. N. (1992). Strategic decision-making. In M. D. Dunnete & L. M. Houge (Eds.). *Handbook of industrial and organizational psychology* (2nd ed., Vol. 3, pp. 961–1008). Palo Alto, CA: Consulting Psychologists Press.

Torbert, W. R. (2013). Listening into the dark: An essay testing the validity and efficacy of collaborative developmental action inquiry for describing and encouraging transformations of self, society, and scientific inquiry. *Integral Review: A Transdisciplinary & Transcultural Journal for New Thought, Research, & Praxis, 9*(2), 264–299.

Voronov, M., & Woodworth, W. P. (2012). OD discourse and domination. In D. M. Boje, B. Burnes, & J. Hassard (Eds.), *The Routledge companion to organizational change* (pp. 440–455). London and New York, NY: Routledge.

Wacquant, L. J. (1989). Towards a reflexive sociology: A workshop with Pierre Bourdieu. *Sociological Theory, 1*, 26–63.

USING ACTION RESEARCH AND ORGANIZATION DESIGN TO PLAN IN-HOME HOSPITAL TREATMENT

Iben Duvald

ABSTRACT

Health-care systems currently face great challenges, including an increasing elderly population. To respond to this problem, a hospital emergency department, three municipalities, and self-employed general practitioners in Denmark decided to collaborate with the aim of reorganizing treatment of elderly acute ill patients. By establishing a small-scale collaborative community and through an action research process, we show, how to jointly explore and develop a new organization design for in-home hospital treatment that enables the health professionals to collaborate in new ways, and at the same time to investigate and improve this cocreation process and codesign of knowledge among multiple different stakeholders.

Keywords: Organization design; action research; health-care challenge; aging population; collaborative community; in-home hospital treatment

INTRODUCTION TO A GREAT CHALLENGE AND A RESPONSE

Health-care systems today face great challenges, e.g., an increasingly aging population. An increasing number of elderly patients will impose considerable demands on health services. This will give rise to clinical and organizational challenges (Mohrman, Shani, & McCracken, 2012). In Denmark, the share of the population over 65 years is expected to rise from 16 percent today to 25 percent in 2042. This demographic development implies an increased number of elderly citizens – many of which will suffer from chronic diseases. This in turn will imply

Research in Organizational Change and Development, Volume 29, 111–142
ISSN: 0897-3016/doi:10.1108/S0897-301620210000029006

a higher demand for health services (Ministry of Health and the Elderly, 2016). Despite the group of elderly medical patients amounting to about 2 percent of the population, their health service consumption amounts to about 15 percent of the municipal cofinanced expenses. Consequently, these are patient groups, whose size and scope in terms of health consumption imply that they are particularly interesting, when it comes to preventive measures (The national association of municipalities, 2013).

Emergency hospitalization is not the best option for all patients. For elderly patients, an emergency admission may prove an upheaval of their daily routine, and often it involves a high risk of both infection and delirium and may entail a significant functional decline – both physically and mentally, which may take a long time to regain (Covinsky et al., 2003; Creditor, 1993; Inouye et al., 1999; Strausbaugh, 2001). Furthermore, many elderly acute medical patients are admitted for only a short period of time, and in many cases, the admission of patients undergoing comparatively uncomplicated treatment could have been avoided had (cooperation with) the home health services been more developed (The national association of municipalities, 2013).

An alternative to hospitalization is in-home treatment. Acute care medical models have been developed in many countries around the world, and the provision of hospital-level care to patients in their homes is one of the fastest-growing alternatives to what has traditionally been referred to as "inpatient" medical care (Sheppard et al., 2016). The international term for this admission-avoidance model is "hospital-at-home" services; the definition of which is a service that provides active treatment by health-care professionals in the patient's home of a condition that otherwise would require acute hospital inpatient care and always for a limited time period. If hospital at home were not available, the patient would be admitted to an acute hospital ward. Many of these services are targeted at elderly medical patients, and they can be organized in various ways and may focus on different patient categories, and be hospital- or municipality-based (Shepperd & Iliffe, 2005). In fact, there is substantial variation between the existing hospital-at-home models with regard to the illnesses treated, acuity of patients, source of admission, composition of the treatment teams, and the amount of physician and nursing care and coverage provided (Leff, 2009; Shepperd et al., 2016; Vale, Franco, Oliveira, Araújo, & Sousa, 2019).

To our knowledge, admission-avoidance hospital at home models do not yet exist in Denmark. However, in 2018, a hospital emergency department (ED), three municipalities, and general practitioners (GPs) decided to collaborate with the aim of reorganizing the treatment of elderly patients in order to avoid hospitalizations and respond to the future problem with an increasingly aging population. Collaboration is a process in which those parties with a stake in a problem actively seek a mutually determined solution. Collaboration involves many barriers that must be overcome, if collaboration is to succeed, especially collaboration across various organizations. However, collaboration is a valuable approach in situations in which a shared goal can only be accomplished by a set of actors, who each provide their complementary contribution to the larger system in a coordinated manner (Bøllingtoft, Donaldson, Huber, Håkonsson, &

Snow, 2012; Gray, 1985). Reorganizing treatment of elderly patients, who often need treatment involving many different professions belonging to different organizational units across sectors, is a situation, where collaboration between multiple actors is needed, if the cocreation of a new organizational form for in-home treatment is going to be a success. To this process of collaboration, new organization designs are suited (Fjeldstad, Snow, Miles, & Lettl, 2012; Mohrman & Lawler, 2012).

Thus, in this research project, we use organization design theory on two levels in order to help various stakeholders to collaborate and to secure the design of the new in-home hospital treatment pathway developed by the collaborators. We established a small-scale collaborative community of organizations in order to create an underlying organization supporting the interorganizational collaboration (Adler & Heckscher, 2006; Fjeldstad et al., 2012). Moreover, with the substantial variation between the existing hospital-at-home models, there are reasons to believe that specific components and processes affect outcomes. Fundamental design principles such as what are the goal, what are the basic tasks, who make which decisions, and what is the structure of communication underlie any well-functioning organization (Burton, Obel, & Håkonsson, 2020). Thus, when designing a new organization to treat patients in their home, a conceptual framework is needed. In this study, we chose the Star Model by Galbraith (2014) to make sure of the performance of the new patient pathway. In order to facilitate the process with developing the new organizational form for in-home hospital treatment in collaboration with multiple different stakeholders, an action research approach was chosen. As Bradbury and Lifvergren (2016) says: an action research orientation to health care exemplifies a shift in mindset that redefines traditional notions of expertise and distributes authority to all key stakeholders across multiple complex systems and directly engages participants in personal reflection on their experiences. Thus, action research is a suitable method to work with stakeholders to understand a context, and where it is necessary to involve all the different occupational groups involved in the treatment of the patient in order to collaboratively discuss and negotiate what the "best" to do is.

This chapter proceeds as follows. Next section presents organization design, including the Star Model introduced by Galbraith and the collaborative community. This is followed by a section, which provides an overview of the research setting and an in-depth description of the action research process as well as the organization of the project. Then we present the findings of the two first action research phases, before we discuss highlights from the process and learning outcomes of both the action research process and the establishment of a collaborative community, and conclude.

ORGANIZATION DESIGN

Organization design is a normative science with the goal of prescribing how an organization's structure, roles, and processes should be created, given a particular set of internal and external factors, to ensure that the organization's goal can be realized. The components within an organization's design have to be aligned, if the organization should function both effectively and efficiently (Burton & Obel, 2004). However, there is not a single best way of organizing, but more options depending on the organization's tasks and environment (Galbraith, 1974).

Traditional organization design, building on an information processing view, involves two complementary problems. First, how to divide a big task of the whole organization into smaller tasks of the subunits, e.g. how to divide the task, in-home hospital treating of patients between collaborators, and allocate these tasks to individuals. Secondly, how to coordinate these smaller subunit tasks, so that they fit together in order to solve the bigger task. Coordinating subtasks requires exchange of information (Burton et al., 2020; Galbraith, 1974; Puranam, Alexy, & Reitzig, 2014). Thus, structure and coordination are the fundamental choices in organizational design (Burton & Obel, 2018).

Given that designing an organization is no simple task and organization design is a decision-making process with numerous steps and many choices to make, it is important to use a guiding conceptual framework, when developing a new organizational form. The literature on organization design offer a number of models building on the information processing view, including Burton and Obel's multicontingency approach (2004), Galbraith's Star Model (2014), and Tushman and Nadler's Information Processing Model (1977). In this project, the Star Model was chosen of more reasons. It is a holistic and frequently used design framework for organizations. Models that are more complex could have been used, including one with more components, e.g., the multicontingency approach by Burton and Obel (2004). However, the initial findings from an ethnographic fieldwork conducted within the constructing phase showed that the components important were the ones included within the Star Model. Moreover, when looking at the essential components, when studying collaboration between various organizations, people, infrastructure/division of labor, and commons, e.g., shared knowledge and standards, are important elements (Fjeldstad et al., 2012). Galbraith's model include all of these elements.

The Star Model (showed in Fig. 1) is a framework, developed by Jay Galbraith in the 1960s, that is used in the development of organizations as a basis for design choices. In this holistic way of thinking about an organization, an organization's design is divided into five essential organizational components: strategy, structure, processes, rewards, and people (Galbraith, 2014; Kates & Galbraith, 2007). For further description of the five components, see Table 1.

These five components should be connected and outlined, in order to lay down a solid base and structure for the organization. When using the Star Model in the phase of an organization's development, the chances of achieving good performance later increase, as well as the chances of a positive corporate culture (Galbraith, 2014).

With the knowledge about the different elements, an organizational design consists of, we move on in this chapter, to *how* we have done in order to plan an organization design for an in-home hospital treatment pathway across and in collaboration with different type of organizations. The point of departure for an organization design process is the unit of analysis (Burton et al., 2020;

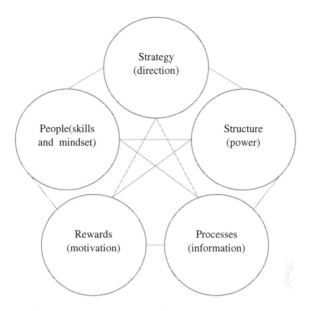

Fig. 1. The Star Model by Galbraith. *Source*: © Jay R. Galbraith.
Reproduced with permission.

Table 1. Description of the Five Components (Galbraith, 2014; Kates
& Galbraith, 2007).

Strategy	The first component to be addressed in the Star Model, as the strategy determines direction: what do the organization(s) wants to accomplish and how to get there?
Structure	Structure is the operationalization of the goal. To get a large number of people to act in an organized way in order to reach the goal of the organization, an organization need a division of labor and power; one to decide what directions the other will take and to coordinate the actions. The processes of collaboration place heavy strains on traditional organization designs, which typically are based on hierarchy, as the primary means of control and coordination. Newer organization designs such as network rely on actor-oriented mechanisms as the primary means of control and coordination.
Processes	Processes are the ways in which work is done in the organization, how the bigger tasks are divided to smaller tasks, and how the smaller tasks are combined/coordinated to meet the organizational goal, which have to do with decision-making, mechanisms for collaboration, and the flow of information. The processes knit the organization together.
Rewards	The system, which influences the motivation of people to behave in ways that will lead to successful execution of the strategy. The purpose of the reward system is to align the goals of the employees with the goals of the organization.
People	The last component, people, is about choosing the skill set and mindset that align with the organization's strategy.

Galbraith, 1974; Van de Ven, Ganco, & Hinings, 2013). The unit of our
analysis is not an organization as a whole, but an organization of a patient
pathway offered by several collaborators and type of organizations.

In order to make the various stakeholders collaborate about designing the new pathway across organizations, we established a collaborative community as the underlying organization. Thus, in this project we found it appropriate to make use of both traditional organization design theories and newer concepts. A collaborative community brings together multiple stakeholders to work collectively to achieve common outcomes, solve shared challenges, and leverage collective opportunities in an environment of trust, respect, empathy, and openness. Building trust is a core value of many collaborations, and especially within collaborative communities without the use of hierarchy as the primary mechanism of control and coordination (Adler & Heckscher, 2006; Snow, Fjeldstad, Lettl, & Miles, 2011). According to Fjeldstad et al. (2012), an actor-oriented organizational architecture has three elements: actors, who have the skills, incentives, and values to self-organize; commons, where the actors accumulate and share knowledge/resources; and protocols, processes, and infrastructures that enable and guide multiactor collaboration. The collaborative communities are often used to large-scale, multiparty collaboration (Fjeldstad et al., 2012; Kolbjørnsrud, 2018). However, in this project, we created a small-scale collaborative community consisting of only five various organizations. However, the developing process included many individuals operating on different levels within these five organizations. Thus, by establishing a collaborative community, we help them to go in the same direction. When relying on lateral, reciprocal relationships and via direct interaction among the actors for control and coordination, an actor-oriented organization often benefit from the presence of a shared services provider, who plays a facilitative role in the community, providing infrastructure and developing data and administrative services that serve the community as a whole (Bøllingtoft et al. 2012; Snow, Håkonsson, & Obel, 2016).

METHODS, CONTEXT, AND PROCESS

This section introduces action research as applied in the present study, and the processes of the action research project, including the different research methods used, are explained, and the setting and underlying organization of the study is presented.

Action research involves close collaboration between practitioners and researchers to bring about change. Since the work of Kurt Lewin (1946), various models with different orientations have developed (Reason & Bradbury, 2008). Coghlan and Shani (2018, p. 4) defined action research as an emergent inquiry process in which applied behavioral science knowledge is integrated with existing organizational knowledge and applied to address real organizational issues. It is simultaneously concerned with bringing about change in organizations, in developing self-help competencies in organizational members and in adding to scientific knowledge. Finally, it is an evolving process that is undertaken in a spirit of collaboration and coinquiry.

Its distinctive characteristics are that it: Focuses on *real organizational issues,* rather than issues created particularly for the purposes of research and, thus, the practitioners experiencing a problem initiate the study; Operates in the people-in-systems domain, and *applied behavioral and organizational science knowledge* is both engaged in and drawn upon; Addresses the twin tasks of bringing about *change in organizations* and in generating robust, *actionable knowledge*, in an evolving process; Is an *emergent inquiry process* it engages in an unfolding story, where data shift because of intervention, and where it is not possible to predict or control what takes place; Is undertaken in a spirit of *collaboration and coinquiry*, whereby research is constructed *with* people, rather than *on* or *for* them; Seeks to contribute to the realm of *practical knowing*, including decisions and actions by practitioners in order to improve situations; and Involves researching in the *present tense* though iterative cycles of constructing, planning, taking action, and evaluating.

Coghlan and Shani (2018) offer a comprehensive framework that comprises four factors:

(1) *Context*: Understanding the external and internal contexts.
(2) *Quality of relationships*: How the action research is research *with* people.
(3) *Quality of the action research process itself*: How action and inquiry progress together through cycles of action and reflection as the project is progressing.
(4) *Outcomes*: The dual outcomes of action research are: (a) improved organizational practice and (b) the creation of actionable theory through the action and inquiry.

Quality in action research may be shown in: how the action research's purpose and rationale, its context, its design, the selection of methodology, and methods of inquiry, and how the narrative and outcomes are described, reflected on, and discussed, and how the extrapolation to a broader context and articulation of actionable knowledge are offered in a manner that demonstrates is rigorous, reflective, and relevant (Coghlan & Shani, 2018).

Grounded in several philosophical traditions and aimed at cogenerating actionable knowledge (useful for practitioners and robust for scholars), action research is scientific because it generates knowledge tested in action and by mobilizing relevant knowledge from those in a position to know.

The action research project presented in this chapter was initiated in February 2018 and is still ongoing (Fig. 2). The chapter describes the results from the constructing and planning action phase, both the facilitated change (the organizational design of an in-home hospital treatment pathway), and the learnings by studying the cocreation process from an outsider perspective.

Using Coghlan and Shani's framework as an overall framework for this action research project allows us to use different appropriate data collection methods within the different phases (an overview of methods used within the constructing and planning phase can be found in Table 2). Within the action research project, the dialog model, especially used within Scandinavian, has inspired us too. The model builds on the understanding that lasting change is best created through network-based and participant involving dialogs (Gustavsen, Hansson, & Qvale, 2008;

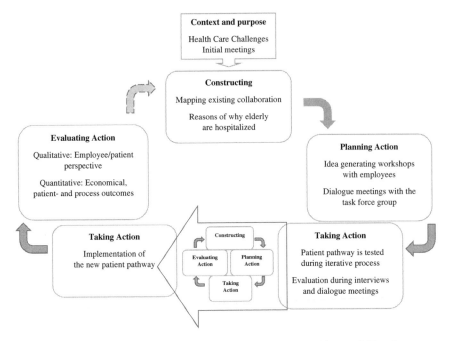

Fig. 2.   Description of How the Project Follows Coghlan and Shani's
Framework.

Pålshaugen, 1998). The aim of this project has been, including all collaborators and through dialogs on various organizational levels, to plan, test, and evaluate an organization for in-home hospital treatment of elderly acute sick patients.

Research Setting and the Three Different Type of Collaborative Organizations

The action research study is carried out in Central Denmark in a collaboration with an ED, three municipalities, and the GPs within the municipalities.

In Denmark, a free, tax-funded health-care system assures that all citizens have unrestricted and equal access to GPs and hospital care. The ED at Viborg Regional Hospital, Regional Hospital Central Jutland, is one of five public emergency hospitals in Central Denmark receiving trauma patients and critically ill patients. The size of Central Denmark Region is 13.142 km^2 with a total population of 1,282,000, out of which the Viborg area, consisting of Skive, Viborg, and Silkeborg municipalities, constitutes approximately 233,000 people. The ED receives patients referred by GPs and patients who have called 112 (the Danish emergency number). Each week, in average, 180 elderly patients are treated within the ED. The ED initiated the study presented in this chapter because they experienced that elderly patients hospitalized in the ED could have been in-home treated if the "right" organization were designed. Moreover, many elderly patients got delirium (acute mental disturbance), when they were hospitalized.

Table 2. Overview of the Methods Used within the First Two Phases of the Research Project.

The Phase	Methods/ Activities	Aim	Participants	Time Span
Constructing phase	Joint seminar – an international known action research consultant presented action research as a way of working	To develop a shared understanding among those involved in the project about the overall research approach	Task force Steering committee Researchers Consultant	November 2018
	Ethnographic fieldwork: 150 hours of participant observation (go along) and 19 semistructured interviews	• To get insights into all aspects of the work practices • To create a common picture and understanding of existing collaboration • To qualify the discussion between the researcher and practitioners • To identify topics and action areas	Researcher workers	August 2018–January 2019
Planning phase	Two one-day workshops with employees planned by the task force	• To get feedback on and discuss the results found in the constructing phase • To let the employees generate ideas about how to design in-home treatment	Workers Researcher	March 2019
	Joint action planning consisted of dialog meetings within the action research group (and the steering committee) Later, individual meetings with task force members Prototyping	• To identify the pre-conditions needed to realize the future in-home patient pathway • To collaborate on developing the new organization design for in-home treating of elderly patients by using the inputs from the workshops • To discuss methods for evaluation	Task force Steering committee Researchers	April 2019–September 2020

GPs have a key role in referring patients to the hospital, since every Danish citizen is registered with a GP, whom they must consult for medical advice. The GP acts as a gatekeeper to the rest of the health-care system, carrying out initial diagnostic investigations and referring patients to hospitals or outpatient clinics when necessary. The GPs are self-employed. They have an agreement with the

Danish authorities, who pay the GPs for every patient who comes to the GPs' office and for the various other services the GPs provide. In addition to this, the practice also gets a set yearly amount per patient assigned to their clinic. The content and conditions for the service provision in general practice is formulated in an agreement signed by the Danish Organization of General Practitioners (PLO) and the Board for Wages and Tariffs of the Regions. GPs organize care coverage for weekends and out-of-hours services. GPs in a given geographical area rotate staffing of regional out-of-hours service centers, where they receive all patient calls. The GP may give a telephone consultation, advise the patient to attend one of the out-of-hours GPs located within the EDs, refer the patient to a hospital or outpatient clinic, or arrange for a home visit. The out-of-hours service operates from 4 p.m. to 8 a.m. from Monday to Friday and 24 hours during weekends and public holidays (Christensen & Olesen, 1998; Larsen, Klausen, & Højgaard, 2020; Pedersen, Andersen, & Søndergaard, 2012). Within the municipalities Viborg, Skive, and Silkeborg, which are the three municipalities in this study, there are about 150 GPs.

The municipalities have the responsibility for home nursing care of patients, and the municipality nurses perform planned tasks. Each municipality also have an acute team, which consists of nurses specialized to admission avoidance. They are called by the hospital to continue treatment of patients in their home after initial treatment at the hospital, by the GPs to visit and evaluate patients, or by municipality nurses to assist them with advanced nursing tasks.

The study benefited from outside researchers from the Department of Management, Aarhus University. Two roles were set up. A professor and expert in organization design is research officer at the project, while an anthropologist, who has been studying organization design challenges within the emergency health-care field and has been affiliated with the ED for the past seven years, were asked to facilitate the cocreation process as project manager. She has been the primary researcher at the project. Thus, having access to both information and individuals that would most likely not be available to an outside researcher. The author of this chapter is the project manager, but named the researcher in the rest of the chapter. Researchers from the Research Center for Emergency Medicine, Aarhus University Hospital, and DEFACTUM, a research and consultant house within the region, are also part of the project.

Context Phase and Purpose

At a joint meeting at the hospital, all potential stakeholders were invited to hear about the initial project idea, addressing the experienced practical concern with an increasing number of elderly. Afterward, the researcher had individual face-to-face meetings with people identified to be potential participants of either the project steering committee or the task force group, people who would be relevant to engage (or needed, because of interdependence in the future task solving) in order to address the issue. As Gray write, the identification of the stakeholders is an important step, when facilitating interorganizational collaboration (1985). The meetings were held at peoples' own offices and were about getting feedback on an early draft of the project description, answering different questions, talking about any concerns about the research project, and to get an understanding of the context. It was a time-consuming process. However, an aim of these initial personal meetings was to foster the trust, which is essential for collaboration (Adler & Heckscher, 2006; Fjeldstad et al., 2012). The meetings allowed people to engage in the project at an early stage and made the first joint meeting easier. They were all familiar with the researcher and had had the opportunity to express their opinions about the project in a comfortable setting. Thus, preliminary expectations were established.

The Constructing Phase: Process and Methods

This study is a joint project, including three municipalities (Skive, Viborg, and Silkeborg), GPs in the three municipalities, and an ED. Thus, different types of organizations (regional, municipalities, self-employed) collaborate in order to solve a mutual challenge with an increasing number of elderly patients. They want to find a new way to collaborate, a new organization design, by leveraging the capabilities of anyone who contributes. In order to qualify the patient pathway and ensure ownership, it was decided that everyone, who contributes and therefore will have a role in the new patient pathway (hospital, municipalities, GPs), should be engaged in the design and evaluation of the new pathway. However, both the hospital and the municipalities are traditionally hierarchical organizations, whereas the GPs are self-employed but united in the political organization, PLO. To secure the collaboration between these various organizations (a series of silos managed by top-down planning) when exploring and designing a new patient pathway, without using the traditionally hierarchical scheme, a collaborative community was created as underlying organization for collaboration.

A steering committee and a task force group have been set up, in which all organizational units that are part of the research project are represented and actively involved. The steering committee members cover the grant holders and include the chief physician and head nurse within the management of the ED, the Heads of Social and Health Services from all three municipalities, and two representatives from the GPs, whereas one of them is the regional vice chair of PLO. In few cases, the directors from the hospital and municipalities have also been involved within the project in order to discuss specific issues. The directors have approved the research project and have been continuously informed about the project. However, the core of the organization is the task force. The task force consists of the managers, who, within traditional organizations based on hierarchy, represent the managerial level closest to the staff. The members are the head of the acute team and the head of the municipality nursing care unit from each of the three municipalities, a physician from the ED, the manager of the hospital visitation, and a GP.[1] The task force group, consisting of 11 different health-care professionals with varying types of knowledge and experience from different sectors, acted within this project as the action research group. With this organization, we created a space for the task force to collaborate more freely and innovatively. As one of the managers expressed it: "In the working group we are

Regional Hospital
Hospital Directors
Department Managers, ED
Manager
Nurses
Manager
Therapists
Manager
Administration
(secretaries)
ED
physicianED
physician
ED physician
Municipality x 3
Municipality Director
Health Director
Managers for different
areas at two different
organizational levels
Manager
Nurses
(home)
Manager
Acute
team
General Practitioners
GP
GP, represent-
tative in PLO
GP, one
representative in
each municipality
GP,
representative
at the hospital
GP
GP

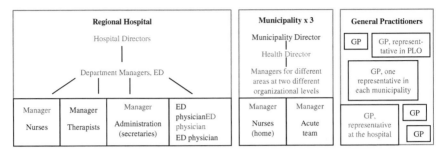

Fig. 3. Overview of the Three Different Collaborators within the Project and Their Participations.

free to develop without thinking about, for example, economics." In Fig. 3, the directors are marked by green (gray in printed version), the steering committee is marked by blue (dark gray in printed version), and the task force is marked by red (light gray in printed version).

In addition to the steering committee and the task force, the formal side of the organization of the project involved of a project group consisting of the affiliated researchers from three different research institutions. In Fig. 4, the organization of the project is illustrated.

The organization itself has been flexible with respect to entering and exiting, and making sure that the right people are invited and stay on. Thus, the configuration is dynamic (Gray, 1985). For example, due to the role, the administrative people within the ED was planned to have in the new patient pathway, the middle manager for the administrative people was invited to take

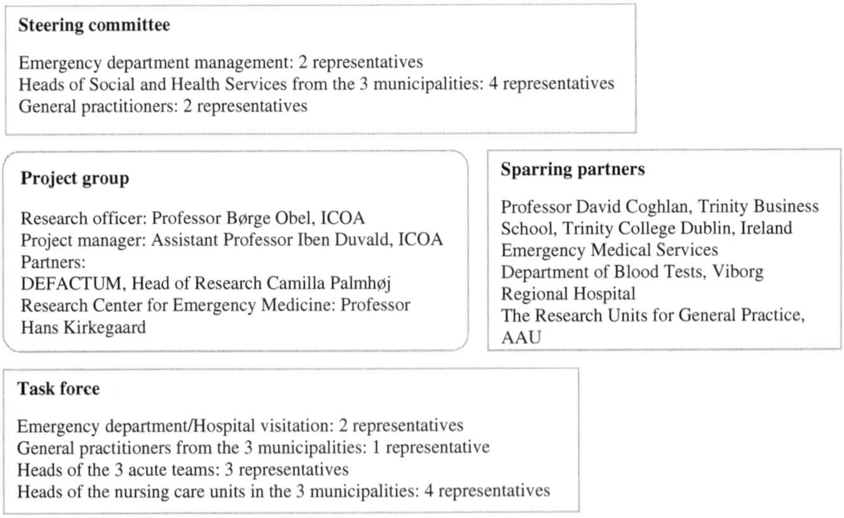

Steering committee
Emergency department management: 2 representatives
Heads of Social and Health Services from the 3 municipalities: 4 representatives
General practitioners: 2 representatives
Project group
Research officer: Professor Børge Obel, ICOA
Project manager: Assistant Professor Iben Duvald, ICOA
Partners:
DEFACTUM, Head of Research Camilla Palmhøj
Research Center for Emergency Medicine: Professor
Hans Kirkegaard
Sparring partners
Professor David Coghlan, Trinity Business
School, Trinity College Dublin, Ireland
Emergency Medical Services
Department of Blood Tests, Viborg
Regional Hospital
The Research Units for General Practice,
AAU
Task force
Emergency department/Hospital visitation: 2 representatives
General practitioners from the 3 municipalities: 1 representative
Heads of the 3 acute teams: 3 representatives
Heads of the nursing care units in the 3 municipalities: 4 representatives

Fig. 4. The Organization of the Project.

part of the task force group in the planning phase. Moreover, the organization has also changed during the process. At one of the steering committee meetings in the planning phase, a chair was established due to a wish of a more agile organization and a need to be able to make faster decisions. A representative from the hospital and one of the municipalities, respectively, were chosen as chairs, due to the size of their role within the new pathway and a recognized interdependence between them.

The researcher introduced action research as a potential helpful approach due to the aim of the project, collaborating across organizations to develop a new treatment pathway and make evidence for the quality of the pathway. In order to make sure that all collaborators, both those involved in the steering committee and those in the task force group, knew about the overall research approach within the project, the researcher invited all to a joint seminar, where an international known action research consultant presented action research as a way of working. The collaborators did not know about the approach and were actively discussing the method and especially the fact that it is allowed to change how to do things along the way and during the project because of the cyclical process.

In the beginning of the project, the local context was explored by the researcher using observation and interviews. Empirical data were gathered through an ethnographic fieldwork consisting of approximately 150 hours of participant observation (Hammersley & Atkinson, 2007; Spradley, 1980) and 19 semistructured interviews (Kvale & Brinkmann, 2009) about the existing treatment of patients, and the collaboration between the ED, the municipalities, and the GPs (the three collaborators within the project). The purpose of the data collection was to identify topics and action areas, when designing the new organizational form.

In order to gain insights into all aspects of the work practices and the current operating model, the researcher participated by following individually employees in their daily activities in shifts at different times of the day and week. By following them from the moment they began their working day until they left for home, the research tool known as go-along was used (Kusenbach, 2003). Oral consent from each employee, who was followed, was obtained prior to the observation. In total, seven municipality nurses, and 10 acute team nurses (five to six nurses in each of the three municipalities), as well as 2 GPs were followed in working days of 6–8 hours. The informants were asked to elaborate on their work practices, and when appropriate, small informal interviews took place (Bernard, 2011). All patients were informed and verbally consented to allow the presence of the researcher. The semistructured interviews (Bernard, 2011; Kvale & Brinkmann, 2009) were performed with 26 employees, including GPs, nurses from the hospital visitation, municipality home care nurses, and acute team nurses from all municipalities. The topics within the interviews, based on the observation data, included the health-care professionals' understanding of their own tasks and role, the collaboration between themselves and each collaborator, strengths and challenges within the existing collaboration with each collaborator, and the collaboration between all the collaborators. The interviews were either individual or duo interviews, lasted between 49 and 85 minutes, and were recorded and transcribed verbatim. All the empirical material was generated between August

2018 and February 2019. The thematic analysis of the empirical material had an explorative and inductive approach (Boyatzis, 1998; Braun, Clarke, Hayfield, & Terry, 2018) and was focusing on an emic perspective – the perspective of the employees, how did they see and experience the collaboration.

Thus, the researcher performed the initial part of the constructing phase herself, the preliminary diagnosis, in order to establish a baseline and qualify the discussion between the researcher and practitioners within the next phase, the planning phase. Initial interactions most be designed to promote valid exchange of information and to search for common ways of framing the problem, when stakeholders hold widely differing perspectives on the problem (Gray, 1985). Though most elderly patients are treated in a collaboration between the GP, the hospital, and the municipalities, the fieldwork showed that each collaborator had various interpretations of the patient pathway, and they only knew about one single piece of the puzzle. This fragmentation often characterizes the health-care system treating acute ill patients (Mohrman et al., 2012). The collaboration was characterized by an "us and them" mindset. The aim of the fieldwork and the presentation of the results were to create a common and a holistic picture and understanding of existing collaboration (the existing situation and operating processes) among the practitioners, and, thus, qualify the planning of the new way of collaboration – the joint (practitioners and researcher) discussions about where to improve. The gap between where they were and where they wanted to go. The results of the fieldwork were discussed in the action research group and presented for the steering committee. During this discussion, the degree of recognized interdependence was confirmed among stakeholders, which is a critical basis for collaboration (Gray, 1985). The ethnographic fieldwork also helped the researcher to understand the field and, thus, to be a facilitator understanding all the different viewpoints of the practitioners, which became an important tool, when managing various discussions at later dialog meetings.

The Planning Phase: Process and Methods

An initial cocreation process, planned by the task force, started this phase. In March 2019, 24 employees were invited to participate in two one-day workshops facilitated by the researcher. The purpose of the 8 hours long workshops was to get feedback on and discuss the results found in the constructing phase, and let the employees based on their experiences generate ideas about and explore collaborative how patients with different symptoms in the future could be in-home hospital treated. Inspired by future creating workshops (Nielsen & Nielsen, 2006), the participants took an active part in the intervention of their own future. Each day, two groups of six people participated. First, on an individual basis, each one generated innovative ideas, and afterward they should do a realization of their ideas in groups by making a step-by-step recipe for an in-home treatment pathway. Each group consisted of a physician from the ED, a nurse from the hospital visitation, a GP, a municipality nurse, an acute team nurse, and a person from the prehospital services. Thus, all participants in each group represented different organizations and had different experiences. In the end of the day, each group presented their idea for the other group, and the workshop ended with a joint discussion about the ideas. The workshops resulted in four roughly described but similar organization designs for patient pathways based on different symptoms. The workshops were video-recorded in order to get in-depth knowledge about the collaborative cocreation process.

After the workshops, the joint action planning consisted of several audio-taped dialog meetings within the action research group (for participants, see the members of the task force). Eleven practitioners and the researcher met every second month face-to-face and later monthly as a group for eight 4-hours sessions over a year (see Fig. 5). Within the meetings, the new organization design for the patient pathway with in-home hospital treatment of elderly patients was slowly created by consolidating, further developing and detailing the initial ideas from the workshops. In a participating dialogue meetings setup created by the researcher, the collaborators were thinking structure and processes of the organization design together across the organizations. Each meeting had an aim (or more than one). It could be in a broader sense, e.g., running through work task descriptions or in a detailed sense, such as how to handle the problem, that the acute team were not allowed to store the medication, they were going to use within the treatment. At each meeting, some questions were answered, but several questions were raised too. The dialog meetings were supplemented with few steering committee meetings. An example of an interesting idea from the steering committee, which affected the work within the action research group, was the idea about the number of pathways. Instead of several pathways focusing on patients with specific symptoms, it should rather be a dialog between the GP and the ED physician about the patients who could benefit from in-home hospital treatment. The researcher acted as a link between the two groups and facilitated the cycles of action and reflection as the project was progressing.

Another decision taking by the steering committee, which affected the work within the task force group, was that the first part of the taking action phase, the pilot test of the patient pathway, should only take place in one municipality. This decision changed the roles within the task force group; some got a bigger role, the managers from the municipality, in which the test should take place, while others got a more peripheral role. As one of the managers stated:

"That process, I think was extremely difficult to be in." "...when I look into our own organization, the fact, that the acute team and the home nurses is organized by two different managers. I think the complexity will be big enough, because how do we get them to collaborate on such a big new task. That we then had to include the other municipalities, which, from my chair, could also say without expense 'it could be nice, we could too, and we should too,' when it was not themselves who had to implement these suggestions. I must say, at that point, I think the task became difficult."

Because of a time pressure, due to that the date for the test came closer, a subgroup within the task force group developed. The speed of the process was set up because the joint meeting process was too slow. As one of the manager said: "Every time we have a task force meeting, I could just feel myself getting more and more breathless overall that we were to achieve in no time." To respond to

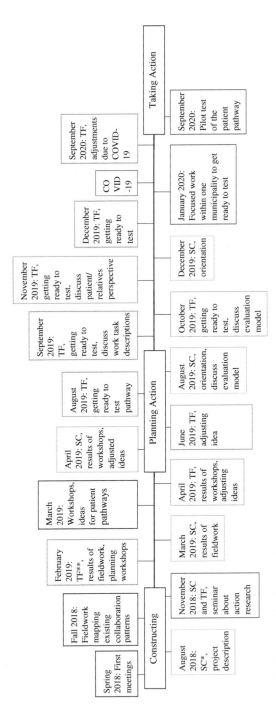

Fig. 5. Process of the Action Research Project.

*SC = The project Steering Committee
**TF = The project Task Force/Action research group

this frustration, the researcher worked intensively together with the individual participants within the task force group, who should implement the new organization, including the various roles and tasks. The aim of the individual meetings was getting the final details in place and talking about how the researcher could help facilitating the implementation. This change within the process helped the involved:

> ...it became easier to focus on, well then we should have done this, and we should have done workflows, and we should have done the introduction material, and we should have figured out how to teach and so forth.... It is us who decide how we do in details. However, it also gives us more responsibility.

The relation between the managers for the acute team and the home nurses in the municipality changed too: "We have been given this task, and it has also expanded and strengthened our collaboration."

In collaboration, we focused on the design to create options and evaluate these options. We used prototyping to test part of the pathway, e.g., one day we tested the flow of information within the patient pathway. Information processing is about creating the connections and knowledge sharing between the collaborating organizations within the pathway. The new patient pathway builds on an increased collaboration between different organizations. Thus, the interdependencies among these increase, and more information must be processed (Galbraith, 1974). By testing the flow of information, we discovered many details on micro level we had to change.

Consequences of the Pandemic

Due to the COVID-19 situation, we had to postpone the first round of the taking action phase, the pilot test of the in-home treatment pathway. Thus, the planning phase was extended from March 2020 to September 2020. The pandemic also created debate within both the steering committee and the task force group. Some of the collaborators had the opinion that you cannot test any new form of organization during a pandemic because the results would not give us a realistic picture, e.g., the use of resources. Others thought that right now due to the pandemic it was important more than ever to run in-home hospital treatment to avoid hospitalization of elderly. Advantages and disadvantages by pilot testing a new organization during a pandemic was discussed, and a majority decided to start testing the new in-home hospital treatment pathway. However, several precautions were taken. The patients had to be tested for COVID-19, when admitted (in a close collaboration between the acute team and the hospital). If they had COVID-19, they had to be admitted to the hospital. Due to limited resources caused by the pandemic, both the acute team and the hospital should be able to press a pause button for a day or more, where new patients were not being admitted to in-home hospital treatment. Once every week, the chairs of the steering committee should meet virtually with the research officer and the project manager to consider the local context, e.g., the situation within the hospital and the municipality (due to) and the current COVID-19 infection rate. Actually, the preparations for running the pilot test during a situation with pandemic showed a new "we-feeling" among the collaborators. A closer relationship has developed. One example, when the ED manager wrote to the manager of the acute team: we should cooperate, when finding a way to test the patients for COVID-19, and maintaining the health of the nurses within the acute team is also in our interest.

Moreover, the pandemic and the following day-to-day changes within the health-care sector may also have a positive effect on this research project. As one manager in the task force explained:

> I think this sudden upheaval, approach, and relationship to some tasks also help us now, when we want to change the organization. The pandemic and all the changes due to the pandemic take the sting out of the horror one would have, when we start hospitalizing citizens in our own homes. We are probably more ready for change now.

FROM CONSTRUCTING PHASE TO PLANNING PHASE BY USING THE STAR MODEL

In collaboration with different type of organizations, an ED, three municipalities, and self-employed GPs, an organization design for in-home hospital treatment was found doing the first two phases of a joint action research project. By using Galbraith's Star Model of organization design in the development of the new organization, the chances of achieving good performance later increase. Table 3 summarizes the main learnings from the constructing phase, when challenges within the existing collaboration were found and decision-making about where to make changes was made, and how these learnings have been addressed in the planning action phase, where the anticipated actions, that can solve the problems, were specified.

By treating patients at home, the ED, the three municipalities, and the GPs create a network for a part of their activities. The collaborators solve and are responsible for different subtasks within the treatment. The ED physician and the acute team are planned to be the key roles, when patients in the future are in-home hospital treated. The process can be divided into three independent components: (1) input, (2) throughput, and (3) output (Asplin et al., 2003). The ED physician is supported by the GP, who performed the objective examination and diagnosed the patient, in the input (admission of the patient), but have the overall responsibility for the patient's treatment though all components and coordinate the treatment with the acute team. The acute team is responsible for the practical execution and coordination of the care and treatment. They can delegate tasks to the municipality nurses, who support the acute team in the throughput (focused care and treatment). All of the employees collaborate in this network organization focusing on a few activities, e.g., the few patients, who can be in-home hospital treated, but at the same time, they have most of their activities, treating all the other patients, within their own organizations, focusing on different aspects of patient care.

Table 3. Summary of the Learnings in the Two First Action Phases, by Using the Star Model.

Elements in the Star Model	Phases within the Project	Illustrative Quotes from the Ethnographic Fieldwork
Strategy (goal, direction)	*Learnings from the constructing phase* • Common interest across the collaborators of solving the problem with increasing number of elderly patients, and a common understanding of that hospitalization is not the best for elderly. • Want to be innovative within the framework of existing health-care system by reorganizing the collaboration. *Learnings addresses within the planning action phase – solutions* • Finding/developing an organization design for in-home hospital treating of elderly patients.	
Structure (organization, key roles, power, and authority)	*Learnings from the constructing phase* • Some patients are treated at home in a collaboration between the acute team and the general practitioner (GP) (within the primary health-care sector). However, it is often due to a series of coincidences. The hospital avoidances depend on the experiences and creativity of the acute team nurse and the willingness of the GP. • Difficulties about getting in touch with a physician, the one responsible for the treatment. An example: when the acute team treat a patient at home and need to consult a physician to complete her task, but the physician do not answer the phone – the nurse is dependent on the decision of the physician to be able to finish her task. • The GPs often know the elderly patients but are only available in daytime on weekdays, whereas the emergency physician does not know the patient, but are available 24/7 and are used to treat acute ill patients. • The acute team has the time and experience to treat acute ill patients in their own home. *Learnings addresses within the planning action phase – solutions* • A team/network structure addressing that the treatment requires lateral coordination across organizations and a more formal integration between the collaborators across the organizational boundaries.	"It is not always about, that we cannot treat them at home. It is due to the organization and the options available" (acute team).

Table 3. (*Continued*)

Elements in the Star Model	Phases within the Project	Illustrative Quotes from the Ethnographic Fieldwork
	• Admitting patients to in-home treatment requires a dialog between the GP, who has the knowledge about the patient, and the emergency physician, who has the time and experiences to treat the patient; can the individual patient be in-home hospital treated, and will the patient benefit from this treatment. • The hospital "outsources" the nurse task to the municipalities. Thus, the municipality nurses are responsible for the practical execution of task. *Learnings from the constructing phase* • Lack of clear responsibility of the existing in-home treatment performed in the primary health-care sector. • Unclear task dividing between the municipality nurses and the acute team. • Four different IT systems. Each collaborator has their own system, in which they document their work, information about the patients are not shared electronic between the collaborators, which is not working together. *Learnings addresses within the planning action phase – solutions* • Detailed descriptions of workflow (work task descriptions) divided between roles/ organizations – informal contracts and mechanisms for coordination to secure the operationalization, when activities/tasks are distributed.Agreements set expectations for actions and foster cooperation. • The emergency physician, who is on duty 24/7, has the responsibility of individual patients' treatment. • The acute team coordinates the treatment within the municipality, and they can delegate tasks to the municipality nurses. • The emergency physician and acute team are parallel personal coordination mechanisms, who secure a lateral flow of information, in order to handle the different information technology (IT) systems, which are not working together. • Secretaries, working at the hospital, secure the flow of written information between the collaborators because of a lack of different IT systems.	"It must be clear, who is responsible for the treatment, is it the GP or is it the physician at the hospital, because few physicians want to take over the responsibility for a treatment initiated by another physician" (acute team). "Sometimes, as a nurse, you may feel that no one will take the responsibility for the in-home treatment you perform (...) it is damn uncomfortable" (acute team).
Processes (decision-making, workflow between roles, mechanisms for collaboration)		

- In all collaboration, it is important to coplan and on a daily basis to coordinate work, such that one gets as simple as possible an interface between the parties involved. This is necessary in order to ascertain that all tasks needed are carried out by someone. The emergency physician and the acute team coordinates tasks across sectors every day at a morning conference.
- Direct phone communication, the nurse can call the emergency physician 24/7, in order to handle that the treatment is coordinated over a distance, i.e. the communicating parties are at different locations and must use some kind of tool to bridge that distance.

Rewards (motivation of people)

Learnings from the constructing phase

- Different incentives to change existing practices in order to collaborate in new ways in order to treat more patients at home.

"We want to use our skills, and not just be a resource" (acute team).

"If we are not treating them at home, they will be here, occupying a bed for days and require more resources" (emergency physician).

Learnings addresses within the planning action phase – solutions

- Possibility for admission avoidance.
- Private benefits, e.g. securing job satisfaction by letting the acute team do the tasks they were supposed to do – the reason why they applied for the position.

Learnings from the constructing phase

- The GPs have the knowledge about the patients.
- The emergency physicians have the time and experiences to treat the patient.
- The municipality nurses perform many tasks within the patients' home.
- Differences between the acute team nurses' skills and size of the team in the three municipalities, the acute teams missing competences.

People (skills and mindset needed, and how to make the best use of skills and resources)

Learnings addresses within the planning action phase – solutions

- Transferring of knowledge from the GP, who know about the patient, to the emergency physician, who has the time and experiences to treat the patient.
- The acute teams are getting more skills – they have to be able to solve the tasks.
- Visualizing the patients in the various IT systems creating shared responsibility for the patients.
- The employees treating patients at home must be relative independent and be able to find solutions.
- The acute team is delegating tasks to the municipality nurses, if they already perform tasks in the home, securing extra resources are not used when offering in-home hospital treatment.

"At night we cannot do the same things as we can during the day. At night, after all, it is me, who is an acute team nurse – without being it" (municipality nurse).

The most significant change is the choice of extended collaboration between the physician within the ED and the nurses employed in the municipalities. The hospital "outsource" the nurse task to the acute team and municipality nurses, and the ED physician and the acute team are going to work as parallel personal coordination mechanisms, who secure a lateral flow of information and coplan the work across sectors on a daily basis (Galbraith, 1974). Thus, the organizational design breaking down the existing siloes between the primary and secondary health-care system was enabled.

DISCUSSION OF LEARNING OUTCOMES

By using Coghlan and Shani's framework (2018) that comprises four factors, I will first discuss the learning outcomes of the two first phases within this action research project. The four factors include context, quality of relationship, quality of the action research process itself, and the outcomes. Secondly, we discuss the learning outcomes by creating a collaborative community, the limitations of this study, and implications, before we conclude.

Context

According to Coghlan (2019), it is important to identify cultural, political, and structural aspects that can act as potential drivers or inhibitors of a change within organizations. These factors are crucial to understand the results of action research.

In this project, an increasing need for treatment of elderly due to demographics initiated the collaboration between a hospital, three municipalities, and GPs in Central Denmark with the aim of developing an in-home hospital treatment pathway for acute ill elderly patients. A common motivation for all the collaborators has been that they rather want to develop a solution to the increasing number of elderly themselves using a democratic process, than to be imposed a political solution to the problem, which may not fit into the local context. It is a political goal, both nationally and locally, to treat more patients in their own home (Health Planning, 2017; Kjeldsen, 2017) – the question has been, how?

Another important part of the context has been the criteria for the development process. At least two criteria have indicated the way to go. Firstly, the existing hospital-at-home literature distinguishes between a hospital and a municipality-based admission avoidance pathway (Sheppard et al., 2016). Due to a decision at director level within the hospital not to work with outgoing employees/teams, the pathway had to be municipality based. Secondly, the pathway should be developed within the framework of the existing health-care system by changing the collaboration patterns between the various stakeholders. Still, it is a huge and complex task. One of the learnings through the first two phases of this action research project has been the visibility of the complexity. As one of the managers from the task force told: "I think the process has been amazingly great to visualize, that all are crying out for more and closer collaboration across regions and municipalities and GPs. However, I have at least noticed how complex a task it is," "It was an insanely exciting task – and it still is – uh, but it's also a big task due to the complexity."

By using Kates and Galbraith's definitions (2007) on innovation initiatives, this complexity becomes evident. According to them, designing an in-home hospital treatment pathway across different organizations can be defined as a breakthrough innovation, an innovation resulting in new products (or here a new service) requiring the development of new knowledge and capabilities. Here the action research process help the collaborators to reach from the idea generation based on the interaction of divergent perspectives to create (and evaluate) a prototype, and in the future may be to commercialization. Moreover, the existing health-care system is not designed to work across organizations. As Mohrman et al. (2012) wrote, the misfit between the existing organization of the health-care system and the services, the health-care system needs to deliver in the changing environment is a common problem. Thus, many barriers have to be overcome if the network structure designed in this project to take care of the elderly is going to work. An example on an organizational issue is the different information technology (IT) systems, which are not compatible. Another issue is trust, which has been discussed within the task force. The ED physician has to trust the GP, who has seen the patient before admission, and the ED physician and acute team nurses have to trust each other, when collaboratively performing the treatment.

Quality of Relationships

Given the involving nature of action research, the researcher has worked closely with practitioners from different organizations (and organizational levels within these organizations) in a process of knowledge generation in the local context of treatment of elderly acute ill patients. The aim was to shed light on some of the challenges, but also possibilities, in order to plan an in-home hospital treatment pathway.

Participants in action research are not subjects of investigation but those who hold the acquired experience. By establishing communities of inquiry within (and across) organizations, they are members of the research group. They just bring another type of knowledge to the inquiry (Eikeland, 2006). The task force, also called the action research group, held an active role and profoundly contributed to the knowledge development throughout the action research process, within both the construction and planning phase. They contributed with their knowledge about practice from different part of the health-care system, and collaboratively, they explored the existing practices and planned the change of practice, according to both work processes and the evaluation of these, by engaging in critical dialogs. An example is how the new patient pathway is going to be evaluated according to heath economics. It is important for both practitioners and researchers to secure a valid result of the health economic consequences of the new way of collaboration, including the hospital's "outsource" of the nurse task to the municipalities, which have been set up in order to in-home hospital treat elderly patients. Thus, together, the researchers and practitioners are developing a micro costing tool, which meets the applicable research standards but which is also possible for the practitioners to perform and incorporate in everyday practice. By bridging practice and academia, the quality of the data collection is expected to increase due to a joint ownership and obligation.

The quality of relationships includes how the action research is with people, that is, both the relationship between the researcher and the practitioner, and also the relationship between the various practitioners (Shani & Coghlan, 2019). By establishing a collaborative community, the collaborators is in a democratic process, rather than a hierarchical development process. As one of the managers from the task force stated:

> To develop this in collaboration, I think that's the cool thing about this project, I have to say. We learn more about each other and have the opportunity to cross some boundaries.

Organizational design has traditionally been a top management decision (e.g., Burton et al., 2020; Donaldson, 2001). However, the combination of establishing a collaborative community and using an action research process to develop the pathway secured active involvement and engagement of all organizational levels from workers to directors. Thus, a shared commitment for the organizational changes was initiated. Especially, the middle managers participating as coresearchers have had an important and active role planning and designing micro dimensions of the new patient pathway. More research on micro approaches to organization design based on knowledge on how people interact in organizations is needed (Puranam, 2018; Van de Ven et al., 2013). This chapter addresses these calls by showing how different organizations on different organizational levels within a collaborative community have codeveloped a new organization design through a series of different involvement methods, including workshops and systematic dialog meetings, initiated by the researcher. However, it has not always been easy for the participants, and it itself has been a learning process, e.g., one manager from the steering committee told the researcher about some solutions, he had thought about himself. She told him that he had to await the solutions developed collaboratively within the task force, to which he replied, that it was not an easy thing to do – it was not, the way he used to work.

Within this project, the researcher helps the practitioners to codevelop and evaluate their new design for in-home hospital treatment. Thus, design is presented as a process involving organizations on all levels, yet the design of the pathway is still building on a traditional organization design model in order to ensure the effectiveness and efficiency of the new organization. In this way, the combination of organization design theory and the action research approach used in this project allows us to examine the coexistence of macro and micro approaches in organizational practice (Puranam, 2018).

Quality of the Action Research Process Itself

As Coghlan (2019) point out, multiple action research cycles are included in an action research project. Some of them are short-term cycles, while others are long-term cycles. The workshops within the planning phase represent a learning cycle itself. The workshops were planned within the action research group, the researcher facilitated the workshops, and the action research group evaluated the results of the workshops. Some of the important results and learnings from the workshops included idea generation of four new patient pathways. However, the organization design for the pathways was quite similar, despite they were developed in four different groups focusing on patients with different symptoms. They wanted to "reuse" things, they experienced as working well. An interesting observation was that when generating ideas, the employees were already thinking about incentives and implementation. Thus, the choices made were dependent on the employees' beliefs about how their colleagues may react on the new design, e.g., they limited the role of the GPs, due to the GPs' heavy workload and their attitude toward intravenous treatment responsibility based on political currents. They were afraid of the GPs' mindset and resistance to the organizational change, and that it could prevent the use of the new patient pathway due to the GPs' gatekeeper position. Thus, the ED physician had to be responsible for the treatment. Another learning point was that the participants did not know that much about each other tasks – they only knew about a specific part of the pathway – their own part. This was already discovered during the fieldwork within the constructing phase. However, it was confirmed during the workshops, and it affected the process. Thus, to get ideas about how to perform in-home hospital treatment, they first had to talk about the existing patient pathway. The starting point for discussions about how to do in the future was how do we do it today. As Coghlan wrote, action research is about the past, now, and future (2019). By collaborating in new ways, the participants believed that more patients could be in-home treated in the future. The participants also stressed the importance of involving them in the process, and it made sense to idea generate in collaboration and across organizations, due to their broad and various expertise concerning the work processes within the organizations. Those employees participating in the workshops learned a lot by meeting health professionals from the other organizations and sharing work experiences, due to their limited knowledge about the others' work practices. Moreover, one GP, who defended some fixed attitudes at the workshop, called the researcher the day after, telling, now that he had had time to think about it, he had changed his mind. Thus, the learning process that began during the workshops did not end when the participants went home.

On management level, a cooperative culture has developed during the joint action research process starting within the constructing phase. An international action research expert introduced all the stakeholders represented in the steering committee and task force group for the action research approach. This presentation was the initial change of the mindset of the practitioners about how knowledge can be created through learning cycles. It has become a mantra, "we can always try it out, we are allowed to make changes – it is an action research project." Moreover, when the researcher presented the results of the initial fieldwork, mapping existing collaboration patterns, a common knowledge about the existing treatment of elderly patients emerged among the stakeholders. In addition, the presentation added value for all the collaborators because challenges within each collaborator's way of working were pointed out, as well as common challenges and benefits of the collaboration between all collaborators. The collaborative community as underlying organization has supported this process.

Outcomes

Despite calls for "useful research" and "engaged scholarship," academics and managers seldom collaborate closely to develop solutions to organizational problems (Miles, 2012). However, researchers should be engaged with practitioners and with the problems, organizations are facing (Mohrman & Lawler, 2012). The aim of this chapter was twofold. We want to present how stakeholders from different organizations with the use of action research collaborative explore and create a new organization design that enables health professionals to collaborate in new ways and offer acute ill elderly patients in-home hospital treatment. At the same time, we have investigated and improved this cocreation process and codesign of knowledge among multiple different stakeholders by establishing a small-scale collaborative community. The collaborators act proactive on a common environmental change, i.e., an increasing number of elderly patients in need of health care, requiring a new form of organizing. The action research approach comprised several changes to the collaborators' practice in order to design a way to perform in-home hospital treatment. The most significant change was the choice of extended collaboration between the ED physician and the nurses employed in the municipalities. Thus, a new organizational design breaking down the existing siloes between the primary and secondary health-care system was enabled. The constructing phase and planning action phase, thus, resulted in a sound theoretical and practical framework to guide the implementation and evaluation phase of the project. Moreover, the journey through the first two phases of the action research study facilitated by the researcher ensured commitment of all stakeholders from different type of organizations, and from different organizational levels within these organizations, mediated a common understanding, allowed continuous learning together, and, thus, secured the cocreation of the new organizational design of treatment. The collaboration and participation of all the different stakeholders with different perspectives and ways of understanding as well as the research cycles and feedback/reflection loops makes the new organization design robust.

Lessons Learned by Establishing a Small-scale Collaborative Community

By establishing a collaborative community as the underlying organization, the researcher helped the ED, three municipalities, and the self-employed GPs to plan through a democratic process a new patient pathway for in-home hospital treatment. The three organizational elements needed to the functioning of a collaborative community are present. The *actors* are the individuals from the five collaborators participating in either the steering committee or the task force group. The researcher acted as the shared services provider within the collaborative community. A facilitative role, who provides *infrastructure* (by arranging meetings for both the steering committee, the chairs, and the task force), secures a shared knowledge (*commons*) (by collecting data to analyze and discuss, and holding an educational seminar by inviting all to hear about action research) and communicates with other important stakeholders (e.g., the department of blood tests). As one from the task force mentioned to a meeting, when discussing learning outcomes from the process so far,

...it is important, that we have you to sit and do all the work, all the coordination. We really want this, but we cannot do it without someone as you, who has the time to do it and the commitment.

Thus, a shared services provider has been crucial to promote the collaborative spirit among the collaborators. Moreover, an inclusive approach created the right mindset and provided an incentive to those who wanted to participate. An initiative to a similar but smaller project has been tried out earlier. However, the organization of that project, which was more traditional and consisted of a small group of initiators, did not manage to get the right support neither from those, who were to perform the tasks, nor managerially. The collaborative community has managed to gather all those, who wanted to participate and create a shared commitment among stakeholders on all organizational levels. The organizational form supported the democratic philosophy within the project. However, a process like this takes time, and it requires managerial support to the bottom-up approach. The project description acts as a *protocol*, in which the aim (development of an in-home hospital treatment pathway) and the formal organization of collaboration are described. The expressed mindset about action research is another example of a protocol guiding the collaborators' thinking. The collaboration does not have a hierarchical management system. The steering committee provides overall guidance, but all the collaborators, both within the steering committee and the task force, are equal within the codevelopment of the patient pathway. Knowledge sharing within the collaborative community could be improved, if the IT systems had been integrated. Thus, it would be easier to evaluate the quality of the new patient pathway developed by the collaborative community. However, the combination of the underlying organization of the collaborators and the action research process has resulted in a plan for a new patient pathway, developed in a democratic nonhierarchical process. The collaborative community as underlying organization secured the commitment, which is essential, when using an action research approach. Thus, the great challenge with more elderly can be solved, if those treating the patients develop new ways of treating the patients, e.g., by moving treatment from the hospitals to the patient's own home, by fostering greater collaboration among hospital, municipalities, and GPs.

A Limitation

In this chapter, we can only present the results of the two first phases of an ongoing action research project. We can design an organization, which looks perfect on the paper, following the organization theory guidelines such as the Star Model, but it is still a "desk solution," which is going to meet the world, the real people, and the real problems. Therefore, we must test the solution and figure out how employees and patients are reacting/doing, and we need to continue to the next phase within the action research cycle, the action taking phase. During the next phase, we will take action and test the new patient pathway and explore how the in-home hospital treatment pathway can be realized, and how the design will be met by employees, patients, and relatives. The phase will consist of two parts: a pilot test of the patient pathway in one municipality before a one-year implementation in all three municipalities. A robust evaluation will allow us to address the question of whether the model is sustainable. The evaluation is planned to include a stepped wedge cluster randomized trial study (SW-CRT) (Hemming, Haines, Chilton, Girling, & Lilford, 2015). We will compare the in-home hospital treatment with traditional in-patient hospital care in the ED, and the effect will be measured on the following parameters: length of stay, readmission rate, mortality rate, functional status, and health-related quality of life. Furthermore, we will investigate if the costs to the health service alter because of providing hospital treatment at patients' own home. Qualitatively, interviews with patients, relatives, and employees will investigate their views and satisfaction. In this way, the action research cycle will be complete, from the generation of theory to its testing out and evaluation in practice.

IMPLICATIONS

In this chapter, we offer in-depth insights into the process of how a collaborative community was established to help various stakeholders to collaborate on different organizational levels with a common goal. We focus on, where organizations are going and how they get there (Mohrman & Lawler, 2012). By studying and showing the process, we create knowledge that is useful to other organizations, both within the health-care setting, in which this project is being utilized, and within other industries. Moreover, we hope, we can stimulate both practice and research to explore further, how the combination of organization design theory and an action research approach can be valuable, when various organizations are exploring solutions to great challenges. Nevertheless, more implications can be mentioned.

Firstly, great challenges cannot be solved by individual organizations themselves. However, within the health-care setting, the existing incentive structures prevent organizations from fostering greater collaboration among hospital, municipalities, and GPs. Newer forms of organization design such as the collaborative community presented in this study are often based on volunteering. Incentives need to be designed such that they reward people and organizations for collaborating. Knowledge about how to create the needed incentive structures is necessary. Secondly, when a collaborative community, as the one presented in this study, exists of various organizations using traditionally hierarchy as control mechanism, future research should investigate the interplay between the control mechanisms within hierarchies and those within collaborative communities. Fjeldstad et al. (2012) also mention this implication. However, this is particularly important, when more organizational levels are included in the process/community, and some of the managers in the steering committee have subordinates sitting in the task force group. In this chapter, we indicate several practical implications for managers. Managers, who want to establish a collaborative community and redesign their organizations to improve the ability to collaborate, both internally and externally, must be aware that to be successful requires an ability to use other forms of control mechanisms than hierarchy. A bottom-up process, including more organizational levels, fosters a higher degree of commitment to the organizational changes. There should be a fit between the organizational form and the philosophy. Moreover, a shared services provider is crucial, when a new collaborative community is established.

CONCLUSION

In this chapter, we present how stakeholders from different organizations with the use of action research collaborative explore and create a new organization design that enables health professionals to collaborate in new ways, and offer acute ill elderly patients in-home hospital treatment. At the same time, we have investigated and supported this cocreation process and codesign of knowledge among multiple different stakeholders in three ways:

- A collaborative community was created as the underlying organization for collaboration;
- An action research approach was used to manage the developing process;
- The Star Model was used to secure the design of the future in-home treatment pathway.

Interorganizational collaboration is critical to find effective solution of complex problems and continuous adaptation to changing environments. The great challenge with more elderly can be solved, if a greater collaboration is fostered among hospitals, municipalities, and GPs. Although the scope of the study is limited, we argue that it has successfully facilitated the development of a user-led model for in-home hospital treatment, which might be relevant in other settings, such as countries with similar health-care systems. To our knowledge, this is the first admission avoidance hospital-at-home model created by using action research engaging three different types of organizations.

ACKNOWLEDGMENT

I would like to thank Professor David Coghlan for sharing his extensive knowledge about action research with me and the collaborators within this action research project. I would also like to thank Professor Børge Obel for reading and commenting on this manuscript.

NOTE

1. The hospital visitation is a gatekeeper function within the emergency department (ED) staffed by nurses. Using formalized rules (and in collaboration with the general practitioner (GP) and consultants at the hospital), they decide where the patients are to be received (e.g., the ED, another hospital department, an outpatient clinic, or a municipal offer).

REFERENCES

Adler, P. S., & Heckscher, C. (2006). Towards collaborative community. In C. Heckscher & P. S. Adler (Eds.), *The firm as a collaborative community: Reconstructing trust in the knowledge economy* (pp. 11–106). New York, NY: Oxford University Press.

Asplin, B. R., Magid, D. J., Rhodes, K. V., Solberg, L. I., Lurie, N., & Camargo, C. A., Jr (2003). A conceptual model of emergency department crowding. *Annals of Emergency Medicine*, *42*(2), 173–180.

Bernard, H. R. (2011). *Research methods in anthropology: Qualitative and quantitative approaches* (5th ed.). Lanham, MD: Altamira Press.

Bøllingtoft, A., Donaldson, L., Huber, G. P., Håkonsson, D. D., & Snow, C. (Eds.). (2012). *Collaborative communities of firms: Purpose, process, and design.* New York, NY: Springer.

Boyatzis, R. E. (1998). *Transforming qualitative information: Thematic analysis and code development.* Thousand Oaks, CA: Sage.

Bradbury, H., & Lifvergren, S. (2016). Action research healthcare: Focus on patients, improve quality, drive down costs. *Healthcare Management Forum*, *29*(6), 269–274.

Braun, V., Clarke, V., Hayfield, N., & Terry, G. (2018). Thematic analysis. In P. Liamputtong (Ed.), *Handbook of research methods in health social sciences.* Singapore: Springer.

Burton, R. M., & Obel, B. (2004). *Strategic organizational diagnosis and design: The dynamics of fit* (3rd ed.). Boston, MA: Kluwer Academic Publishers.

Burton, R. M., & Obel, B. (2018). The science of organizational design: Fit between structure and coordination. *Journal of Organ Dysfunction*, *7*(5), 1–13.

Burton, R. M., Obel, B., & Håkonsson, D. D. (2020). *Organizational design: A step-by-step approach* (4rd ed.). Cambridge: Cambridge University Press.

Christensen, M. B., & Olesen, F. (1998). Out of hours service in Denmark: Evaluation five years after reform. *British Medical Journal*, *316*, 1502–1505.

Coghlan, D. (2019). *Doing action research in your own organization* (5rd ed.). London: SAGE Publications.

Coghlan, D., & Shani, A. B. (2018). *Conducting action research for business and management students.* Los Angeles, CA: SAGE Publications.

Covinsky, K. E., Palmer, R. M., Fortinsky, R. H., Counsell, S. R., Stewart, A. L., & Kresevic, D. (2003). Loss of independence in activities of daily living in older adults hospitalized with medical illnesses: Increased vulnerability with age. *Journal of the American Geriatrics Society*, *51*(4), 451–458.

Creditor, M. C. (1993). Hazards of hospitalization of the elderly. *Annals of Internal Medicine, 118*(3), 219–223.

Donaldson, L. (2001). *The contingency theory of organizations*. Thousand Oaks, CA: Sage Publications.

Eikeland, O. (2006). Validity of action research and validity in action research. In K. A. Nielsen & L. Svensson (Eds.), *Action and interactive research: Beyond practice and theory* (pp. 193–240). Maastricht and Aachen: Shaker.

Fjeldstad, Ø. D., Snow, C. C., Miles, R. E., & Lettl, C. (2012). The architecture of collaboration. *Strategic Management Journal, 33*, 734–750.

Galbraith, J. (1974). Organization design: An information processing view. *Interfaces, 4*(3), 28–36.

Galbraith, J. R. (2014). *Designing organizations. Strategy, structure and process at the business unit and enterprise levels* (3rd ed.). San Francisco, CA: Jossey-Bass.

Gray, B. (1985). Conditions facilitating interorganizational collaboration. *Human Relations, 38*(10), 911–936.

Gustavsen, B., Hansson, A., & Qvale, T. U. (2008). Action Research and the challenge of scope. In P. Reason & H. Bradbury (Eds.), *The Sage handbook of action research: Participative inquiry and practice* (2nd ed.). London: SAGE.

Hammersley, M., & Atkinson, P. (2007). *Ethnography: Principles in practice* (3rd ed.). London; New York, NY: Routledge.

Health Planning. (2017). Strategy for the Central Denmark Region's role in the near and cohesive healthcare system. A report in Danish.

Hemming, K., Haines, T. P., Chilton, P. J., Girling, A. J., & Lilford, R. J. (2015). The stepped wedge cluster randomised trial: Rationale, design, analysis, and reporting. *British Medical Journal, 350*, h391.

Inouye, S. K., Bogardus, S. T., Jr, Charpentier, P. A., Leo-Summers, L., Acampora, D., & Holford, T. R. (1999). A multicomponent intervention to prevent delirium in hospitalized older patients. *New England Journal of Medicine, 340*(9), 669–676.

Kates, A., & Galbraith, J. R. (2007). Designing your organization. In *Using the star model to solve 5 critical design challenges*. San Francisco, CA: Jossey-Bass.

Kjeldsen, S. B. (2017). Langtflerepatienterskalbehandlesiegethjem [Far more patients need to be treated in their own homes]. *Sygeplejersken, 10*, 34–37. (The nurse, a Danish journal).

Kolbjørnsrud, V. (2018). Collaborative organizational forms: On communities, crowds, and new hybrids. *Journal of Organ Dysfunction, 7*(11), 1–21.

Kusenbach, M. (2003). Street phenomenology: The go-along as ethnographic research tool. *Ethnography, 4*(3), 455–485.

Kvale, S., & Brinkmann, S. (2009). *InterViews: Learning the craft of qualitative research interviewing*. Los Angeles, CA: Sage.

Larsen, A. T., Klausen, M. B., & Højgaard, B. (2020). *Primary health care in the Nordic countries. Comparative analysis and identification of challenges*. A report published by VIVE – The Danish Center for Social Science Research.

Leff, B. (2009). Defining and disseminating the hospital-at-home model. *Canadian Medical Association Journal, 180*(2), 156–157.

Lewin, K. (1946). Action research and minority problems. *Journal of Social Issues, 2*(4), 34–46.

Miles, R. (2012). The centrality of organization design. *Journal of Organ Dysfunction, 1*(1), 12–13.

Ministry of Health and the Elderly. (2016). *Strengthened efforts for the elderly medical patient, national action plan 2016*. A report in Danish.

Mohrman, S. A., & Lawler, E. E. (2012). Generating knowledge that drives change. *Academy of Management Perspectives, 26*(1), 41–51.

Mohrman, S. A., Shani, A. B., & McCracken, A. (2012). Organizing for sustainable health care: The emerging global challenge. In S. A. Mohrman & A. B. Shani (Eds.), *Organizing for sustainable health care* (pp. 1–40). Bingley: Emerald Group Publishing.

Nielsen, B. S., & Nielsen, K. A. (2006). Methodologies in action research – action research and critical theory. In L. Svensson (Ed.), *Action research and interactive research – Beyond practice and theory* (pp. 63–88). Maastricht: Shaker Publishing.

Pålshaugen, Ø. (1998). *The end of organization theory?* Philadelphia, PA: John Benjamins Publishing Company.

Pedersen, K. M., Andersen, J. S., & Søndergaard, J. (2012). General practice and primary health care in Denmark. *The Journal of the American Board of Family Medicine, 25*, 34–38.

Puranam, P. (2018). *The micro structure of organizations.* Oxford: Oxford University Press.

Puranam, P., Alexy, O., & Reitzig, M. (2014). What's 'new' about new forms of organizing? *Academy of Management Review, 39*(2), 162–180.

Reason, P., & Bradbury, H. (2008). *The Sage handbook of action research: Participative inquiry and practice* (2nd ed.). Los Angeles, CA: SAGE.

Shani, A. B., & Coghlan, D. (2019). Action research in business and management: A reflective review. *Action Research*, 1–24. Retrieved from https://journals.sagepub.com/doi/pdf/10.1177/1476750319852147

Shepperd, S., & Iliffe, S. (2005). Hospital at home versus in-patient hospital care. *Cochrane Database of Systematic Reviews, 3*, 1–67.

Shepperd, S., Iliffe, S., Doll, H. A., Clarke, M. J., Kalra, L., Wilson, A. D., & Gonçalves-Bradley, D. C. (2016). Admission avoidance hospital at home (review). *Cochrane Database of Systematic Reviews, 9*(9).

Snow, C. C., Fjeldstad, Ø. D., Lettl, C., & Miles, R. E. (2011). Organizing continuous product development and commercialization: The collaborative community of firms model. *Journal of Product Innovation Management, 28*, 3–16.

Snow, C. C., Håkonsson, D. D., & Obel, B. (2016). A smart city is a collaborative community: Lessons from smart Aarhus. *California Management Review, 59*(1), 92–108.

Spradley, J. P. (1980). *Participant observation.* Belmont, CA: Wadsworth.

Strausbaugh, L. S. (2001). Emerging health care-associated infections in the geriatric population. *Emerging Infectious Diseases, 7*(2), 268–271.

The national association of municipalities. (2013). Effective municipal prevention - Focusing on prevention of admissions and readmissions. A report in Danish.

Tushman, M. L., & Nadler, D. A. (1977). Information processing as an integrating concept in organizational design. *Academy of Management Review, 3*(3), 613–624.

Vale, J. S., Franco, A. I., Oliveira, C. V., Araújo, I., & Sousa, D. (2019). Hospital at home: An overview of literature. *Home Health Care Management & Practice*, 1–6.

Van de Ven, A. H., Ganco, M., & Hinings, C. R. (2013). Returning to the frontier of contingency theory of organizational and institutional designs. *The Academy of Management Annals, 7*(1), 393–440.

OPENING THE DOORS OF THE IVORY TOWER: ACTION RESEARCH AS A TOOL SUPPORTING COOPERATION BETWEEN UNIVERSITIES AND EXTERNAL ORGANIZATIONS

Beata Jałocha, Ewa Bogacz-Wojtanowska, Anna Góral, Grażyna Prawelska-Skrzypek and Piotr Jedynak

ABSTRACT

In this chapter we discuss how, as a tool for organizational change, action research can affect the development of cooperation between a traditional university and the external environment. The case analyzed was a two-year action research project carried out in cooperation with over 20 employers. This project was carried out at multiple levels and had several essential goals. Apart from its emancipatory role in the shift in the way students carry out their master's theses (toward application, implementation, where organizations become the research subject instead of the research object), the project's aim was to open up the university to cooperation with its environment and conduct useful research. The results indicate that action research through the democratization of the process of introducing changes and its bottom-up nature influences the development of real cooperation between the university and external organizations. Additionally, they contribute to the emancipation of university knowledge, its democratization, dehierarchization, as well as cocreation and sharing with cooperating organizations.

Research in Organizational Change and Development, Volume 29, 143–171
Copyright © 2022 Emerald Publishing Limited
ISSN: 0897-3016/doi:10.1108/S0897-301620210000029007

Keywords: Action research; useful research; higher education; stakeholders; university management; organizational change

INTRODUCTION

The cooperation of universities with the external environment is described as the so-called third mission of the university. It entails cooperation with nongovernmental, public, and business organizations, as a result of which students develop competences that are in line with the needs of the labor market, economy, and society. It is worth emphasizing that the need to intensify cooperation with the environment forces organizational change at universities, which are related to the intensification of cooperation with external partners and can be initiated both top-down (through government programs, a system of incentives in the form of grant programs, etc.) and bottom-up (through initiatives and projects carried out by employees in cooperation with the industry). It takes various forms: (1) introducing practical fields of studies, implemented in cooperation with the employer, (2) dual education, (3) an extensive system of internships.

On the other hand, by creating relations with businesses, universities disseminate and popularize the results of research, implement innovative ideas, and often commercialize them. However, the implementation of the "third mission" is not an easy task, especially in the case of "traditional" universities, focused primarily on research and teaching – especially in the areas of social sciences, humanities, and partly natural sciences. These processes are often characterized by the belief in an authoritarian role of the university, both as the initiator as well as the implementer. The changes, in recent decades, in the way of thinking about the university and its relations with the environment have drawn attention to such aspects of cooperation as dialogue, partnership, and cocreation. At the same time, cooperation between scientists and practitioners is still not developing sufficiently, including in business schools, where this process might be expected to be completely natural. First of all, scientists do not share their research with practitioners, and the language of their publications is impenetrable. Secondly, the most successful books on management are often those written by CEOs or consultants where research findings are rarely reported. Thirdly, business schools focus on conducting research, the results of which are to be primarily published in key scientific journals, and not, for example, in trade journals (Latham, 2011).

The concept that combines the need for rigorous scientific research with cooperation with the world of practice is *useful research* – defined as a research that is useful for both theory and practice (Mohrman & Lawler III, 2011). Useful research is influenced by practice in organizational settings and influences it (Latham, 2011). Moreover, the assumptions of useful research also say that organizations are not inanimate objects and therefore they and their members "cannot be studied as subjects in a way that distances the researcher from the context and its participants" (Mohrman &Lawler III, 2011). Bridging the gap between research and the world of practice requires the use of other approaches that differ from traditionally used positivist methods of fundamental research. Following the traditional understanding of the world of science and the world of practice as two separate entities, researchers are focused on creating and publishing generalizable knowledge based on rigorous research. In turn, practitioners create knowledge in the course of solving practical organizational problems (Mohrman & Lawler III, 2011).

> Theory is when you know everything but nothing works. Practice is when everything works but no one knows why. In this room, theory and practice come together: Nothing works and no one knows why. (Hackman, 2011, p. 103)

These words, which Herb Kelman, professor emeritus at Harvard, put on the door of his office well sum up the fundamentally difficult dilemma faced by researchers in the field of management and organizational sciences – how to enable theory and practice to inform one another? (Hackman, 2011). There are various methodological approaches that allow for combining scientific research with creating organizational changes in the world of practice and resulting in the creation of actionable knowledge. Actionable knowledge contributes to the ability of organizational actors to redesign the system of practice to accomplish their purposes (Mohrman & Lawler III, 2011). According to Beer (2011), the best way to develop actionable knowledge is to use Action Research. We also chose Action Research, a less frequently used and less formalized form of cooperation between the University and the world of practice, to develop links between our research and practitioners. Therefore, in this chapter we address the following research question:

As a tool for organizational changes, how can action research affect the development of cooperation between a traditional university and the external environment?

An instrumental case study was the research strategy chosen for this project. The case analyzed was a two-year action research project carried out in cooperation with over 20 employers. This project was carried out at multiple levels and had several essential goals. Apart from its emancipatory role in the shift in the way students carry out their master's theses (toward application, implementation, where organizations become the research subject instead of the research object), the project's aim was to open up the university to cooperation with its environment and conduct useful research.

The university where the project was implemented is a public European university. A key assumption, the basis of the identity of the university under study, which is a typical traditional Humboldtian European university, is the integrity of education and research. At the same time, the university under consideration is a unique autopoietic system. According to M. Lenartowicz (2015), universities as autopoietic systems have their own distinctive identity pattern. At the same time

...being open systems, are yet operationally closed, as all their activities and interactions with
the environment are aspects of just one process: the recursive production of themselves,
according to a pattern of their own identity. (Lenartowicz, 2015)

As noted by Ripkey (2017), universities as organizations continue many cultural rituals and traditions that were established or were significant in the context
of the time they emerged, when their identity was formed. New members of the
academic community – students, scientists, and administrative staff learn
(actively and passively) the language, the rituals of tradition, and the deeply
entrenched cultural norms as they join the organization (Ripkey, 2017). In the
case presented, organizational change takes place in a very specific context and
situation – when an organization with a centuries-old tradition and very complex
organizational structures implements new practices to continue its activities in the
face of ongoing changes.

In this chapter, we would like to share our experiences in a project where the
academics followed a bottom-up approach that was not imposed by anyone in
any way. It is entirely consistent with the activities of self-organization, mutual
support, cooperation with the socioeconomic environment, building open and
critical attitudes of students and academics toward the changing world, as well as
with the implementation of the mission of the university that is open to these
changes and is changing along with its environment. As a result, not only the
method of education and the implementation of cooperation between the university and environmental organizations underwent a transformation but also the
approach of academic teachers to the implementation of the education process
carried out in true partnership between the student, their thesis supervisor, and
the organization in which they carried out their research. Action research was
adopted as the form of introducing changes – combining research on one's own
practice while at the same time implementing changes.

While the project described by us was an innovative undertaking compared to
other Polish universities, there are numerous, similar examples of activities in the
field of cooperation between universities and business around the world. They
often combine didactic activity with an attempt to support organizations that
cocreate the environment of universities in the processes of initiating and
implementing organizational changes, thus referring to E. Schein's Philosophy of
Helping, who, while developing his philosophy, focused on the process of helping
human systems, often referring to managerial education, postulated that students
be sent into organizations as helpers (Schein & Bennis, 1965). Examples of such
activities can be found, among others in the didactic practice of the School of
Nursing & Midwifery at Trinity College in Dublin (Ireland), Brown University
(USA), which has been implementing The LAB Education Alliance for several
decades, or in the practices of Finnish universities that implement action research
programs, e.g., in cooperation with schools (Kalliola, Niemelä, & Eskelinen,
2017; Niemi, 2019).

The structure of this chapter is as follows. The chapter begins with a discussion
on the contemporary university, its third mission, and the specific context of the

functioning of Polish universities. Then we discuss organizational change and its implementation through action research. To illustrate the aforementioned change, we present the project "Research for practice," and we analyze the process that allowed for the enhancement of cooperation between the university and its environment.

THE CONTEMPORARY UNIVERSITY AND ITS THIRD MISSION: COOPERATION OF THE UNIVERSITY WITH THE EXTERNAL ENVIRONMENT

Massification of higher education at the turn of the twentieth and twenty-first centuries, combined with the rapid increase in the importance of scientific research as well as research-implementation activities in the processes of building competitive advantages for the economy, gave a new impulse to strengthen the role of states in the management of higher education and science (Altbach, Reisberg, & Rumbley, 2009; OECD, 2009). Being aware of the role that universities play in positioning countries and their economies in global competition (Alvesson, 2013), it was the main argument in favor of maintaining public funding for most research (especially basic research), as well as controlling the subject matter of such research.

These processes were repeatedly, more or less critically analyzed all over the world – mostly in the context of the public finance crisis of the 1980s and the beginning of the twenty-first century (Kwiek, 2005). They were very specific and particularly dynamic in countries undergoing a profound political, economic, and social transformation during this period, such as Poland and other Central and Eastern European countries. Its course was influenced not only by the opening up of possibilities for the global functioning of the economy (and at the same time – education) with the support of international structures and organizations but also by the national culture of these countries (Minkov, 2011). Among its many characteristics, this culture was distinguished by a high level of social consent to the centralization of the management of transformation processes, combined with a years-long favorable climate for a neoliberal approach to shaping social and economic relations.

This social attitude – also visible in the university environment – created a climate for the introduction of further reforms (ongoing since 1990) of higher education in Poland. Initially, despite the radical overhaul of the management system of higher education, these changes were very favorably received. In the early 1990s, the most important thing for universities was their institutional autonomy and political noninterference of the state in research and education. This political autonomy has been maintained right up to the most recent reform of 2018 which introduced representatives of organizations in the environment into university governing bodies, as well as sophisticated tools for centralized control and supervision over universities (USTAWA, 2018).

The arguments in favor of stronger ties linking research and education with social and economic needs were received less favorably in the academic community because in this aspect Polish universities were Humboldtian in nature, with a rather poor approach toward the needs of its environment (Szadkowski, 2015). However, the growing scale of education, access to positive foreign experiences linking education and research with practice, the pressure exerted by newly established private universities, and above all, its drop in global rankings of the economy and science, as well as the difficulty in adapting to a new situation (overwhelmed by teaching and lack of funds for research) created a climate of awaiting change. The most problematic issue in the current transformation of universities, especially public universities, is the implementation of the "third mission." To implement it, it is not enough to put additional requirements on research and education, or to create façade university councils or administrative structures related to commercialization but not integrated with the academic community. M. Kwiek (2012), identifies five elements of the "third mission of the university": relations with the immediate territorial environment of the university inscribed in its social, economic, and cultural aspirations; academic entrepreneurship which leads to generating new sources of income; responding to the needs of the environment in terms of human resources, consulting, solving specific problems, fostering the development of awareness, knowledge and civic attitude, supporting and contributing to innovation processes. A significant part of the implementation of the "third mission" is related to education.

Policy toward higher education and science in Poland remains the domain of the central authorities. It is developed and implemented according to a top-down model, in which the participation of interested groups is limited to submitting nonbinding proposals and consultation about them. The state develops the system and creates mechanisms to control it based primarily on the principle of competitive financing. At present, while giving the universities a high degree of institutional autonomy, it also forces them to create specific organizational structures of the universities – both internal as well as those concerning relations with their environment (university councils). The emphasis is on supervisory instruments, into which even evaluation has been incorporated – thus missing the opportunity to rebuild the organizational culture toward a culture of evaluation, mutual support, self-improvement, and increased trust. The work of the university was made subservient to the implementation of various metrics of the quality of education and science, scientific productivity, and commercialization. This new supervision system was superimposed on the preexisting bureaucratic system and consequently led to its monstrous proportions.

In exchange for managerial autonomy, universities have been forced to accept change and implement them primarily through institutional changes: (1) set up new units – cooperation with the environment, commercialization of research, support for project activities, support for academic entrepreneurship, student career offices, (2) formulate rules, standards, and complex decision-making procedures covering almost all processes related to research, research-implementation activities, education, and multidimensional cooperation with the environment, (3) create opportunities for employees to improve their skills in order to move freely in the new bureaucratic reality and undertake new activities, and (4) supervise the activities of internal units in terms of the fulfillment of formal requirements set for universities by the central administration and its agencies (exercising quality control of education and research and determining the availability of funds for research and education, as well as determining the scientific and teaching credentials of universities).

Contrary to the dominant official narrative, the intention of the above-mentioned management activities in universities – especially in traditional universities – is to demonstrate that they meet the requirements of central administration, and not to actually change the organizational culture, transforming it into an entrepreneurial or socially responsible university model. Thus, they behave like typical autopoietic organizations (Lenartowicz, 2015), which do not change their identity but regroup their forces to adapt to external requirements. This management strategy has an impact on scientists who are overwhelmed by formal, bureaucratic obligations; they have to examine exactly what the money in competitions is for, organize research processes in a manner imposed from above, which often heightens mutual competition and animosity, and increases job insecurity. Education focuses more and more on its practical effects, without squandering time on deepening the understanding of the organizational reality and the problems of the socioeconomic environment, missing out on the shaping of civic attitudes, as well as solidarity and responsibility for the changing world in which students live and which they will shape in the future.

To sum up, Polish universities, as well as universities around the world, are subject to permanent processes of change that originate both outside and inside the organization.

ACTION RESEARCH AS A MEANS OF INTRODUCING ORGANIZATIONAL CHANGE

The problem of "change" is a real challenge in management sciences, which is emphasized by, e.g., Boston (2002), By (2005) or Buono and Kerber (2010). It requires departing from tried and tested and therefore "safe" procedures and solutions functioning in organizations. Hence change is often perceived as a threat resulting from uncertainty, which gives rise to resistance and fear among those it concerns (Pieterse, Caniels, & Homan, 2012). In addition, the organization's awareness of how to deal with change management often starts to activate when it is too late, i.e., when the changes have already led to various types of adverse reactions, for example, anxiety and resistance from employees. Giving "change" a utilitarian form and transforming it into a positive phenomenon is a challenge that the management staff of different organizations continually face (Cummings, Bridgman, & Brown, 2016). The inability to adjust to rapid change and adapt to new conditions is perceived by the environment of the organization as its weakness (Sutterfield, Friday-Stroud, & Shivers-Blackwell, 2006). It is also worth noting that according to Smith (2003), in his review of four studies and a total of 284 cases, only 19% of organizations were successful in implementing organizational change. A McKinsey study reported by Isern and Pung (2007) showed that in a survey of 1,536 executives, only 38% of transformational change initiatives were successful. This is often due to the conviction that the directions of changes and the ways of their implementation should be based on the decisions of the authorities – be it the organization's management having power over how the organization works or external experts – researchers who have the competence, as recognized by a certain community, to judge the organization (Grant, Nelson, & Mitchell, 2008). This reduces the role of members of the organization and its environment in the processes of change management, both at the stage of initiating as well as implementing new solutions. It is worth noting, however, that the authority of the latter – having to a large extent only theoretical knowledge – does not translate into the ability to cope with management practice. This has led to a loosening of the academy's ties with its environment in recent decades.

Among the key factors conducive to the effective implementation of changes in organizations, researchers indicate, above all, the readiness of the organization to undertake change (Armenakis, Harris, & Mossholder, 1993). There are several aspects to this readiness, among which Rafferty, Jimmieson, and Armenakis (2013) identified both individual and collective factors, such as external pressures, internal factors, and personal characteristics that lead to readiness for cognitive and affective change. Another aspect of change was described by Tushman and Romanelli (1985), who noted that inertia is a force that builds resistance to changes in periods of equilibrium, and change often requires a contextual crisis, otherwise, it may not work. The research of Sastra (1997) is also important in this respect, as he showed that the ability to change is inversely proportional to inertia, thus highlighting the role of organization members in change management processes.

In recent years, the growing interest in the issues of organizational change is also visible among researchers – not only on theoretical grounds, but primarily in terms of practice, which reflects contemporary trends in social science philosophy. Coghlan, Shani, and Hay (2019) draw attention to the recently dominant belief that social science is an activity that is inextricably engaged with society and not isolated from it. In their deliberations, Delanty and Strydom (2003) distinguish several turns in the philosophical thought behind social sciences such as logical turn, historical-cultural turn, or the so-called knowledge (cognitive) turn that views science as a meaning-making enterprise that reflects current social and historical trends. However, these approaches, according to Coghlan et al. (2019), do not fit in with the contemporary understanding of the role of social sciences in society. Therefore, these researchers add the so-called action turn to the classification put forward by Delanty and Strydom (2003). Reason and Torbert (2001) point out that the nature and goal of researchers representing this line of thought in social sciences is to contribute "directly to the blossoming of people, their communities and the ecosystems they are part of" (Coghlan et al., 2019, as cited in Reason & Torbert, 2001, p. 6). This trend emerged from the study on how it is possible to actually change the social and organizational reality through research. What distinguishes action turn is, above all, the belief that science should serve practice, oriented toward the future and cooperation. It should be agnostic and situational, oriented toward development, thus generating an action-based theory (Susman & Evered, 1978).

The philosophy of action research is grounded in action turn. Its roots go back to the early twentieth century and the tradition of pragmatic philosophy that inspired Kurt Lewin (McTaggart, 1991). On the one hand, this trend is an attempt to bring the world of science and practice closer together by showing the possibility of cooperation based on different rules than before. On the other hand, it emerged from the desire to develop an effective model for initiating and implementing real changes in organizations. Action research is most often presented in the literature as a research concept that aims to combine research with solving specific social problems leading to the initiation of change in a particular environment (Rapport, 1970). Stephen Kemmis defines action research as "a form of collective self-reflective inquiry undertaken by participants in social situations in order to improve the rationality and justice of their own social or educational practices, as well as their understanding of these practices and the situations in which these practices are carried out" (Kemmis, 2010, p. 45). He also emphasizes that contemporary "reflection on research in action is increasingly emphasizing the social" (Kemmis, 2010, p. 46), thus clearly emphasizing the role of collectivity and cooperation in the research process, which, in a way, confronts the hitherto known research concepts, in which the emphasis was placed on the researcher – most often the scientist and his authoritarian role in the research process. As asserted by Hynes, Coghlan, and McCarron (2012) in the epistemological sense, researching with others means that inquiry is based on participants' understanding of the unfolding process and joint meaning-making rather than through the lens of a lead researcher's personal worldview. Thus, the idea of participation in action research is understood as conducting joint research, or research with people, and not on people, the latter being characteristic of research in the positivist trend (Hynes et al., 2012 after: Reason & Bradbury, 2008). Hynes et al. (2012) point out that, by adopting an epistemological approach, joint, participatory action research is characterized by the understanding by all participants of the process in which they participate and by sharing meanings of the observed phenomena, not only through the prism of the knowledge and experience of the lead researcher. Cherns, Clarks, and Jenkins (1976, p. 35) emphasizing this idea at the basis of action research "question the position of the representative of social sciences as a privileged observer, analyst and critic." Participation understood in this way means full commitment combined with mutual understanding and acceptance for the diversity of knowledge and competences of participants. On the other hand, the active inclusion of participants in the research process, their emancipation, and empowerment are factors that foster change (Jeon, Kim, & Koh, 2011).

The idea of action research centers around the will to implement changes (Craig, 2009), the implementation of which is the result of cooperation based on mutual trust, respect, recognition of mutual competences, knowledge and experiences, as well as the belief in the importance of all participants in this process (Grant et al., 2008; Hynes et al., 2012; Zuber-Skerritt, 2005). Putting this idea into practice, according to Kurt Lewin, requires looking at it from the perspective of a process that consists of successive specific stages (Dickens & Watkins, 1999, p. 133). It is worth emphasizing that this process, according to the researcher, is not closed within a specific time frame and, as David Coghlan also points out, should be repeated (the so-called spiral of action research cycles) until the participants of the research process – the researcher and members of the organization involved in research – consider the result of their work to be satisfactory and the problem that is the subject of their work as solved (Coghlan & Brannick, 2014), which will be tantamount to introducing a change. Importantly, whether or not the research problem – the subject of the change – is defined before starting the research, the process of its identification is in itself one of its stages. It may change in the course of the research if its participants recognize that the problems considered so far are not relevant after all and at the same time pay attention to the issues they consider more important. Thus, the action research project extends over time, adapting to the needs of its participants, and its goals, individual stages, or the tools used represent the subject of current arrangements of research participants. Similarly, the success of a research project is not defined in advance, and the basic criterion for achieving it is the participants' sense of initiating or implementing a change in their everyday practice (Greenwood & Levin, 1998).

To sum up, while in the traditional research approach the aim of the research is primarily to expand knowledge (Creswell, 2013), action research is aimed not only at generating knowledge on a certain subject but also at individual and organizational development – a change that is to allow for the improvement of what is done together with people associated with the environment studied (Góral, Jałocha, Mazurkiewicz, & Zawadzki, 2019; Herr & Anderson, 2005) in the spirit of respect for democracy and support for emancipatory processes of all participants of the action research project. Although strongly grounded in practice, there have been several elaborations of how action research may be considered to be scientific (Argyris, Putnam, & Smith, 1985; Cassell & Johnson, 2006; Coghlan, 2011; Coghlan & Shani, 2018).

CASE STUDY: PROJECT "RESEARCH FOR PRACTICE" CARRIED OUT BY THE UNIVERSITY IN COOPERATION WITH EXTERNAL ORGANIZATIONS

Research Methods

The research strategy used to present the results of the research carried out in this chapter was an instrumental case study. The case study is a research strategy that focuses on understanding the dynamics of single "settings" (Eisenhardt, 1989). The case analyzed was an action research project in which the university and its representatives (students, researchers) collaborated with external organizations. Simons (2009, p. 21), defines a case study as an in-depth study of the complexity and uniqueness of a specific project, policy, institution, program, or system from different perspectives and using different methods. Stake (1995) notes, on the other hand, that case studies do not serve to understand other cases – their overriding aim is to understand a single case under study.

The instrumental approach was selected from among the three basic types of case studies (autotelic, instrumental, and multiple (Stake, 1995). It is based on the fact that the researcher studies a specific case in order to get a broader understanding of it – the specific case is thus intended to deepen the knowledge of a wider phenomenon or to draw more general conclusions (Stake, 2005). The case, which is the basis for the analysis in this research, was selected not because it is representative of other cases, but because of its uniqueness, which is cognitively extremely interesting – it enables us to understand how action research can influence organizational change in the university.

The data on which our study was based were collected throughout the duration of the project, i.e., from September 2017 to November 2019. The following techniques and methods were used to collect data: surveys, interviews, document analysis, and participant observation. This text is based only on a fragment of the collected data, which were analyzed in terms of the research problem posed.

In this study, we focus on the following data sources:

(1) Surveys addressed to project stakeholders: students, thesis supervisors, and representatives of cooperating organizations. The surveys were carried out at the beginning (September 2017 – 139 surveys) and at the end of the project (November 2019 – 111 surveys).
(2) In-depth interviews with 14 key project stakeholders (scientists, representatives of cooperating organizations). The interviews were conducted between April and November 2019.

During the data analysis, an answer was sought to the question – As a tool for organizational changes, how can action research affect the development of cooperation between a traditional university and the external environment? The analysis of the data, both from the surveys as well as the interviews, was qualitative in nature, as the surveys containing open-ended questions were not intended to describe a given problem statistically.

Project and Its Context

The project, which is the subject of analysis in this text, was carried out between 2017 and 2019 at the Faculty of Management and Social Communication of the

Jagiellonian University. It consisted in introducing implementation master's theses, carried out in cooperation with external organizations, as a standard of didactic work. The Jagiellonian University is one of the largest and oldest Polish universities – over 40,000 students study here, almost 4,000 scientists work here, and its history dates back 650 years. The Faculty of Management is one of the 16 faculties of the university and at the same time one of the youngest organizational units. The faculty has an excellent scientific background, highly qualified staff, and a sound financial situation. At the same time, like all scientific units, it must confront problems such as bureaucratization, clientelism, and challenges related to the process of teaching. Due to the specific nature of the Faculty, it is extremely important for it to cooperate with the social and economic environment. Although there are constant attempts to establish relations with the environment, the didactic process is often carried out in isolation from the real needs of the world of practice. An example of this were master's theses, in which students usually addressed abstract, theoretical problems, without deepening the practical understanding of the challenges of the organizations studied. This problem resulted not only from the choices made by students but also from the lack of such expectations on the part of the university, and the lack of encouragement given to students to cooperate with external organizations.

The project attempts to make the master's theses more practical through their joint implementation with employers, and thus introduce an organizational change: opening the university to more intensive cooperation with the environment. For this purpose, cooperation was established with over 20 organizations, in which a group of over 40 students began to cocreate their design and implementation master's theses. At the same time, this project had a second goal, which was to implement an organizational change at the university level, as well as at the level of attitudes and approach to the implementation of didactic tasks by individual employees/thesis supervisors. The aim was to change the way the university cooperates with external entities: greater openness to practitioners, establishing real cooperation with them. As a result of the project, based on the action research conducted, a model was created, which was adopted by the Faculty Council (collegial decision-making body) as one of the ways of carrying out implementation of master's theses and shaping cooperation with the external environment.

The action research that was carried out as part of the project had many dimensions. First, each student carried out a separate action research in cooperation with the thesis supervisor and an external organization. Secondly, a project team composed of university employees conducted research on their own practice and designed organizational change. To show the complexity of these processes, we will first present three vignettes presenting a selection of student projects, and then in the next section, we will proceed to the analysis of the process of introducing organizational change at the university level.

Vignette 1: Museum

The public history museum of the city hosts exhibitions, carries out educational, publishing, and artistic activities, and popularizes culture.[1] The museum has 18 branches and subsidiaries and employs over 300 people. Each of the museum's activities – events, book publishing, temporary and permanent exhibitions, construction of new facilities or renovations – is treated as a project, and the museum carries out over 90 such projects annually.

The Diagnosed Problem

The museum is a project-oriented organization, where a number of basic functions and activities, including strategic ones, are implemented through projects. Different people are responsible for individual projects, often carrying out multiple projects simultaneously, at the same time performing their duties resulting from the functional structure of the organization. Projects are carried out without sufficient knowledge of methodology, i.e., the level of knowledge about project management among employees differs widely and project management is not systematized and not formalized. The diagnosed research problem concerned how to improve the project knowledge management process in the organization.

The Implementation Process of Action Research

Museum employees were involved in the process of implementing action research, and on the part of the university – a student and a thesis supervisor were involved in the process. After formulating the research problem, the student conducted observations of the project teams. She also studied project and organizational documents. The student conducted individual interviews with employees involved in implementing projects and developed a questionnaire, the aim of which was to check what competences the employees lack, what tools are the most useful for sharing knowledge, and if there are any actions that could be improved. As a result of the research, it was confirmed that the process of sharing project knowledge in a museum needed to be improved. The employees of the organization pointed out that they did not acquire knowledge from already completed projects, and the organization lacked practices of sharing knowledge within projects and between teams.

Results

Some of the problems observed were addressed during the course of the action research – for example, a special team was appointed to develop a new methodology for project management processes in the organization.

As a result of the project, an implementation plan, which included ideas for solving existing problems, was prepared in cooperation with the organization.

Recommendations were developed for implementation, which were divided into short- and long-term ones. People responsible for the change and the necessary resources were identified. A schedule for implementing changes and success indicators were also developed. Additionally, an analysis of factors favoring and threatening the implementation of changes in the museum was conducted.

It was planned, among other things, to organize training courses for employees in the field of project management, supporting the planning and management of the team's work or in the subsequent evaluation of projects. A system was designed to motivate employees to share knowledge with other colleagues and to organize team meetings aimed at integration and facilitating the knowledge sharing process. Moreover, a project management office was designed to manage project documentation, supervise the progress of work, develop project management in the organization, collect best practices, and organize training in project management for employees.

Vignette 2: Nongovernmental Organization

The nongovernmental organization actively works to support the development of tourism and promote a positive image of the region where it operates on domestic and foreign tourism markets. The organization has its headquarters in a large city, but most of its activities are carried out in rural areas and in smaller towns in the region. It employs 15 people on a permanent basis, and several dozen employees are employed seasonally to implement projects. The organization's activities are based on various projects – short term and long term – for which it has to obtain funds in the form of grants from various external sources.

The Diagnosed Problem

The flagship project of the organization is the management of the regional cultural trail, which consists of over 200 facilities scattered throughout the region. This project has been carried out for several years by order of the regional government. The owners of individual facilities on the trail are public organizations, nongovernmental organizations, and often private individuals who implement their own ideas and activities. Belonging to the trail is a chance for them to better promote and participate in additional activities aimed at attracting new tourists. Every year, as part of expanding the accessibility of the trail, guides are employed in some of the sites, funded by and under the auspices of the organization managing the trail, to make the site available to visitors. However, due to the seasonality of this work, a large labor turnover can be observed. Moreover, people employed in the facilities are not always equipped to serve tourists, especially those with special needs, including people with disabilities. The diagnosed research problem was concerned with how to improve the accessibility of facilities on the cultural trail for people with special needs, with particular emphasis on the deaf.

The Implementation Process of Action Research

Employees of the nongovernmental organization were involved in the process of implementing action research – those involved in the management of the trail, as well as guides employed in the facilities on the trail, and on the side of the university – a student and a thesis supervisor. In addition, deaf people were invited to join. After formulating the research problem, the student conducted numerous observations and interviews with the guides on the trail and members of the trail management team. The student also conducted interviews with deaf people who actively participate in the cultural program of the region. The research also included the analysis of documents of the organization and Polish and foreign best practices in terms of making the cultural program available to the deaf. As a result of the research carried out, it was shown that the management of the accessibility of facilities on the trail needed improvement. A few ideas emerged that could help solve the diagnosed problem. Ultimately, however, it was decided to start the changes "from scratch." Particular attention was paid to the lack of knowledge of guides about the limitations of deaf people and ways of communicating with them, which repeatedly led to fear and reluctance of the guides to serve this group of tourists, and the consequence of this was the absence of deaf people on the trail.

Results

As a result of the project, in cooperation with the organization, a handbook for guides was prepared, which was to introduce them to the "world of silence" and contained the basic principles of savoir vivre in serving tourists with hearing impairment. The handbook was printed and distributed free of charge to all guides providing access to facilities on the trail and employees of the organization involved in the trail project. The electronic version of the guide was published on the organization's website. Additionally, a meeting for guides was organized during which they were presented with the solution developed within the project.

---

[1]Based on: Bogacz-Wojtanowska, Jedynak, Wrona, and Pluszyńska (2019).

Vignette 3: A Philharmonic

The object of the research was a philharmonic, a winner of the medal of merit for Polish culture, which has been operating uninterruptedly since the early 1930s. Currently, it consists of 8 ensembles presenting 7 year-round serial events, including concerts performed under the educational program. It includes 7 different cycles starting from the development of audiation by means of concerts for children and youth of various ages, combined with learning a foreign language, carried out in schools all over the region, directed toward disabled children in their places of residence, as well as meetings with musicians and the conductor as part of a tour to the philharmonic.

The Diagnosed Problem

This highly regarded public institution of music, with its high operating costs, is struggling to reconcile its artistic aspirations with its economic requirements, while at the same time wishing to attract young music lovers. One such music lover was a management student, a lover of the philharmonic, who decided to help this institution she idealized, to reach out to children and the youth. In the course of her research, she became convinced of the importance of this goal, in the face of a significant reduction in artistic education within main-stream education, reformed in the spirit of a neoliberal approach to the pro-vision of public services. She realized that the education of the youngest plays a key role in preparing future viewers and listeners to benefit from cultural programs on offer.

The Implementation Process of Action Research

Joining the organization, the first observations and conversations were related to the demythologization of the philharmonic under study, the student detecting internal conflicts, interest groups, and games being played. This reality came as a surprise to her, but at the same time she deferred to the organization and began to identify and analyze various problems signaled by the respondents. She focused on those related to educational activities.

To get a better understanding, she conducted observations by participating in concerts for children and youth, and confronted the results during inter-views with various employees. She was aware that listeners without musical education sometimes clap at the wrong moment, thus disrupting the concert, but what she experienced during the concerts for children came as a complete shock to her and determined her choice of the organizational problem for which she decided to find a solution. It was the problem of inappropriate behavior during musical events, especially on the part of the youngest lis-teners, but also parents and guardians accompanying them. The problem was noticed by most of the employees, who spoke of it as a chronic problem hindering their work, but above all, it was against the mission of the phil-harmonic, with which they strongly identified themselves. For this reason, they enthusiastically joined in clarifying the essence of the problem and then developing and implementing a solution. At certain stages of the study, the student expanded it to include other musical institutions in Poland, in order to establish the conviction that the identified problem was not specific to only the philharmonic under study, and also sound out how other similar institutions deal with the same issue. At the stage of exploring the problem and looking for a solution, the student described her situation as an action researcher in this way: the relationship in which there are three – the thesis supervisor, the tutor on the part of the organization, and I – where the researcher was, and still is, an extremely important relationship. Basically, without mutual interaction, consultation, exchange of plans, and expectations the project would not have existed (Malczyk, 2019, p. 33).

Results

Designing the solution was a multistage process, during which emerging ideas were consulted with the organization and confronted with its capabilities as well as solutions used in other musical institutions. As a result, a common idea for solving the problem that emerged was to conduct a competition in schools, entitled: "Class and style – cultured behavior." The competition involved recording a film of up to 2 minutes duration, presenting good manners, the rules of appropriate behavior in the philharmonic as chosen by the pupil/class. The student-researcher prepared the draft regulations of the competition and a promotional leaflet, which were perfected in the Philharmonic and supple-mented with the announcement of awards for the competition. One of the highlights is the screening of the winning entry before the start of the concert. The winners of the first edition were declared in June 2019. At the same time, the Philharmonic, in response to the incoming signals, took its own actions to overcome this previously ignored problem.

The above examples illustrate the challenges faced by students involved in the implementation of practical projects effecting change in organizations. At the same time, the process of change also took place at the university level, and this process is presented in detail in the next section.

ORGANIZATIONAL CHANGE IN THE AREA OF COOPERATION BETWEEN THE UNIVERSITY AND EXTERNAL ORGANIZATIONS USING ACTION RESEARCH

Prior to this project, the Jagiellonian University did not use the action research approach extensively. Widely recognized forms of university cooperation as part of action research, such as: community–university partnerships, extensive formal cooperation networks, doctoral programs, or special organizational units dedicated to action research (Bogacz-Wojtanowska, Jedynak, Wrona, & Pluszyńska, 2019; London et al., 2017) were not prevalent at the Jagiellonian University until the implementation of the project *Action Research*. Instead,

- Action research was a part of informal collaboration, where individual researchers, through their personal relationships and collaborative networks, participated in action research carried out in their environment. It occurred in the form of ad hoc consultancy and cooperation between scientists and practitioners, as well as participation in large projects.
- There were classes devoted to action research, where students carried out microprojects within this approach, without establishing formal relationships with other organizations.

Prior to the initiation of cooperation as part of the project, one of the elements linking the University and the organizations operating in its environment was a common need and interest in introducing a change in a specific area of operations. In the case of the University, it was about introducing changes in didactic practice and relations with the social and economic environment, which was only possible thanks to cooperation with other organizations. In the case of NGOs and public organizations, it was about cooperation with a prestigious university and conducting research in their organizations, which could lead to the desired organizational changes.

As regards the forms of cooperation between the university and the environment, the project, *Research for Practice*, was a scientific and implementation project, where the university team, in cooperation with other organizations, used action research. It is important to point out here that it was of a formal nature – the university (in our case 2 organizational units) participated in the implementation of projects that deal with issues important to local communities or organizations as a leader or as a partner along with other organizations.

In our project, the strategy of action research was proposed to organizations as a way to develop relations between universities and organizations, identify organizational problems, and solve them. Therefore, the university established a relationship with a specific organization, with a proposal for the involvement and participation of the following parties in the process: representatives of the organization as well as thesis supervisors and students (as representatives of the university).

The cooperation between the university and organizations within the framework of the project was a process that consisted of individual stages (Fig. 1). Each stage was attended by representatives of organizations, thesis supervisors, and students. These stages were developed as an original model of interorganizational cooperation as part of action research. They focused on the most important issues from the point of view of the organization and the university while taking into

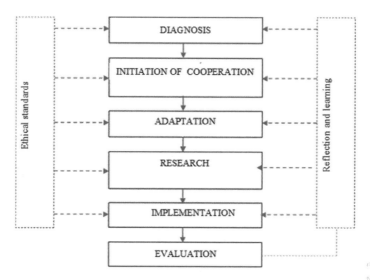

Fig. 1. Process of Cooperation between the University and Organizations within the Framework of the Project. *Source*: Own study.

account the relationship between the organization's representatives and the student and the thesis supervisor involved in the research.

The first stage of the process of cooperation between the university and public and nongovernmental organizations was the *diagnosis*. In the case of our project, it consisted in identifying the needs of cooperation, including a critical assessment of the needs of the organization in terms of their further development and the development of teaching and satisfying the needs of students, in the case of a university. The stage of diagnosis and identification of needs was also the time of checking whether the organizations were ready to start cooperation with the university, awareness of its causes and effects, its benefits, as well as its limitations. It is worth adding that in the case of our project, the diagnosis phase began before the formal start of cooperation. For the university, it started during the preparation of the project, acquiring funding for its implementation, and for the cooperating organizations, it started after the initial invitation to cooperate and before the formal signing of the contract.

The second stage was the *initiation* of cooperation, which in our project consisted in recruiting organizational partners for the project. For this purpose, detailed criteria for selecting the organization and the organization database were created. This database of organizations consisted of new organizations with which the university employees had previously cooperated only on an individual basis, organizations in which students had so far carried out research, practical training, or internships, as well as from organizations that expressed their willingness to participate in the project. Here, the motivating factors for the organizations to start cooperation within the project were their trust in the university and its credibility, especially individual scientists, as well as their previous experience of cooperation with the university. In the case of our project, the list of organizations that decided to cooperate with the university was intended to support students looking for organizations where they could conduct action research. In the event that the student communicated with an organization not featuring in this list and justified their choice, and the thesis supervisors did not have any cause for concern (e.g., sudden withdrawal of the organization from the project), their choice was accepted by the university.

After signing formal agreements with organizations, the initiation also included a series of meetings between the representatives of the university and the organizations, during which we discussed the details of the project, but more importantly, we shared knowledge about action research. A common understanding of the idea of action research was vital for the initiation of cooperation. During the initiation phase, the thesis supervisors undertook study trips to research centers where action research has been carried out for years in order to learn best practices of conducting action research with students.

The third stage of the cooperation process was *adaptation*, which in our project consisted in launching and "getting used to" the cooperation of thesis supervisors from the university with the students, as well as with the mentors for students designated by the organization. Adaptation was a multistage process and included, in particular: formal and informal meetings of thesis supervisors and representatives of the organization, students and thesis supervisors, students and representatives of the organization, as well as workshops organized for all participants of the project, during which all parties had the opportunity to give presentations, and they often gave presentations together.

Research, the fourth stage, lasted the longest during the cooperation. It included the following phases: seeking and formulating a research problem, conducting research and developing the results, as well as preparing conclusions, recommendations, and drawing up an implementation plan. Students, thesis supervisors, and representatives of the organization were all involved in each of these phases.

Implementation, i.e., the fifth stage of our cooperation process, meant turning the plan into action or introducing planned changes into the life of the organization. This stage, taking place inside the cooperating organization, was beyond the control of the university. It was the organization that decided when, how, and whether to implement the prepared plan and whether it would decide to regularly examine and evaluate the results of these changes. The implementation itself could be guided only by the students or only by the organization or jointly by both. If the student had ended the cooperation at the planning stage of implementation, in accordance with the previously concluded agreement, they could be invited back by the organization for further cooperation under a new agreement.

As regards the university, implementation consisted of an organizational change at the university level, as well as at the level of attitudes and approaches to the realization of teaching tasks by individual employees/thesis supervisors. Changes were introduced to methods of cooperation with public and nongovernmental organizations so as to effect genuine cooperation. As a result of the project, based on the action research conducted, a model was created, which was adopted by the Faculty Council (collegial decision-making body) as one of the ways of carrying out implementation master's theses and shaping cooperation with the external environment.

The final stage is the *evaluation* of the introduced changes, both at the university and in cooperating organizations. In our project, we conducted several types of evaluation, i.e., *ex ante, ongoing,* and *ex post.* In order to carry out *ex ante* and then *ex post* studies, we marked the main project objectives on the matrix and proposed indicators for their measurement. We wanted to agree on what information we need to be able to measure how we implemented our project assumptions in relation to three groups: students, organizations, and thesis supervisors. As a result, we conducted two different surveys aimed at representatives of organizations and students, the purpose of which was to learn their opinions and expectations regarding cooperation. The third group of respondents, thesis supervisors, was asked to fill out a self-reflection form, which contained a list of questions to help with self-evaluation. These questions were related to work at seminars, communication with project partners, our role in cooperation, and the development of competences and knowledge.

The *ongoing* evaluation was conducted using a survey and interview technique. The survey addressed to the thesis supervisors concerned the ongoing evaluation of the model of the implementation thesis based on action research at the university. In addition, a survey addressed to students, organizations, and thesis supervisors was conducted. It pertained to conclusions about cooperation between partners participating in the survey, suggested changes, and identifying benefits of working in the action research model. Interviews were also conducted with thesis supervisors, the aim of which was to get to know their opinions and reflections on working in the action research model, opportunities and limitations, as well as benefits and difficulties of cooperation. On the other hand, the interviews with students and employers pertained to the evaluation of relations between the collaborating partners.

The *ex post* evaluation took into account questionnaires that were compatible with those conducted *ex ante.* Thesis supervisors, students, and organizations evaluated the project's activities and shared opinions on barriers and opportunities for interorganizational cooperation.

Parallel to the successive stages of cooperation, a continual complementary process of *reflection and learning* took place, both in the university as well as in cooperating organizations (Fig. 1). In the course of the cooperation, on the part of thesis supervisors and students, there was also a constant focus on meeting certain *ethical standards*, with respect to the diagnosis, initiation of, and adaptation to the cooperation, in particular the conduct of research.

The model approach/generalized approach to the process of student action research and the cooperation of universities with external organizations somewhat oversimplifies the reality, ignoring various specific problems resulting from the particularities of the situation and the people involved. First and foremost, the students – conducting action research for their thesis – found themselves in a position where they were the "main players." Through their own observations and research conducted in cooperation with the employees of the organization, they were to find its significant problems, recognize them, and design their solution. In many cases, they had to repeat this process several times, partly because the organization could not or did not want to deal with all the problems. The situation required the student to be independent, creative, responsible, and conciliatory. It was difficult for many students who quickly became discouraged and would have preferred to follow clear instructions of their supervisor. It was also a challenge for the thesis supervisor to support the student and at the same time refrain from giving instructions and being overprotective while maintaining the students' enthusiasm and stimulating openness to different opinions, creativity, and a sense of autonomy. Many students had idealized the organizations they had chosen and experienced a shock when delving into their organizational reality – especially when they saw conflicts, incomprehensible social relations, or power games. Here, the important role of the thesis supervisor was to sensitize the students to the power games being played out in the organization, and above all, to be in constant contact with the student and to listen to them. It was also difficult for the thesis supervisors to persuade students toward deeper reflection on the essence of the identified problems. They swelled with pride that they were able to face the real problem of the organization, cooperating with people in a completely new environment. In this situation, the question of whether other similar organizations have similar problems and how they deal with them, and above all, where such problems arise from seemed to be a question that was unnecessary, or perhaps even one trying to discredit their achievements. And yet students completing their master's studies in business school should be able to think critically, and be aware of how external conditions affect the functioning of the organization. Forcing them to deepen their understanding of the issues under study required the initiation of abductive reasoning and contextual thinking. Reflectiveness, which permeated the entire process of action research and cooperation with the thesis supervisor, also included the broader context of the problems and organizations under study.

During the project, we identified a number of benefits, both from the side of the university as well as the organizations cooperating with it, as part of the action research approach. On the side of the cooperating organizations, and their leaders involved, the following benefits were noted:

- A fresh look at the organization from the outside, by a researcher who is not involved in its internal organizational processes or in the organizational culture. The researcher's "alienation" triggers reflection on their own practice because it breaks down organizational routines, allows a problem to be seen – one which was previously unnoticed, marginalized, or that members of the organization had gotten used to. Thus, the researcher gives the organization a picture of how it is perceived inside and also how it is seen by its environment.
- Launching processes effecting change in the organization, where the first step is the presence of the researcher in the organization and identification of areas that need improvement or rectification. Commonly noticeable problems or areas of improvement covered vastly different organizational areas, different

levels of significance or importance, as well as different orders of priority in the organization.

- The development of implementation plans containing detailed descriptions of how to solve the problem or improve certain processes. Many organizations cooperating with the Jagiellonian University under the project would otherwise not be able to organize such cooperation due to financial and organizational limitations on both sides. The project allowed for the launch of cooperation, and became its catalyst.
- In the case of public organizations, raising the involvement of employees, or volunteers and members, in the functioning of the organization. Due to the fact that the action research in the implemented project was participatory, often in organizations, there was a process of generating ideas and information and problems, which had not been previously formulated.

It was noticed that the University also received a number of benefits from this cooperation including, in particular:

- The possibility of mutual learning, both for the university scientists, their students, and the representatives of cooperating organizations. In particular, there emerged a sense of community among the thesis supervisors (Prawelska-Skrzypek, Ćwikła, Barańska, & Kołodziejczyk, 2019).
- The cooperation under action research allowed the students to break the shackles imposed by their thesis supervisors who conduct their students' master's theses under a strict time regime, often involving anonymous respondents or organizations. Additionally, an emerging sense of agency and educational reality has led to a different way of working with students, which was previously less known.
- Thanks to the development of the competences of its academics as part of the action research approach, the University has acquired a new approach to conducting seminars and master's theses. This approach is not widespread in Polish universities. The development and implementation of a model for the preparation of implementation theses in the field of humanities or social sciences has enriched the academic practice, including the work conducted by the thesis supervisors. It has also allowed for the expansion of the didactic toolset as well as the launch of new student activities – playing the role of researcher-consultants in organizations as part of action research.
- As a part of the cooperation in the action research project, the University hosted meetings and consultations with representatives of cooperating organizations. Therefore, the "opening" of the University to the socioeconomic environment was not just symbolic, but turned out to be a substantive experience for academics. Establishing ties and deeper relationships allows for the continuation of collaboration with cooperating organizations and the realization of subsequent theses by students.

The project also encountered a number of difficulties such as communication and information barriers, blocking of access to data about the organization, unreliable and sloppy fulfillment of obligations both on the part of the organization as well as university students. Nevertheless, the benefits of the cooperation outweighed the difficulties faced by both sides.

Summing up, when we wrote "University," in relation to the project and the implementation of action research, we really meant one department of the University where the above-described cooperation process was launched. Although it is the largest faculty of the University, the areas of scientific activity of its employees include mainly social sciences and humanities. It is worth noting, however, that the changes related to this project apply to the entire University. The formal introduction of didactic changes in one faculty gives the possibility of introducing them in another, in accordance with the University's statute. The good practice of cooperation within action research is transferred not only to social science departments but also to departments of natural science and medicine. New research ideas are born, reinforced by the strong policy of the University's central authorities, implementing a large program strengthening the interdisciplinarity of research (implemented from 2020). Additionally, faculty employees carry out classes outside their own faculty and transfer their practices and experience in cooperation within action research to other organizational units. The process of changes and thinking about cooperation with the environment using action research at the University is not rapid, but it fits in with the thinking that is traditional and constantly maintained in organizational culture at the University about its role of service in relation to the environment.

CONCLUDING DISCUSSION

The very first research conducted by Kurt Lewin and his associates showed that the democratic implementation of organizational change is more effective than the autocratic imposition of solutions (Góral et al., 2019; Marrow, 1969). Burton Clark, in his work "The Higher Education System" – now considered a classic – identified four different ways of transforming universities, where change is made under the dominant influence of one of four forces: bureaucratic coordination (the state and its apparatus), academic oligarchy, political coordination in the clash of interest groups, market forces, and competition mechanisms (Clark, 1983, pp. 201–203). At the same time, he tried to go beyond these four types of change management, looking for examples in which universities as academic communities, as complex social systems, would carry out their autonomous transformations from the bottom up. This approach, therefore, refers to the sources of the university's identity as an organization. Our case seems to be a good illustration of Clark's search for practices, the search by the academic community of a traditional university for the path of its own transformation from the bottom up, from within the university's social system. At the same time, the case proves that it is possible to change the university, which is accused of consolidating the social hierarchy through control over knowledge and by claiming to seek the truth (Deer, 2003; Ospina, Hoffman-Pinilla, & El Hadidi, 2008).

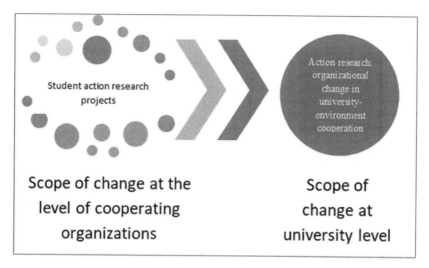

Student action research projects

Action research: organizational change in university-environment cooperation

Scope of change at the level of cooperating organizations

Scope of change at university level

Fig. 2. Areas of Change at External Organization and University Levels.

Referring to the research problem posed (As a tool for organizational changes, how can action research affect the development of cooperation between a traditional university and the external environment?), it should be noted that action research through the democratization of the process of introducing changes and its bottom-up nature influences the development of real cooperation between the university and external organizations. Additionally, they contribute to the emancipation of university knowledge, its democratization, dehierarchization, as well as cocreation and sharing, in our case, with cooperating organizations. The change initiated as a result of a joint effort undertaken by representatives of the academic community (lecturers, students) and external organizations may result in real cooperation. The source of the change we described was scientists who experienced the problems that resulted from the incarceration of the university in the proverbial "ivory tower," and not political decision-makers imposing ready-made solutions from above.

The organizational learning that came about through the coimplementation of the action research projects by students and employers with the support of thesis advisors resulted in a change at the level of cooperating organizations. Action research made it possible to develop a project of organizational change at the university level in a reactive way, thanks to which the change taking place had a multilevel character (see Fig. 2).

The desired change was cocreated through dialogue and cooperation. From this point of view, the common organizational learning has overcome another criticism of the university, which is considered to be the one that "produces" knowledge, while practitioners and the environment are the subject of research and their consumer, that is, the knowledge produced by the university "is consumed" (Bradbury, 2007; Gibbons et al., 1994). The collaboration of scientists with practitioners in useful research, including designing changes in organizations, refutes the myth of a university creating elite knowledge, sometimes useless to anyone. Thanks to the cooperation, actionable knowledge was created and those who are de facto users were included rather than excluded.

It is also worth noting that the implementation of action research projects described by us had a clear emancipatory dimension not only in the case of young student-researchers and scientists but also in relation to the employees of the organizations participating in the project. Often, it was only during the project that these employees got the chance to share their thoughts about their work or at least to talk, and in some cases also the chance for real actions that improved their work environment or the effectiveness of their activities. The project participants became cocreators of the so-called *communities of practice*, which Yonthan Mizrachi defines as a group of people who are involved in a certain activity in order to both solve a specific problem and to learn from each other through regular interaction and exchange of ideas (Coghlan & Brydon-Miller, 2014, p. 135), which for many researchers is an even more important goal in action research than solving a specific research problem (Coghlan, 2001).

Our research, presenting an example of the implantation of organizational change in an autopoietic, traditional university, is part of the OD discussion on organizational culture and introducing changes. From the perspective of organizational change at universities, it should be emphasized that the adaptation of cooperation processes using action research offers potential opportunities for the development of knowledge that goes beyond individual cases of research carried out in organizations (Mohrman, Mohrman, Cohen, & Winby, 2008) and may be of value to research conducted by the university. At the same time, this type of cooperation should be viewed as a natural way of implementing the university's third mission. Universities often organize various types of activities for their environment, which "wrest" them out of natural research processes. Moreover, referring to the words of Ghoshal (2005), the purpose of researchers in business schools should be "to make the world a better place" (Mohrman & Lawler III, 2011), and we do believe that useful research and action research may be the ways to achieve this goal.

NOTES

1. Based on: Bogacz-Wojtanowska, Jedynak, Wrona, and Pluszyńska (2019).

REFERENCES

Altbach, P. G., Reisberg, L., & Rumbley, L. E. (2009). *Trends in global higher education: Tracking an academic revolution*. Paris: UNESCO.

Alvesson, M. (2013). *The triumph of emptiness. Consumption, higher education, and work organization*. Oxford: Oxford Unversity Press.

Argyris, C., Putnam, R., & McLain Smith, D. (1985). *Action science: Concepts, methods, and skills for research and intervention*. San Francisco, CA: Jossey-Bass.

Armenakis, A. A., Harris, S. G., & Mossholder, K. W. (1993). Creating readiness for organizational change. *Human Relations, 46*(6), 681–703.

Beer, M. (2011). Making a difference and contributing useful knowledge:principles derived from life as a scholar-practitioner. In A. S. Mohrman, E. Lawler, III, & Associates (Eds.), *Useful research: Advancing theory and practice* (pp. 147–168). San Francisco, CA: Berrett-Koehler Pub Inc.

Bogacz-Wojtanowska, P., Jedynak, P., Wrona, S., & Pluszyńska, A. (2019). *Action research w kształtowaniu współpracy uczelni z interesariuszami. Korzyści, szanse i wyzwania.* Kraków: Wydawnictwo Uniwersytetu Jagiellońskiego.

Boston, J. (2002). The challenge of evaluating systemic change: The case of public management reform. *International Public Management Journal, 3*(1) 23–46.

Bradbury, H. (2007). Quality and "Actionability": What action researchers offer from the tradition of pragmatism. In A. B. R. Shani, S. A. Mohrman, W. A. Pasmore, B. Stymne, & N. Adler (Eds.), *Handbook of collaborative management research* (pp. 583–600). Thousand Oaks, CA: Sage Publications.

Buono, A., & Kerber, W. (2010). Creating a sustainable approach to change: Building organizational change capacity. *SAM Advanced Management Journal, 75*(2), 4.

By, R. T. (2005). Organisational change management: A critical review. *Journal of Change Management, 5*(4), 369–380.

Cassell, C., & Johnson, P. (2006). Action research: Explaining the diversity. *Human Relations, 59*(6), 783–814.

Cherns, A. B., Clark, P. A., & Jenkins, W. I. (1976). Action research and the development of social sciences. In A. W. Clark (Ed.), *Experimenting with organizational life* (pp. 33–42). New York, NY: Springer US.

Clark, B. R. (1983). *The higher education system. Academic organization in cross-national perspective.* Berkeley, CA: University of California Press.

Coghlan, D. (2001). Insider action research projects. Implications for practising managers. *Management Learning, 32*(1), 49–60.

Coghlan, D. (2011). Action research: Exploring perspective on a philosophy of practical knowing. *Academy of Management Annals, 5*, 53–87.

Coghlan, D., & Brannick, T. (2014). *Doing action research in your own organization.* London: SAGE.

Coghlan, D., & Brydon-Miller, M. (2014). *The SAGE encyclopedia of action research.* Thousand Oaks, CA: SAGE Publications Ltd.

Coghlan, D., Shani, A. B., & Hay, G. W. (2019). Toward a social science philosophy of organization development and change. *Research in Organizational Change and Development, 27*, 1–29.

Coghlan, D., & Shani, R. (2018). Action research in business and management: A reflective review. *Action Research*, 1–24.

Craig, D. V. (2009). *Action research essentials.* San Francisco, CA: Jossey-Bass, A Wiley Imprint.

Creswell, J. W. (2013). *Qualitative inquiry and research design. Choosing among five approaches* (3rd ed.). London: Sage.

Cummings, S., Bridgman, T., & Brown, K. G. (2016). Unfreezing change as three steps: Rethinking Kurt Lewin's legacy for change management. *Human Relations, 69*(1), 33–60.

Deer, C. (2003). Bourdieu on higher education: The meaning of the growing integration of educational systems and self-reflective practice. *British Journal of Sociology of Education, 24*(2), 195–207.

Delanty, G., & Strydom, P. (2003). *Philosophies of social science.* Maidenhead: Open University Press.

Dickens, L., & Watkins, K. (1999). Action research: Rethinking Lewin. *Management Learning, 30*(2), 127–140.

Eisenhardt, K. M. (1989). Building theories from case study research. *Academy of Management Review, 14*(4), 532–550.

Ghoshal, S. (2005). Bad management theories are destroying good management practices. *Academy of Management Learning and Education, 4*, 75–91.

Gibbons, M., Limoges, C., Nowotny, H., Schwartzman, S., Scott, P., & Trow, M. (1994). *The new production of knowledge: The dynamics of science and research in contemporary societies.* London: Sage Publication.

Góral, A., Jałocha, B., Mazurkiewicz, G., & Zawadzki, M. (2019). *Badania w działaniu. Książka dla kształcących się w naukach społecznych.* Kraków: Wydawnictwo Uniwersytetu Jagiellońskiego.

Grant, J., Nelson, G., & Mitchell, T. (2008). Negotiating the challenges of participatory action research: Relationships, power, participation, change and credibility. In P. Reason & H.

Bradbury (Eds.), *The SAGE handbook of action research: Participative inquiry and practice* (2nd ed., pp. 589–601). Londyn: SAGE Publications Ltd.

Greenwood, D., & Levin, M. (1998). *Introduction to action research: Social research for social change.* Thousand Oaks, CA: SAGE Publications Ltd.

Hackman, R. J. (2011). Comentary:Walking on three legs. In A. S. Mohrman, E. Lawler, III, & Associates (Eds.), *Useful research: Advancing theory and practice* (pp. 103–112). San Francisco, CA: Berrett-Koehler Pub Inc.

Herr, K., & Anderson, G. L. (2005). *The action research dissertation. A guide for students and faculty.* Thousand Oaks, CA: Sage Publications, Inc.

Hynes, G., Coghlan, D., & McCarron, M. (2012). Participation as a multi-voiced process: Action research in the acute hospital environment. *Action Research, 10*(3), 293–312.

Isern, J., & Pung, C. (2007). Harnessing energy to drive organizational change. *McKinsey Quarterly, 2007*(1), 16–19.

Jeon, S., Kim, Y. G., & Koh, J. (2011). An integrative model for knowledge sharing in communities-of-practice. *Journal of Knowledge Management, 15*(2), 251–269.

Kalliola, S., Niemelä, J., & Eskelinen, O. (2017). How to reconcile work and university studies – An action research case from Finland. *International Journal of Action Research, 13*(3), 221–239. doi:10.3224/ijar.v13i3.03

Kemmis, S. (2010). Teoria Krytyczna I Uczestniczące Badania W Działaniu. In H. Červinková & B. Gołębniak (Eds.), *Badania W Działaniu.Pedagogika I Antropologia Zaangażowane.* Wrocław: Wydawnictwo Naukowe Dolnośląskiej Szkoły Wyższej.

Kwiek, M. (2005). The university and the state in a global age. Renegotiating the traditional social contract? *European Educational Research Journal, 4*(4), 324–341.

Kwiek, M. (2012). Universities, regional development and economic competitiveness. The Polish case. In R. Pinheiro, P. Benneworth, & G. A. Jones (Eds.), *Higher education and regional development* (pp. 69–85). London: An Assessment of Tensions and Contradictions.

Latham, G. P. (2011). Commentary: Observations concerning pathways for doing "useful research". In A. S. Mohrman, E. Lawler, III, & Associates (Eds.), *Useful research: Advancing theory and practice* (pp. 309–318). San Francisco, CA: Berrett-Koehler Pub Inc.

Lenartowicz, M. (2015). The nature of the university. *Higher Education, 69*(6), 947–961.

London, J., Schwarz, K., Cadenasso, M., Cutts, B., Mason, C., Jr, Lim, J., … Smith, H. (2017). Weaving community-university research and action partnerships for environmental justice. *Action Research, 16*(2), 1–17.

Malczyk, K. (2019). *Promowanie kulturalnego zachowania wśród odbiorców wydarzeń muzycznych.* MA Thesis, Jagiellonian University in Kraków.

Marrow, A. J. (1969). The practical theorist. In *The life and work of Kurt Lewin.* New York-London: Basic Books.

McTaggart, R. (1991). Principles for participatory action research. *Adult Education Quarterly, 41*(3), 168–187.

Minkov, M. (2011). *Cultural differences in a globalizing world.* Bingley: Emerald Publishing Limited.

Mohrman, A. S., & Lawler, E., III, & Associates (2011). *Useful research: Advancing theory and practice.* San Francisco, CA: Berrett-Koehler Pub Inc.

Mohrman, S., Mohrman, A., Jr, Cohen, S., & Winby, S. (2008). The collaborative learning cycle: Advancing theory and building practical design frameworks through collaboration. In A. Shani, S. Mohrman, W. Pasmore, B. Stymne, & N. Adler (Eds.), *Handbook of collaborative management research* (pp. 509–530). Los Angeles, CA: SAGE Publications, Inc. Retrieved from https://www.doi.org/10.4135/9781412976671

Niemi, R. (2019). Five approaches to pedagogical action research. *Educational Action Research, 27*(5), 651–666. doi:10.1080/09650792.2018.1528876

OECD. (2009). *Higher education to 2030, Vol. 2, globalisation.* Paris: Centre for Educational Research and Innovation OECD.

Ospina, S., Hoffman-Pinilla, A., & El Hadidi, W. (2008). Cooperative inquiry for learning and connectedness. Proceedings of the 4th International Barcelona conference on higher education, vol. 8. Higher education and citizenship, participation and democracy. Retrieved from http://www.guni-rmies.net

Pieterse, J. H., Caniels, M. C. J., & Homan, T. (2012). Professional discourses and resistance to change. *Journal of Organizational Change Management, 25*(6), 798–818.

Prawelska-Skrzypek, G., Ćwikła, M., Barańska, K., & Kołodziejczyk, J. (2019). *Badania w działaniu jako podejście w realizacji procesu promotorskiego.* Kraków: Wydawnictwo Uniwersytetu Jagiellońskiego.

Rafferty, A. E., Jimmieson, N. L., & Armenakis, A. A. (2013). Change readiness: A multilevel review. *Journal of Management, 39*(1), 110–135.

Rapport, R. (1970). Three dilemmas in action research: With special reference to the tavistock experience. *Human Relations, 23*(6), 499–513.

Reason, P., & Bradbury, H. (2008). Introduction. In P. Reason & H. Bradbury (Eds.), *The SAGE handbook of action research: Participative inquiry and practice* (2nd ed., pp. 1–10). Londyn: SAGE Publications Ltd.

Reason, P., & Torbert, W. (2001). The action turn: Toward a transformational social science. *Concepts and Transformation, 6*(1), 1–3.

Ripkey, S. L. (2017). Organizational change and ambidexterity in higher education: A case study of institutional merger. In *Research in organizational change and development* (Vol. 25, pp. 285–317). Bingley: Emerald Publishing Limited.

Sastry, M. A. (1997). Problems and paradoxes in a model of punctuated organizational change. *Administrative Science Quarterly, 42*(2), 237–276.

Schein, E. H., & Bennis, W. G. (1965). *Personal and organizational change through group methods.* New York, NY: John Wiley & Sons.

Simons, H. (2009). *Case study research in practice.* Thousand Oaks, CA: SAGE.

Smith, M. E. (2003). Changing an organisation's culture: Correlates of success and failure. *Leadership & Organization Development Journal, 24*(5), 249–261.

Stake, R. (2005). Qualitative case studies. In A. Bryman & R. G. Burgess (Eds.), *Qualitative research* (pp. 443–467, 3rd ed.). Thousand Oaks, CA: The Sage Publications.

Stake, R. E. (1995). *The art of case study research.* Thousand Oaks, CA: Sage.

Susman, G. I., & Evered, R. D. (1978). An assessment of the scientific merits of action research. *Administrative Science Quarterly, 23*, 582–603. doi:10.2307/2392581

Sutterfield, J. S., Friday-Stroud, S. S., & Shivers-Blackwell, S. L. (2006). A case study of project and stakeholder management failures: Lessons learned. *Project Management Journal, 37*(5), 26–35.

Szadkowski, K. (2015). *Uniwersytet jako dobro wspólne. Podstawy krytycznych badań nad szkolnictwem wyższym.* Warszawa: Wydawnictwo Naukowe PWN.

Tushman, M. L., & Romanelli, E. (1985). Organizational evolution: A metamorphosis model of convergence and reorientation. In L. L. Cummings & B. M. Staw (Eds.), *Research in organizational behavior* (Vol. 7, pp. 171–222). Greenwich, CT: JAI Press.

USTAWA. (z dnia 20 lipca 2018 r). Prawo o szkolnictwie wyższym i nauce. *DZIENNIK USTAW RZECZYPOSPOLITEJ POLSKIEJ.* Warszawa, dnia 30 sierpnia 2018 r. Poz. 1668.

Zuber-Skerritt, O. (2005). A model of values and actions for personal knowledge management. *Journal of Workplace Learning, 17*(1), 49–64.

DESIGNING FOR COLLABORATION: DON'T JUST FOCUS ON THE TEAM, FOCUS ALSO ON THE CONTEXT IN WHICH TEAMS WORK

Brenda A. Barker Scott and Michael R. Manning

ABSTRACT

Ask leaders what their organizations need more of to thrive, and many will identify collaboration. Yet many collaborative efforts fail. A focus on the inner workings of teams, to the exclusion of the ecosystem in which teams work, has masked the importance of a collaborative context. We undertook a single case study of an exemplar firm with the intent of offering a nuanced illustration of the collaborative workplace. We illustrate how three contextual factors related to work, relationships, and behaviors shift the setting from a place where collaboration is hard to do, to one that embodies collaboration as a widespread competence.

Keywords: Collaboration; organization change; organization design; collaborative capacity; cross-boundary collaboration; collaborative leadership

INTRODUCTION: LOOKING FOR COLLABORATION IN ALL THE WRONG PLACES

What makes organizations collaborative? Years ago, we noticed an emerging pattern among our clients. Independent of their size, industry, or sector, they were all seeking to become more collaborative. While leaders understood that cross-boundary collaboration was essential for meeting evolving expectations, solving complex problems, and linking essential services, typically, their quest for

Research in Organizational Change and Development, Volume 29, 173–199
ISSN: 0897-3016/doi:10.1108/S0897-301620210000029008

collaboration followed conventional wisdom to charter cross-functional teams. Yet, despite good intentions and solid efforts, more often than not, teams did not produce the intended results.

The reasons varied and yet rang familiar. Leaders were not aligned with the collective goals, teams were not resourced properly, accountabilities were unclear, and people simply did not know how to work across diverse domains. The aha was that if collaboration is the aim, the focus must shift from the collaborative effort, to also the environment in which teams and peers collaborate. Simply put, if you want collaboration, don't just focus on the single team, focus also on the environment in which the collaborators are meant to interact.

As we turned to the literature, we found that our experience matched a growing pattern. A large body of research suggested that attempts to insert collaborative efforts into traditional contexts failed. To explain failed collaborative outcomes, a host of organizational barriers were identified, including inadequate communication systems, incompatible rewards, authority imbalances, and diverse goals, among others (Agranoff, 2012; Gratton, Voigt, & Erickson, 2007; Hackman, 2007; Kezar, 2006; Rhoten, 2003). Searching for answers, scholars have tended to treat the sources of collaborative inertia as independent factors to be overcome. Whereas incompatible leadership was addressed by *adding-on* collaborative leadership, the antidote to incompatible rewards was to *add-on* supportive rewards. Needless to say, the *adding-on* approach has not contributed to a contextualized and holistic understanding of the collaborative workplace. As work increasingly requires the blending of talents and efforts, and in ever-shifting configurations of collaborators, the focus of interest too must shift from the single collaborative effort to the environment in which multiple sets of peers interact (DeChurch & Zaccaro, 2010; Mortensen & Haas, 2018; Tannenbaum, Mathieu, Salas, & Cohen, 2012; Wageman, Gardner, & Mortensen, 2012). Simply put, collaboration requires a collaborative ecosystem in which to thrive.

Our quest, to uncover the organizational factors that combine to support widespread collaboration, led to a case study undertaken as Barker Scott's dissertation (Barker Scott, 2020). With the aim of offering a nuanced illustration of the collaborative workplace, we share the case of the Consumer Tax Group (CTG) of Intuit Canada, an exemplar firm well known for collaboration. We begin with an exploration of the literature to reveal important insights around how collaboration is changing and how it is supported, before illustrating the factors that presented at our research site.

APPROACHING INQUIRY WITH A HEAD FULL OF THEORIES

Reasoning that "it takes richness to grasp richness" (p. 16), Karl Weick (2007) advises researchers to approach the study of complex social phenomena with a *head full of theories*. Much can be learned about our social worlds, Weick suggests, when we expand our capacity for seeing. In the spirit of seeing widely, we approached the collaboration literature from a varied and unique set of lenses.

Our first lens explored how collaboration manifests in the contemporary knowledge-based firm. We reasoned that before we could understand the factors that promote collaboration, we first needed to understand what collaboration is and how it is changing. We referred to this first literature as the *inside-out lens*, as scholars place the changing nature of contemporary collaboration inside, or central to, the inquiry before exploring how the outside contextual elements are pulled to afford it. With a focus on local, peer-led interactivity, this literature was represented by three perspectives: the team learning (e.g., Edmondson, 2012a, 2018), social network (e.g., Cross, Ehrlich, Dawson, & Helferich, 2008), and social learning (e.g., Wenger, McDermott, & Snyder, 2002) literatures.

Our second lens explored the collaborative work context as an ecological whole. We referred to this second line of inquiry as the *outside-in approach*, as scholars give primacy to how factors in the *outer* collaborative context combine to support collaboration. Three holistic frameworks were identified and explored: the collaborative community (e.g., Adler & Heckscher, 2018), the organizational ecology (e.g., Becker, 2007; Davis, 2019), and the reconfigurable, team-based organization (e.g., Galbraith, 2010; Mohrman, Cohen, & Mohrman, 1995; Pasmore, Winby, Mohrman, & Vanasse, 2019). Beyond features, the ecological view cast the organization itself as being in perpetual motion to adapt to changing priorities and to embrace ever-evolving technological and social advances.

Together, our dual lenses offered a fuller lens from which to explore how collaborative efforts manifest, as well as how organizational elements are aligned to afford it. Below, we share insights from each lens and conclude with a reflection on how the insights offered an expanded, evidence-based lens for our inquiry.

Inside-out Approach: Exploring Collaboration as a Cross-boundary Competence

How does collaboration manifest in contemporary knowledge-based firms? We share three themes that underscore collaboration as dynamic efforts that coevolve at the point of need, to fluidly engage the right mix of talent, around learning-oriented efforts. Together, the insights reveal how collaborative efforts promote impactful change as well as how the localized context enables the dynamic interactivity.

Collaborative efforts dynamically evolve: Perhaps the only thing routine about collaborative arrangements in contemporary firms is that they routinely shift. A first theme of contemporary cross-boundary collaboration is that efforts evolve dynamically at the point of need. Traditionally, team structures have emphasized permanence and relative stability to promote enduring strategic and operational value. Indeed, stable teams of people who work well together have yielded, and still do, tremendous value for organizations (Edmondson, 2012b). Yet in today's dynamic contexts, where market needs and opportunities shift, often in unpredictable ways, it follows that collaborative arrangements must follow in kind (Hackman, 2007; Mortensen & Haas, 2018; Tannenbaum et al., 2012).

Scholars have noted this shift for quite some time. Based on their decade-long exploration into how firms in fast-moving contexts compete, Eisenhardt and

Gulanic (2000) observed that collaborative efforts coevolved as opportunities presented and priorities shifted. Having observed this same phenomenon in her extensive fieldwork, Edmondson (2012b, 2013) describes the dynamic formation as *teaming*; an activity more like players self-organizing for a pickup basketball game than an established team with set plays. From a social network perspective, the coevolving dynamic has been described in terms of hubs of "dynamic participation" (Mortensen & Haas, 2018, p. 347) or networks that rapidly form and dissolve at the nexus of need (Cross et al., 2008). And within the social learning tradition, collaborative interactions are described as communities of practice (Lave & Wenger, 1991; Wenger et al., 2002) which form as participating peers surface and attend to needs (Brandi & Elkjaer, 2011; Brown & Dugid, 1991, 2000). Core to the idea that collaborative interactions coevolve is that they do so around value-added initiatives, for it is the local players who are best positioned to notice and attend to the problems before them (Cross, Rebele, & Grant, 2016; Cross & Gray, 2013; Dewar, Keller, Lavoie, & Weiss, 2009; Mariotti & Delbridge, 2012).

Cross-boundary collaborative configurations are fluid: A second theme of contemporary collaboration is that collaborative configurations – who's involved and for how long – are fluid. Traditionally scholars have emphasized the importance of stable membership to collaborative performance, whereby members developed a shared learning context (e.g., Moreland & Myaskovsky, 2000) and adopted sustained roles and responsibilities (e.g., Hackman, 1990, 2002). In dynamic contexts, however, what's becoming important is that collaborative boundaries are porous and membership fluid, so as to access and integrate useful expertise (Amelkin, Askarisichani, Kim, Malone, & Singh, 2018; Cross et al., 2008; Edmondson, 2018; Edmondson, Casciaro, & Jang, 2019; Mortensen & Haas, 2018; Tannenbaum et al., 2012).

Fluid boundaries appear to serve two interrelated purposes. The first is the ability to access expertise (knowledge, talents, perspectives) that resides outside of the collaborating core. This means that rather than having an inward focus and operating as a self-contained unit, collaborators benefit from seeking advice, knowledge, and perspective, and coordinating strategies with others. Such access to external competence has been found to be essential for a wide variety of purposes, including learning and innovation (Amelkin et al., 2018; Edmondson, 2018; Pentland, 2012), as well as coordination with others in the value stream (Ancona & Bresman, 2007; Cross, Gray, Cunningham, Showers, & Thomas, 2010).

A second purpose of fluid boundaries is to adjust the actual makeup of the collaborating core. Given the competing demands for knowledge workers' time and talents, the aim is to target their involvement to the contributions they can best make. Edmondson (2012b) found that the tasks associated with recalibrating teams – figuring out who should serve, for how long, and when their expertise was best freed up to be utilized elsewhere – were continuous and iterative. As Edmondson (2012b) explains, when organizations tackle out-of-the-ordinary initiatives, "It's just not possible to identify the right skills and knowledge in advance and to trust that the circumstances will not change" (p. 77). Under these conditions, the emphasis has shifted from composing stable teams to enabling fluid membership matched to evolving needs. Jeffery's (2003) study of the makeup and level of interactivity among a cross-functional research group over an eight-month period is illustrative. Referring to the project as a "constantly maturing agenda" (p. 553), he observed that over time, the core group shifted from 10 members to 3, meetings became more informal, and the depth of interactivity among the core group increased. Rather than a planned occurrence, Jeffery noted, "it was just the way that things happened" (p. 554), in an effort to tap and target the right mix of expertise as the work evolved.

Contemporary collaboration relies on collective learning: A third theme associated with the changing nature of contemporary collaboration is that it is learning oriented. Traditionally, organizations have favored work approaches that rely on planning and execution over learning and innovation (Edmondson, 2003, 2008). Yet, as workplace challenges become more complex and the problem space more volatile, new approaches that favor learning and innovation are spreading from creative firms to a wide variety of contexts (Beckman & Barry, 2007; Edmondson, 2012a, 2013; Kellogg, Orlikowski, & Yates, 2006). Underpinning this movement is the recognition that cross-boundary challenges are by nature complex and collaborative (e.g., Chan, Beckman, & Lawrence, 2007) requiring collective learning to produce novel solutions (Edmondson & Lei, 2014; Pennington, 2008, 2010). As Cummings and Kiesler (2005) explain, collaborations across boundaries "are expected to increase the likelihood of innovation due to their juxtaposition of disciplinary expertise, perspectives, approaches, tools, and technologies" (p. 704). In other words, the very reason for joining collaborators across boundaries is to integrate and build on their domain capabilities in service of novel insights and solutions.

Contextual enablers of fluid, coevolving collaboration: If collaborative efforts coevolve at the point of need, engage players fluidly, and rely on collective learning, *what are the contextual factors that enable such collaborative dynamism?* A first and foundational condition is that local players must be entrusted to determine where, when, and how to collaborate. The reasoning is pragmatic. If local players are ideally situated to notice, interpret, and solve the problems in front of them, then they must be free to coalesce, exchange knowledge, and experiment with solutions (Edmondson, 2012a; Eisenhardt & Gulanic; 2000).

Beyond local latitude, the team learning and social network literatures identify a number of social-relational properties inherent in the community or network that support collaborators to seek, access, and integrate expertise with others. A first property is the development and maintenance of trusting relationships. Perceptions of trust have been found to support knowledge exchange across role and unit boundaries by fostering both seeking behaviors – whereby members are open to acquiring the knowledge of others – and helping behaviors – whereby members are accessible and willing to share what they know (Borgatti & Cross, 2003; Cross, Edmondson, & Murphy, 2020; Levin & Cross, 2004). How are trusting relationships built? Having asked that question, Abrams, Cross, Lesser, and Levin (2003) found a simple, yet powerful answer. Respondents shared that as people get to know each other through personal chitchat, a sense of social ease translates into relatability and approachability. And as people take the time to help each other, the exchange builds trust. On point, Borgatti and Cross (2003) found that trust-builders were welcoming and accessible; in addition to inspiring confidence in their competence, they were open to receiving queries and helping others. Pointing to the inordinate influence that trust-builders play in their organizations, scholars have referred to them as *energizers* (Cross et al., 2010, 2020) and *pilus priors* or first lancers (De Toni & Nonino, 2010).

A second relational property that supports collaborators to connect across boundaries concerns the strength and focus of ties, or linkages, among members. While strong ties denote frequent and ongoing interactivity among peers (Borgatti & Cross, 2003), weak ties connect members to nonredundant expertise (Granovetter, 1973). The more that solutions rely on the help or agreement of distant players, the more important weak ties are to the network (Cross et al., 2005, 2010; Levin & Cross, 2004). Fieldwork reveals that leaders can promote ties and steward connectivity in a number of overlapping ways. Social forums – for example summits and celebrations – cross-pollinate people with potentially useful talents (Abrams et al., 2003; Cross et al., 2020), while open offices make it more likely for people to fortuitously encounter others (Elsbach & Bechky, 2007). Core roles, often assumed voluntarily, act as integrators of people around a common cause, bridge subcultures, and promote the exchange of information across boundaries (Cross et al., 2020; Jang, 2017; Long, Cunningham, & Braithwaite, 2013). Formally, leaders – as unifiers, role models, and coaches – have been identified as essential boundary-spanning catalysts (Cross et al., 2020; Edmondson, 2019). By way of example, at IDEO, designers are guided to "set up at least two introductory brainstormers to get the best minds in the company, the collective consciousness of the office, working on your problem" (as cited in Hargadon & Bechky, 2006, p. 491). At IDEO, help-seeking is a value espoused by leaders and a protocol that nudges collaborators to seek out relevant intelligence.

A third set of contextual enablers support collaborating peers to learn together. While collective learning is the aim, collaborators joining from different parts of an organization necessarily work from a place of diversity and difference (Agranoff, 2012; Corporaal, Ferguson, & De Gilder, 2015; Edmondson & Lei, 2014; Klotz, 2018; Siedlok & Hibbert, 2014). Here, contextual aids that equip and align collaborators to practice together surface in importance. It is through joint practice – whereby collaborators converse, experiment, and iterate – that collaborators are guided to externalize what they know, as well as to test how their knowledge relates to and combines with others (Nonaka, 1994; Pennington, 2008). Edmondson (2012b) describes the tools and processes that enable collective learning and problem-solving as scaffolds, in that they offer a "light, temporary structure" (p. 77) that equips and enables collaborators to learn and progress together. Typically those aids include a learning-oriented problem-solving approach that guides members to prototype and test potential solutions (Edmondson, 2003, 2012a, 2013) and supportive protocols that promote seeking diverse input and testing with real-time data (Edmondson, 2012a, 2013; Hargadon & Bechky, 2006; Hargadon & Sutton, 1997). In many settings, core roles are embedded in the problem-solving methodology – such as facilitators, coaches, or project managers – to guide and align the collaborators as they work.

Summary of learnings from the inside-out lens: Our review of the inside-out literatures revealed three significant themes characterizing how cross-boundary collaboration manifests in contemporary knowledge-based enterprises. A first theme, coevolving formation, enables collaborative efforts to form around impactful needs. A second theme, fluid composition and engagement, enables collaborators to access the necessary talent as the work unfolds. A third theme, a learning orientation, enables collaborators to share and integrate their domain knowledge to produce novel solutions.

In what ways does the organizational context support the collaborative dynamism? Three contextual factors created an enabling context for the collaborative dynamism; they included: (1) the localized autonomy of players to freely mix and problem-solve, (2) a social-relational climate of helpfulness among peers, built from protocols, practices, and roles that engender trust and foster boundary-spanning interactivity, and (3) a set of dependable tools and approaches to scaffold collaborators to learn and work collectively. Importantly, leaders played an outsized role as shapers and role models of a welcoming collaborative context.

Outside-in Approach: Designing the Collaborative Organizational Context

Our second line of inquiry, referred to as the *outside-in approach*, explored scholarly frameworks that treat the collaborative context as an ecological whole. A foundational principle underpinning the outside-in approaches is that widespread collaboration requires a holistically supportive context (Adler & Heckscher, 2018; Agranoff, 2012; Kezar, 2006; Kislov, Hyde, & McDonald, 2017). Trist (1977) was one of the earliest voices to identify the need for the collaborative workplace. Arguing that higher levels of interdependence, complexity, and uncertainty were surpassing the capability of the traditional organization to cope, Trist reasoned that widespread collaborative efforts required a reimaged organizational foundation, built from participative and democratic principles.

In answer to the call, academics are conceptualizing the workplace as an organizational ecosystem in which social, technological, and physical subsystems interrelate to promote and afford collaborative efforts. While frameworks vary, the common aim is to shape organizational elements to afford useful interactivity patterns for knowledge sharing, innovation, and agility. Becker (2007) has characterized the workplace ecology as being in *dynamic harmony* when the elements are mutually aligned to support organizational goals. Its opposite, *dynamic constraint*, represents a system where elements are in conflict, thereby thwarting intended efforts. To support the dynamism, the organizational elements are idealized to be in continuous flux to align with emerging goals (Adler & Heckscher, 2018; Becker, 2004, 2007; Davis, 2019; Pasmore et al., 2019). As to the elements that make up an organizational ecosystem, our examination is represented by three distinct organizing logics as represented by community (Adler & Heckscher, 2018; Heckscher & Adler, 2006), workspace ecology

(Becker, 2004, 2007; Davis, 2019), and the reconfigurable team-based organization (Galbraith, 2010; Mohrman et al., 1995). Below, the features of each are explored, followed by a summary of core themes.

The collaborative community: Adler and Heckscher (Adler, Kwon, & Heckscher, 2008; Adler & Heckscher, 2018; Heckscher, 2007; Heckscher & Adler, 2006) have offered the community as the ideal organizing logic for the collaborative firm, alongside a wide group of co-contributors (e.g., Fjeldstad, Snow, Miles, & Lettl, 2012; Snow, 2015; Snow, Fieldstad, Lettl, & Milles, 2011). Based on membership, a shared purpose and set of trust-based values provide a foundation for communal efforts. While a collaborative purpose defines collective goals and shapes efforts, an ethic of contribution (Adler & Heckscher, 2018; Heckscher & Adler, 2006) encourages people to contribute beyond roles to the common good. A set of shared protocols, processes, and tools form a *cooperative infrastructure* to equip collaborators and align efforts (Adler & Heckscher, 2018; Kolbjørnsrud, 2018). Authority is both participative – as it flows to those who are best positioned to contribute – and also centralized – as efforts are guided and coordinated by lead roles and designated experts. A final element, the deliberate design of human resources practices, selects for, develops, and motivates collaborative behaviors.

The collaborative workspace ecology: A second variant, the collaborative ecology, puts workspace at the core. While the role of physical space has long been recognized in shaping and affording collaborative interactivity patterns (e.g., Allen, 1977; Porras & Robertson, 1992), scholars taking a whole systems perspective view workspace as an integral element of organizational design. Frank Becker (2004, 2007), a pioneer of the movement, has conceptualized the workplace as an organizational ecology in which the physical environment interacts with social and technological subsystems to generate collaborative potential. Well-publicized examples of firms employing the design of workspace to bolster their innovative and collaborative work practices, protocols, and technologies include Google, 3M, and IDEO among others (Danielsson, 2019; Fuzi, Clifton, & Loudon, 2014; Groves, 2010). All foster relaxed yet stimulating atmospheres, designed to generate openness, playfulness, and employee well-being.

A central premise of a well-functioning ecology is that it is eco-diverse, or flexibly designed, to accommodate a wide range of interactivity needs (Becker, 2004, 2007; Davis, 2019). A wealth of scholarship examines how the design of workspace affords the fluidity of collaborative efforts, whereby peers shift seamlessly from solitary efforts, to short bursts of interactive problem-solving, to more formal and ongoing teamwork (Heerwagen, Kampschroer, Powell, & Loftness, 2004). By way of example, workspaces that promote openness and transparency enable knowledge and decisions to flow and prime peers for co-contributing (e.g., Davis, 2019; Hua, Loftness, Heerwagen, & Powell, 2011). Work pods designed to human scale promote the necessary socialization for exchange, coordination, and innovation. Neutral zones stretch people to mix beyond their home locales to widen the circle for fortuitous collaborative encounters (e.g., (Becker, 2007; Hua et al., 2011). Easy access to breakout spaces and project rooms afford privacy for collective problem-solving and complex decision-making (Becker, 2007; Davis, 2019; Heerwagen et al., 2004; Hua et al., 2011). And increasingly virtual workspaces mimic and enhance the features of the physical environment and enable remote colleagues to blend with their on-site peers (O'Hara, Kjeldskov, & Paay, 2011).

The reconfigurable team-based organization: Working within the stream of organization development, Susan Mohrman and colleagues from the Center for Effective Organizations were among the first scholars to design an organization holistically for collaboration (Mohrman et al., 1995). Their team-based organization employed Galbraith's (1973) star model as a way to shape and integrate social and technical elements to build widespread collaborative capacity. More recently, the expression of the team-based form has evolved to match the needs of today's complex, fast-moving world. In this renewed conception, teams form dynamically (or reconfigure) around emergent opportunities, flowing from the organization's strategic priorities. Importantly, those priorities are shaped as outcomes – typically a product or service or process innovation – and allocated to teams and networks, so configured to include the necessary mix of talent (Galbraith, 2010; Harris & Beyerlein, 2008; Pasmore et al., 2019; Winby & Mohrman, 2018).

Paradoxically, a central feature of the reconfigurable team-based organization is that a stable platform of approaches enables the highly emergent teams to work (Galbraith, 2010; Pasmore et al., 2019; Winby & Mohrman, 2018). A sophisticated governance framework scans for environmental drivers, shapes new priorities, and adapts team assignments (Galbraith, 2010; Harris & Beyerlein, 2008; Mohrman et al., 1995). Once formed, team efforts are linked through a wide array of integrating mechanisms including roles (such as project leads and cross-team coordinators), forums for shared interactivity, and communication protocols. Decision-making flows to teams who, at the same time, are guided by leaders who follow progress, coach efforts, and ensure overall alignment (Galbraith, 2010; Pasmore et al., 2019; Winby & Mohrman, 2018). A collaborative philosophy guides leaders to promote involvement, build trust, develop people, and work collectively, and rewards are tied to the value team members create, both to the overall business and to local team results (Galbraith, 2010; Harris & Beyerlein, 2008; Mohrman et al., 1995).

Summary of learnings from the outside-in lens: Our review of the outside-in literatures offered three frameworks for the design of the collaborative organizational ecosystem, each offering a unique organizing logic by way of community (e.g., Adler & Heckscher, 2018; Heckscher & Adler, 2006), or ecology (e.g., Becker, 2007; Davis, 2019), or platform (e.g., Galbraith, 2010; Mohrman et al., 1995; Pasmore et al., 2019).

Collectively the collaborative frameworks offered a range of organizational elements that clustered into five general categories: (1) a shared purpose and strategy to align collaborators around a common cause and high-priority work, (2) integrating processes including common work-related tools to guide, align, and equip collaborators and linking roles, forums, and processes to align efforts, (3) the design of physical space to afford easy connectivity, (4) people practices such as behavioral protocols, rewards, and performance management to promote collaborative contributions, and (5) leadership, whereby leaders play a host of essential roles from shapers of teams, to providers of resources, to climate setters.

FROM THEORY TO PRACTICE

Our review of the literatures exploring collaborative work and workplaces revealed that collaboration is indeed an essential source for innovation and renewal. The inside-out literatures depicted collaboration as a highly dynamic effort that forms at the nexus of need and engages collaborators in learning-oriented activities to produce novel solutions. A second line of inquiry, the *outside-in approach*, shifted the focus from the collaborative efforts, to how organizations must be transformed to support collaborative dynamism as a widespread competence.

Together the literatures revealed an emerging logic of the collaborative firm that is fundamentally different from that of the traditional organization. Rather than promoting the division of labor, organizational boundaries are permeable in favor of connectedness and collaboration. Rather than allocating work to distinct factions to execute, work is shaped and integrated to achieve holistic outcomes across boundaries. People are not accountable for individual job tasks per se, but to collective outcomes, bolstered by emotional bonds that develop as people help each other and leaders who embody a collaborative philosophy.

Armed with a head full of theories and a keen sense of curiosity, we sought an exemplar organization who would welcome our real-world inquiry. We found our match with the CTG of Intuit Canada.

The Case of the Consumer Tax Group of Intuit Canada

Widely recognized in the popular press for their collaborative capacity (e.g., Grenier, 2018), our pre-research correspondence with the CTG of Intuit Canada confirmed that collaboration was not simply added on, but essential to how the group innovated, delivered, and supported their products and services. Two examples are illustrative. Approximately one year prior to the research, the leadership team made the difficult decision to colocate two head offices into one, all in service of promoting real-time collaboration among the product development, design, customer care, and marketing teams. As a leader explained, the geographical separation made collaboration inefficient:

> We found ourselves uncomfortably split between the sites. Collaboration became very difficult, really inefficient. Everything was on video, or phone calls, or flying back and forth. We made a decision about a year ago to bring the whole team together and to bring people into open and collaborative workspaces. Now, you can walk up and down the hall, grab people, and go to a boardroom and start writing on the wall.

So colocated, the design team inspired a move from the group's cubicles to a large empty space on CTG's main floor. Unauthorized and to the chagrin of the facilities staff, the team borrowed tables and chairs from the cafeteria, curated toys and supplies from their basements, painted the walls so they could write on them, and started a movement that other teams followed:

> So, this space was actually open, and we literally just started stealing desks from the cafeteria and working here. And it was funny, we referred to it as tent city. ... Gradually, more and more people wanted to sit here. And people were coming over and it was just nicer; we gravitated towards each other.

As explanation, we learned that the migration to the open space was the design team's way of promoting the aims of the colocation to achieve easy, boundary-free collaboration: "In order for us to think like teams, we had to all be together." The chief executive officer (CEO) proudly touted the move as an employee-initiated living experiment and a symbolic embodiment of the organization's commitment to collaboration. We were intrigued to proceed.

Our study focused on the collaborative interactions among a subset of 40 or so people within the CTG as they completed the final month of their tax season and transitioned to the planning and design season. Informants included: (a) a product development team, (b) the marketing team, (c) the experience design team, (d) a series of teams that work across functions, including mission teams and the scrum of scrums team, among others, and (e) core roles including senior leaders, team leads, scrum masters, product managers, and a process manager. The first author spent approximately 400 hours over 50 days, observing the CTG organization. Using a constructivist approach, the study collected data with semistructured interviews, supported by observation and document analysis. This was followed by a multistep and iterative process to reflect on the data, draw out themes, and identify emerging patterns (Barker Scott, 2020).

Below, we illustrate the core factors and associated principles that were revealed from our inquiry. Equipped with our dual lenses for inquiry, we were attuned to how collaborative efforts manifested (as highlighted through the inside-out literatures) as well as how organizational elements were aligned to afford them (as highlighted through the outside-in literatures). Consequently, our logic model presents as a scalable viewfinder. A zoomed-in view exploring the nature of collaborative work revealed a set of collaborative properties for how work was shaped, assigned, and conducted. As we zoomed-out to explore the wider collaborative context, two additional factors were revealed; they are how collaborative relationships and behaviors were promoted and afforded.

Three Factors Shape the Collaborative Workplace: Collaborative Work, Relationships, and Behaviors

In all, three organizational factors were found to generate the makeup of the collaborative firm at our study site; they are how work, relationships, and behaviors were shaped to promote and support collaborative efforts. While how work was conceived and shaped created a unified focus for collaborative efforts, the nature of relationships defined how collaborators interacted, and behaviors shaped how people were primed to co-contribute. Essentially, the leaders of the CTG were both architects, in that they purposefully shaped each factor to promote collaboration, and also cultivators, in that they led the work, encouraged the relationships, and role modeled and rewarded collaborative contributions.

Below, we share the factors, as illuminated by our case study. A full reporting of the data underlying these three factors and how they interrelated to shape collaboration at the study site is offered in Barker Scott (2020) and Barker Scott and Manning (2021).

Collaborative Work Factor

A central learning from our case study is that collaboration, fundamentally, is built from a collective aim. At the CTG, that collective aim started as a set of strategic initiatives, referred to as missions to denote their purposeful and collective nature. Missions guided the efforts of two broad categories of work: (1) the strategic work which engaged cross-functional teams in identifying the highest impact customer-focused innovations and (2) the delivery work which engaged all core functions, from engineering to customer care, in the design and delivery of those high-impact innovations. Beyond goal setting, it was how work was shaped, assigned, and approached that bolstered its collaborative potential.

Collaborative work was shaped to mobilize collaborative thinking and effort: At the CTG, work was shaped to focus efforts and elevate thinking beyond role-related activities to achieve a common set of aims. Beginning each year with the setting of five strategic priorities, or missions, each mission was assigned to a cross-functional team, so tasked to discover the most impactful way to innovate a product for the upcoming tax season. A feature highlighted in the literature (e.g., Galbraith, 2010; Heckscher & Adler, 2006), the shaping of the mission priorities was in and of itself a collaborative effort, with input from cross-functional groups charged with exploring a provocative customer-focused question. So set, the strategic missions were understood to be messy, learning-oriented efforts, akin to Edmondson's (2003, 2008) concept of *framing for learning*. In recounting how the leadership team described her team's assignment, a mission team member shared:

> They said, you four people go away and work on one of our five big bets this year. ...We're not diving deep into it. We're not finding the insights. We're not savoring the surprises. We're asking you to collaborate with us.

Missions mobilized collaborative thinking and effort well beyond the mission teams. As soon as the missions were framed and the teams chartered, all employees were invited to a full-day immersion event. The dual goal was to "give everyone a strong feeling around what we are doing," and to build a common context for how each employee's work contributes, "because obviously when you understand what you are building and why, it helps you to be thinking about that bigger picture." A broad understanding of the missions was important because as mission teams worked, they regularly tapped their functional peers to assist. The transparency of the mission goals and progress continued as the work unfolded. Through regular town hall meetings, employees were kept apprised of the mission-related progress; a condition respondents attributed to keeping everyone *in the know*, so that it was virtually impossible to be unaware of big goals, presenting issues and progress. So focused, mission and functional team members alike reported that the experience of working across functions on strategic goals helped to "broaden," "expand," and "rewire" their thinking and develop a "greater appreciation" and "totally different perspective" of their collective work.

While the strategic missions generated focused activity around a clear *what*, in turn, those priorities aligned functional peers as they diverged to deliver the *how*; the execution of the product and service innovations. Here too, the work was understood to be highly interdependent, with each functional unit contributing their domain expertise – that is, product management, experience design, customer care, and marketing. Yet, as the work landed with the functional teams to execute, it was understood that those with the expertise in their crafts were best positioned to identify issues requiring alignment and to join with colleagues to share information, experiment, and problem-solve. As a respondent explained:

> So, once you start to get into something, the level of complexity goes up exponentially. So, I'll pull up to [name] and go, 'What did you do to fix this?' And he can show me in two minutes.

Consistent with the literature describing collaboration as emergent, needs-based, and localized (e.g., Edmondson, 2012a; Mortensen & Haas, 2018) it was the peers themselves who identified and shaped the collaborative efforts.

Collaborative work was assigned to align and empower: Once defined, mission work was purposefully assigned to mobilize fast-moving, cross-boundary collaborative effort. Missions were purposefully assigned to multifunctional teams, always involving a product manager, and depending on the challenge, a member from the experience design, engineering, marketing, and customer care teams. With each assignment, the responsibility for doing the work and making associated decisions followed. In explaining the connection between accountability and commitment, a mission team member explained: "We've done the thinking, the exploration, the why, what, and how. ... So there is a level of ownership that adds to the overall collaboration and willingness to engage."

Quite practically, local accountability afforded collaboration by simply freeing people to connect with each other as they pursued their work (e.g., Edmondson, 2012b). As one respondent explained:

> If you want something, you don't have to go up the ladder and down the ladder to the other side to get something done. You just go and talk to the person and get the conversation rolling.

In turn, given that their efforts mattered, colleagues engaged meaningfully "because you are not just putting in a recommendation and waiting for someone higher up to make a decision, you can go pretty deep on solving a problem."

While peers and teams were accountable, their latitude was counterbalanced by procedural boundaries and leadership coaching. Similar to Adler and Heckscher's (2018) notion of *participative centralization*, whereby accountability is both distributed to the most knowledgeable people *and also* centralized through leadership oversight, leadership coaching and guidance brought rigor to how the teams worked and ensured that efforts were progressing in alignment. The coaching was rigorous, described by team members as intense, like presenting before a panel of judges on "Intuit's Got Talent" yet developmental "to help us see things ... it sharpens our toolkit." While both latitude *and* oversight may appear to be counterintuitive, it led to a condition whereby teams owned their work *and also* were guided to achieve aligned progress.

Collaborative work approaches aligned and equipped peers to work collectively: Consistent with research demonstrating how dependably common approaches scaffold or support collective efforts (Adler & Heckscher, 2018; Edmondson, 2012, 2013), the approaches at the study site fostered collaborative efforts in two overlapping ways. First, common techniques and tools guided peers to learn together. A common approach to how work was conducted, variously described as "agile," "lean," and "design thinking," guided and equipped team members for learning collectively. Acting as a playbook for how we do things around here, the agile approach defined key roles including project leads, chunked work into weekly sprints, structured daily briefings, and promoted a data-driven approach to discovering customer priorities. To support teams to work iteratively, leaders provided a host of tools and resources, including an iterative learning process and toolkit called *design for delight* and innovation champions who coached the teams as they experimented with the tools.

Second, a seasonality to mission work aligned the stages, pace, and tempo of teams to progress in tandem. Beginning fresh each May, the first phase of the work, described as a *broadening* phase, required the teams to slow down and step back to understand their challenges. As the season unfolded, teams shifted to a narrowing phase where they worked actively with the delivery teams to prioritize, build, and market the chosen product and service innovations. The pace and subsequent sense of urgency along with the destination of a tax filing deadline acted as a unifier that "kind of forces collaboration, because people can't sit and let it get sorted out at their own pace." Sharing how the seasonality of work aroused a sense of collective resolve, a respondent explained: "It creates pressure, focus, the need for speed, and a competitive spirit. It requires all hands on-deck."

Summary collaborative work factor: Work at the study site was designed to mobilize cross-boundary thinking and effort. The collaborative potential of work came from how the work was shaped, assigned, and approached. Strategic missions were shaped as a quest to define and deliver the highest impact customer-focused innovations, assigned to distribute accountabilities across the wider community, and supported with common approaches that guided and equipped collaborating peers to learn and progress together. Importantly, this work demonstrates how a set of shared priorities provided a common aim for both strategic and delivery-oriented efforts. Deftly, the leadership team set a clear direction via a set of mission-oriented aims. In turn, cross-functional mission teams tackled those aims to define the high-priority agenda for product and service innovation. Following, the functional teams were charged to integrate their efforts to design and deliver those high priority innovations.

Collaborative Relationships Factor

While collaborative work shaped the focus of collaborative efforts, a relational structure defined the nature of interactivity and the enabling linking mechanisms. Given that collaborative work was both strategic and delivery focused, two mutually supportive relational structures emerged. While mission team linkages forged a tightly orchestrated alignment among the teams tasked with creating the strategic innovation agenda, local linkages among peers responsible for delivering those innovations relied on a supportive social climate. A third element of the relational structure, the design of physical space, afforded both relational structures, practically and symbolically.

A robust relational structure aligned peers to set a strategic agenda for innovation: Given the high degree of interdependencies among the mission teams and with their functional peers, a robust set of formal linking mechanisms enabled members to share information, coordinate efforts, and stay informed and aligned as decisions were made. Highlighted by the outside-in literatures as a cooperative infrastructure (Adler & Heckscher, 2018; Heckscher, 2007) or an integrating platform (e.g., Galbraith, 2010; Pasmore et al., 2019), scholars have identified a wide range of mechanisms that support peers to connect around their collective work including integrating roles, processes flows, technology platforms, forums, and information-sharing protocols (e.g., Adler & Heckscher, 2018; Galbraith, 2010; Heckscher, 2007; Valentine & Edmondson, 2015).

At the study site, a robust set of formal linking mechanisms kept the mission community in dynamic alignment in two important ways. First the visibility of each team's work naturally kept the work collaborative. Through daily and weekly forums – within teams, across teams, and with the leadership team – the mission community remained aware of how their issues and progress impacted others, as well as who needed to be looped in as decisions were contemplated. Second, the preset schedule and rhythm via which the teams met ensured that teams progressed in tandem. As teams reported progress, issues were identified for decision-making, barriers were attended to, and help was offered to those who were lagging. Third, a prioritization structure linked the discovery-focused mission work with the delivery-focused product development work. Essentially, the mission team priorities were funneled to the functional teams through project managers, who as the "connective tissue" and "drivers of progress" lead a forum to prioritize the agenda for designing and delivering the product innovations.

In all, a robust set of linking roles and forums guided the mission community for moving fast and remaining in alignment as critical, time-sensitive decisions were made.

A supportive social fabric afforded impromptu, peer-led interactivity: The need to integrate work efforts across functions extended beyond mission teams to the functional organization as well. Here the work was intentionally decentralized and the linkages opportunistic. At the CTG, a social fabric built to breed both belongingness and rapport readied peers for peer-led, organic interactivity. Consistent with the outside-in literatures that emphasized a communal sense of togetherness through an ethic of contribution (Adler & Heckscher, 2018; Heckscher & Adler, 2006) or spirit of volunteering (Mohrman et al., 1995), respondents reported that a sense of belongingness to the wider community promoted them to think and contribute beyond their functional roles. Through a wide array of social opportunities – from all-hands meetings to clubs and recreational activities – people developed a sense that they were "all in this together" and "part of something bigger."

Concurrently, a social rapport, built from peers getting to know each other personally, readied them to reach out to each other and genuinely engage while doing so. Knowing a fellow employee beyond their work role shifted the interactions from formulaic to personal, whereby people were more willing to ask for and offer help: "So, by getting to know and respect each other, we go that extra mile for each other." Akin to the importance of trust-based bonds identified in the social learning and social network literatures (e.g. Cross et al., 2010; Edmondson, 2018), with rapport, people shared that they felt safe and supported to "put themselves out there," "speak their minds," and "fire ideas back and forth and push back," all in service of learning from each other and advancing new insights. To foster rapport, leaders supported a wide range of activities, from common volunteering activities, to team-building sessions, to supporting travel to meet colleagues working in different settings, to the design of open workspaces. Respondents emphasized how rapport was enriched when peers were able to see, hear, and easily connect with each other, "Like, that rapport that you get with someone you sit next to, that you never ever get, even if you video-conference every day. And I don't know why."

The insight is that impromptu, yet highly useful interactivity among peers relies on a social fabric. Whereas social rapport among participating peers generates a safe and welcoming climate for interactivity, a sense of belongingness appears to bind people as insiders to a wider community and prime people to think and contribute beyond boundaries.

The design of workspace made it easy for peers to connect and convene: At the CTG, the design of workspace formed part of the relational platform from which people interrelated. Having colocated from two head offices to one, and following the move from cubicles to an open office environment, respondents reported that the design of physical space afforded both planned and in-the-moment, opportunistic linkages among peers. Practically, the design of workspace made it easy for peers to connect and convene. In keeping with the advice of the ecosystems frameworks (Becker, 2007; Davis, Leach, & Clegg, 2011; Heerwagen et al., 2004; Hua et al., 2011), that work hubs should be designed to human scale for easy peer access, respondents emphasized that being able to see that a helper was readily available prompted them to reach out to each other, and that by overhearing each other's conversations, they were drawn to intervene.

Related to easy access, a wide array of gathering spaces made it easy for peers to coalesce as the need arose, a finding emphasized by scholars who have noted the fluidity in which knowledge workers shift from individual to collective work (Becker, 2007; Heerwagen et al., 2004; Hsiao, Tsai, & Lee, 2012; Hua et al., 2011). The ease of being able to transition from working independently to gathering the right group of peers was widely touted as "allowing quick, spontaneous collaboration with minimal commitment." And for teams requiring dedicated spaces, well-equipped project rooms with web-ex tools enabled teams to work with colleagues virtually. To support virtual connectivity with off-sight peers, all meeting rooms were equipped with two large screens, one for a close-up image of the virtual participants "to bring the virtual players into the room" and the other to display the work being discussed.

In addition to the practical ease via which people interacted, participants emphasized how the physical space symbolized connectedness over separation, referring to the "open space here" as "a metaphor for how we collaborate." Referring to the felt sense of openness as an "approachability factor," respondents shared how peers felt like they were "automatically included" in the conversations occurring around them. And finally, the bright and vibrant décor created a space that people found energizing and inspiring: a place they wanted to be in together.

In all, practically and symbolically, the design of physical space formed a relational platform from which mission teams and their functional peers interrelated. Given that peers worked fluidly within and across mission and functional teams, the spatial layout was designed to match and afford a wide array of interactivity.

Summary of the collaborative relationship factor: While the collaborative work factor defined *what* work people performed together, the relational factor defined the mechanisms by which people connected around that work. Given that collaborative work was understood to be both strategic and delivery oriented, the relational linkages were designed in kind. Alongside the highly programmed roles and forums linking the mission community, an informal social fabric readied peers for impromptu yet useful connectivity. The design of workspace afforded easy interactivity both practically and symbolically.

Collaborative Behaviors Factor
With collaborative work setting the collective focus, and collaborative relationships affording essential linking patterns, the collaborative behaviors factor guided how peers contributed together. A common theme among the explored literatures is that people, and their ability to contribute collectively, are essential to the well-functioning collaborative organization. Rather than simply executing independent job tasks, collaborators must attend to wider organizational goals, integrate their skills and coordinate activities with others, and redirect efforts as new priorities emerge (e.g., Becker, 2007; Cross et al., 2008; Davis, 2019; Edmondson, 2012a; Lave & Wenger, 1991; Mohrman et al., 1995). At the CTG, the contributions of collaborators were guided and promoted in three ways. While a customer-focused purpose unified and inspired efforts, protocols guided peers to be personally accountable in service of collective success, and people practices hired and recognized people for their technical competence as well as their collaborative orientation. People embraced these tone-setting practices and appreciated the efforts of leaders to promote and preserve them.

A shared purpose unified and focused collaborative efforts: A core tenet well emphasized in the outside-in literatures is that collaborative organizations are bound by a unifying purpose (e.g., Adler & Heckscher, 2018; Davis, 2019;

Mohrman et al., 1995; Pasmore et al., 2019). Adler and Heckscher (2018) argue that *a distinctly collaborative type of purpose* is required to align and motivate effort among locally empowered actors. That purpose, they suggested, must imbue people with a sense of meaning around the value they collectively create and foster an ethic of working collectively for the greater good. Beyond meaning, purpose must be a practical pursuit that defines collective aims, shapes strategic priorities and work assignments, and causes members to continuously reflect on and evolve how they practice.

At the CTG, a purpose to solve customer problems was central to how the strategic missions were formed (as customer-focused innovations), how mission-related efforts were prioritized (around customer impact), and how functional efforts were focused to deliver those innovations (to generate holistic customer solutions). So embedded, employees referred to "solving customer problems quickly, faster, efficiently, effectively" as being "in our DNA." To sharpen the focus on purpose, leaders designed opportunities for people to interact with customers and their needs often. Through an annual immersion event, all employees learned about their role in supporting the customer-focused missions. Routinely, face-to-face touchpoints with customers supplemented customer analytics to keep customer needs real. And regular forums kept people informed about and linked around mission-focused progress.

Protocols encouraged both individual and collective responsibility: A host of collaborative protocols associated with being open, curious, helpful, and learning oriented, among others, have been identified as supporting peers to contribute collectively (e.g., Adler & Heckscher, 2018; Borgatti & Cross, 2003; Edmondson & Nembhard, 2009). At the CTG two protocols worked synergistically to foster productive peer-led interactivity: one protocol promoting individualism and the other interdependence.

A first protocol for voice, or for speaking up, encouraged people to think independently and to offer input and suggestions beyond their roles. Referred to as "pushing," peers were encouraged to challenge assumptions, ask provocative questions, and offer alternative options, all in service of promoting the best possible outcomes for customers. Framed as a core value for boundaryless participation, a respondent explained:

> Don't be afraid to participate, criticize, offer suggestions for improvement, even for things that have nothing to do with your direct work…. And then expect to be challenged. … but it's in the aim of perfecting and being better.

On the flip side, having considered the ideas of others, a protocol for deci-siveness caused peers to thoughtfully consider the input of others, while main-taining ownership for and a knowledge-based stance around their own work. As a respondent shared:

> It's really useful to have people offering different views and insights, however the owner then needs to take the insights and integrate them. You can have your input, but we leave it to the people to do their crafts.

Importantly, the protocols fostered both independence *and* interdependence of thought and action. A protocol for sharing and welcoming input promoted peers to assume collective accountability beyond role boundaries, while the protocol for personal decisiveness ensured that the responsible players applied their professional judgment having considered that input.

People practices selected for and recognized collaborative contributions: Two frameworks, the collaborative community (e.g., Adler & Heckscher, 2018) and the reconfigurable, team-based organization (Galbraith, 2010; Mohrman et al., 1995) attend directly to the importance of designing people practices that select for, develop, and motivate collaborative behaviors and mindsets. At the CTG, a top theme, widely shared by employees, was that the attributes of their peers made collaborating easy. Respondents expressed genuine appreciation for their colleagues, who were described as "open," "generous," "competent," "conscientious," and "nice"; in short, they were easy to work with. Respondents attributed the practice of hiring people for their technical and interpersonal skills to creating a competent and like-minded workforce with the right balance of "IQ and EQ to deliver as a team." Once hired, people were recognized more for *how* they contributed to the wider goals than to results with leaders celebrating "the process of getting to the ahas." A practice of cross-unit role mobility encouraged people to move freely between teams to create a sense of boundarylessness opportunity. Collectively, the people practices caused employees to feel seen by their leaders and genuinely appreciated for their contributions: "It's more than just saying that they value employees. It's like they have a true appreciation for us."

Summary of the collaborative behaviors factor: Collectively, purpose, protocols, and practices created a behavioral code for widespread cross-boundary collaboration at the study site. People were guided by a customer-focused purpose that unified and inspired efforts. Protocols guided peers to be personally accountable, yet in service of collective success. Supportive people practices ensured that people were hired and recognized for their technical competence as well as their collaborative orientation.

Collaborative Leadership

The role of leadership in fostering widespread collaboration across levels and boundaries is a factor well-identified in the examined literatures. Collaborative leaders not only design the factors to support a collaborative context (Adler & Heckscher, 2018; Becker, 2007; Davis, 2019; Mohrman et al., 1995) but also shape and assign the collaborative efforts (Edmondson, 2018; Galbraith, 2010; Pasmore et al., 2019; Mohrman et al., 1995) and set the expectation for collaborative contributions through their coaching and role modeling (Adler & Heckscher, 2018; Edmondson, 2018; Mohrman et al., 1995).

At the CTG, two core leadership roles were found to underpin a myriad of supportive leadership activities: the roles of architect and cultivator. As architects, leaders purposefully designed the collaborative context; it was the leaders who shaped the purpose, work priorities, approaches, protocols, people practices, and the like. As cultivators, leaders inspired and nurtured collaborative activities through their daily activities as coaches, role models, and performance drivers; they guided and steered the mission team efforts, fostered widespread contributions among the delivery network, and equipped and enabled efforts through a platform of collaborative supports. In this way, leaders were the keepers of culture (Schein, 1992); they shaped and role-modeled the basic assumptions from which people worked and codified those assumptions into essential design elements that supported collaborative work, relationships, and behaviors.

IMPLICATIONS FOR RESEARCH AND PRACTICE

Traditionally, managers have been advised to think locally about their collaborative efforts. In seeking teamwork, the advice has been to charter local, discrete teams. However, when efforts cross organizational boundaries, teams are often stymied by the formal structure. Our work shows that while cross-boundary teams are valuable and indeed required in the contemporary workplace, it is the wider organizational context that must be designed to support them. In other words to support cross-boundary efforts widely, design the collaborative context to enable them.

A second insight from this work concerns the formal and informal nature of cross-boundary collaboration. In recent years, advice flowing from the social learning, social network, and office design literatures has suggested that collaboration emerges organically, without formal roles, protocols, or linking mechanisms, as long as peers have the freedom and opportunity to connect. Our work shows that both formal and informal peer-led interactivity are desirable. Paradoxically, we found that informal peer-led interactivity was built from a base of formal and centrally guided interactivity around strategic goals. The insight is that both formal and informal collaboration can be purposefully supported through organizational design.

In all, the major learning for organizational designers is that if you want collaboration, you need to design the organizational context for collaboration. Through our review of the examined literatures and our case analysis of an exemplar firm, we discovered a unique set of factors that combine to generate the collaborative context. We offer three factors for the designer to attend to: (1) collaborative work, (2) collaborative relationships, and (3) collaborative behaviors.

Our framework prompts designers to think about each factor, yet the specific set of design choices will be unique to each firm. What's important is that each factor is attended to and coaligned. While these insights are articulated as part of the case study analysis, below we offer four propositions for the organizational designer to test, adapt, and employ.

P1. Collaborative organizations design work as a collaborative effort. Work is designed as a collaborative effort when: (1) it focuses and aligns the participating players around a set of interdependent outcomes in which they must interrelate, (2) it is distributed so that participating players are empowered to deliver, as defined by roles and accountabilities that are in service of each other, and (3) it enables and aligns the participating players through common approaches.

Commentary: This work shows that the collaborative potential of work is defined by three interrelated properties; how work is shaped, assigned, and approached. Essentially, both strategic and delivery-oriented work can be shaped to elevate work from a set of independent tasks to a collective contribution to a common cause. Designers will be well served by carefully attending to how goals, roles, and responsibilities are assigned to facilitate a mutual compatibility, so that the local autonomy of peers is balanced with leadership coaching and procedural standards to guide, elevate, and align progress. Importantly, how work is conducted is an important aligning tool. A common platform of tools, processes, and protocols equips and aligns how peers work together – including their work stages, pace, and activities.

P2. Collaborative organizations shape relationships to support collaborative work and promote collaborative encounters. Relationships are designed to support collaborative efforts when they enable the requisite patterns of interactivity among the participating players. Ideally the relational structure will provide for formal linking mechanisms to support formal collective efforts, a welcoming social fabric to enable opportunistic, peer-led collective efforts, and be bolstered by the physical and virtual workspace.

Commentary: If the collaborative work is the *what*, the focus of the collective efforts, collaborative relationships enable the requisite patterns of interactivity among the participating players. Our work found that the relational structures, can and perhaps should, be intentionally designed to support both centrally driven strategic work and also peer-led work. The lesson is that organizational designers will benefit from attending to two different but equally important types of relational structures. While a robust set of formal roles and forums link peers around highly interdependent strategic work, an informal social fabric readies local peers for impromptu yet useful interactivity. To build belongingness and rapport, designers are advised to eliminate boundaries by promoting intentional opportunities for social interactivity and opportunities for working peers to relate beyond their work responsibilities. Another learning from this work is that designers will be well served by thinking about the design of their office environments as an essential linking mechanism. Collaborative organizations design their physical and virtual workspaces to enable productive interactions, both formal and opportunistic. The design of workspace can fulfill the dual role of creating a symbolic sense of togetherness as well as, quite practically, enabling easy, timely, and useful interactivity among peers.

P3. Collaborative organizations cultivate the collaborative contributions of their people. Collaborative organizations carefully nurture the collaborative potential of their people. People are primed to work collaboratively when they are bound by a galvanizing common cause, guided by protocols to think and work across boundaries, and prompted to work collaboratively via organizational practices that recognize and reinforce their collaborative efforts.

Commentary: This work shows that collaborative organizations rely on a shared purpose to bind employees around a common cause and motivate collective effort. Done well, purpose gives people a deep sense of why their work matters, sets the foundation for unifying goals, and sets the tone for an ethic of mutuality whereby peers contribute beyond roles and take collective responsibility. Designers will be well served to shape a set of protocols that foster purposeful contributions beyond boundaries, a condition necessary for peers to informally and opportunistically connect for information-sharing, problem-solving, and co-planning. A delicate balance of protocols can create the conditions for people to practice in a way that honors their disciplinary independence *while also* seeking and integrating the input of others. As a final element, collaborative organizations build their talent pools with collaboratively oriented people by designing practices to select for and nurture their collaborative potential. The lesson for designers is to use and align a variety of people practices – from hiring to rewards to performance management – to set a clear expectation for how people are meant to contribute and interrelate.

P4. Collaborative leadership is essential to a collaborative organization. Collaborative organizations rely on leaders to fulfill a dual role as the architects of the collaborative ecosystem, as well as the cultivators of how people contribute.

Commentary: An essential learning from the study site is that formal leaders, beginning with the example set by the senior leadership team, are foundational to the collaborative enterprise. As architects, leaders design how work is collaboratively shaped, distributed, and approached, how participants are linked around the collaborative work, and how contributions are defined and nurtured. As cultivators, leaders promote collaborative contributions by role-modeling and guiding collaborative efforts. In this way, leaders are the cultural keepers of the collaborative ecosystem, so much so, that this work should not be attempted without it.

Future field research is called for to test the usefulness of our collaborative framework across a variety of settings and over time. One approach might be to explore how practitioners use the framework to diagnose their organization's collaborative capacity or to plan for how to enhance it. Another approach might be to illustrate how the factors manifest and compare over a wide variety of settings. A third approach might be to explore the applicability of the framework to the virtual workplace. Ripe for testing given the need for many organizations to work remotely during the COVID-19 pandemic, we suspect that the factors will remain useful as a guide for leaders as they contemplate how to generate collaborative outcomes. For example, if a shared purpose and climate of helpfulness remain important, how can they be fostered in a virtual world? And, over time, as organizations naturally adopt and experiment with new technologies, it will be interesting to follow how those advances permit new ways for peers to interact and innovate together, in both virtual and blended settings. In any event, we fully expect that technological advances will permit social advances in how people work collaboratively, and vice versa. It will be important for field researchers to follow these advances to illustrate the ever-evolving capacity for collaborative work and workplaces. As organizations experiment with virtual and blended settings, the questions become which principles remain relevant, how do they manifest, and what additional or alternative principles are becoming relevant?

Closing Remarks

Our starting premise was that as collaboration shifts to a widespread co-evolving activity, the organizational context must also shift to afford it. Through a careful analysis of two literatures – defined as the inside-out and outside-in approaches – and the case study of an exemplar firm, we revealed a unique and expanded evidence-based lens from which to design the collaborative workplace. Illustrated by the case of the CTG of Intuit Canada, we show that a collaborative workplace is built from how organizational leaders and designers construct work, relationships, and behaviors. While each firm's specific set of design choices will be unique, what's important is that each factor is attended to and coaligned to support the organization's needs for interactivity.

ACKNOWLEDGEMENTS

Thank you to the employees of the Consumer Tax Group (CTG) of Intuit Canada who welcomed us into their collaborative space, participated in interviews, answered our many questions, and ever so kindly invited us into hackathons, meetings, stand-ups, luncheons, and celebrations. A special thank you to the leadership team for opening your doors for this work.

REFERENCES

Abrams, L., Cross, R., Lesser, E., & Levin, D. (2003). Nurturing interpersonal trust in knowledge sharing networks. *Academy of Management, 17*(4), 64–77.

Adler, P. S., & Heckscher, C. (2018). Collaboration as an organization design for shared purpose. In L. Ringel, P. Hiller, & C. Zietsma (Eds.), *Toward permeable boundaries of organizations? (Research in the sociology of organizations)* (Vol. 57, pp. 81–111). Bingley: Emerald Publishing Limited.

Adler, P., Kwon, S., & Heckscher, C. (2008). Perspective-professional work: The emergence of a collaborative community. *Organization Science, 19*(2), 359–376.

Agranoff, R. (2012). *Collaborating to manage: A primer for the public sector.* Washington, DC: Georgetown University Press.

Allen, T. J. (1977). *Managing the flow of technology: Technology transfer and the dissemination of technological information within the R&D organization.* Cambridge, MA: MIT Press.

Amelkin, V., Askarisichani, O., Kim, Y., Malone, T., & Singh, A. (2018). Dynamics of collective performance in collaboration networks. *PLoS ONE, 13*(10). Retrieved from https://journals.plos.org/plosone/article?id=10.1371/journal.pone.0204547

Ancona, D., & Bresman, H. (2007). *X-teams: How to build teams that lead, innovate, and succeed.* Boston, MA: Harvard Business Press.

Barker Scott, B. A. (2020). *Designing for collaboration: An examination of the organizational elements that support cross-boundary collaboration.* Doctoral dissertation, Available from ProQuest Dissertations & Theses Global database.

Barker Scott, B. A. & Manning, M. R. (2021). Designing the collaborative organization: How shaping work, relationships and behaviors builds collaborative capacity. "Manuscript in preparation".

Becker, F. (2004). *Offices that work: Workspace strategies that add value and improve performance.* San Francisco, CA: Jossey-Bass.

Becker, F. (2007). Organizational ecology and knowledge networks. *California Management Review*, *49*(2), 42–61.

Beckman, S., & Barry, M. (2007). Innovation as a learning process: Embedding design thinking. *California Management Review*, *50*(1), 25–56.

Borgatti, S., & Cross, R. (2003). A social network view of organizational learning: Relational and structural dimensions of 'know who'. *Management Science*, *49*(4), 432–445.

Brandi, U., & Elkjaer, B. (2011). Organizational learning viewed from a social learning perspective. In M. Easterby-Smith & M. A. Lyles (Eds.), *Handbook of organizational learning and knowledge management* (pp. 23–41). Chichester: John Wiley & Sons.

Brown, J. S., & Duguid, P. (1991). Organizational learning and communities-of-practice: Toward a unified view of working, learning, and innovation. *Organization Science*, *2*(1), 40–57.

Brown, J. S., & Duguid, P. (2000). *The social life of information*. Boston, MA: Harvard Business School Press.

Chan, J., Beckman, S., & Lawrence, P. (2007). Workplace design: A new managerial imperative. *California Management Review*, *49*(2), 6–22.

Corporaal, G. F., Ferguson, J. E., & De Gilder, D. (2015). A cross-boundary coordination perspective on managing complexity in multiparty collaboration. *Academy of Management Proceedings*, *2015*(1), 18119.

Cross, R., Edmondson, A., & Murphy, W. (2020). A noble purpose alone won't transform your company. *MIT Sloan Management Review*, *61*(2), 37–43.

Cross, R., Ehrlich, K., Dawson, R., & Helferich, J. (2008). Managing collaboration: Improving team effectiveness with a network perspective. *California Management Review*, *50*(4), 78–99.

Cross, R., & Gray, P. (2013). Where has the time gone? Addressing collaboration overload in a networked economy. *California Management Review*, *56*(1), 50–66.

Cross, R., Gray, P., Cunningham, S., Showers, M., & Thomas, R. J. (2010). The collaborative organization: How to make employee networks really work. *MIT Sloan Management Review*, *52*(1), 83–90.

Cross, R., Liedtka, J., & Weiss, L. (2005). A practical guide to social networks. *Harvard Business Review*, *83*(3), 124–132.

Cross, R., Rebele, R., & Grant, A. (2016). Collaborative overload. *Harvard Business Review*, *94*(1), 74–79.

Cummings, J., & Kiesler, S. (2005). Collaborative research across disciplinary and organizational boundaries. *Social Studies of Science*, *35*(5), 703–722.

Danielsson, C. (2019). Holistic office design. From an organizational and management perspective. In R. Ayoko & N. Ashkanasy (Eds.), *Organizational behavior and the physical environment* (pp. 37–57). Oxon: Routledge.

Davis, M. C. (2019). Socio-technical systems thinking and the design of contemporary workspace. In R. Ayoko & N. Ashkanasy (Eds.), *Organizational behavior and the physical environment* (pp. 128–146). Oxon: Routledge.

Davis, M. C., Leach, D. J., & Clegg, C. W. (2011). The physical environment of the office: Contemporary and emerging issues. In G. P. Hodgkinson & J. K. Ford (Eds.), *International review of industrial and organizational psychology* (Vol. 26, pp. 193–237). Chichester: Wiley-Blackwell.

De Toni, A., & Nonino, F. (2010). The key roles in the informal organization: A network analysis perspective. *The Learning Organization*, *17*(1), 86–103.

DeChurch, L., & Zaccaro, S. (2010). Perspectives: Teams won't solve this problem. *Human Factors*, *52*(2), 329–334.

Dewar, C., Keller, S., Lavoie, J., & Weiss, L. M. (2009). *How do I drive effective collaboration to deliver real business impact?* (McKinsey & Company report). Retrieved from https://studylib.net/doc/8772492/how-do-i-drive-effective-collaboration

Edmondson, A. C. (2003). Framing for learning: Lessons in successful technology implementation. *California Management Review*, *45*(2), 34–54.

Edmondson, A. C. (2008, July–August). The competitive imperative of learning. *Harvard Business Review*. Retrieved from https://hbr.org/2008/07/the-competitive-imperative-of-learning

Edmondson, A. C. (2012a). *Teaming: How organizations learn, innovate, and compete in the knowledge economy*. San Francisco, CA: John Wiley & Sons.

Edmondson, A. C. (2012b). Teamwork on the fly. *Harvard Business Review, 90*(4), 72–80.

Edmondson, A. C. (2013). *Teaming to innovate*. San Francisco, CA: John Wiley & Sons.

Edmondson, A. C. (2018). *The fearless organization: Creating psychological safety in the workplace for learning, innovation, and growth*. Hoboken, NJ: John Wiley & Sons.

Edmondson, A. C. (2019). The role of psychological safety. *Leader to Leader, 2019*(92), 13–19. Retrieved from https://onlinelibrary.wiley.com/doi/abs/10.1002/ltl.20419

Edmondson, A. C., Casciaro, T., & Jang, S. (2019). Cross-silo leadership. *Harvard Business Review, 97*(3), 130–139.

Edmondson, A. C., & Lei, Z. (2014). Psychological safety: The history, renaissance, and future of an interpersonal construct. *Annual Review of Organizational Psychology and Organizational Behavior, 1*(1), 23–43.

Edmondson, A. C., & Nembhard, I. M. (2009). Product development and learning in project teams: The challenges are the benefits. *Journal of Product Innovation Management, 26*(2), 123–138.

Eisenhardt, K., & Gulanic, C. (2000, January–February). Coevolving: At last, a way to make synergies work. *Harvard Business Review*. Retrieved from https://hbr.org/2000/01/coevolving-at-last-a-way-to-make-synergies-work

Elsbach, K., & Bechky, B. A. (2007). It's more than a desk: Working smarter through leveraged office design. *California Management Review, 49*(2), 80–101.

Fjeldstad, Ø. D., Snow, C. C., Miles, R. E., & Lettl, C. (2012). The architecture of collaboration. *Strategic Management Journal, 33*(6), 734–750.

Fuzi, A., Clifton, N. & Loudon, G. (2014). New in-house organizational spaces that support creativity and innovation: The co-working space. In R & D Management Conference, June 3–6, 2014, Stuttgart.

Galbraith, J. (1973). *Designing complex organizations*. Boston, MA: Addison-Wesley.

Galbraith, J. (2010). The multi-dimensional and reconfigurable organization. *Organizational Dynamics, 39*(2), 115–125.

Granovetter, M. S. (1973). The strength of weak ties. *American Journal of Sociology, 78*(6), 1360–1380.

Gratton, L., Voigt, A., & Erickson, T. J. (2007). Bridging faultlines in diverse teams. *MIT Sloan Management Review, 48*(4), 22–29.

Grenier, A. (2018, May). Best workplaces in Canada legends: Great workplace cultures that stand the test of time. Retrieved from https://www.greatplacetowork.ca/en/resources/articles/best-work-places-in-canada-legends-great-workplace-cultures-that-stand-the-test-of-time-2

Groves, K. (2010). *I wish I worked there! A look inside the most creative spaces in businesses*. London: John Wiley & Sons.

Hackman, J. R. (1990). *Groups that work (and those that don't): Creating conditions for effective teamwork*. San Francisco, CA: Jossey-Bass.

Hackman, J. R. (2002). *Leading teams: Setting the stage for great performances*. Boston, MA: Harvard Business School Publishing.

Hackman, J. R. (2007, January). Why teams don't work. *Leader to Leader, 1998*(7), 24–31.

Hargadon, A., & Bechky, B. A. (2006). When collections of creatives become creative collectives: A field study of problem solving at work. *Organization Science, 17*(4), 484–500.

Hargadon, A., & Sutton, R. (1997). Technology brokering and innovation in a product design firm. *Administrative Science Quarterly, 42*(4), 716–749.

Harris, C., & Beyerlein, M. (2008). Team-based organization: Creating an environment for team success. In M. A. West, D. Tjosvold, & K. G. Smith (Eds.), *International handbook of organizational teamwork and cooperative working* (pp. 187–210). Malden, MA: John Wiley & Sons.

Heckscher, C. (2007). *The collaborative enterprise: Managing speed and complexity in knowledge-based businesses*. New Haven, CT: Yale University Press.

Heckscher, C., & Adler, P. S. (2006). *The firm as a collaborative community: The reconstruction of trust in the knowledge economy*. New York, NY: Oxford University Press.

Heerwagen, J. H., Kampschroer, K., Powell, K., & Loftness, V. (2004). Collaborative knowledge work environments. *Building Research & Information, 32*(6), 510–528.

Hsiao, R. L., Tsai, D. H., & Lee, C. F. (2012). Collaborative knowing: The adaptive nature of cross-boundary spanning. *Journal of Management Studies, 49*(3), 463–491.

Hua, Y., Loftness, V., Heerwagen, J., & Powell, K. (2011). Relationship between workplace spatial settings and occupant-perceived support for collaboration. *Environment and Behavior, 43*(6), 807–826.

Jang, S. (2017). Cultural brokerage and creative performance in multicultural teams. *Organization Science, 28*(6), 993–1009.

Jeffery, P. (2003). Smoothing the waters. Observations on the process of cross-disciplinary research collaboration. *Social Studies of Science, 33*(4), 539–562.

Kellogg, K. C., Orlikowski, W. J., & Yates, J. (2006). Life in the trading zone: Structuring coordination across boundaries in post bureaucratic organizations. *Organization Science, 17*(1), 22–44.

Kezar, A. (2006). Redesigning for collaboration in learning initiatives: An examination of four highly collaborative campuses. *The Journal of Higher Education, 77*(5), 804–838.

Kislov, R., Hyde, P., & McDonald, R. (2017). New game, old rules? Mechanisms and consequences of legitimation in boundary spanning activities. *Organization Studies, 38*(10), 1421–1444.

Klotz, F. (2018). The unique challenges of cross-boundary collaboration. *MIT Sloan Management Review, 59*(4), 1–5.

Kolbjørnsrud, V. (2018). Collaborative organizational forms: on communities, crowds, and new hybrids. *Journal of Organizational Design, 7*(11), 1–5. https://doi.org/10.1186/s41469-018-0036-3

Lave, J., & Wenger, E. (1991). *Situated learning: Legitimate peripheral participation.* New York, NY: Cambridge University Press.

Levin, D., & Cross, R. (2004). The strength of weak ties you can trust: The mediating role of trust in effective knowledge transfer. *Management Science, 50*(11), 1477–1490.

Long, J., Cunningham, F., & Braithwaite, J. (2013). Bridges, brokers and boundary spanners in collaborative networks: A systematic review. *BMC Health Services Research, 13,* 158. doi: 10.1186/1472-6963-13-158

Mariotti, F., & Delbridge, R. (2012). Overcoming network overload and redundancy in interorganizational networks: The roles of potential and latent ties. *Organization Science, 23*(2), 511–528.

Mohrman, S., Cohen, S., & Mohrman, A. (1995). *Designing the team-based organization: New forms for knowledge work.* San Francisco, CA: Jossey-Bass.

Moreland, R., & Myaskovsky, L. (2000). Exploring the performance benefits of group training: Transactive memory or improved communication? *Organizational Behavior and Human Decision Processes, 82*(1), 117–133.

Mortensen, M., & Haas, M. R. (2018). Rethinking teams: From bounded membership to dynamic participation. *Organization Science, 29*(2), 341–355.

Nonaka, I. (1994). A dynamic theory of organizational knowledge. *Organization Science, 5*(1), 14–37.

O'Hara, K., Kjeldskov, J., & Paay, J. (2011). Blended interaction spaces for distributed team collaboration. *ACM Transactions on Computer-Human Interaction, 18*(1), 3. Retrieved from https://dl.acm.org/doi/abs/10.1145/1959022.1959025

Pasmore, W., Winby, S., Mohrman, S., & Vanasse, R. (2019). Reflections: Sociotechnical systems design and organization change. *Journal of Change Management, 19*(2), 67–85.

Pennington, D. (2008). Cross-disciplinary collaboration and learning. *Ecology and Society, 13*(2), 8. Retrieved from http://www.ecologyandsociety.org/vol13/iss2/art8

Pennington, D. (2010). The dynamics of material artifacts in collaborative research teams. *Computer Supported Cooperative Work, 19*(2), 175–199.

Pentland, A. (2012). The new science of building great teams. *Harvard Business Review, 90*(4), 60–69.

Porras, J. I., & Robertson, P. J. (1992). Organizational development: Theory, practice, and research. In M. D. Dunnette & L. M. Hough (Eds.), *Handbook of industrial and organizational psychology* (pp. 719–822). Palo Alto, CA: Consulting Psychologists Press.

Rhoten, D. (2003). *A multi-method analysis of the social and technical conditions for interdisciplinary collaboration.* (The Social Science Research Council report). Retrieved from https://www.ssrc.org/publications/view/a-multi-method-analysis-of-the-social-and-technical-conditions-for-interdisciplinary-collaboration/

Schein, E. H. (1992). *Organizational culture and leadership.* San Francisco, CA: Jossey-Bass.

Siedlok, F., & Hibbert, P. (2014). The organization of interdisciplinary research: Modes, drivers, and barriers. *International Journal of Management Reviews, 16*(2), 194–210.

Snow, C. C. (2015). Organizing in the age of competition, cooperation, and collaboration. *Journal of Leadership & Organizational Studies, 22*(4), 433–442.

Snow, C. C., Fieldstad, O. D., Lettl, C., & Milles, R. E. (2011). Organizing continuous product development and commercialization: The collaborative community of firms model. *Journal of Product Innovation Management, 28*(1), 3–16.

Tannenbaum, S., Mathieu, J., Salas, E., & Cohen, D. (2012). Teams are changing: Are research and practice evolving fast enough? *Industrial and Organizational Psychology, 5*(1), 2–24.

Trist, E. (1977). Collaboration in work settings: A personal perspective. *The Journal of Applied Behavioral Science, 13*(3), 268–278.

Valentine, M., & Edmondson, A. C. (2015). Team scaffolds: How mesolevel structures enable role-based coordination in temporary groups. *Organization Science, 26*(2), 405–422.

Wageman, R., Gardner, H., & Mortensen, M. (2012). The changing ecology of teams: New directions for teams research. *Journal of Organizational Behavior, 33*(3), 301–315.

Weick, K. (2007). The generative properties of richness. *Academy of Management Journal, 1*(50), 14–19.

Wenger, E., McDermott, R. A., & Snyder, W. (2002). *Cultivating communities of practice: A guide to managing knowledge.* Boston, MA: Harvard Business School Press.

Winby, S., & Mohrman, S. A. (2018). Digital sociotechnical system design. *The Journal of Applied Behavioral Science, 54*(4), 399–423.

CONTEXT-LEVELS-CULTURE: A DIAGNOSTIC FRAMEWORK FOR CONSULTING TO DIVERSITY, EQUITY, AND INCLUSION CHANGE IN ORGANIZATIONS

Frank D. Golom and Mateo Cruz

ABSTRACT

Scholarship on workplace diversity, equity, and inclusion (DEI) is volumi-nous. Nevertheless, there is relatively little work that examines DEI from an organization development and change (ODC) or systems perspective. As a result, there is no unified framework ODC practitioners can use for DEI diagnosis and intervention. The purpose of this chapter is to review the ODC literature with respect to DEI and propose a diagnostic Context-Levels-Culture (CLC) framework for understanding and addressing diversity-related challenges in organizations. We also present a case example of how this framework can be used in DEI consulting, including implications for future research and practice.

Keywords: Diversity; equity; inclusion; organization development; organi-zation change; systems thinking; organizational diagnosis; consulting

After decades of theory and research in the social, organizational, and manage-ment literatures (Roberson, Ryan, & Raggins, 2017) and billions of dollars spent annually on diversity, equity, and inclusion (DEI) initiatives (Mehta, 2019), what began as a niche area of inquiry (Anand & Winters, 2008) is now a workplace imperative. The fact that the global and local US workforce will continue to diversify is a fundamental assumption of workplace DEI scholarship and practice

Research in Organizational Change and Development, Volume 29, 201–234
ISSN: 0897-3016/doi:10.1108/S0897-301620210000029009

(Roberson, 2019). The growing number of women and people of color in the US labor market (Toossi, 2015) combined with changing attitudes related to generational values, religious tolerance, sexual orientation, and gender identification (Hout, 2020) now mean that more and more individuals will find themselves working with others whose backgrounds and worldviews are different from their own. As a result, there is a need, both in science and practice, to examine the consequences of diversity and consider its implications for individuals and organizational systems.

In this regard, there is no shortage of DEI research. Several prominent reviews of workforce diversity have been conducted in the last decade (e.g., Guillaume, Dawson, Woods, Sacramento, & West, 2013; Holmes et al., 2021; Joshi, Liao, & Roh, 2011; Triana, Gu, Chapa, Richard, & Collela, 2021), providing a robust set of meta-analytic and integrative findings around which our current understanding now hinges. Organizational scholars and practitioners know a fair amount about racial and gender dynamics in the US workplace, including the impact of an employee's race and gender on a number of important human resource judgments and decisions (Triana et al., 2021). Literatures on age, disability, religion, and sexual orientation are smaller by comparison, but growing (Triana et al., 2021).

There is also a steadily increasing base of knowledge regarding diversity-related interventions in organizations (Ferdman, 2021). This includes, but is not limited to, research on how to improve climates for diversity (Cachat-Rosset, Carillo, & Klarsfeld, 2019; Groggins & Ryan, 2013; Komaki & Minnich, 2016) and inclusion (Nishii & Rich, 2014) as well as how to develop inclusive leaders (Perry, Block, & Noumair, 2020; Roberson & Perry, 2021; Shore & Chung, 2021). Diversity training also continues to receive attention (Chang et al., 2019; Cheng et al., 2019; Lindsey, King, Amber, Sabat, & Ahmad, 2019; Ragins & Ehrhardt, 2021; Rawski & Conroy, 2020), despite inconclusive evidence regarding its overall effectiveness (Devine & Ash, 2022; Kalinoski et al., 2013). And, microaggressions, the "brief and commonplace daily verbal, behavioral, and environmental indignities, whether intentional or unintentional, that communicate hostile, derogatory or negative slights and insults to the target person or group" (Sue et al., 2007, p. 273), continue to gain traction in DEI theory and practice (Kim, Block, & Nguyen, 2019).

For organization development and change (ODC) scholars and practitioners who engage in DEI work, there is no shortage of scholarship that can be used to inform client interactions. There is, however, a shortage of work, both in research and in practice, that approaches DEI from a systems perspective (Block & Noumair, 2017; Golom, 2018). In their call for papers for a special issue of *The Journal of Applied Behavioral Science* devoted to understanding diversity dynamics, Block and Noumair (2015) remark that although there has been a "great deal of research on understanding the causes of this persistent social inequality in organizational settings," there is far less attention to "the role of the organizational context or system where these persistent inequalities occur" (p. 5–6). In fact, relative to decades of research on workplace diversity and discrimination (Triana et al., 2021), there is little research that addresses DEI as an organization development, change, or systems issue (Ferdman, 2014; Golom, 2018; Gonzalez, 2010). Existing work offers insights into the influence of social identity variables on human resource judgments (e.g., Perry et al., 2017), the attitudes, behaviors and cognitive processes of members of minority and majority groups (e.g., Deitch et al., 2003), the impact of interventions targeting individual biases or empowering members of underrepresented groups (e.g., Wilton, Good, Moss-Racusin, & Sanchez, 2015), and the impact of group or organizational-level diversity on organizational processes and outcomes (e.g., Richard, Kirby, & Chadwick, 2013). Yet far less is known about (1) how to understand DEI issues as systemic challenges embedded in an organization's culture, (2) how to diagnose such challenges using a systemic, organization change frame, (3) how such a diagnosis might lead to different and more effective interventions than those suggested by current DEI research and practice, and (4) how such interventions might ultimately create sustainable, whole system change.

The purpose of this chapter is to address the first two of these gaps and answer the question of how to frame DEI issues from a systems perspective and how to approach diagnosing those issues using a systemic, organization change frame. In the first part of the chapter, we provide a limited overview of current approaches to managing DEI in organizations, which research continually demonstrates lead to mixed results and which often fail to frame workplace diversity as an organizational change issue. We then review the relatively few studies that explore DEI work from an ODC and systems perspective in effort to inform a more holistic and diagnostic approach. Based on this review, we suggest that the lack of a systems, organizational change frame is one possible explanation for the insufficient evidence associated with the long-term success of many popular individual-level DEI interventions (e.g., diversity training).

In the second part of the chapter, we propose a conceptual framework to understand and diagnose issues of workplace diversity from a systems, organization change perspective. Building on previous work by Gonzalez (2010) and Golom (2018), we argue that ODC practitioners must account for the influence of (1) context, (2) multiple levels of analysis, and (3) organizational culture in their diagnostic work with clients, which we label the Context-Levels-Culture (CLC) framework. In the final section of the paper, we provide a short case example to illustrate the application of the CLC framework to a professional services firm struggling with diversity and inclusion. Throughout the chapter, we rely on a fundamental premise of the ODC literature frequently championed by thought leaders in the field (Burke, 2017; Burke & Noumair, 2015) and echoed by a growing number of DEI scholars and practitioners (Block & Noumair, 2015, 2017; DiTomaso, 2010; Gonzalez, 2010; Stephens, Rivera, & Townsend, 2020) – individual-level interventions do not bring about systems-level change. Because DEI issues are fundamentally about the deep structure of an organization (Gersick, 1991), they are, first and foremost, systems-level issues and need to be diagnosed as such, particularly if we hope to achieve successful and sustainable organizational transformation.

Last, although we acknowledge the intimate link between diagnosis and intervention in ODC consulting practice (Burke & Noumair, 2015), this chapter intentionally focuses on the diagnostic phase of the consulting cycle and not on intervention. Given the limited research exploring DEI as a systemic culture change issue, we believe it is important to address the notable lack of theorizing on how DEI challenges can be understood and approached from a systems perspective. We are also not aware of published work that presents a diagnostic frame that can be used to consult to DEI issues. To that end, Ferdman (2020), in a recent special issue of *Consulting Psychology Journal* on the state of diversity and inclusion initiatives, writes:

> Although I would have liked to see additional contributions more systematically addressing how consulting psychologists, in particular, approach D&I initiatives, their absence may in itself indicate that this work has not yet become a core element of what many consulting psychologists do or are prepared to do. (p. 245)

By focusing on diagnosis, this chapter and the framework we propose directly answer Ferdman's call. We hope that the chapter can serve as a guide for consulting psychologists and ODC scholars and practitioners as they begin DEI work with their clients.

DEI AND ORGANIZATIONAL CHANGE

The existing empirical literature on organizational DEI challenges is voluminous, spans the mainstream management, psychology, and organizational behavior fields, and covers the last six decades (Roberson, 2019; Triana et al., 2021). Although there has been limited attention in this literature to examining the effectiveness of diversity management interventions (Roberson, Ryan, & Ragins, 2017), several scholars have noted the mixed and sometimes negative outcomes (Dobbin & Kalev, 2016, 2018; Kalev, Dobbin, & Kelly, 2006; Leslie, 2019; Stephens et al., 2020; Yadav & Lenka, 2020) associated with common individual-level diversity initiatives, including frequently employed diversity and unconscious bias training (Dobbin & Kalev, 2018) as well as organizational grievance policies and standardized performance evaluations or hiring tests (Dobbin & Kalev, 2016). Additionally, the mainstream literature does not often frame diversity as an issue that requires a fundamental change in the organizational culture or system (Block & Noumair, 2015, 2017; Gonzalez, 2010), which may in fact account for the lack of progress on key DEI issues over the last several decades.

Before developing our systems framework further, we therefore consulted the few studies that do explore DEI from an ODC perspective. We conducted a systematic literature search of papers published in science-to-practice journals as designated by the 2018 Academic Journal Guide (AJG). The 2018 AJG is a guide used to evaluate the quality of journals in business and management based on expert review across 22 subject areas (Chartered Association of Business Schools, 2018, March). For the purpose of this paper, we identified 25 science-to-practice journals across two AJG categories: organizational studies (ORG STUD) and workplace psychology (PSYCH-WOP-OB). Additionally, we included five journals either not ranked or listed in these categories because of their focus on ODC and/or DEI: *Consulting Psychology Journal: Practice and Research*; *Equality, Diversity and Inclusion: An International Journal*; *OD Practitioner*; *Organization*

Development Journal; and *The Organization Development Review* (for a full list of journals searched, see Table 1).

To execute the review, we performed an abstract search using keywords: "diversity," "diversity and change," "diversity and intervention," "inclusion," and "inclusion and change" (see Appendix 1). We included the term "intervention" because it is often used synonymously with change in the research literature. We limited the search to articles published in the past 10 years (2010–2021) because we are interested in *current* approaches to DEI and organizational change (see Yadav & Lenka, 2020, for a review of "diversity management" 1991–2018). We accessed corresponding databases (i.e., APA PsychArticles,

Table 1. Science-to-practice Journals Searched from 2010 to 2021 in Alphabetical Order.

Journal	2018 AJG Designation
Applied Psychology: An International Review	PSYCH-WOP-OB
Consulting Psychology Journal: Practice and Research	Not ranked
Equality, Diversity and Inclusion	ETHICS-CSR-MAN
Group & Organization Management	ORG STUD
Group Dynamics: Theory, Research and Practice	PSYCH-WOP-OB
Group Processes and Intergroup Relations	ORG STUD
Human Relations	ORG STUD
International Review of Industrial and Organizational Psychology	PSYCH-WOP-OB
Journal of Applied Psychology	PSYCH-WOP-OB
Journal of Applied Social Psychology	PSYCH-WOP-OB
Journal of Business and Psychology	ORG STUD
Journal of Managerial Psychology	ORG STUD
Journal of Occupational and Organizational Psychology	PSYCH-WOP-OB
Journal of Organizational Behavior	PSYCH-WOP-OB
Journal of Organizational Behavior Management	ORG STUD
Journal of Organizational Change Management	ORG STUD
Journal of Vocational Behavior	PSYCH-WOP-OB
Leadership and Organization Development	ORG STUD
OD Practitioner	Not ranked
Organization	ORG STUD
Organization Development Journal	Not ranked
Organization Science	ORG STUD
Organization Studies	ORG STUD
Organizational Behavior and Human Decision Processes	PSYCH-WOP-OB
Organizational Dynamics	ORG STUD
Research in Organizational Behavior	ORG STUD
Systemic Practice and Action Research	ORG STUD
The Journal of Applied Behavioral Science	PSYCH-WOP-OB
The Leadership Quarterly	ORG STUD
The Organization Development Review	Not ranked

Business Source Complete, Google Scholar, JSTOR, ProQuest One Academic, ProQuest One Business) and searched abstracts within each specific journal. In this process, we found 186 articles with "diversity and change" in the abstract, 163 with "diversity and intervention," and 193 with "inclusion and change" (note, search results were not mutually exclusive). Upon closer examination, only 67 of the articles identified addressed DEI and organizational change simultaneously. We coded the 67 article abstracts to determine (1) the DEI "problem" under examination and (2) the approaches to intervention taken. What follows is a summary of themes surfaced about DEI and organizational change from a science-to-practice perspective. These 67 articles are marked with an asterisk in the reference section.

IDENTIFYING THE DEI "PROBLEM"

Of the 67 articles examined, 28 adopted a conceptual approach (42%) (i.e., theories and frameworks, commentaries, or literature reviews) and 39 (58%) employed empirical methods to examine DEI and organizational change (i.e., survey research, participatory action research, case studies, interviews and focus groups, quasi-experimental designs, meta-analyses). Conceptual papers focused on the state of the DEI and change literature (e.g., Akpapuna, Choi, Johnson, & Lopez, 2020; Holck, Muhr, & Villeseche, 2016; Roberson et al., 2017; Yadav & Lenka, 2020; Yang & Konrad, 2011) and/or the need for more theory development (e.g., Block & Noumair, 2017; Coleman et al., 2017; Ferdman, 2017; Gagnon, Augustin, & Cukier, 2021; Gonzalez, 2010; Heracleous & Bartunek, 2021; Nkomo, 2020, 2021; Pringle & Ryan, 2015). Other conceptual pieces provided resources and recommendations for implementing DEI change in organizations (e.g., Hayes, Oltman, Kaylor, & Belgudri, 2020; McCluney, King, Bryant, & Ali, 2020; Stephens et al., 2020; Thomas & Ashburn-Nardo, 2020).

Of the empirical papers reviewed, representation appeared to be the primary DEI problem under investigation. More specifically, papers identified the lack of women and people of color throughout the organizational hierarchy as the main problem to be "fixed" (e.g., Cavanaugh & Green, 2020; Sekaquaptewa, Takahashi, Malley, Herzog, & Bliss, 2019; Vos, Celik, & de Vries, 2016). The second most common problem examined pertained to dominant majority attitudes, perceptions, and experiences in response to DEI change initiatives. These papers either focused on the change leader themselves (organizational leaders, consultants, DEI leads) or organizational members. The third most common problem addressed concerned the (in)effectiveness of DEI interventions. These papers examine phenomena such as resistance to DEI change (Velasco & Sansone, 2019), why DEI change initiatives may backfire or fail to stick (e.g., Burchiellaro, 2020; Carrillo Arciniega, 2021; Evans, 2014; Holck, 2016; Solebello, Tschirhart, & Leiter, 2016; van den Brink, 2020), and/or the factors that allowed some DEI change efforts to work (e.g., Bilimoria & Singer, 2019; Cavanaugh & Green, 2020; Chrobot-Mason & Aramovich, 2013; Downey, van der Werff, Thomas, &

Plaut, 2015; Easley, 2010; Gavino et al., 2010; Groggins & Ryan, 2013; Jansen, Otten, & van der Zee, 2015; Komaki & Minnich, 2016).

APPROACHES TO INTERVENTION

We should first note that only 13 of the 39 empirical studies published document an organizational DEI intervention in situ, grossly limiting what we know about effective interventions. Of these studies, most engage interventions at the individual level. This is likely related to how DEI problems are diagnosed. Meaning, studies that identify recruitment and retention as the main DEI "problem" target decision-makers or DEI hires in the design of the intervention. For example, a university may train faculty search committees about implicit biases (Cavanaugh & Green, 2020), implement Faculty Learning Communities to increase the retention and advancement of underrepresented minority (URM) faculty (O'Meara, Nyunt, Templeton, & Kuvaeva, 2019), or develop leadership workshops to influence faculty attitudes about hiring practices (Sekaquaptewa et al., 2019; Yen et al., 2019). Though each of these programs helps shift attitudes and increase the hiring and retention rates of URM faculty, they facilitate change at the individual level more than the institutional level. Additionally, most of these interventions occur at a single site (for exceptions, see Bilimoria, & Singer, 2019; Dahanayake, Rajendran, Selvarajah, & Ballantyne, 2018), typically in a university or nonprofit setting. Few studies examine DEI interventions in business settings. Likewise, methodologically, the majority of studies published adopt a case-based approach, using qualitative or mixed-methods data. Few studies employ an experimental design (for an exception see Hennes et al., 2018), impeding our ability to make causal claims.

In sum, over the past 10 years, the main problems identified in the DEI and organizational change literature have been (1) the lack of representation of women and people of color in organizations; (2) dominant majority attitudes toward DEI change; and (3) why some DEI interventions are effective and others not (e.g., a focus on the individual level). These studies are invaluable to our understanding of DEI and organizational change. At the same time, there are notable gaps in how DEI problems are framed. For example, few studies describe the diagnostic process engaged to better understand the problem to be solved. Most assume the numbers are sufficient to indicate the need for change or are commissioned by a larger granting agency (i.e., National Science Foundation, NSF) that uses representation as the primary metric for success. Consequently, problems tend to be specific to diversity (i.e., recruitment, retention, promotion) more than equity or inclusion. Second, because of the overlap between organizational role (leader, manager, consultant) and social identity group membership (White, male), DEI studies privilege the perspective of members from the dominant majority group, *not* those whom the DEI efforts are intended to help (for exceptions, see Beba & Church, 2020; Carter-Sowell, Vaid, Stanley, Petitt, & Battle, 2019; Chin, Desormeaux, & Sawyer, 2016; Easley, 2010; Hanappi-Egger, 2012; Holck, 2016; Nkomo & Kriek, 2011). As a result, only part of the system is represented in the diagnosis, leading to the implementation of narrowly focused interventions.

FRAMING DEI FROM A SYSTEMS PERSPECTIVE

As the limited literature on DEI and organizational change makes clear, there is a need for a more robust and complete conceptual framing of DEI work, as scholars consider how to increase and assess the efficacy of common diversity management practices. Although several methodological and conceptual explanations have been put forth for the mixed results associated with diversity training (Cheng et al., 2019; Dobbin & Kalev, 2016, 2018; Kulik & Roberson, 2008), implicit bias training (Forscher et al., 2019), and other attempts to control or mitigate individual employee or managerial bias (Dobbin, Schrage, & Kalev, 2015), the explanations offered by the mainstream organizational psychology, organizational behavior, and management literatures rarely include attention to viewing DEI work from an ODC or systems perspective (Block & Noumair, 2017). In fact, Cheng et al. (2019) note that the main conclusion they can draw from their review of the diversity training literature is that "most interventions are not grounded in theory or backed by empirical support" (p. 2), which, although true, is not a systems-level analysis.

Outside the mainstream literature, there has been increasing emphasis on the need to conceptualize and approach diversity management systemically and from an ODC perspective (Block & Noumair, 2017; Golom, 2018; Gonzalez, 2010; Vinkenburg, 2017). For example, in their article examining participant attitudes toward their organizations' progress on structural racism, Abramovitz and Blitz (2015) found that mixed organizational success may be due to a "heavy concentration on individual differences and characteristics rather than addressing systemic issues" (p. 98). This line of thinking is echoed by Stephens et al. (2020), who argue that "the individual-level changes that have been observed in some studies do not translate into achieving the ultimate goal of increasing organizational-level diversity" (p. 8). In fact, the common slate of diversity interventions in organizations often leaves problematic organizational cultures and norms unaddressed and focuses too heavily on fixing biased employees or empowering the targets of such bias (Block & Noumair, 2015; Vinkenburg, 2017).

To that end, while potential explanations for the lack of documented success for many DEI initiatives could be their lack of grounding in psychological or management theory or their mixed empirical support (Cheng et al., 2019), a more likely explanation is that such interventions do not position the entire organizational system as the target for change. Consequently, these interventions do not alter important reinforcing mechanisms related to bias, discrimination, and unequal distributions of power that are embedded in the larger organizational system and that either undermine or run directly counter to the intended attitudinal, behavioral, or skill-based outcomes associated with individual-level diversity interventions (Vinkenburg, 2017). As Gonzalez (2010) notes,

"Diversity policies are not effective unless they are backed up by organizational culture change" (p. 198). In order to avoid the middling success of many DEI initiatives and shift the engrained norms, routines, and practices that differentially impact employees from underrepresented groups (van den Brink, 2020), the entire organizational system must become the target of DEI change.

Such a notion is consistent with decades of scholarly work on the nature of change in organizations (Burke, 2017), which suggests that change must be transformational (versus developmental or transitional) if it is to lead to permanent shifts in the organization beyond continuous improvement (Anderson & Ackerman Anderson, 2001). For example, Bartunek and Moch (1987) distinguish between first-order, second-order, and third-order change, with first-order change referring to incremental improvement and second-order and third-order changes referring to the kind of transformational shifts that are absent in many DEI interventions. Weick and Quinn (1999) also distinguish between episodic and continuous change, with the emphasis of episodic change again being on organizational transformation and strategic disruption, in part "because programs are replaced rather than altered, and initiated at higher levels in the organization" (p. 368). Although other models of transformational change exist in the literature (e.g., Anderson & Ackerman Anderson, 2001), they have not necessarily crossed over into the DEI space (Block & Noumair, 2015), likely for two reasons. First, transformational change is highly complex and all-encompassing, demanding "a shift in human awareness that completely alters the way the organization and its people see the world, their customers, and their work" and requiring "a shift of culture, behavior, and mindset to implement successfully and sustain over time" (Anderson & Ackerman Anderson, 2001, p. 39). This is especially difficult for DEI challenges given entrenched identity-based intergroup and power relations in US social and organizational contexts (Plaut, 2010).

Second, and more importantly, approaching DEI issues from an ODC or transformational change perspective requires practitioners to develop a shared understanding of systems approaches to DEI, which may not be standard training for consultants (Ferdman, 2020). Although there are multiple ways of conceptualizing systems in the literature (i.e., Burke & Litwin, 1992; Meadows, 2008; Syvantek & Brown, 2000), Senge's (1990) distinction between the structural, functional, and behavioral elements of any system may be helpful when considering the intersection of systems theory, organization change, and DEI. Senge (1990) defines a system as "anything that takes its integrity, form and definition from the ongoing interaction of its elements...all of which have a common purpose and behave in common ways" (p. 137). Said another way, a system is a set of elements "interconnected in such a way that they produce their own pattern of behavior over time" (Meadows, 2008, p. 2). From an ODC perspective, the structural element of any system is the most critical and refers to "the basic interrelationships that control behavior and translate perceptions, goals, rules, and norms into action," including hierarchies, information flows, and general decision-making processes (Senge, 1990, p. 40). The functional element describes the long-term response tendencies or patterns of behavior between actors that often result from the organization's structural makeup. And, the behavioral element refers to an organization's specific, individual responses to a given situation, including specific events embedded in its overall pattern of behavior (Golom, 2018).

In DEI initiatives as traditionally researched and practiced, the tendency is to focus on this short-term behavioral element by responding to and addressing bias-related events as they arise but ignoring the more long-term response patterns and structures that support such events in the first place. As Davidson (1999) notes, organizations frequently require training in response to biased or insensitive behavior among their employees. They also engage in affinity group programming or targeted leadership development sessions in response to feedback or pushback from employees from various underrepresented groups (Block & Noumair, 2015). In both cases, the pull is to conceptualize change by focusing on the individual behavioral elements in isolation, rather than thinking about the patterns and structures that lock seemingly disconnected elements together or cause them (Burke, 2017; Senge, 1990). From a systems perspective, organizations that approach DEI work in this way often "appear actively and reactively busy, calming isolated and even repeated crises" (Golom, 2018, p. 14) without ever addressing the "cultures, routines, and structures" that contribute to those crises in a much more sustainable way (van den Brink, 2020, p. 380).

As has been noted elsewhere (Golom, 2018), the failure to target the entire organizational system is the death knell of many change initiatives (Katzenbach, Steffen, & Kronley, 2012), resulting in an oft-cited 60% failure rate (Burke, 2017) that likely holds in the DEI space (Block & Noumair, 2017; Dobbin & Kalev, 2016; Foldy & Buckley, 2017; van den Brink, 2020; Vinkenburg, 2017). Despite this, there are few systemic approaches in the ODC literature to understand issues of DEI and almost no models that can be used to diagnose DEI issues from a systems perspective in OD consulting work (Ferdman, 2020). In order to facilitate a shift from individual-level approaches to managing diversity to one focused on creating change in the organizational system, we draw from supportive conceptual frameworks and propose an integrated systems model for diagnosing DEI issues in organizations: the CLC framework.

A SYSTEMS APPROACH TO DIAGNOSING DEI ISSUES: THE CONTEXT-LEVELS-CULTURE FRAMEWORK

Although there are no specific ODC consulting frameworks for diagnosing DEI issues from a systems perspective, there have been several attempts to move the field toward an understanding of DEI work that deliberately incorporates systems thinking (DiTomaso, 2010; Finckh & Reich, 2016; Gonzalez, 2010; Gotsis & Kortezi, 2015; Vinkenburg, 2017). For example, Gonzalez (2010) advocated a conceptual approach to diversity change in organizations that views such change as a systemic, multilevel, and nonlinear process. From his perspective, diversity change is considered (1) systemic insofar as it takes into account both the organization's external environment and its internal context, (2) multilevel insofar as it accommodates the impact of group and organization-level variables on individual and organizational DEI outcomes, and (3) nonlinear insofar as it acknowledges the existence of backlash, reactivity, and self-reinforcing feedback loops "that build change on change and can gain momentum in either an upward or downward direction" (p. 202). Although such framing is helpful, Gonzalez (2010) does not provide a diagnostic model or mechanism for using his conceptual writing in a DEI consulting intervention.

Similarly, Finckh and Reich (2016) stressed the importance of using a systems approach to diversity and inclusion through their Systemic Constellation process. Such an approach has three key features, including (1) employing a holistic view of the system, (2) acknowledging the importance of relationships, and (3) allowing for the contextualized construction of reality within the system (Finckh & Reich, 2016). In line with Senge (1990), this approach focuses on the relationships between and among systemic elements rather than on the singular elements themselves. As Finckh and Reich note, interdependent "relations determine the structure of the system" (p. 20). By deliberately incorporating context and different levels of analysis (macro, meso, and micro), their systems frame is presented as superior to traditional DEI management practices, which the authors argue "are of limited use when trying to deal with problematic situations in diversity management" (Finckh & Reich, 2016, p. 23). Similar to Gonzalez (2010), Finckh and Reich (2016) do not provide a diagnostic model or clear mechanism for applying their ideas to consulting work.

An emphasis on context and levels of analysis also appears in Gotsis and Kortezi (2015), who offer a critical diversity framework for implementing new DEI practices in organizations. Based on a relational view of diversity management, they advocate for an approach to DEI work that "takes into account the contextual, structural, and individual factors shaping diversity management strategies" (p. 75). Although their perspective is based more on critical management theory than on an ODC frame, the authors support moving from "a labor market-driven and business-case oriented diversity management to one presupposing a substantial change in organizational priorities" (p. 80). Similar to Gonzalez (2010) and Finckh and Reich (2016), they suggest that such a shift is achieved by (1) displaying contextual sensitivity when implementing standard HR DEI policies, (2) acknowledging how multilevel factors impact diversity-related interventions, and (3) incorporating paradigms that move beyond viewing diversity "as a static dimension [of difference] in binary terms" to one that examines interactions and power relations between and among various identity groups (p. 84). Similarly, they do not translate their ideas into an actionable model that can be used for DEI diagnosis and consultation.

Finally, Golom (2018) proposed three perspectives higher education DEI practitioners could use to engage their work from an organization change or systems perspective. Rather than focus on particular individual-level crisis events that tend to promote cyclical attention to DEI issues on college campuses (Harvey, 2016), practitioners were encouraged to consider how organizational context, levels of analysis, and systems dynamics impact both the manifestation and amelioration of difficult DEI-related university issues. To that end, practitioners were encouraged to (1) think systemically by holding at bay their reactions to specific events and (2) approach DEI work from a culture change perspective by examining the patterns, interrelationships, and feedback mechanisms that contribute to social inequity and exclusion.

While the disciplinary perspectives and fields of practice of these scholars differ, their critiques of the current diversity management literature all independently support moving toward an understanding of DEI change that is (1) contextually situated, (2) multilevel-focused, and (3) dynamically or relationally oriented. Said another way, they each promote a systems approach to DEI that encourages scholars and practitioners to attend to context, levels of analysis, and organizational culture in their diagnostic and intervention work. Based on this literature and building on the conversational framework developed in Golom (2018), we integrate the various ideas across these disparate approaches into a CLC framework for DEI consulting, diagnosis, and change.

Context

The importance of accounting for context when engaging in DEI research and practice has long been established by scholars and practitioners alike (Gonzalez, 2010; Joshi & Roh, 2009). In fact, context is the one dimension of the CLC framework shared by the various authors cited above, all of whom advocated for an organization change/systems approach to DEI. Gonzalez (2010) incorporates context into his framing of diversity change as systemic, concluding that "environmental drivers [often] provide the impetus that shapes the magnitude of diversity change" (p. 200). In addition to external environmental pressures, context has also been defined to include an organization's internal systems, policies, and procedures (Golom, 2018; Gonzalez, 2010). Such an approach is consistent with the interactionist perspective (Chatman, 1989) that defines much of social and organizational psychology, which states that behavior in organizations is jointly determined by two factors – those related to individual actors/ units and those related to the larger group and organizational contexts in which those actors reside (Chatman, 1989; Lewin, 1951). As noted in Golom (2018), this interactionist perspective is critical for navigating modern organizations, as it forces the recognition that the organizational context can be as strong an influence on organizational behavior as individual-level variables (Chatman, 1989), and provides answers to important qualifying questions related to when and for whom diversity impacts workplace outcomes.

From a DEI perspective, context complements what would otherwise be a myopic focus on the individual level (Block & Noumair, 2015). The critical question is what counts as context in an organizational setting and what should be taken into account in terms of DEI diagnosis and intervention. From a purely empirical and research-based perspective, context functions as important intervening variables that "help better explain when and how diversity affects work outcomes" (Guillaume et al., 2013, p. 134). For example, Joshi and Roh (2009) examined the impact of occupational, industry, and team-level moderators on the relations between demographic diversity and performance outcomes. They found greater negative impacts of diversity on performance in occupations heavily dominated by men and White employees, suggesting an important role for the larger industry or occupational context of many localized diversity efforts. The demographic composition of the surrounding community has also been shown to impact diversity effects within specific organizations, particularly the impact of the organization's racial composition on perceptions of diversity climate (Pugh, Dietz, Brief, & Wiley, 2008).

Taken together, such findings suggest that accounting for contextual variables is likely to nuance DEI practitioners' understanding of the interpersonal or performance-related dynamics between members of different identity groups within the organization. Though the empirical literature points to various examples of contextual variables that have been studied empirically as moderators of diversity effects, those writing about diversity change as a practice note the importance of context as well. The organization's regulatory environment (Gonzalez, 2010), its geographic location (Pugh et al., 2008), its business model, mission and strategy (Burke, 2017), specific policies and procedures (Gotsis & Kortezi, 2015), its management practices (Dobbin et al., 2015), and localized climate perceptions around diversity and inclusion (Nishii & Rich, 2014), among others, can all influence the nuanced ways in which DEI issues are likely to manifest in organizations. To be successful at producing sustainable organizational change, these variables must be taken into account and directly assessed in the contracting and diagnosis process with clients (Burke & Noumair, 2015; Joshi & Roh, 2009).

Levels of Analysis

In addition to context, DEI practitioners can also expand their focus to incorporate phenomena at the group, organizational, or institutional levels of analysis to improve their diagnostic capabilities (Gonzalez, 2010; Gotsis & Kortezi, 2015). First, research suggests that changes at one level of analysis can often impact outcomes at other levels (Klein, Dansereau, & Hall, 1994; Roberson et al., 2017). Additionally, studies show that certain variables, like demographic faultlines (Lau & Murningham, 1998), do not exist at the individual level, while others, like team cohesion, may be better understood by examining them as group- or organization-level constructs (Salas, Grossman, Hughes, & Coultas, 2015). For example, Salas et al. (2015) found that more significant outcomes were associated with team cohesion when it was measured at the team level than when it was measured at the individual level. Similarly, Joshi and Roh (2009) note that the relationship between demographic diversity and performance worsens when various team-level variables are taken into account, particularly team interdependence or longevity. These findings suggest that a rich tapestry of nuance can emerge by thinking beyond individual identities, biases, or prejudices, allowing DEI practitioners to develop a deeper understanding of diversity dynamics within an organization and also the ability to more directly target their change interventions.

Beyond methodological or empirical imperatives, another critical argument in favor of attending to levels of analysis is related to the nature of organizational change itself. As previously mentioned, individual-level interventions do not produce systems change. Not only is there little evidence in the organizational literature that changing individuals results in a changed organizational system (Burke, 2017), there is some consensus among DEI practitioners that diversity interventions are often reactive and do not occur as part of an overall DEI strategy (cf. Thomas, 2004). Change can also occasionally occur in the opposite direction of what is intended, as some common individual-level diversity interventions have been shown to create backlash or decrease the representation of underrepresented groups in leadership roles (Dobbin & Kalev, 2016; Kalev et al., 2006).

For these reasons, multilevel considerations should be as paramount as attending to context when creating change. DEI practitioners interested in a systems approach to their work should consider how phenomena at the micro (individual), meso (team), and macro (organizational) levels interact to impact diversity dynamics within a particular organization (Gotsis & Kortezi, 2015). Too heavy of a focus on the individual level ignores other dynamic forces that exist in any organization, including higher-order group, unit, organization, industry, and societal and national forces that influence organizational members (Golom, 2018). At the very least, diversity management practices focused on specific units (i.e., group training or group coaching) may be more effective than those that attempt to educate individuals, as they encourage the development of group norms and shared mental models that can remain in place after a psychoeducational event has concluded (Golom, 2018; Liang, Moreland, & Argote, 1995; Roberson et al., 2013).

Organizational Culture

Although attending to larger contextual and levels of analysis issues is important, no systems approach to DEI work would be complete without examining the critical role of organizational norms in creating, reinforcing, and maintaining behavior in workplace settings. For this reason, exposing and changing implicit, taken-for-granted norms and assumptions are at the heart of all ODC initiatives (Burke, 2017), and DEI interventions should be no exception (Beba & Church, 2020; Golom, 2015). Gonzalez (2010) makes this point explicitly, writing that "variations in the organization's diversity-related *cultural* elements, such as new and emerging attitudes, values, and beliefs about diversity or specific social groups," ought to be an essential driver and outcome of diversity change initiatives (p. 201). This sentiment is also echoed across the writings of other scholars, who collectively point to some dynamic, relational, and largely implicit force that systematically influences DEI work in organizations, whether it be "routines and structures" (van den Brink, 2020, p. 380), "day-to day organizational practices and norms" (van den Brink, 2020, p. 381), "organizational policies, routines, and hierarchies" (Gotsis & Kortezi, 2015, p. 73), "overt and covert processes" (Block & Noumair, 2017, p. 7), "system dynamics and self-reinforcing mechanisms"

(Vinkenburg, 2017, p. 215), and "relations between individuals...abstract elements and persons" (Finckh & Reich, 2016, p. 20). For the purpose of the CLC framework, we refer to these forces as organizational culture.

According to Schein (2016), culture is defined as the organizational "beliefs, values, and behavioral norms that come to be taken for granted as basic assumptions and drop out of awareness" even as they are implicitly "taught to new members as the correct way to perceive, think, feel, and behave in relation to problems" (p. 6). Colloquially, culture is often referred to as "the way we do things around here" (Burke, 2017; Cameron & Quinn, 2011). Although it has many uses in a workplace context, one key feature of organizational culture is that it provides an interpretative framework for understanding the daily events that occur in organizations, in part by exposing the localized attitudes, values, and beliefs that create, reinforce, maintain, and connect them (Schein, 2016). To that end, organizational culture is conceptually similar to the structural element of a system as described by Senge (1990) or the work on deep structure that permeates the organization change literature (Burke, 2017; Gersick, 1991; Heracleous & Bartunek, 2021). All three concepts relate to the implicit rules or norms that govern the relationships between and among the actors in a system and produce patterns of internal mechanisms that pull organizations to return to their status quo (Cameron & Quinn, 2011; Schein, 2016; Vinkenburg, 2017). As a result, all three are integral to understanding and navigating organizational change. Because culture is structurally stable, deeply unconscious, pervasively broad, and subtly integrating of disparate events and activities (Schein, 2016), it must be fully understood and mined for the insights and leverage points needed to sustain organizational transformation. As Cameron and Quinn (2011) note, "efforts to improve organizational performance fail because the fundamental culture of the organization – values, ways of thinking, managerial styles, paradigms, approaches to problem solving – remains the same" (p. 12).

Given the entrenched history of social identity-related biases and power relations in organizations and in US society (Plaut, 2010) and the pervasive role of culture as a stabilizing force born of past organizational and leadership decisions (Schein, 2016), attending to change in the organization's culture is the most critical feature of any successful DEI intervention (Golom, 2015). It is also the aspect of the CLC framework most closely linked to utilizing a systems approach (Meadows, 2008; Senge, 1990) to understand and diagnose DEI workplace issues. To that end, to think in systems is not only to attend to context and level of analysis but also to the structural interdependence, interrelatedness, and patterns between and among different aspects of the system, both in any given moment and over time (Gonzalez, 2010; Heracleous & Bartunek, 2021; Meadows, 2008). Sustainable organization change cannot occur without targeting the organization's culture or deep structure (Burke, 2017), and most change efforts fail precisely because they do not (Heracleous & Bartunek, 2021). We believe failing to take a systems approach is the main reason why DEI initiatives in organizations have not achieved the representation, climate, or performance-based goals they have set for the past several decades (Block & Noumair, 2017). Without a frame that accounts for context, levels of analysis, and organizational culture, a systems diagnosis cannot occur, revolutionary change (Gersick, 1991) is less likely to be successful, and a lack of progress on key organizational initiatives is almost guaranteed. Fundamentally altered organizational behavior requires an altered system (Golom, 2015), which cannot be produced by individual-level DEI interventions alone. Organizational culture is perhaps the best vehicle for operationalizing, understanding, and producing such systems transformation (Cameron & Quinn, 2011).

For an example of how traditional individual-level diversity interventions might be enhanced by attending to context, levels of analysis, and organizational culture, see Table 2.

Table 2. Common Diversity, Equity, and Inclusion (DEI) Interventions Reconsidered Using the Context-Levels-Culture Diagnostic Framework.

Challenge	Individual-Level Interventions	Context Considerations	Levels Considerations	Culture Considerations
Several employees are concerned about the lack of queer individuals in senior leadership roles.	In the next recruitment cycle, HR devotes additional resources to identifying and targeting queer candidates.	Is the climate in the organization favorable for queer-identified individuals, and how is prior experience working on queer issues viewed?	How would the inclusion of queer employees in certain departments or units impact group cohesion, communication, conflict, and trust?	How might institutional heterosexism be manifest in formal and informal organizational policies, procedures, and systems?
A group of female employees, unsatisfied with what they perceive as a negative workplace climate, post a series of social media videos to voice their experiences of microaggressions.	Senior leaders, in response to increased social media attention and pressure, implement mandatory gender diversity training for employees.	Does the organization's diversity programming include multiple opportunities for learning about issues of social justice, diversity, equity, and inclusion?	How does training support an overall vision, strategy, and action plan for DEI efforts at the organizational level?	What are the potential points of resistance to mandatory training around issues of gender diversity, and how and where are they likely to manifest in the organization?
A new employee of color has complained about her supervisor's biased behavior, including racially and politically insensitive comments.	The employee is encouraged to file a formal bias complaint or grievance, which is then investigated by HR.	How is this dynamic reflective of or influenced by current (or historical) organizational, regional, or national patterns and trends?	Are the supervisor's actions an isolated event, or do they imply something about the climate for inclusion in this employee's department?	What implicit norms are present in the organization that tacitly condone or allow supervisors to remain ignorant of issues of racial justice?

Source: Adapted from Golom (2018).

CASE STUDY: APPLYING THE CLC FRAMEWORK TO A PROFESSIONAL SERVICES FIRM

The CLC framework provides a unique lens through which consultants can diagnose DEI challenges in organizations. To illustrate how the framework can be used, we present the following case example. The case takes place in a boutique professional services firm (hereafter known as "the Firm") headquartered in the Washington, DC metropolitan area. Our consulting engagement with the Firm is ongoing and currently in the data analysis/feedback stage of the ODC consulting cycle. Below, we present the initial contracting and data collection/diagnosis phases of the engagement through the application of the CLC framework.

Background

The Firm in question provides marketing, advertising, and information management services to an impressive array of Fortune 500 companies. It was founded in the 1970s and has been remarkably consistent in both its business model and the services it provides over the last four decades. The Firm was founded by its current Chairman and CEO, who describes himself as a "reluctant CEO and founder." Nevertheless, he has led the organization for over 40 years after starting the company with a friend as somewhat of a passion project. To that end, despite the impact of the COVID-19 pandemic on US businesses, the Firm had the most profitable year in its history in 2020 and has expanded considerably over the last five years, with a full-time staff of nearly 50 employees spread across three main office locations. Several employees are also embedded at client locations in the United States and abroad.

A member of the Firm's newly formed diversity and inclusion (D&I) committee contacted the lead author in the summer of 2020 through a referral from a mutual colleague. The contact client (Schein, 1999) sought support from someone who could assist the Firm with "cultural and systemic issues." In our exchange, it became clear that the organization was responding in part to the murder of George Floyd, an unarmed Black US citizen, and its aftermath, which prompted widespread civil unrest and demands for racial justice throughout the United States and the world. The Firm's D&I committee felt strongly that this was a critical moment to address issues of race and DEI work at the Firm and thus sought external support to make recommendations to senior leadership on how to advance.

Contracting

During the contracting phase, the contact client stated that the D&I committee was seeking

> ...an objective and brutally honest look at where our organization currently is – in terms of culture, D&I, and related progress – and any advice on steps we can take to make positive change in the coming months/years.

At the first in-person meeting, the contact client indicated that the D&I committee had been formed two weeks prior. Though the impetus for its formation was related to the larger systemic racial injustice issues plaguing the country, it also became clear that the Firm's culture was in need of examination. The culture was described as evolving yet toxic, particularly for women. The leadership team was exclusively White and male, despite a roughly 50/50 balance of men and women at lower levels of the organization. The contact client also described the Firm as having "zero LGBT individuals and zero people of color," which he considered an urgent problem given the larger sociopolitical climate. Thus, in parallel with other studies cited on DEI and organizational change, the presenting problem was representation.

The contact client shared that the primary goal of a possible consulting engagement was to take a hard look at "culture or D&I" related to representation. In particular, he requested tangible recommendations for a "D&I strategy roadmap," to address training, selection, and performance management. The internal D&I committee did not feel "equipped to lay out this roadmap" and therefore wanted the assistance of a third party to conduct an audit of their current practices and ensure "accountability." The contact client emphasized that the work should not be "exclusively D&I focused but should incorporate D&I." The lead author was asked to draft a short proposal for the consulting engagement to share with senior leadership. In addition to recommendations, the contact client communicated that the proposal should put a clear monetary value on the work.

The lead author sent a scope of work to the client two weeks after the initial contracting conversation. Consistent with the CLC framework, he recommended a two-phased approach. Phase One would include an audit of the entire organizational system (cf. Selzer & Foley, 2018) in an effort to surface the ways that the context, levels of analysis issues, and culture interrelate and influence DEI opportunities at the Firm. There were several reasons to pursue this strategy in lieu of focusing solely on DEI in Phase One. First, although issues of representation were highlighted in the initial request for services, focusing on recruitment and selection would have been counterproductive. Data indicating that the Firm had difficulty retaining women and employees of color suggested a systemic diagnosis was needed. Second, we noticed ambivalence on the part of the contact client regarding the degree to which the engagement should focus exclusively on DEI. This ambivalence seemed like a relevant data point about the organization's culture, considering that the death of George Floyd had sparked the formation of the D&I committee, and that the initial conversation highlighted representation as the presenting challenge. Finally, as discussed, failure to adopt a systems approach is likely why there was a lack of progress on DEI issues at the Firm in the first place.

Phase Two of the proposal entailed the development of a "diversity roadmap," grounded in data from the systems audit and guided by best practices in the diversity management literature. This roadmap would offer tangible recommendations related to areas previously identified as needing attention, including training, recruitment, selection, and performance management. The development of the roadmap would also include accountability mechanisms designed to ensure systematic progress and alignment across different DEI initiatives. The goal in offering this approach was to help develop a strategy directly informed by and aligned with the Firm's culture.

We sent the proposal to the contact client and scheduled a meeting with the D&I committee. During the meeting, the committee questioned the lead consultant about the following: Why should the Firm hire an individual contractor (versus a DEI consultancy)? Why recommend a two-phased approach (versus providing direct attention to DEI issues)? Why request an 8-month timeframe (versus "banging it out" quickly)? Why not provide tentative recommendations before the end of the fiscal year? And, why not establish "quick wins" along the way? We communicated the importance of a whole system organization change approach to DEI work and how interventions undertaken without a full understanding of the organization's culture could be both mistargeted and unsustainable. We also emphasized that DEI work is in part about the differential application of workplace norms and practices to different constituent and identity groups, and that to improve the experiences of those groups in tangible ways, a full explication and examination of those norms and practices would be required. This latter point was made to emphasize that DEI work *is* culture work, a consistent refrain echoed throughout the engagement.

Two months later, we were informed that the Firm wished to move forward. The D&I committee had attended a two-day training by a diversity consultancy and examined proposals from large DEI consulting firms. They agreed that the two-phased approach aligned better with their needs, and that it was the most customized and least "boilerplate" proposal offered. The contact client indicated he was authorized to hire us, pending the solicitation of references and a final interview with a member of the senior leadership team who was tasked with overseeing the D&I committee's work on this project and who we were told would simply "sign off" on the committee's recommendation. That "sign off" process was more complicated than the contact client had indicated, involving multiple conversations and proposal revisions between the lead consultant and the senior leadership team and suggesting that the D&I committee was not being fully authorized by senior leadership to make a hiring recommendation.

Data Collection and Diagnosis

As is often the case with OD work, phases of the consulting process are neither discrete nor linear (Burke & Noumair, 2015). Phase One began as we attempted to agree on the data sources to inform the systems audit. It would take another two months to finalize the contract, resulting in an overall contracting period of four months before the contract was signed and five months before the audit began. Several sources of tension emerged during the latter half of this period, including a lack of alignment between the senior leadership team and the D&I committee regarding the purpose of the engagement, a demand for "actionable" reports and recommendations, and a requirement to see sample deliverables from the consultants' previous DEI engagements with other clients. Each of these sources of tension represented dynamics above and beneath the surface (Nou-mair, Pfaff, John, Gipson, & Brazaitis, 2017), reflecting logistical requests that are both reasonable and also may indicate sources of resistance. In particular, the lack of alignment between senior leadership and the D&I committee about how much the engagement should focus on DEI was particularly noteworthy. Despite the contact client decrying a lack of representation as a primary concern, and members of the D&I committee advocating for a more explicit DEI approach in the proposal, the senior leader charged with overseeing the D&I committee stated that "the success of the Firm's journey is not about D&I, but about uncovering all kinds of needs, opportunities and insights." Somewhat ironically, this lack of alignment between senior leaders and the D&I committee actually made it easier to implement a systems frame, as it leveraged the ambivalence toward DEI located within the Firm's all-male and all-White senior leadership team.

The CLC framework guided both the data collection and diagnosis phases of the systems audit, while anecdotal data points regarding the Firm's culture continued to emerge from interpersonal interactions between the client and the consultants. Consistent with an ODC approach, those interactions reflected the very norms and practices the audit would also surface. Thus, it became critical to ensure that the audit assessed important contextual and cultural factors across levels of the organization in an attempt to determine how DEI issues were manifesting. Planning for the systems audit was done in full collaboration with the D&I committee and the organization's senior leadership, consistent with an action research approach to organizational diagnosis and change (Coghlan, 2019). Over the course of two hour-long meetings, the consultant and the com-mittee discussed various focal areas that were likely to influence the organiza-tion's D&I work and contribute to its current state (e.g., the Firm's overall climate for inclusion, top management support for change). Additionally, several members of the D&I committee felt that assessing possible sources of readiness and resistance would be an important component to any subsequent D&I strategy. A complete list of focal areas generated by this process, and the asso-ciated measures and items used to assess them, is included in Table 3.

We employed two phases of data collection, consistent with OD practice (Burke & Noumair, 2015). First, we sent an organization-wide survey to all employees. To assess context, employees responded to a series of open-ended questions about the nature of their work, the services they provide, and prevalent factors in the external environment (Gonzalez, 2010). We also included quanti-tative assessments related to change readiness (Holt, Armenakis, Field, & Harris, 2007) and perceptions of climate for inclusion (Nishii, 2013). To address levels of analysis, we included items designed to assess group and organization-level variables that might impact individual outcomes (Joshi & Roh, 2009), including perceptions of the Firm's management practices, mission, and strategy (Burke & Litwin, 1992). We also collected demographic data to examine differ-ences between groups and units based on social and functional identities and to aggregate climate data to the unit-level of analysis. Finally, to address culture, we used Cameron and Quinn's (2011) Organizational Culture Assessment Instru-ment (OCAI), a validated measure of organizational culture. We also added

Table 3. Sample Measures and Items for Use with the Context-Levels-Culture Diagnostic Framework.

	Context	Levels	Culture
Existing scales	Change Readiness (Holt et al., 2007) Climate for Inclusion (Nishii, 2013)	Mission/Strategy Leadership Management Practices Work Unit Climate (Burke & Litwin, 1992)	Organizational Culture Assessment Instrument (Cameron & Quinn, 2011)
Select open-ended items	What are the barriers and hindrances that prevent you from doing the kind of work you feel you should or want to be doing?	Demographic questions pertaining to functional role, organizational rank, and tenure.	What three words or phrases would you use to describe the way things are done in this organization?
Select focus group/ interview items	How would you describe the nature of the work you do? How would having a diverse workforce enhance your work?	How do you feel the senior leadership team functions?	What does it feel like to be a woman in this organization? One theme that arose in the survey data was a culture of bullying; can you help me better understand this?

several open-ended questions that asked employees to describe the Firm's current and ideal culture.

To ensure full participation, all data were collected directly and anonymously by the lead consultant using an external platform to host the survey (Qualtrics), and all employees were informed that their responses would be kept strictly confidential. They were also told that no identifying information would be presented, and that all data shared with the organization would be shared in the aggregate. The lead consultant conducted all quantitative and qualitative data analyses. Quantitative data were examined using standard descriptive statistics (means, standard deviations, and frequencies), and basic mean comparisons were conducted to determine if significant differences existed between organizational demographic groups on some of the scales measured. Qualitative data were content analyzed for common themes, with a theme being classified as a similar response shared by at least five organizational members.

Themes from the open-ended survey data informed the second phase of the systems audit, which included four different employee focus groups and interviews with the Firm's five senior leaders. With the exception of the climate for inclusion measure, only one of the quantitative or qualitative survey items directly addressed employee perceptions of DEI at the Firm. Despite this, most survey responses organically indicated DEI challenges in some way. In fact, results from the survey suggested that new employees (i.e., tenure of less than five years), female employees, and employees from the technical side of the Firm (versus the creative side) experienced the Firm's culture as challenging to navigate. For this reason, focus groups were set up for three constituent groups, women, newer employees and those from a specific technical function, in addition to a general focus group for all employees. We designed eight focus group questions to further explore key themes in the open-ended survey data and attended to DEI issues in these questions more explicitly. For example, we asked each focus group to reflect on what it felt like to be a member of their specific demographic group in the organization (e.g., "What does it feel like to be a woman in this organization?"). Each group was also asked how having a diverse workforce might enhance the nature of the Firm's work. We asked senior leaders the same questions as focus group participants, in addition to four other questions related to the Firm's business model, vision and strategy, and the overall functioning of the senior leadership team. We interviewed the Firm's Chairman and CEO last.

Although data analysis is ongoing, several immediate themes emerged from the open-ended survey, focus group, and interview data that reinforce the benefit of a systems approach to DEI and organizational change. First, and foremost, it became clear that DEI issues at the Firm sit at the nexus of social identity and organizational culture. Although the lack of employees of color and openly LGBTQ+ employees is notable and problematic, the data revealed how the culture conspires to make the workplace environment particularly inhospitable to members of marginalized or low power groups. For example, several employees referred to the culture as "aggressive" and "bullying," a perception acknowledged and in some cases appreciated by the Firm's senior leaders. Separately, representation challenges and an aggressive culture are not particularly revelatory organizational problems. Taken together, however, they reveal a complex masculinity contest culture (Berdahl, Cooper, Glick, Livingston, & Williams, 2018) that serves to marginalize women, LGBTQ+ employees, and employees of color whose values and approaches to the workplace may not align with the Firm's norms and practices and the taken-for-granted assumptions and behaviors of its senior leaders.

Second, the lack of alignment between senior leadership and the D&I committee uncovered during the initial contracting phase foretold a general lack of alignment between and within numerous competitive factions in the Firm, including misalignment between the Firm's five senior leaders regarding its future directions, the nature of the consulting engagement, and how employee concerns at the Firm should be addressed and managed. Relatedly, it became clear that newer employees and those with advanced tenure had markedly different perceptions of the organizational climate and the consulting engagement, with several long-standing members of the organization confiding that the Firm had hired other consultants before for "this type of thing" and that "nothing would come of it," particularly with the Firm's founder and CEO remaining in his role. To that end, there was a general sense among some that senior leaders were paying lip service to D&I issues, but would not commit to the work of change on this issue.

Finally, the entire systems audit process revealed fairly significant leadership and succession planning issues as core drivers of the Firm's current challenges that were somewhat masked by the initial focus on D&I and the lack of diverse representation among the Firm's staff. A deeper analysis of the data revealed concerns with the Firm's most senior leaders and a general feeling of powerlessness to address those concerns. This feeling of powerlessness was juxtaposed in the data with a sense that a change in leadership was needed, and that organizational survival required significant attention to succession planning, innovation, and diversity to ensure the Firm remained competitive. This was unsurprising to us as consultants, considering that senior leadership had confidentially disclosed that a succession plan was being implemented and a new organizational structure would be announced the following year, despite the fact that a preliminary analysis of the data was not yet available. In this way, the systems audit process itself became caught in the misalignment between the founder and CEO, the senior leadership team, and the D&I committee, reflecting the very masculinity contest culture the audit had begun to reveal.

See Table 4 for a timeline of consultant activities related to the entire consulting engagement.

Implications of the Case for the CLC Framework

As is often the case with DEI work, the presenting problem brought before the consultants was born of two factors – an organizational response to a crisis in the external environment and a lack of diverse representation among the Firm's employees. The use of a systems, organization change approach, as operationalized by the CLC framework, allowed the consultants to contract with the client to collect data on a wide range of organizational factors so that a more nuanced, contextualized understanding of the presenting DEI problem could be surfaced. In theory, this understanding should allow for the design of organizational interventions that are both better targeted to the actual problem and also better designed to produce transformational shifts in the organization's culture or deep structure. It is doubtful that any traditional, individual-level DEI intervention, such as training, recruitment, selection, mentoring, or networking, would have had a significant or sustainable impact on the lived experiences of underrepresented employees in this organization or that an individual-level intervention would influence the differential application of the implicit workplace norms and practices that keep the faultlines of organizational DEI challenges active. To that end, the CLC framework helps illustrate why increasing the numbers of women and people of color in an organization is an insufficient metric of success for DEI work. A true metric for success must also include the development of different structural and relational patterns between and among all of the actors in the system. As Cameron and Quinn (2011) articulate, without "new values, ways of thinking, managerial styles, paradigms, and approaches to problem solving," (p. 12) there is little chance that sustainable progress on issues of workplace DEI will ever occur.

Implications of the CLC Framework for ODC Research and Practice

Given our review of the current literature on DEI and organizational change, the CLC framework offers a number of implications for research and practice. First, our approach provides a unifying framework through which scholars and

Table 4. Timeline of Consulting Activities with the Firm.

Task	Responsible Parties	Timing
• Initial scouting conversations	Contact client; lead consultant	Early July
• First proposal sent	Lead consultant	Mid July
• Interview with full D&I committee	D&I committee; lead consultant	Early August
• Meeting with senior leadership representative	Sr. leader; lead consultant	Early September
• Ongoing communication with senior leadership representative and contact client about proposal concerns/revisions	Sr. leader; contact client; lead consultant	September/ October
• Final agreement signed	Sr. leader; lead consultant	Mid November
• Systems audit kickoff meeting	Sr. leader; D&I committee; lead consultant	Late November
• Audit survey planning	Sr. leader; D&I committee; lead consultant	Late November
• Discussion with entire senior leadership team about audit survey	Sr. leadership; lead consultant; HR representative	Early December
• Culture audit survey finalized and distributed to organization	Lead consultant	Mid December
• Focus group planning	Lead consultant; D&I committee; Sr. leader	Early January
• Focus groups conducted	Lead consultant	Mid January
• Senior leader interviews conducted	Lead consultant	Mid January
• Data analysis	Lead consultant	February/ March
• Preliminary data feedback meeting	Lead consultant; Sr. leadership; D&I committee	Early April
• Action planning	D&I committee; Sr. leadership; lead consultant	Q2–Q3
• D&I roadmap	Lead consultant; D&I committee	TBD

practitioners can conceptualize and study workplace diversity as a dynamic organization change issue instead of a static, individual-level phenomenon (Block & Noumair, 2017; Gonzalez, 2010). Currently, empirical studies focused on DEI change efforts adopt a wide range of diagnostic processes to inform interventions. Some interview key stakeholders about the DEI challenges they see in their organizations (e.g., Chin et al., 2016; Nkomo & Kriek, 2011). Others present a mixed-methods case study approach drawing from archival data, participant observations, focus groups, and survey data in an effort to assess and intervene (e.g., Bilimoria & Singer, 2019; O'Meara et al., 2019). Many studies examine DEI interventions at the individual level. However, our systematic review of the literature revealed that scholars rarely use the same methods (e.g., interview protocols, survey measures) for diagnosis, nor are they guided by a single, coherent conceptual or diagnostic framework that approaches DEI change from a multilevel systems perspective. As a result, it is difficult, if not impossible, to draw generalizable conclusions from the existing literature, compare findings across different studies, or build a cumulative conceptual and practical knowledge base regarding how to approach DEI change systemically. The CLC framework directly addresses these limitations.

Second, the framework integrates the perspectives of several conceptual critiques of the current DEI change literature (e.g., Golom, 2018; Gonzalez, 2010; Gotsis & Kortezi, 2015; Vinkenburg, 2017) into three dimensions, each of which can be further developed using the mainstream management literature, the ODC-focused DEI literature, and the ODC literature writ large, including more recent work on complex adaptive systems (Olson & Eoyang, 2001) and dialogic OD (Bushe & Marshak, 2014). For example, research examining contextual moderators of workplace demography effects (Joshi & Roh, 2009) or cross-level models of workplace diversity (Roberson et al., 2017) can be used to incorporate additional variables into the CLC framework beyond those used in the current client example (e.g., climate for inclusion, external environment, change readiness). In this way, the CLC framework provides a structure for diagnosis that is both prescribed and customizable, allowing it to be tailored to specific organizational contexts while remaining conceptually unified around three core dimensions of DEI systems change.

Third, the framework offers an explicit consulting tool that ODC practitioners can use when they approach critically important, and likely sensitive, DEI projects, satisfying a need recently highlighted by Ferdman (2020). As the case example and our systematic review reveal, the temptation when addressing DEI challenges in organizations is to conceptualize and treat them as if they result from psychoeducational gaps at the individual level or a lack of representation. Yet, if the dominant conceptual frame on DEI work is an individual-level one, then the interventions that follow will likely be at the individual level as well (Golom, 2018). For ODC scholars and practitioners who recognize the central role that system-wide interventions play in creating successful transformational change, the need for a coherent systems framework to guide these interventions is essential. Said another way, without a comprehensive systems diagnosis and subsequent systems-level intervention, the organization's fundamental culture will remain unchanged and any DEI goals and initiatives are likely to fail (Cameron & Quinn, 2011).

Relatedly, a common critique of systems approaches to change is that they lend themselves more easily to diagnosis than they do to intervention and action (Golom, 2018; Meadows, 2008). However, as ODC scholars and practitioners often note (Burke & Noumair, 2015), the act of diagnosing a client system is itself an intervention. As the case illustrates, employees and senior leaders at the Firm both influenced and were subtly influenced by the data gathering and diagnostic process, even though formal interventions based on the systems audit have yet to be proposed. Additionally, the CLC framework has other implications for the content and process of intervening in a client system and creating change around DEI. For example, both Schein (2016) and Cameron and Quinn (2011) offer models of managed culture change in their respective books on organizational culture. These models recommend that consultants walk their clients through phases (unfreezing, cognitive restructuring, refreezing) or discrete steps of the change process. However, they do not explicitly incorporate assessment content related to DEI concerns and are not based on a thorough, multilevel diagnostic of the entire organizational system. As a result, they do not necessarily allow for explicit attention to the contextual and multilevel factors that we argue are likely to influence how DEI issues manifest in organizations and that should inform any DEI intervention. Similar tensions exist between other content-based (Burke & Litwin, 1992) and process-based (Kotter, 2007) models of change, suggesting that one potential implication of the CLC framework for future ODC research and practice could be its integration with well-regarded intervention models for designing an organizational culture change process.

Finally, and perhaps most importantly, given the middling effectiveness of most contemporary DEI workplace initiatives and their lack of impact on both employee behavior and sociodemographic representation, we hope that the CLC framework provides a potentially fruitful path forward toward sustainable DEI change that is conceptually grounded in the systems literature and broad enough to be applicable to a range of specific client contexts. To that end, we recognize the degree to which any one model offers both a limited and a limiting perspective on the realities of organizational life (Noumair et al., 2017). This is particularly true with respect to the complex, multifaceted, multilevel, and deeply embedded nature of DEI issues in organizations. Overly specific models and frameworks are likely to be ineffective at encouraging people to think about the interdependent and contingent norms and relationships that lock organizations into entrenched patterns of exclusion. Encouraging DEI practitioners and their clients to shift their mindsets toward thinking systemically is a stronger leverage point for change than any specific individual-level DEI intervention or a list of pre-determined organizational change steps. While work with the Firm is ongoing, there is enough data to suggest, both in the case and in the DEI and organizational change literatures writ large, that approaching diversity and inclusion issues as simply issues of representation, bias, or social identity is to miss them at best or create intractable in-group/out-group dynamics at worst.

CONCLUSION

The goal of this chapter was to address how to frame DEI issues from a systems perspective and how to conduct an ODC diagnosis of workplace diversity and inclusion challenges within that framing. While it is too soon to declare "*you don't do diversity work by doing diversity work"* (similar to the adage that *"you don't change culture by trying to change culture"*), the CLC framework may expand our ability to conceptualize workplace DEI initiatives from a whole system, organizational culture change perspective instead of an individual-level diversity and difference one. The framework offers a more uniform approach to diagnosing DEI challenges in organizations that, if used across a wide range of institutional contexts, may be better able to detect common barriers and target more effective system-wide solutions, thereby increasing the likelihood that organizations experience the type of transformational change they believe they seek.

ACKNOWLEDGMENTS

The authors would like to thank the editors of *ROCD* for their insightful, constructive, and helpful feedback. It is a better chapter for your efforts.

REFERENCES

Note: Works identified with an * signify that they were part of our literature search but may not be cited directly in this chapter.

Abramovitz, M., & Blitz, L. V. (2015). Moving toward racial equity: The undoing racism workshop and organizational change. *Race and Social Problems*, *7*(2), 97–110.

*Akpapuna, M., Choi, E., Johnson, D. A., & Lopez, J. A. (2020). Encouraging multiculturalism and diversity within organizational behavior management. *Journal of Organizational Behavior Management*, *40*(3–4), 86–209.

Anand, R., & Winters, M. F. (2008). A retrospective view of corporate diversity training from 1964 to the present. *Academy of Management Learning & Education*, *7*(3), 356–372.

Anderson, D., & Ackerman Anderson, L. S. (2001). *Beyond change management: Advanced strategies for today's transformational leaders*. San Francisco, CA: Jossey-Bass.

Bartunek, J. M., & Moch, M. K. (1987). First-order, second-order, and third-order change and organization development interventions: A cognitive approach. *The Journal of Applied Behavioral Science*, *23*(4), 483–500.

*Beba, U., & Church, A. H. (2020). Changing the game for women leaders at PepsiCo: From local action to enterprise accountability. *Consulting Psychology Journal: Practice and Research*, *72*(4), 288–302.

Berdahl, J. L., Cooper, M., Glick, P., Livingston, R. W., & Williams, J. C. (2018). Work as a masculinity contest. *Journal of Social Issues*, *74*(3), 422–448.

*Berry, J. W. (2020). How shall we all work together? Achieving diversity and equity in work settings. *Organizational Dynamics*, *50*, 100750.

*Bilimoria, D., & Singer, L. T. (2019). Institutions developing excellence in academic leadership (IDEAL). *Equality, Diversity and Inclusion: An International Journal*, *38*(3), 362–381.

Block, C. J., & Noumair, D. A. (2015). Call for papers: Understanding diversity dynamics in systems: Social equality as an organization change issue. *The Journal of Applied Behavioral Science*, *51*, 5–9.

*Block, C. J., & Noumair, D. A. (2017). Understanding diversity dynamics in systems: Social equality as an organization change issue. *The Journal of Applied Behavioral Science*, *53*(2), 150–155.

*Brewis, D. N. (2019). Duality and fallibility in practices of the self: The 'inclusive subject' in diversity training. *Organization Studies*, *40*(1), 93–114.

*Burchiellaro, O. (2020). Queering control and inclusion in the contemporary organization: On 'LGBT-friendly control' and the reproduction of (queer) value. *Organization Studies*, *41*(7), 1–25.

Burke, W. W. (2017). *Organization change: Theory and practice*. Los Angeles, CA: Sage Publications.

Burke, W. W., & Litwin, G. H. (1992). A causal model of organizational performance and change. *Journal of Management, 18*(3), 523–545.

Burke, W. W., & Noumair, D. A. (2015). *Organization development: A process of learning and changing*. Indianapolis, IN: FT Press.

Bushe, G. R., & Marshak, R. J. (2014). The dialogic mindset in organization development. *Research in Organizational Change and Development, 22*, 55–97.

Cachat-Rosset, G., Carillo, K., & Klarsfeld, A. (2019). Reconstructing the concept of diversity climate–A critical review of its definition, dimensions, and operationalization. *European Management Review, 16*(4), 863–885.

Cameron, K. S., & Quinn, R. E. (2011). *Diagnosing and changing organizational culture: Based on the competing values framework*. New York, NY: Wiley.

*Carrillo Arciniega, L. (2021). Selling diversity to white men: How disentangling economics from morality is a racial and gendered performance. *Organization, 28*(2), 228–246.

*Carter-Sowell, A. R., Vaid, J., Stanley, C. A., Petitt, B., & Battle, J. S. (2019). ADVANCE scholar program: Enhancing minoritized scholars' professional visibility. *Equality, Diversity and Inclusion: An International Journal, 38*(3), 305–327.

*Cavanaugh, C., & Green, K. (2020). Training faculty search committees to improve racial and ethnic diversity in hiring. *Consulting Psychology Journal: Practice and Research, 72*(4), 263–274.

Chang, E. H., Milkman, K. L., Gromet, D. M., Rebele, R. W., Massey, C., Duckworth, A. L., & Grant, A. M. (2019). The mixed effects of online diversity training. *Proceedings of the National Academy of Sciences, 116*(16), 7778–7783.

Chartered Association of Business Schools. (2018, March). Academic journal guide 2018 methodology. Retrieved from https://charteredabs.org/wp-content/uploads/2018/03/AJG2018-Methodology.pdf

Chatman, J. A. (1989). Improving interactional organizational research: A model of person-organization fit. *Academy of Management Review, 14*(3), 333–349.

*Cheng, S., Corrington, A., Dinh, J., Hebl, M., King, E., Ng, L., … Traylor, A. (2019). Challenging diversity training myths: Changing the conversation about diversity training to shape science and practice. *Organizational Dynamics, 48*(4), 1–11.

*Chin, J. L., Desormeaux, L., & Sawyer, K. (2016). Making way for paradigms of diversity leadership. *Consulting Psychology Journal: Practice and Research, 68*(1), 49–71.

*Chrobot-Mason, D., & Aramovich, N. P. (2013). The psychological benefits of creating an affirming climate for workplace diversity. *Group & Organization Management, 38*(6), 659–689.

Cocchiara, F. K., Connerley, M. L., & Bell, M. P. (2010). "A GEM" for increasing the effectiveness of diversity training. *Human Resource Management, 49*(6), 1089–1106.

Coghlan, D. (2019). *Doing action research in your own organization*. Thousand Oaks, CA: Sage Publications.

*Coleman, P. T., Coon, D., Kim, R., Chung, C., Bass, R., Regan, B., & Anderson, R. (2017). Promoting constructive multicultural attractors: Fostering unity and fairness from diversity and conflict. *The Journal of Applied Behavioral Science, 53*(2), 180–211.

*Dahanayake, P., Rajendran, D., Selvarajah, C., & Ballantyne, G. (2018). Justice and fairness in the workplace: A trajectory for managing diversity. *Equality, Diversity and Inclusion: An International Journal, 37*(5), 470–490.

Davidson, M. N. (1999). The value of being included: An examination of diversity change initiatives in organizations. *Performance Improvement Quarterly, 12*, 164–180.

Deitch, E. A., Barsky, A., Butz, R. M., Chan, S., Brief, A. P., & Bradley, J. (2003). Subtle yet significant: The existence and impact of everyday racial discrimination in the workplace. *Social Relations, 56*, 1299–1324.

Devine, P. G., & Ash, T. L. (2022). Diversity training goals, limitations, and promise: A review of the multidisciplinary literature. *Annual Review of Psychology, 73*, 1.1–1.27.

DiTomaso, N. (2010). A sociocultural framework on diversity requires structure as well as culture and social psychology. *Psychological Inquiry, 21*(2), 100–107.

Dobbin, F., & Kalev, A. (2016). Why diversity programs fail. *Harvard Business Review, 94*(7), 52–60.

Dobbin, F., & Kalev, A. (2018). Why doesn't diversity training work. *Anthropology Now, 10*(2), 48–55.

Dobbin, F., Schrage, D., & Kalev, A. (2015). Rage against the iron cage: The varied effects of bureaucratic personnel reforms on diversity. *American Sociological Review, 80*(5), 1014–1044.

*Dobusch, L. (2014). How exclusive are inclusive organisations? *Equality, Diversity and Inclusion: An International Journal, 33*(3), 220–234.

*Downey, S. N., van der Werff, L., Thomas, K. M., & Plaut, V. C. (2015). The role of diversity practices and inclusion in promoting trust and employee engagement. *Journal of Applied Social Psychology, 45*(1), 35–44.

*Easley, C. A. (2010). Expanding a conversation: Is how we live as a culturally diverse society congruent with our underlying assumptions, methodologies, and theories regarding change? *The Journal of Applied Behavioral Science, 46*(1), 55–72.

Ely, R. J., & Thomas, D. A. (2001). Cultural diversity at work: The effects of diversity perspectives on work group processes and outcomes. *Administrative Science Quarterly, 46*(2), 229–273.

*Evans, C. (2014). Diversity management and organizational change. *Equality, Diversity and Inclusion: An International Journal, 33*(6), 482–493.

*Ferdman, B. M. (2014). Toward infusing diversity and inclusion as core elements of OD. *OD Practitioner, 46*(4), 44–46.

*Ferdman, B. M. (2017). Paradoxes of inclusion: Understanding and managing the tensions of diversity and multiculturalism. *The Journal of Applied Behavioral Science, 53*(2), 235–263.

Ferdman, B. M. (2020). The state of progress in diversity and inclusion initiatives: Perspectives for consulting psychology. *Consulting Psychology Journal: Practice and Research, 72*(4), 243–246.

Ferdman, B. M. (2021). Inclusive leadership: The fulcrum of inclusion. In B. M. Ferdman, J. Prime, & R. E. Riggio (Eds.), *Inclusive leadership: Transforming diverse lives, workplaces, and societies* (pp. 3–24). New York, NY: Routledge.

Finckh, C., & Reich, K. (2016). Systemic constellations in diversity management. *The International Journal of Organizational Diversity, 16*(4), 17–38.

*Foldy, E. G., & Buckley, T. R. (2017). Reimagining cultural competence: Bringing buried dynamics into the light. *The Journal of Applied Behavioral Science, 53*(2), 264–289.

Forscher, P. S., Lai, C. K., Axt, J. R., Ebersole, C. R., Herman, M., Devine, P. G., & Nosek, B. A. (2019). A meta-analysis of procedures to change implicit measures. *Journal of Personality and Social Psychology, 117*(3), 522–559.

*Gagnon, S., Augustin, T. J., & Cukier, W. (2021). EXPRESS: Interplay for change in equality, diversity and inclusion studies. *Human Relations, 1–50.

*Gassam, J. Z., & Salter, N. P. (2020). Considerations for hiring external consultants to deliver diversity trainings. *Consulting Psychology Journal: Practice and Research, 72*(4), 275–287.

*Gavino, M. C., Eber, J. E., & Bell, D. (2010). Celebrating our diversity: Creating an inclusive climate in a US university. *Equality, Diversity and Inclusion: An International Journal, 29*(4), 395–405.

Gersick, C. J. (1991). Revolutionary change theories: A multilevel exploration of the punctuated equilibrium paradigm. *Academy of Management Review, 16*(1), 10–36.

Golom, F. D. (2015). Creating systemic change around lesbian, gay, bisexual and transgender (LGBT) issues: A case analysis and recommendations. In J. C. Hawley (Ed.), *Expanding the circle: Creating an inclusive environment in higher education for LGBTQ students and studies* (pp. 107–126). Albany, NY: State University of New York (SUNY) Press.

Golom, F. D. (2018). Reframing the dominant diversity discourse: Alternate conversations for creating whole system change. *Metropolitan Universities, 29*(1), 11–27.

*Gonzalez, J. A. (2010). Diversity change in organizations: A systemic, multilevel, and nonlinear process. *The Journal of Applied Behavioral Science, 46*(2), 197–219.

Gotsis, G., & Kortezi, Z. (2015). Operationalizing critical diversity theories: A contextual framework of implementing new diversity practices. In *Critical studies in diversity management literature* (pp. 69–98). Dordrecht: Springer.

*Greene, R. D., & Berthoud, H. (2015). OD is diversity. *OD Practitioner, 47*(4), 36–41.

*Groggins, A., & Ryan, A. M. (2013). Embracing uniqueness: The underpinnings of a positive climate for diversity. *Journal of Occupational and Organizational Psychology, 86*(2), 264–282.

Guillaume, Y. R., Dawson, J. F., Woods, S. A., Sacramento, C. A., & West, M. A. (2013). Getting diversity at work to work: What we know and what we still don't know. *Journal of Occupational and Organizational Psychology, 86*, 123–141.

*Hanappi-Egger, E. (2012). "Shall I stay or shall I go"? *Equality, Diversity and Inclusion: An International Journal, 31*(2), 144–157.

Harvey, W. B. (2016, February 21). How many protests will it take to finally diversify our campuses? *The Chronicle of Higher Education.* Retrieved from http://www.chronicle.com

*Hayes, T. L., Oltman, K. A., Kaylor, L. E., & Belgudri, A. (2020). How leaders can become more committed to diversity management. *Consulting Psychology Journal: Practice and Research, 72*(4), 247–262.

*Heitner, K. L., Kahn, A. E., & Sherman, K. C. (2013). Building consensus on defining success of diversity work in organizations. *Consulting Psychology Journal: Practice and Research, 65*(1), 58–73.

*Hennes, E. P., Pietri, E. S., Moss-Racusin, C. A., Mason, K. A., Dovidio, J. F., Brescoll, V. L., … Handelsman, J. (2018). Increasing the perceived malleability of gender bias using a modified video intervention for diversity in STEM (VIDS). *Group Processes & Intergroup Relations, 21*(5), 788–809.

*Heracleous, L., & Bartunek, J. (2021). Organization change failure, deep structures and temporality: Appreciating Wonderland. *Human Relations, 74*(2), 208–233.

*Herdman, A. O., & McMillan-Capehart, A. (2010). Establishing a diversity program is not enough: Exploring the determinants of diversity climate. *Journal of Business and Psychology, 25*(1), 39–53.

*Holck, L. (2016). Putting diversity to work. *Equality, Diversity and Inclusion: An International Journal, 35*(4), 296–307.

*Holck, L., Muhr, S. L., & Villeseche, F. (2016). Identity, diversity and diversity management: On theoretical connections, assumptions and implications for practice. *Equality, Diversity and Inclusion: An International Journal, 35*(1), 48–64.

Holmes IV, O., Jiang, K., Avery, D. R., McKay, P. F., Oh, I. S., & Tillman, C. J. (2021). A meta-analysis integrating 25 years of diversity climate research. *Journal of Management, 47*(6), 1357–1382.

Holt, D. T., Armenakis, A. A., Field, H. S., & Harris, S. G. (2007). Readiness for organizational change: The systematic development of a scale. *The Journal of Applied Behavioral Science, 43*(2), 232–255.

Hout, M. (2020). *A new compendium of trends in the general social survey, 1972–2018: Period and cohort trends and differences by race, gender, education, urban-rural, and region for 276 repeating items.* (GSS Social Change Report 64). National Opinion Research Center. Retrieved from http://gss.norc.org/Documents/reports/social-change-reports/SC64%20A%20new%20compendium%20of%20trends.pdf

*Jansen, W. S., Otten, S., & van der Zee, K. I. (2015). Being part of diversity: The effects of an all-inclusive multicultural diversity approach on majority members' perceived inclusion and support for organizational diversity efforts. *Group Processes & Intergroup Relations, 18*(6), 817–832.

Joshi, A., Liao, H., & Roh, H. (2011). Bridging domains in workplace demography research: A review and reconceptualization. *Journal of Management, 37*(2), 521–552.

Joshi, A., & Roh, H. (2009). The role of context in work team diversity research: A meta-analytic review. *Academy of Management Journal, 52*(3), 599–627.

Kalev, A., Dobbin, F., & Kelly, E. (2006). Best practices or best guesses? Assessing the efficacy of corporate affirmative action and diversity policies. *American Sociological Review, 71*(4), 589–617.

*Kalinoski, Z. T., Steele-Johnson, D., Peyton, E. J., Leas, K. A., Steinke, J., & Bowling, N. A. (2013). A meta-analytic evaluation of diversity training outcomes. *Journal of Organizational Behavior, 34*(8), 1076–1104.

Katzenbach, J. R., Steffen, I., & Kronley, C. (2012). Culture change that sticks. *Harvard Business Review, 90*(7), 110–117.

*Katz, J. H., & Miller, F. A. (2016). Defining diversity and adapting inclusion strategies on a global scale. *OD Practitioner, 48*(3), 42–47.

*Katz, J. H., & Miller, F. A. (2018). Diversity and inclusion in OD. *OD Practitioner, 50*(4), 16–21.

Kim, J. Y. J., Nguyen, D., & Block, C. (2019). The 360-degree experience of workplace microaggressions: Who commits them? How do individuals respond? What are the consequences? In G. C. Torino, D. P. Rivera, C. M. Capolilupo, K. L. Hadal, & D. W. Sue (Eds.), *Microaggression theory: Influence and implications* (pp. 159–178). San Francisco, CA: John Wiley & Sons, Inc.

Klein, K. J., Dansereau, F., & Hall, R. J. (1994). Levels issues in theory development, data collection, and analysis. *Academy of Management Review, 19*(2), 195–229.

*Koall, I. (2011). Managing complexity: Using ambivalence and contingency to support diversity in organizations. *Equality, Diversity and Inclusion: An International Journal, 30*(7), 572–588.

*Komaki, J. L., & Minnich, M. L. (2016). A behavioral approach to organizational change: Reinforcing those responsible for facilitating the climate and hence promoting diversity. *Journal of Organizational Behavior Management, 36*(2–3), 154–184.

Kotter, J. P. (2007). Leading change: Why transformation efforts fail. *Harvard Business Review, 86*, 97–103.

Kulik, C. T., & Roberson, L. (2008). Common goals and golden opportunities: Evaluations of diversity education in academic and organizational settings. *Academy of Management Learning & Education, 7*(3), 309–331.

Lau, D. C., & Murnighan, J. K. (1998). Demographic diversity and faultlines: The compositional dynamics of organizational groups. *Academy of Management Review, 23*(2), 325–340.

Leslie, L. M. (2019). Diversity initiative effectiveness: A typological theory of unintended consequences. *Academy of Management Review, 44*(3), 538–563.

*Leslie, L. M., Bono, J. E., Kim, Y. S., & Beaver, G. R. (2020). On melting pots and salad bowls: A meta-analysis of the effects of identity-blind and identity-conscious diversity ideologies. *Journal of Applied Psychology, 105*(5), 453–471.

Lewin, K. (1951). *Field theory in social science.* New York, NY: Harper.

Liang, D. W., Moreland, R., & Argote, L. (1995). Group versus individual training and group performance: The mediating role of transactive memory. *Personality and Social Psychology Bulletin, 21*(4), 384–393.

Lindsey, A. P., King, E., Amber, B., Sabat, I., & Ahmad, A. S. (2019). Examining why and for whom reflection diversity training works. *Personnel Assessment and Decisions, 5*(2), 82–90.

*Madera, J. M. (2018). Situational perspective taking as an intervention for improving attitudes toward organizations that invest in diversity management programs. *Journal of Business and Psychology, 33*(3), 423–442.

*McCluney, C. L., King, D. D., Bryant, C. M., & Ali, A. A. (2020). From "Calling in Black" to "Calling for Antiracism Resources": The need for systemic resources to address systemic racism. *Equality, Diversity and Inclusion: An International Journal, 40*(1), 49–59.

Meadows, D. H. (2008). *Thinking in systems: A primer.* White River Junction, VT: Chelsea Green Publishing.

Metha, S. (2019, November 21). Despite spending billions, companies can't buy diversity. *The Washington Post.* Retrieved from https://www.washingtonpost.com/outlook/despite-spending-billions-companies-cant-buy-diversity/2019/11/21/d8907b92-fb1a-11e9-ac8c-8eced29ca6ef_story.html

*Nadiv, R., & Kuna, S. (2020). Diversity management as navigation through organizational paradoxes. *Equality, Diversity and Inclusion: An International Journal, 39*(4), 355–377.

Nishii, L. H. (2013). The benefits of climate for inclusion for gender-diverse groups. *Academy of Management Journal, 56*(6), 1754–1774.

Nishii, L. H., & Rich, R. E. (2014). Creating inclusive climates in diverse organizations. In B. M. Ferdman & B. R. Deane (Eds.), *Diversity at work: The practice of inclusion* (pp. 330–363). San Francisco, CA: Jossey-Bass.

*Nkomo, S. M. (2020). Intersecting viruses: A clarion call for a new direction in diversity theorizing. *Equality, Diversity and Inclusion: An International Journal, 39*(7), 811–821.

*Nkomo, S. M. (2021). Reflections on the continuing denial of the centrality of "race" in management and organization studies. *Equality, Diversity and Inclusion: An International Journal, 40*(2), 212–224.

*Nkomo, S. M., & Kriek, D. (2011). Leading organizational change in the 'new' South Africa. *Journal of Occupational and Organizational Psychology*, *84*(3), 453–470.

Noumair, D. A., Pfaff, D. L., John, C. M. S., Gipson, A. N., & Brazaitis, S. J. (2017). X-ray vision at work: Seeing inside organizational life. In A. B. R. Shani & D. A. Noumair (Eds.), *Research in organizational change and development*. Bingley: Emerald Publishing Limited.

*Olsen, J. E., Parsons, C. K., Martins, L. L., & Ivanaj, V. (2016). Gender diversity programs, perceived potential for advancement, and organizational attractiveness: An empirical examination of women in the United States and France. *Group & Organization Management*, *41*(3), 271–309.

Olson, E. E., & Eoyang, G. H. (2001). *Facilitating organization change: Lessons from complexity science*. San Francisco, CA: Pfeiffer.

*O'Meara, K., Nyunt, G., Templeton, L., & Kuvaeva, A. (2019). Meeting to transgress. *Equality, Diversity and Inclusion: An International Journal*, *38*(3), 286–304.

*Opie, T., & Livingston, B. (2021). Shared Sisterhood™: Harnessing collective power to generate more inclusive and equitable organizations. *Organizational Dynamics*, 100833.

*Ortlieb, R., & Sieben, B. (2013). Diversity strategies and business logic: Why do companies employ ethnic minorities? *Group & Organization Management*, *38*(4), 480–511.

Perry, E. L., Block, C. J., & Noumair, D. A. (2020). Leading in: Inclusive leadership, inclusive climates and sexual harassment. *Equality, Diversity and Inclusion: An International Journal*, *40*(4), 430–447.

Perry, E. L., Golom, F. D., Catenacci, L., Ingraham, M. E., Covais, E. M., & Molina, J. J. (2017). Talkin' 'bout your generation: The impact of applicant age and generation on hiring-related perceptions and outcomes. *Work, Aging and Retirement*, *3*(2), 186–199.

Plaut, V. C. (2010). Diversity science: Why and how difference makes a difference. *Psychological Inquiry*, *21*, 77–99.

*Pringle, J. K., & Ryan, I. (2015). Understanding context in diversity management: A multi-level analysis. *Equality, Diversity and Inclusion: An International Journal*, *34*(6), 470–482.

Pugh, S. D., Dietz, J., Brief, A. P., & Wiley, J. W. (2008). Looking inside and out: The impact of employee and community demographic composition on organizational diversity climate. *Journal of Applied Psychology*, *93*(6), 1422–1428.

Ragins, B. R., & Ehrhardt, K. (2021). Gaining perspective: The impact of close cross-race friendships on diversity training and education. *Journal of Applied Psychology*, *106*(6), 1–26.

*Ravazzani, S. (2016). Understanding approaches to managing diversity in the workplace. *Equality, Diversity and Inclusion: An International Journal*, *35*(2), 154–168.

Rawski, S. L., & Conroy, S. A. (2020). Beyond demographic identities and motivation to learn: The effect of organizational identification on diversity training outcomes. *Journal of Organizational Behavior*, *41*(5), 461–478.

Richard, O. C., Kirby, S. L., & Chadwick, K. (2013). The impact of racial and gender diversity in management on financial performance: How participative strategy making features can unleash a diversity advantage. *The International Journal of Human Resource Management*, *24*(13), 2571–2582.

Roberson, Q. M. (2006). Disentangling the meanings of diversity and inclusion in organizations. *Group & Organization Management*, *31*(2), 212–236.

Roberson, Q. M. (2019). Diversity in the workplace: A review, synthesis, and future research agenda. *Annual Review of Organizational Psychology and Organizational Behavior*, *6*, 69–88.

Roberson, L., Kulik, C. T., & Tan, R. Y. (2013). Effective diversity training. In Q. M. Roberson (Ed.), *The Oxford handbook of diversity and work* (pp. 107–126). Oxford: Oxford University Press.

Roberson, Q., & Perry, J. L. (2021). Inclusive leadership in thought and action: A thematic analysis. *Group & Organization Management*, 10596011211013161.

*Roberson, Q., Ryan, A. M., & Ragins, B. R. (2017). The evolution and future of diversity at work. *Journal of Applied Psychology*, *102*(3), 483–499.

Salas, E., Grossman, R., Hughes, A. M., & Coultas, C. W. (2015). Measuring team cohesion: Observations from the science. *Human Factors*, *57*(3), 365–374.

Schein, E. H. (1999). The concept of client. In E. H. Schein (Ed.), *Process consultation revisited* (pp. 64–83). Boston, MA: Addison-Wesley.

Schein, E. H. (2016). *Organizational culture and leadership* (5th ed.). Hoboken, NJ: Wiley.

*Sekaquaptewa, D., Takahashi, K., Malley, J., Herzog, K., & Bliss, S. (2019). An evidence-based faculty recruitment workshop influences departmental hiring practice perceptions among university faculty. *Equality, Diversity and Inclusion: An International Journal, 38*(2), 188–210.

Selzer, R., & Foley, T. (2018). Implementing grassroots inclusive change through a cultural audit. *Qualitative Research in Organizations and Management: An International Journal,* 1–19.

Senge, P. M. (1990). *The fifth discipline: The art and practice of the learning organization.* New York, NY: Doubleday.

Shore, L. M., & Chung, B. G. (2021). Inclusive leadership: How leaders sustain or discourage work group inclusion. *Group & Organization Management,* 1059601121999580.

Shore, L. M., Cleveland, J. N., & Sanchez, D. (2018). Inclusive workplaces: A review and model. *Human Resource Management Review, 28*(2), 176–189.

Shore, L. M., Randel, A. E., Chung, B. G., Dean, M. A., Holcombe Ehrhart, K., & Singh, G. (2011). Inclusion and diversity in work groups: A review and model for future research. *Journal of Management, 37*(4), 1262–1289.

*Solebello, N., Tschirhart, M., & Leiter, J. (2016). The paradox of inclusion and exclusion in membership associations. *Human Relations, 69*(2), 439–460.

Stephens, N. M., Rivera, L. A., & Townsend, S. S. (2020). What works to increase diversity? A multilevel approach. *Research in Organizational Behavior,* 1–51.

Sue, D. W., Capodilupo, C. M., Torino, G. C., Bucceri, J. M., Holder, A., Nadal, K. L., & Esquilin, M. (2007). Racial microaggressions in everyday life: Implications for clinical practice. *American Psychologist, 62*(4), 271–286.

Syvantek, D. J., & Brown, L. L. (2000). A complex systems approach to organizations. *Current Directions in Psychological Science, 9*(2), 69–74.

Thomas, D. A. (2004, September). Diversity as strategy. *Harvard Business Review.*

*Thomas, K., & Ashburn-Nardo, L. (2020). Black lives matter…still: Moving beyond acknowledging the problem toward effective solutions in graduate training and education. *Equality, Diversity and Inclusion: An International Journal, 39*(7), 741–747.

Toossi, M. (2015, December). Labor force projections to 2024: The labor force is growing, but slowly. *Monthly Labor Review.* U.S. Bureau of Labor Statistics. https://doi.org/10.21916/mlr.2015.48

Triana, M. D. C., Gu, P., Chapa, O., Richard, O., & Colella, A. (2021). Sixty years of discrimination and diversity research in human resource management: A review with suggestions for future research directions. *Human Resource Management, 60*(1), 145–204.

*van den Brink, M. (2020). Reinventing the wheel over and over again: Organizational learning, memory and forgetting in doing diversity work. *Equality, Diversity and Inclusion: An International Journal, 39*(4), 379–393.

*Velasco, M., & Sansone, C. (2019). Resistance to diversity and inclusion change initiatives: Strategies for transformational leaders. *Organization Development Journal, 37*(3), 9–20.

*Vinkenburg, C. J. (2017). Engaging gatekeepers, optimizing decision making, and mitigating bias: Design specifications for systemic diversity interventions. *The Journal of Applied Behavioral Science, 53*(2), 212–234.

*Vos, M., Çelik, G., & de Vries, S. (2016). Making cultural differences matter? Diversity perspectives in higher education. *Equality, Diversity and Inclusion: An International Journal, 35*(4), 254–266.

Weick, K. E., & Quinn, R. E. (1999). Organization change and development. *Annual Review of Psychology, 50,* 361–386.

Wilton, L. S., Good, J. J., Moss-Racusin, C. A., & Sanchez, D. T. (2015). Communicating more than diversity: The effect of institutional diversity statements on expectations and performance as a function of race and gender. *Cultural Diversity and Ethnic Minority Psychology, 21*(3), 315–325.

*Yadav, S., & Lenka, U. (2020). Diversity management: A systematic review. *Equality, Diversity and Inclusion: An International Journal, 39*(8), 901–929.

*Yang, Y., & Konrad, A. M. (2011). Understanding diversity management practices: Implications of institutional theory and resource-based theory. *Group & Organization Management, 36*(1), 6–38.

*Yen, J., Riskin, E. A., Margherio, C., Spyridakis, J. H., Carrigan, C. M., & Cauce, A. M. (2019). Promoting gender diversity in STEM faculty through leadership development. *Equality, Diversity and Inclusion: An International Journal, 38*(3), 382–398.

APPENDIX 1

SEARCH TERMINOLOGY USED

It is important to clarify terminology as it relates to our literature search. First, as Yadav and Lenka (2020) note, there is no shared agreement among scholars about the definition of "diversity." At face value, diversity is synonymous with difference. In the management and organizational literatures, dimensions of difference can be broadly categorized as visible/observable (surface level) and invisible/nonobservable (deep level) (Roberson, 2019). Yadav and Lenka (2020) further classify these attributes as job-relevant (e.g., role, function, knowledge, experience) or relational (e.g., sex, race, values, attitudes). For the purpose of this paper, we pulled articles that describe "diversity" as differences in cultural identities (observable or not) *in the context of power and status* (Ely & Thomas, 2001, emphasis added). We add the qualification of "power and status" because we are interested in change efforts that focus on differences in cultural identities in the context of social hierarchies (e.g., race, ethnicity, gender, sexual orientation, age, disability, religion).

Related to this distinction is how we conceptualize a DEI organizational "change" effort or intervention. We used the term "intervention" because it is often used synonymously with change in the research literature. Drawing from an ODC perspective, we conceive of organizational change as a planned process compared to an unplanned one (Burke & Noumair, 2015). Likewise, we only examined articles that directly address DEI and organizational change through a process of planned intervention. This differs from the "diversity management" literature which focuses on diversity as a process, both planned and spontaneous, via antecedents, consequences, moderators, and mediators at the individual, group, and organizational levels (Yadav & Lenka, 2020). In fact, Yadav and Lenka *excluded* papers about diversity change initiatives (practices, programs, and trainings) in their literature review on diversity management.

Last, we added the term "inclusion" to our search because it is considered a distinct construct from diversity (Roberson, 2006). While diversity denotes cat-egorical differences in social identity group membership, inclusion reflects the perception or experience of belonging in an organization. More specifically, Shore et al. (2011) define inclusion as

> ...the degree to which an employee perceives that he or she is an esteemed member of the work group through experiencing treatment that satisfies his or her needs for belonging and uniqueness. (p. 1265)

Shore, Cleveland, and Sanchez (2018) further distinguish the two terms by arguing that "diversity" change efforts focus on getting people in the door, but "inclusion" change efforts create the organizational practices and processes that make people want to stay. An organization change effort or intervention focused on inclusion may not appear in a literature search for "diversity" and change. Yet, the process of creating an inclusive organization is directly related to our frame on DEI and organizational change.

ALIGNING STRATEGY AND DIGITAL TECHNOLOGY IN GOVERNMENT ORGANIZATIONS: A CALL TO ACTION

Joe McDonagh

ABSTRACT

For the last four decades, the alignment of strategy and digital technology has persisted as one of the most critical and bothersome issues for senior government executives. Against this backdrop and drawing on the fruits of an extended program of collaborative research between 1995 and 2020, this chapter draws attention to how government organizations foster effective alignment and how this is achieved through four distinct cycles of alignment work. Considering that this work is heavily people- and organization-centric, the chapter calls for greater involvement of organization development and change scholars and practitioners in this important area of organizational life and work.

Keywords: Alignment work; collaborative inquiry; digital technology; ICT; strategy work; digital strategy

INTRODUCTION

Government organizations are under constant pressure to renew and reform. This is predicated on the relentless pursuit of value for money along with the delivery of enhanced social and public value. The focus on value brings strategy work center stage since it emphasizes the astute allocation of scarce resources in pursuit of priority goals, objectives, actions, and outcomes. Exemplary strategy work has the potential to make an invaluable contribution to ensuring that government

Research in Organizational Change and Development, Volume 29, 235–260
ISSN: 0897-3016/doi:10.1108/S0897-301620210000029010

organizations build the necessary resources and capabilities, harness their value to the full, and maximize the delivery of value-based outcomes.

With regards to information and communications technology (ICT)-related resources and capabilities, exemplary strategy work seeks to both build and exploit these in pursuit of an organization's vision, mission, values, and mandate along with its priority goals, objectives, actions, and outcomes. There are a myriad of choices here ranging from exploiting ICT to transform: performance at individual, group, and intra- and interorganization levels; the organization and distribution of work; the configuration of intra- and interorganizational functions and processes; the symmetry between people, work, and technology; the equilibrium between social and enterprise technologies; and the organization's capability and capacity to deliver on all of the above. Making wise choices here and harnessing the transformational potential of ICT are considered to be within the purview of alignment work, that is the alignment of strategy and ICT.

While alignment work is central to strategizing in relation to ICT in professional practice, it is also one of the most critical and worrisome issues for senior government executives. A recent survey by the Society for Information Management not only confirms this but also suggests that its enduring nature is a function of capability gaps in the areas of strategy and change in organizations (Kappelman et al., 2020). Of course, the critical and bothersome nature of this issue is not new as it has featured prominently across the last four decades in all major studies of critical ICT management issues in organizations (Ball & Harris, 1982; Kappelman et al., 2017; Luftman & Derksen, 2012; Luftman & McLean, 2004).

Having regard for the centrality of alignment work along with its bothersome nature, it is not so surprising that it looms large once again in accounts of failed ICT-enabled change initiatives in government organizations. A brief perusal of publicly available reports produced by a range of government oversight and accountability offices (e.g., Government Accountability Office, USA; National Audit Office, UK; Comptroller and Auditor General, Ireland) confirms the inordinately troublesome nature of large-scale ICT-enabled change initiatives and the perception that poor or ineffective alignment of strategy and ICT is regularly one of the most significant contributing factors (McDonagh, 2004, 2006; National Audit Office, 2013).

Recognizing the inherent value of good strategy work and the manner in which it can be used productively to shape the direction and development of government organizations, the central question around which this chapter is now organized is as follows: "How can government organizations foster greater alignment between strategy and ICT?". The interest in and focus on government organizations is a product of pragmatism, ease of access, and the researcher's relationship with senior government executives cultivated over the last 25 years. By their nature, government organizations are open and transparent, operate in complex environments, and are accountable to a multiplicity of stakeholders. They provide a rich arena in which to inquire into the alignment of strategy and ICT.

The chapter is organized as follows. The section on *aligning strategy and digital technology* draws from a range of related literature in the information systems (IS) discipline, offers six significant points of departure, and concludes with an invitation for new approaches to inquiry that have the potential to both inform and transform professional practice. By way of responding to this invitation, *the case for collaborative inquiry* is presented in the next section where it is argued that the distinctive hallmarks of such inquiry are reflected in its clinical, appreciative, and processual nature. Collaborative inquiry is considered essential in order to meet the twin objectives of informing and transforming professional practice in a real-world setting while simultaneously contributing to the production of knowledge for the wider academic and practitioner communities (Avison, Davison, & Malaurent, 2018; Davison, Martinsons, & Malaurent, forthcoming; Gable, 2020).

The section on the *practice of collaborative inquiry* explores the evolution of a major thematic research program over the last 25 years. It explores its genesis based on observations in professional practice, an initial phase of research between 1995 and 2000, a subsequent phase between 2000 and 2010 which embodied a whole system perspective on development and change, and a more recent phase between 2010 and 2020 which favored getting up close and personal with individual government organizations. Attention is focused on the manner in which the practice of collaborative inquiry is deepened and enriched as the researcher increases proficiency over time.

Drawing on the richness of this research, the section on *the fruits of collaborative inquiry* provides insights into how government organizations foster greater alignment between strategy and ICT through the adoption of four distinct but overlapping cycles of alignment work including *discovery*, *renewal*, *empowerment*, and *orchestration*. Each cycle is presented and considered from both social and technical viewpoints. This is followed by a series of *reflections* that focus on the role of organization development and change (OD&C) scholars, the practice of collaborative inquiry, and new avenues in alignment research. By way of *conclusion*, attention is drawn to the pressing need for OD&C scholars to step forward and embrace the nexus between strategy, change, and ICT and to challenge the dominant social systems and embedded ideologies that marginalize the people and organizational aspects of development and change as they relate to the adoption of ICT in government organizations.

ALIGNING STRATEGY AND DIGITAL TECHNOLOGY

Digital Foundations

The current interest in and pervasive influence of digital technologies, as in ICT, in organizations is not new. This interest has been central to the field of *computing* which has changed its name several times over the last seven decades (Denning, 2003, 2010; Rosenbloom, 2004). In the 1940s it was called *automatic computation* and in the 1950s, *information processing*. In the 1960s, as it moved into academia, it was known as *informatics* in Europe and *computer science* in the United States.

By the 1980s, *computing* comprised a complex web of interrelated fields including *computer science, informatics, computational science, computer engineering, software engineering, information systems,* and *information technology*. By the 1990s, the term *computing* had become the standard for referring to this core group of disciplines (Denning, 2010).

While the field of computing has been greatly influenced by the fields of engineering, mathematics, and computational-oriented science, the core principles of computing which define the field have remained stable across the decades. As defined by Denning (2010), they include: computation (what can and cannot be computed); communication (reliably moving information between locations); coordination (effectively using many autonomous computers); recollection (representing, storing, and retrieving information from media); automation (discovering algorithms for information processes); evaluation (predicting performance of complex systems); and design (structuring systems and software for reliability and dependability). It is important to note that all digital technologies and related systems and platforms reflect a combination of these stable underlying principles.

The emergence of digitalization as a pervasive theme in the field of management and organization studies over the last decade (e.g., digital business, digital strategy, digital technology, digital change, digital transformation) is often matched with a poor understanding of the history of computing within and between organizations. Advances in ICT manifest themselves in the form of systems of record, systems of engagement, and systems of insight, and their collective impact is to enhance performance, productivity, and predictability at multiple levels within and between organizations. The challenge for organizations is to determine where to invest with a view to delivering value, irrespective of whether that value is classified as being of an economic, social, or public nature.

Of course, this has always been a challenge and there is nothing new here. It remains a challenge in the current era marked by the pervasive influence of digital technologies and platforms and their implications for the design of increasingly sophisticated and distributed work systems (Pasmore, Winby, Mohrman, & Vanasse, 2019; Winby & Mohrman, 2018). These work systems are underpinned by complex systems of interconnected digital systems and networks (Chen & Clothier, 2003; Haines, 2012) that offer the possibility of creating greater symmetry between people, work, and technology. Notwithstanding this new emphasis on systems of systems, it remains that an organization must still choose where to invest in order to deliver best possible outcomes for its range of stakeholders. This is a strategy-related matter.

The Place of Strategy

Against the backdrop of an ever-evolving *computing* domain, the IS discipline emerged with a central focus on the evolution and adoption of ICT in organizations from the 1950s onwards (Hirschheim & Klein, 2012; Taylor, Dillon, & van Wingen, 2010). Throughout its rich history, the structure of knowledge within the IS discipline has afforded a unique place to the study of strategizing and the nexus between strategy and ICT in its various guises and forms

(Sidorova, Evangelopoulos, Valacich, & Ramakrishnan, 2008). As noted by Bharadwaj, El Sawy, Pavlou, and Venkatraman (2013a, p. 472), strategizing in relation to ICT encompasses a *strategy formulated and executed by leveraging digital resources to create differential value*. This has been true for the electronic data processing era in the 1950s/1960s, the management information systems era in the 1970s, the strategic information systems era in the 1980s, the integrated enterprise era of the 1990s, the extended enterprise era of the 2000s, and the digital transformation era of 2010s and beyond (Bharadwaj et al., 2013a, 2013b; Merali, Papadopoulos, & Nadkarni, 2012). Throughout these eras, the IS discipline has viewed strategizing as the great work of organizations and deemed it pivotal to shaping and giving effect to an organization's agenda for ICT-enabled change (Besson & Rowe, 2012; Merali et al., 2012; Vial, 2019).

Of course, the central challenge in strategizing is to determine what level of investment to make in ICT systems in their various forms (e.g., systems of record, systems of engagement, systems of insight) in order to deliver on an organization's vision, mission, values, and mandate along with its supporting strategic goals, objectives, actions, and outcomes. In essence, there is a need to achieve a high degree of alignment between the strategic direction and development of an organization and its related investments in ICT resources and capabilities. While this alignment work is essential to giving purpose and shape to an organization's agenda for ICT-enabled change, it is unfortunate that many such change initiatives pay little if any heed to strategy (Block, Blumberg, & Laartz, 2012).

The Alignment Challenge

While the IS discipline recognizes strategizing as being central to advancing the agenda for ICT-enabled change in organizations, what insights does the literature offer in relation to the current state of professional practice? In relation to strategizing, the alignment of business and ICT strategies has been and remains one of the most critical and worrisome issues for senior executives over the last four decades (Ball & Harris, 1982; Luftman & Derksen, 2012; Luftman & McLean, 2004; Kappelman et al., 2017, 2020). What is it about alignment work that keeps it as the most critical and worrisome issue for senior executives? Why is it that the requisite strategizing capabilities deemed so essential to exploiting ICT are considered both *soft* and *most difficult to find* in practice (Kappelman et al., 2020, p. 79)?

Throughout the last four decades, researchers within the IS discipline have generated a steady flow of alignment-related research (Teubner & Stockhinger, 2020). This work has clarified the factors that precede, enable, and impede alignment (Hu & Huang, 2006; Luftman & Brier, 1999) while also producing a large volume of models that capture alignment's key dimensions (Benbya & McKelvey, 2006; Earl, 1989; Henderson & Venkatraman, 1993, 1999; Scott-Morton & Rockart, 1984). As an evidence base, there is little consistency among these models, and they appear not to offer insights into either the strategy processes or related practices that underpin them. With regards to how these models might be used to either inform or transform professional practice, the literature is rather silent.

Much of this scholarly work on alignment has been heavily criticized for being far too conceptual and divorced from professional practice (Chen, Mocker, Preston, & Teubner, 2010; Ciborra, 1997; Williams, Torres, & Carte, 2018). It appears not to be grounded in the real-world challenges of aligning strategy and ICT in organizations and in the everyday lived experiences of senior managers who must engage with this challenge in professional practice. The mind of the strategist is conspicuously missing as is any serious treatment of the people dimension of strategizing. It would seem that this stream of literature with its many frameworks and models exhibits a strong engineering orientation, a cleaving to its technical roots and underpinnings, and no attention afforded to alignment as a continuous process of OD&C. As an evidence base, one wonders whether there is reason to question the trustworthiness and value of this cumulative scientific knowledge (Kepes, Bennett, & McDaniel, 2014).

With regards to this body of knowledge which has emerged over the last four decades, this chapter accommodates six significant points of departure which are informed by a knowledge of the literature and the researcher's sustained interest in the nexus between strategy, change, and ICT in government organizations over the last 25 years. The points of departure relate to aligning families of strategies; engaging leadership teams and networks; adopting a values-based perspective; harnessing developmental opportunities; instilling a people-centered approach; and uncovering patterns and rhythms. They are presented below:

First, the IS literature speaks directly to the alignment of business and ICT strategies, and it considers the essential challenge as one of aligning related goals, objectives, actions, and outcomes (Reich & Benbasat, 1996). Alignment is framed in terms of a two-way interplay between two distinct realms of strategizing, with most scholarly work speaking to private sector organizations. But this conception is exceptionally narrow and dated. The strategic direction and development of a government organization is influenced and shaped by both its internal and external *families of strategies* which evolve through time. There are a multiplicity of strategies which must be considered when alignment work comes into play. Alignment work must consider not only the organization but also the wider government ecosystem in which it is embedded (Pasmore et al., 2019; Winby & Mohrman, 2018). While Teubner and Stockhinger (2020) have recently drawn attention to this shortcoming in the literature, the manner in which it is framed does not really speak to the context of government ecosystems.

Second, working within a rather narrow conception of alignment, the principal protagonists in the alignment space are considered to be the most senior executive officer and the most senior ICT officer (Chen et al., 2010; Edwards, 2000; Moon, Choi, & Armstrong, 2018; Preston & Karahanna, 2005; Reich & Benbasat, 1996; Shao, 2019). There is an enormous amount of research that speaks to this space including significant work on the CEO–CIO relationship

(Benlian & Haffke, 2016; Johnson & Lederer, 2010). While the scholarly work at times moves beyond this narrow focus to embrace a top management team perspective (Krotov, 2015; Preston & Karahanna, 2009), it is still very deficient. This narrow emphasis is perpetuated through time in the literature, and it reinforces a view of ICT strategy work as being of a functional rather than organizational nature (Bharadwaj et al., 2013a). The alignment of strategy and ICT in a government organization is far more complex than this. It involves *leadership teams and networks* (from both within the organization and the wider government ecosystem) working in unison to emerge with a shared blueprint for the future.

Third, the adoption of a *values-based perspective* on strategy work is important in government organizations. It is considered essential to open up strategy work (Matzler, Füller, Hutter, Hautz, & Stieger, 2016; Stadler, Hautz, & von den Eichen, 2020) and to infuse it with values and principles that promote openness and transparency; equality, diversity, and inclusion; engagement and collaboration; and distributed and democratic decision-making. There is a strong emphasis on being in this together, working at this together, and cocreating and coowning the strategic direction and development of the organization together. Striking a healthy gender balance in strategizing is deemed critical work (Morgan & Knights, 1991). Yet, the IS stream of literature on alignment is fixated on the ICT artifact and gives scant attention to the role of core values and principles in shaping alignment work in government organizations. This is a significant omission.

Fourth, in government organizations, the practice of strategizing offers unrivalled opportunities for on-the-job *leadership and career development* and directly contributes to the development goals and objectives of individuals and groups involved. Strategy work itself is developmental by its very nature, and it is essential to harness its hidden potential. By building the capability of individuals and groups, government organizations grow their strategizing capability and enhance their level of proficiency (basic, novice, intermediate, advanced, expert) over time. It is inappropriate to assume that individuals and groups engaged in strategizing have the requisite capabilities. Such capabilities must be actively nurtured and developed. The developmental nature of strategizing and its related capability building agenda have not been appropriately addressed in the IS literature to date (McDonagh, 2015b).

Fifth, the need to adopt a *people-centered approach* to alignment work is pressing. Seven decades of research in the field of computing and more specifically in the field of IS provide unassailable evidence to support the assertion that people and organizational aspects of strategy and change are routinely marginalized and ignored when dealing with the evolution and adoption of ICT in organizations (McDonagh, 2015a; McDonagh & Coghlan, 1999). Both IS scholarship and professional practice are dominated by a technical mode of thinking in relation to ICT. This mode of thinking is partial and impoverished and has undoubtedly contributed to the recurring narratives of failed change initiatives that mar the landscape of government organizations (Beer & Eisenstat, 2000; Bostrom & Heinen, 1977a, 1977b; Carlton, 2019; Chanias, Myers, & Hess,

2019; Clegg et al., 1996a, 1996b; Correani, De Massis, Frattini, Petruzzelli, & &Natalicchio, 2020; Crittenden & Crittenden, 2008; Davenport & Westerman, 2018; Lyytinen & Hirschheim, 1987; Tomeski & Lazarus, 1975).

The dominance of a technical mode of thinking and the marginalization of people and organizational aspects of strategy and change result in change initiatives that are partial and fragmented from the outset. Failed change initiatives are characterized by a distinct inability to coordinate and integrate varied forms of wisdom, knowledge, skill, and expertise that are widely distributed across diverse occupational communities (Coghlan & McDonagh, 2001; McDonagh, 2015a; Schein, 1992, 1996). They are also characterized by an equally distinct inability to coordinate and integrate strategic, organizational, and technological aspects of development and change (National Audit Office, 2013; Sage et al., 2014). While the adoption of modern program management practices was for a time viewed as the panacea to address this organizational ill, such practices have had a rather limited impact due to the dominance of a mechanistic approach to change (McDonagh, 2015a).

Sixth, alignment work in government organizations unfolds to a discernible *pattern or rhythm* (a theme that is addressed in greater detail later in this paper). This rhythm encapsulates specific developmental challenges and supporting strategy practices that speak to both the social and technical dimensions of strategizing (McDonagh, Burke, & O'Leary, 2018). It is in attending to the social dimension of strategizing that the interests and influences of diverse actors, embedded in their respective occupational communities (Schein, 1992, 1996), can be accommodated and reconciled while also being fashioned into a purposeful agenda for strategic, organizational, and technological change (McDonagh & Coghlan, 1999). As strategy work progresses through these cumulative cycles, it is here that the work of alignment takes place in practice; that organizational strategies are framed in the form of goals, objectives, actions, and outcomes; that the capability of individuals and groups to strategize well is enhanced; and that the interests and influences of diverse actors are reconciled and accommodated. This perspective on alignment work presented here is without doubt understated in the IS literature.

The Need for Fresh Approaches

Cognizant of the unique and disparate ways in which occupational communities shape the work of strategizing in relation to ICT in organizations (Coghlan & McDonagh, 2001; Schein, 1992, 1996), mindful of the related propensity to marginalize and ignore the people and organizational aspects of development and change, and taking note of the points of departure considered above, how might one productively attend to the central research question in this chapter: *How can government organizations foster greater alignment between strategy and ICT?*. Having reflected for a time and having considered the range of people and organizational issues that one might encounter in work of this nature, there is a strong case for adopting a collaborative and deliberately interventionist approach to inquiry.

THE CASE FOR COLLABORATIVE INQUIRY

To positively influence the practice of strategizing in relation to ICT in government organizations and to instill a people-centered approach to development and change in that regard, there is a compelling case for harnessing the wisdom, knowledge, skill, and expertise of scholars and practitioners alike (Boyer, 1990; Van de Ven, 2007; Van de Ven & Johnson, 2006). Sound scholarship has the potential to support a step change in the practice of strategizing in the key areas identified earlier. Such scholarship offers a firm basis for both informing and transforming professional practice (Jacelon, Donoghue, & Breslin, 2010; Parke, Stevenson, & Rowe, 2015). Achieving a step change of this nature requires a strong commitment to collaborative inquiry where scholars and practitioners work in unison over extended periods of time (Shani & Coghlan, 2021).

Having engaged collaboratively for the last 25 years (1995–2020) with government organizations at the nexus between strategy, change, and ICT, what are the defining characteristics of collaborative inquiry that contribute to positive development and change in such organizations? While it is beyond the scope of this chapter to provide a comprehensive view on the practice of collaborative inquiry over time, three key perspectives are afforded priority attention here. They include the adoption and interweaving of clinical, appreciative, and processual perspectives on development and change in organizations.

From a clinical perspective, the nature of the relationship between the scholar and practitioner is of the utmost importance (Schein, 1995). It is the practitioner who invites the scholar to collaborate with a view to achieving purposeful change in relation to ICT. The nature of that relationship is such that the practitioner is willing to reveal ALL relevant and pertinent information and the scholar is seen as one to whom ALL information can be made available without question (Schein, 1995). It is assumed that the work of the scholar is values-based and values-led and embodies the principles of stewardship and service. It is also assumed that the scholar has the ability to remain hidden in plain sight while quietly instructing, teaching, counseling, and watching over others as part of the collaborative research endeavor. As a welcome contemporary development of action research, the clinical perspective reflects an embodiment and an enactment of clinical inquiry as espoused by Schein (Coghlan, 2009; Coghlan & McDonagh, 2001; Schein, 1991, 1995).

From an appreciative perspective, inquiry is infused with and sustained by a spirit of humility (Schein, 2013) that gives preference to the exercise of gratitude, grace, and compassion (Fehr, Fulmer, Awtrey, & Miller, 2017; Wasylyshyn & Masterpasqua, 2018) in human affairs. It places individuals and groups at the center of inquiring together and it seeks to engage, enable, and empower them to frame and enact their agenda for positive development and change (Cameron & McNaughtan, 2014; Copperrider & Srivastva, 1987, 2017). In the context of any given inquiry, the appreciative perspective seeks to call forth and name all that is excellent and to make explicit the rich store of psychological resources already available to the organization. The language of development and change is not problem-centric in the here and now. Rather, it is future focused and seeks to clarify the small number of affirmative actions that have the potential to create positive change and to transition the organization toward an increasingly desirable future. The appreciative perspective recognizes and honors the richness that flows in, through, and around individuals and groups in organizations. It seeks to tap into, channel, and direct that richness in pursuit of purposeful change. Like the clinical perspective, the appreciative perspective is also a welcome contemporary development of action research (Copperrider & Srivastva, 1987, 2017).

From a processual perspective, inquiry into the practice of strategizing and the related nexus between strategy and ICT unfolds as a sequence of actions, interactions, and reactions over time. Achieving step change in the area of alignment work must of necessity focus on the underlying action sequences as they unfold. Moreover, what is particularly important here is how individuals and groups are engaged in continuous cycles of *joint diagnosis*, *joint action planning*, *joint intervention*, and *joint evaluation*. Here, the role of the scholar is twofold. First, the scholar ensures that these continuous cycles are infused with scholarly insights as appropriate. Second, the scholar helps channel the energy of individuals and groups into affirmative and productive action. The processual perspective on strategizing naturally accommodates and promotes action-oriented inquiry. This is the heartbeat of action research, an approach to inquiry that is established and valued within the IS discipline (Avison et al., 2018; Davison et al., forthcoming; Gable, 2020).

Operating within a clinical paradigm, adopting an appreciative perspective, and accommodating a processual viewpoint on development and change all contribute to a rich approach to collaborative inquiry. But, for such collaboration to be effective, the scholar must do more than simply focus on the continuous cycles of *joint diagnosis*, *joint action planning*, *joint intervention*, and *joint evaluation*. With others, the scholar must also help nurture an organizational climate that supports working across boundaries, foster team characteristics deemed essential for effective collaboration, nurture collaborative processes essential for success, and be clear about intended collaborative outcomes from the outset (McDonagh, 2008).

THE PRACTICE OF COLLABORATIVE INQUIRY

Earlier in this chapter, it was noted that individuals and groups engaged in strategy work in government organizations grow their capability and enhance their level of proficiency over time. It was suggested that such levels might be classified as basic, novice, intermediate, advanced, and expert. It is a central point in this chapter that the most natural place to strengthen one's ability to strategize well is through immersion in strategy work in one's own organization. Capability building and enhancing related levels of proficiency equally apply to the practice of collaborative inquiry. As one journeys through the seasons of a scholar's life, one transitions from the early application of the rudiments of collaborative inquiry to a time when one's way of being with others is synonymous with the spirit and practice of such inquiry.

The researcher's interest in the nexus between strategy and ICT is long-standing. It was a feature of his work between 1976 and 1992 when he held a series of technology-related development, advisory, and management roles with organizations such as Imperial Chemical Industries, Price Waterhouse, Continental, and Philips. During these years in professional practice, the researcher observed a tendency among senior managers to view strategy work in relation to ICT as the domain of technology specialists and not one to which they could readily or easily contribute. The researcher also observed that senior managers had a tendency to garner personal praise and narrate their personal involvement when ICT-related change was considered successful. When such change was hanging in the balance and countenancing the prospect of failure, the same senior managers tended to wash their hands of such initiatives and to view ICT professionals as the principal protagonists in narratives of failed change.

Having pondered at length the relationship between senior managers and the introduction of ICT in organizations, the researcher committed to an extensive program of related research between 1995 and 2020 (see Table 1 for a description of the program and its phases and timelines). Executed between 1995 and 2000, the initial phase of this research focused on an exploration of the roles of executive leaders in shaping strategic change initiatives. It adopted a model of collaborative inquiry with particular emphasis on its clinical and processual dimensions. Following a longitudinal research design, the study traced the evolution and development of large-scale strategic change initiatives that depended on the effective exploitation of modern ICT systems. The study revealed that executive leaders tend to influence large-scale change in rather diverse and predictable ways. While the study shed light on the four distinct roles deemed essential to delivering large-scale change, it noted that strategy work was central to only one of these roles. It also noted that the absence of any one of these roles in a large-scale change initiative contributed to significant underperformance and failure. In hindsight, the researcher's practice of collaborative inquiry throughout this period was principled and bore many of the hallmarks of the novice at work.

Table 1. Collaborative Research Program: Phases and Timelines.

Phase	Focus	Participating Organizations	Timeline
I	Inquiry into the diverse roles of executive managers in leading large-scale change, especially change underpinned by modern ICT systems.	One government organization (drawn from Western Europe).	1995–2000
II	Inquiry into factors that contribute to misalignment and underperformance on large-scale ICT-enabled change initiatives.	Twenty-five government organizations (drawn from Western Europe and the United Nations).	2000–2010
III	Inquiry into the nature of exemplary strategy work and its role in fostering effective alignment between strategy and ICT.	Twelve government organizations (drawn from Western Europe).	2010–2020

Note: ICT, information and communications technology.

Armed with insights and perspectives from this academic study and satisfied that it had yielded a rich explanation for what had been observed and experienced in professional practice, the researcher engaged in a more systematic program of collaborative inquiry between 2000 and 2010. The program remained focused on the diverse roles of executive leaders in shaping large-scale change, particularly change enabled by modern ICT systems. The purpose of the program was to build a stronger and more compelling evidence base beyond that of the single government organization included in the original doctoral study. In building this evidence base, the study sought to continue in the spirit of coinquiry and to both inform and transform professional practice in the process.

The period from 2000 to 2010 was marked by extensive engagement and collaboration with executive leadership teams in government organizations in Ireland (IRL), United Kingdom and Northern Ireland (UK&NI), and the United Nations (UN). Collaborative research progressed throughout this period gave rise to a series of 25 evaluations of large-scale change initiatives that were encountering challenges at the time. For example, in an IRL context, the research program included an evaluation of the REACH initiative which was focused on exploiting ICT in support of integrated service delivery (McDonagh, 2004) and the PPARS initiative which sought to exploit ICT in modernizing the human resource function in autonomous regional health authorities (McDonagh, 2006). In a UK&NI context, it included a review of the capability and capacity of central government departments to shape and deliver large-scale trans-formational change programs (McDonagh, 2009, pp. 1–28). In a UN context, it included a review of the capability and capacity of UN organizations to shape and deliver large-scale ICT-enabled change initiatives (McDonagh, 2010, pp. 1–38). These are but a sample of the formal reviews and evaluations completed throughout this decade.

All of the reviews and evaluations completed between 2000 and 2010 were as a result of invitations from government organizations to collaborate as part of significant renewal and reform initiatives. They all benefited from extensive engagement and collaboration. In all cases, formal reports evolved in tandem with shared dialogue between the scholar and practitioners involved, and they were viewed as a defining component of the continuous cycles of *joint diagnosis*, *joint action planning*, *joint intervention*, and *joint evaluation*. The reports were deemed essential to building a shared understanding among actors engaged in the cycle of collaborative inquiry from diagnosis through to subsequent evaluation. Upon reflection, the scholar's practice of collaborative inquiry deepened throughout this decade and most likely mirrored that at an intermediate or advanced level. The model of inquiry was dominated by its clinical and proces-sual dimensions, with the need for an appreciative perspective yet to take firm hold.

While the program of collaborative inquiry continued apace throughout the period 2010–2020, it clearly manifested some new characteristics when compared with the previous decade. Around 2010, the researcher reflected at length on progress with this collaborative research program and concluded that some practitioners may not have been sufficiently engaged and inspired to address the magnitude of change in their own organizational settings. A number of the more significant studies carried out in the previous decade were positioned at a whole system level (e.g., Regional Health Authorities in IRL, Central Government Departments in the UK&NI, and the UN System and its major Agencies) and as a result may not have been sufficiently up close and personal for individual organizations. In addition, there were some instances in which formal reviews were leaked for less than noble purposes, or at least that is how it seemed (https://www.irishtimes.com/news/ppars-fiasco-could-happen-again-says-report-1.10 23500).

By way of learning from experience and making some important midpoint corrections, the researcher decided to focus attention for the next decade on individual organizations and to weave an appreciative perspective into the practice of collaborative inquiry. The researcher also decided to disengage from evaluating and reviewing problematic change initiatives and to focus instead on organizations about to embark on a journey of significant development and change. For practical reasons, the researcher focused on Western European government organizations throughout this decade, especially those that sought to integrate key aspects of leadership, strategy, and change when addressing the challenge of ICT. The implementation of these decisions resulted in a fruitful and fulfilling decade. This has involved collaborating with 12 large government organizations committed to evolving and developing their executive leadership capabilities through engagement in critical cross-organizational work, including the alignment of strategy and ICT. It has also involved serving as an independent external expert overseeing capability reviews of government organizations while also serving in a mentoring capacity to a number of government executive leadership networks.

By increasingly infusing collaborative inquiry with an appreciative perspective over the last decade, the practice of such inquiry has definitely transitioned to a more advanced or expert level. It has involved working with individuals and groups to empower them to shape and give effect to change initiatives in their own organizational settings. For example, in the case of one major government organization, it has involved supporting the evolution and development of both senior and middle management networks and exploiting the potential of strategy work (including the exploitation of ICT) in this regard (McDonagh et al., 2018). It has also involved supporting the evolution and development of a range of people and ICT strategies in other large government organizations.

THE FRUITS OF COLLABORATIVE INQUIRY

Throughout the period 1995–2020, the focus of this research has always been on the nexus between strategy, change, and ICT in government organizations. While many themes of interest have waxed and waned throughout this period, the alignment of strategy and ICT has remained a constant. With regards to how government organizations foster greater alignment between strategy and ICT, this is addressed in greater detail below and undoubtedly responds to recent calls for studies of this nature within the IS discipline (Chan, 2001; Street, Gallupe, & Baker, 2018; Yeow, Soh, & Hansen, 2018).

Cycles of Alignment Work

Reflecting on the program of research carried out between 1995 and 2020, there is strong evidence that government organizations committed to fostering greater alignment between strategy and ICT engage in four distinct *cycles of alignment work* as depicted in Fig. 1. Labeled *DISCOVERY, RENEWAL, EMPOWERMENT*, and *ORCHESTRATION*, these cycles are iterative, interdependent, and cumulative by nature. The presentation of the cycles here is biased toward encouraging OD&C scholars to actively engage with the alignment of strategy and ICT and the related agenda for ICT-enabled change in government organizations. The cycles are detailed below.

The Discovery Cycle

The discovery cycle offers a powerful vantage point from which to explore matters of alignment or misalignment as the case may be. It involves taking stock of the organization's experience with the alignment of strategy and ICT and identifying those areas in which affirmative action might best be pursued into the future. Reflecting on and learning from experience is the central activity here in the knowledge that this can form the basis for productive action into the future. The discovery cycle roots and grounds practitioners in their everyday lived experience, and it seeks to uncover rich wisdom, knowledge, skill, and expertise from within the organization. Discovery work can happen at any time and no new strategy-making endeavor should be countenanced without first engaging in this critical work. This cycle of alignment work has the potential to demystify ICT for everyone involved.

The discovery cycle encapsulates one or more large-group interventions in the form of a discovery conference or a structured learning symposium. Irrespective of what the event is called, the researcher plays a central role here in helping structure the event and in helping practitioners to evaluate their individual and collective experience. The most effective way to proceed with an event of this nature is to select a mix of five to eight change initiatives and have each champion

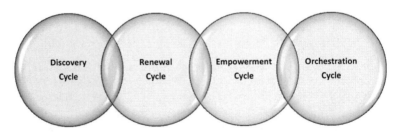

Fig. 1.   Cycles of Alignment Work in Government Organizations.

answer the same set of questions in relation to their particular initiative. For example, champions may be briefed on the context, content, process, and outcome dimensions of change and asked to critique their initiative in this regard. Having champions present their findings in a brief presentation to a discovery conference is invaluable. When all champions and their teams are present and when all members of leadership teams and networks are also present, the learning that takes place is transformative. The five to eight presentations reveal the very soul of the organization, demonstrate where strategy work sits in its psyche, and provides rich insights into the organization's approach to development and change.

A discovery conference always leads to an emerging game plan in relation to renewal and reform of professional practice. Effective alignment of strategy and ICT is the product of exemplary strategy practices. Where alignment is deemed to be ineffective, it always points to the need to transform strategy practices at some level in the organization. Here, the discovery cycle makes an inviable contribution to organizational health by tapping into the root of misalignment and addressing it at its very core. A day spent in a discovery conference is always a day well spent for all involved. Beyond helping structure an event of this nature and guiding participants to prepare well, the researcher also plays a central role in supporting the free flow of group dialogue and helping making sense of what is emerging.

The Renewal Cycle

The renewal cycle is shaped by the outcomes of the discovery cycle in the form of an emerging game plan for the renewal of professional practice. The researcher has a central role here in determining how best to engage a range of leadership teams and networks in assessing the current state of practice, determining ideal practice, and planning to transition toward that ideal at some point in the future. The renewal of strategy practices at varying levels across an organization is the heartbeat of this cycle. Working collaboratively, leadership teams and networks seek to achieve a step change in strategy practice in the full knowledge that it will contribute directly to an increasingly healthy organization. Engaging leadership teams and networks in work of this nature demands skill and patience.

Fostering greater alignment between strategy and ICT in government organizations will almost always involve leadership teams and networks in advancing an agenda for renewal and reform of professional management practices. This work leaves an enduring imprint on an organization's landscape. Well architected and executed, it contributes to a more cohesive and integrated family of organizational strategies of which ICT is but one. It also lays the foundation for reaping greater dividends from strategy work into the future. Advancing work of this nature through leadership teams and networks is empowering for corporate support functions such as human resources and ICT as they often struggle with similar alignment issues and challenges.

For the researcher committed to coinquiring with leadership teams and networks in work of this nature, a great starting point is to empower them to evaluate the form and function of their respective groups and to determine where strategy work sits in this regard. Considering that leading strategy and change is one of the most critical leadership competencies for senior managers in government organizations, this is a great starting point. Never start with a conversation on ICT as too many senior managers see that as sitting within the realm of ICT professionals and not one to which they can easily contribute. But such thinking is misguided. Senior managers need to excel at strategy work and ICT is nothing more than one resource available to deliver on the organization's vision, mission, and mandate, and supporting strategic goals and objectives.

The Empowerment Cycle

The renewal cycle, where leadership teams and networks work productively together to transform professional practice, legitimizes the empowerment cycle which seeks to humanize the strategy process from beginning to end. Adopting a values-based approach to development and change, this cycle fosters deep engagement in strategy work and seeks to generate a strategy that is cocreated and coowned by a multitude of actors across the organization. This cycle places a particular emphasis on opening up strategy work, freely inviting organizational members in, and seeks to match the leadership and career development goals of individuals involved with developmental opportunities emerging through engaging in strategizing. The intentions are to democratize strategy work; engage, enable, and empower individuals and groups; and to build strategy-related capabilities in the process. By harnessing the collective wisdom, knowledge, skill, and expertise of such a diverse array of actors, the language of ICT becomes increasingly demystified and organizational members become comfortable with the idea of achieving greater symmetry between people, work, and technology.

For the researcher, this cycle is demanding as organizational members frequently need guidance on what open strategy looks like; what democratizing strategy work means; how a values-based approach to development and change can be made real; why cocreation and coownership are essential to good strategizing; and how to use strategy work as part of on-the-job leadership development. Of course, these are but a sample of the developmental themes of interest to organizational members in this cycle. This work is real, tangible, and very demanding. Yet, it delivers enormous value in terms of aligning people with the strategy process and aligning the process with the organization's approach to development and change. This is foundation work deemed essential to making any significant progress with the actual alignment of strategy and ICT. There is a major commitment to reeducation as part of this cycle of alignment work.

The essential work that constitutes the empowerment cycle is always progressed with and through a small, focused strategy development team that is sensitized to the range of issues involved and guided toward making critical choices that deliver on the organization's desired legacy from this cycle of alignment work. The researcher give priority attention to this team in the full knowledge that it needs to be enabled to lead out on this cycle. It is this team that will make all the calls for engagement in strategy work; guide the formation of cross-organizational teams; and exploit the power of peers (i.e., mentoring, coaching, evaluation, learning, and networking) throughout the process.

The Orchestration Cycle

All of the earlier cycles of alignment work enrich the orchestration cycle. Here, the emphasis is on cocreating and coowning a robust strategy process that brings together the fruits of all the earlier work. What this means in practice is moving from the early initiation stage of the strategy process through to the final transition stage which sees the launch of the strategy and the immediate mobilization of resources in support of execution. It is in the orchestration cycle that all of the work comes together, that individuals and groups are engaged and developed, and that the actual alignment of strategy and ICT takes place in practice. This involves a comprehensive program of work which eventually yields a multiyear strategic framework and supporting action plan along with an implementation road map and resourcing plan that have been cocreated and coowned by a myriad of actors across the organization.

It is in this cycle of work that strategic issues are identified and responded to; that goals and objectives are framed; that choices in relation to systems of record, engagement, and insight are determined; that the shape of increasingly sophisticated and distributed work systems is determined and matched by the capabilities of complex systems of interconnected digital systems and networks (Pasmore et al., 2019; Winby & Mohrman, 2018); and that achieving symmetry between people, work, and technology is progressed. Harnessing the collective wisdom, knowledge, skill and expertise of the whole organization is critical in this work as is accessing expertise in the broader government and digital ecosystems.

The cycle is busy with a lot of work going on at any given time. A key challenge for the strategy development team is to keep the strategy work moving to plan and to address issues as they emerge. For the researcher, the challenge is to retain a bird's-eye view of the unfolding strategy process and to weave together scholarly and practice-based insights into clear guidance notes that support the strategy development team and other actors involved. Again, this can be onerous for the researcher as guidance notes of this nature are always particular to the circumstances of a given organization.

Deep and Demanding

These four cycles of alignment work are deep and demanding. They take focused energy, time, and resources. They commence with engaging the social system and in due time emerge with critical choices that have a long-term impact on both the social and technical dimensions of a government organization and the wider ecosystem in which it is embedded. The four cycles provide clarity on how government organizations foster alignment between strategy and ICT, but that is not to suggest that all government organizations engage in work of this nature.

REFLECTIONS

The narrative presented above provides a basis for a focused discussion which is organized here as a series of reflections on the role of OD&C scholars, the practice of collaborative inquiry, and new avenues in alignment research. Together, these reflections are intended to stimulate the interests of OD&C scholars and to encourage more active engagement at the nexus between strategy, change, and ICT in government organizations. In some small way, it is hoped that the reflections will add to Cummings and Cummings's (2020) call to reignite the field of OD&C and to help return it to its rightful place in the academy and in professional practice.

Reflections on the Role of OD&C Scholars

This chapter presents rich insights into the nature of alignment work and the manner in which it unfolds in government organizations. It has demonstrated that a people-centered, values-laden approach to such work has the potential to engage individuals and groups in reflecting on their experience; leadership teams and networks in the renewal of professional practice; and the whole organization in cocreating and coowning a strategy process and related strategy framework and action plan that fully aligns investments in ICT resources and capabilities with the strategic direction and development of the organization. Considering that alignment work is all about individuals, groups, teams, and networks and their choices in relation to both the renewal and reform of professional practice and the related alignment of strategy and ICT, this is clearly within the ambit of OD&C scholars and the broader OD&C community. They have a unique and vital role to play here.

That this work involves critical choices in the design of work systems and related choices in terms of systems of interconnected digital systems and networks are not reasons for the OD&C community to disengage from this critical area of scholarship and professional practice. A good understanding of the stable underlying principles of all digital technologies (Denning, 2003, 2010) helps demystify this terrain fast as does a firm grounding in the nature of ICT systems in organizations (e.g., systems of record, systems of engagement, systems of insight). It does not take a lot of time to familiarize oneself with the rules of engagement here. And indeed, there are many well-established industry frameworks available which provide a quick route to what is perceived as being important in this space.

Considering that the people and organizational aspects of development and change are routinely marginalized and ignored when dealing with the multifaceted nature of ICT in organizations and considering that the field of OD&C is exceptionally strong here, surely there is a strong case to be made for the OD&C community to give priority attention to the nexus between strategy, change, and ICT in government organizations. In addition, having due regard for the distinctive influences of both the executive and ICT communities when dealing with ICT (Coghlan & McDonagh, 2001; Schein, 1992, 1996), the case for the OD&C community to engage is even more compelling.

The Practice of Collaborative Inquiry

To be effective in the practice of collaborative inquiry, the researcher needs to be committed to engaging with practitioners and their organizational contexts over extended periods of time. While the work of the researcher undoubtedly contributes to positive development and change in any given context in the short term, there is also a need for a longitudinal view where the researcher observes the dynamics of change and related patterns both within and across government organizations over time. Being committed for the long haul, engaging in longitudinal thematic research that is interventionist by design, and developing the capability to collaborate well with practitioners all pose significant opportunities for a researcher's development and growth. The pursuit of engaged scholarship is without doubt a worthy and lifelong mission as is the wise stewardship of the researcher's self and all that has been entrusted to its care as it journeys through seasons of inquiry.

Over time, the practice of collaborative inquiry becomes increasingly agile and reflexive. As the practice becomes progressively affirmative, the tone and texture of the cycles of *joint diagnosis, joint action planning, joint intervention,* and *joint evaluation* evolve in significant ways. It becomes easier to flow together in envisaging a new future, easier to commend together all that is truly excellent, and use this as a basis for continued growth and development. It becomes natural to draw on very different ways of knowing individually and collectively and to integrate these in a manner that attends to and honors the distinctiveness of all involved. Indeed, the researcher shapes and is shaped by an ever-evolving repertoire of collaborative inquiry know-how.

Of course, the practice of collaborative inquiry is all about people, people, people. Even when dealing with matters of strategy and ICT, it remains that collaborative inquiry is still all about people, people, people. It takes time and patience along with continuous reflection to develop a healthy and life-giving practice of collaborative inquiry. It requires an endless reservoir of fortitude and grace combined with an ability to quickly recognize and simply set aside that which is unimportant and unhelpful. It takes a transformed self to continuously place others at the center, to hold them in profound honor and respect, to teach them how to hold strength and weakness in balance and to respect them equally, and to teach how to use adversity as a basis for being increasingly well formed over time. It takes a transformed self to continuously exercise gratitude, compassion, and grace in human affairs and to teach others to do likewise as part of the process of collaborative inquiry. The wise stewardship of one's self combined with a commitment to taking the deeper inner journey of transformation are essential for scholars committed to the practice of such inquiry.

From a processual perspective, the practice of collaborative inquiry unfolds to a discernible pattern akin to that espoused by Shani and Coghlan (2021). Their six phases of inquiry along with related practices and activities represent an excellent depiction of how such inquiry evolves real time in practice. Yet, it must be noted that collaborative inquiry emerges as an integral and underpinning element of exemplary strategy work. It does not stand apart from it. For a more detailed treatment of the six phases of collaborative inquiry and related practices and activities, see Shani and Coghlan (2021, pp. 67–85).

New Avenues in Alignment Research

That alignment continues to be a critical and worrisome issue for senior government executives (Kappelman et al., 2020), that the outcomes of ICT-enabled change are regularly disappointing (Davenport & Westerman, 2018), that the inability to align strategy and ICT is considered to be one of the most critical factors contributing to such disappointment (National Audit Office, 2013), which all suggest that many government organizations have yet to discover the enormous value of attending to and executing high-value alignment work. The root of the dilemma lies in a poor understanding of the central role of strategy work in shaping the direction and development of government organizations, not in any particular issue with ICT as such. All too often, this poor understanding and related capability deficits are widely shared by the executive and ICT communities alike (Schein, 1992, 1996).

Looking toward the future, there is merit in sticking the course with this collaborative research program and attending to new research themes emerging from the four cycles of alignment work. Specific areas of interest include:

(1) The role of collaborative learning and reflective practice (Lee & Bonk, 2014) in the *discovery cycle*. This will undoubtedly respond in part to the stream of calls from IS scholars (Chan, 2001; Hu & Huang, 2006; Moon et al., 2018; Reich & Kaarst-Brown, 2003; Schlosser, Beimborn, Weitzel, & Wagner, 2015) to address the informal nature of organizations and organizing and the related linkages with alignment.

(2) The role of collaborative dialogue within and between leadership teams and networks (Day, 2001; Hope & Reinelt, 2010) in the *renewal cycle*.

(3) The role of collaborative development in the *empowerment cycle*. This will move beyond existing strategy and IS scholarship which emphasize the strategy itself rather than the developmental journey underpinning it (Bryson, Edwards, & Van Slyke, 2018; Rahimi, Møller, & Hvam, 2016; Van Grembergen, 2004).

(4) The role of collaborative change in the *orchestration cycle*.

These four themes are congruent with the model of interventionist research and represent a fertile frontier for both informing and transforming professional practice while simultaneously generating new knowledge of interest to the academy. The themes are of particular interest and suited to both OD&C scholars and practitioners alike. While they may not appear as interesting to IS scholars, new partnership between OD&C and IS scholars would undoubtedly yield fruitful results in due time.

CONCLUSIONS

This chapter introduced the alignment of strategy and ICT as a critical and worrisome issue for senior executives in government organizations. It highlighted the enduring nature of this issue and the perception that it is somehow linked to capability deficits in the areas of strategy and change. It further noted that poor outcomes from ICT-enabled change initiatives invariably point to ineffective alignment of strategy and ICT. Against this backdrop, the chapter sought to explore how government organizations foster alignment of strategy and ICT.

Drawing on evidence collected from a program of collaborative research spanning the period 1995–2020, the chapter illuminated *four cycles of alignment* work deemed essential to tackling this enduring issue. The design and execution of these cycles draw heavily on the world and worldview of OD&C scholars and practitioners, a world which is rarely understood and drawn from by IS scholars and practitioners. Two worlds with their embedded worldviews that rarely meet in either scholarly or practice-based contexts.

Responding to Cummings and Cummings's (2020) call to action, there is a pressing need for OD&C scholars to step forward and embrace the nexus between strategy, change and ICT and to challenge the dominant social systems and embedded ideologies that marginalize the people and organizational aspects of development and change as they relate to the adoption of ICT in government organizations. OD&C scholars would do well to examine established orthodoxy that guides change in relation to ICT in government organizations.

Government organizations make extensive use of a range of frameworks such as COBIT (https://www.isaca.org/resources/cobit), TOGAF (https://www.opengroup.org/togaf), and SFIA (https://sfia-online.org/en) to support their strategy and change work in relation to ICT. These frameworks espouse best practice and are widely used by a number of the largest management consulting firms in the world. Yet, their embedded perspectives on development and change appear incomplete. They so often miss the human dimension. Is it any surprise then that the narratives of failure with strategic, organizational, and technological change programs continue unabated in government organizations?

REFERENCES

Avison, D. E., Davison, R. M., & Malaurent, J. (2018). Information systems action research: Debunking myths and overcoming barriers. *Information & Management, 55*, 177–187. doi: 10.1016/j.im.2017.05.004

Ball, L., & Harris, R. (1982, March). SMIS members: A membership analysis. *MIS Quarterly, 6*(1), 19–38.

Beer, M., & Eisenstat, R. A. (2000). The silent killer of strategy implementation and learning. *MIT Sloan Management Review, 41*(4), 29–40.

Benbya, H., & McKelvey, B. (2006). Using co-evolutionary and complexity theories to improve IS alignment: A multi-level approach. *Journal of Information Technology, 21*(4), 284–298. doi: 10.1057/palgrave.jit.2000080

Benlian, A., & Haffke, I. (2016). Does mutuality matter? Examining the bilateral nature and effects of CEO – CIO mutual understanding. *Journal of Strategic Information Systems, 25*(2), 104–126. doi:10.1016/j.jsis.2016.01.001

Besson, P., & Rowe, F. (2012). Strategizing information systems-enabled organizational transformation: A transdisciplinary review and new directions. *Journal of Strategic Information Systems, 21*(2), 103–124. doi:10.1016/j.jsis.2012.05.001

Bharadwaj, A., El Sawy, O. A., Pavlou, P. A., & Venkatraman, N. (2013a). Digital business strategy: Toward a next generation of insights. *MIS Quarterly, 37*(2), 471–482.

Bharadwaj, A., El Sawy, O. A., Pavlou, P. A., & Venkatraman, N. (2013b). Visions and voices on emerging challenges in digital business strategy. *MIS Quarterly, 37*(2), 633–634.

Block, M., Blumberg, S., & Laartz, J. (2012). Delivering large-scale ICT projects on time, on budget, and on value. *McKinsey Digital*. Retrieved from https://www.mckinsey.com/business-functions/mckinsey-digital/our-insights/delivering-large-scale-it-projects-on-time-on-budget-and-on-value#

Bostrom, R. P., & Heinen, J. S. (1977a). MIS problems and failures: A socio-technical perspective – Part I: The causes. *MIS Quarterly, 2*(3), 17–32.

Bostrom, R. P., & Heinen, J. S. (1977b). MIS problems and failures: A socio-technical perspective – Part II: The application of socio-technical theory. *MIS Quarterly, 2*(4), 11–28.

Boyer, E. L. (1990). *Scholarship reconsidered: Priorities of the professoriate*. Princeton, NJ: The Carnegie Foundation for the Advancement of Teaching.

Bryson, J. M., Edwards, L. H., & Van Slyke, D. M. (2018). Getting strategic about strategic planning research. *Public Management Review, 20*(3), 317–339. doi:10.1080/14719037.2017.1285111

Cameron, K., & McNaughtan, J. (2014). Positive organizational change. *Journal of Applied Behavioral Science, 50*(4), 445–462. doi:10.1177/0021886314549922

Carlton, D. (2019). Situational incompetence: The failure of governance in the management of large-scale IT projects. *The Journal of Modern Project Management, 7*(2). Retrieved from https://www.journalmodernpm.com/index.php/jmpm/article/view/JMPM02004

Chan, Y. E. (2001). Why haven't we mastered alignment? The importance of the informal organization structure. *Journal of Strategic Information Systems, 10*, 77–99. Retrieved from https://aisel.aisnet.org/misqe/vol1/iss2/2

Chanias, S., Myers, M. D., & Hess, T. (2019). Digital transformation strategy-making in pre-digital organizations: The case of a financial services provider. *Journal of Strategic Information Systems, 28*(1), 17–33.

Chen, P., & Clothier, J. (2003). Advancing systems engineering for systems-of-systems challenges. *Systems Engineering, 6*(3), 170–183.

Chen, D. Q., Mocker, M., Preston, D. S., & Teubner, A. (2010). Information systems strategy: Reconceptualization, measurement, and implications. *MIS Quarterly, 34*(2), 233–259.

Ciborra, C. U. (1997). De profundis? Deconstructing the concept of strategic alignment. *Scandinavian Journal of Information Systems, 9*(1), 2. Retrieved from http://aisel.aisnet.org/sjis/vol9/iss1/2

Clegg, C. W., Axtell, C., Damodaran, L., Farbey, B., Hull, R., Lloyd-Jones, R., Nicholls, J., … Stewart, T. (1996a). *The performance of information technology and the role of human and organizational factors*. Report to the Economic and Social Research Council, United Kingdom, January.

Clegg, C. W., Coleman, P., Hornby, P., Maclaren, R., Robson, J., Carey, N., & Symon, G. (1996b). Tools to incorporate some psychological and organizational issues during the development of computer based systems. *Ergonomics, 39*(3), 482–511.

Coghlan, D. (2009). Toward a philosophy of clinical inquiry/research. *Journal of Applied Behavioral Science, 45*(1), 106–121. doi:10.1177/0021886308328845

Coghlan, D., & McDonagh, J. (2001). Research and practice in IT-related change: The case for clinical inquiry. In R. Woodman & W. Pasmore (Eds.), *Research in organizational change and development* (Vol. 13, pp. 195–211). Oxford: Elsevier.

Copperrider, D. L., & Srivastva, S. (1987). Appreciative inquiry in organizational life. In W. A. Woodman & R. W. Passmore (Eds.), *Research in organizational change and development* (Vol. 1, pp. 129–169). Oxford: Elsevier.

Copperrider, D. L., & Srivastva, S. (2017). The gift of new eyes: Personal reflections after 30 years of appreciative inquiry in organizational life. *Research in Organizational Change and Development, 31*, 81–142. doi:10.1108/S0897-301620170000025003

Correani, A., De Massis, A., Frattini, F., Petruzzelli, A. M., & Natalicchio, A. (2020). Implementing a digital strategy: Learning from the experience of three digital transformation projects. *California Management Review, 62*(4), 37–56.

Crittenden, V. L., & Crittenden, W. F. (2008). Building a capable organization: The eight levers of strategy implementation. *Business Horizons, 51*(4), 301–309.

Cummings, T. G., & Cummings, C. (2020). The relevance challenge in management and organisation studies: Bringing organization development back in. *The Journal of Applied Behavioral Science, 56*(4), 521–546. doi:10.1177/0021886320961855

Davenport, T., & Westerman, G. (2018, March). Why so many high-profile digital transformations fail. *Harvard Business Review*, p. 2–5.

Davison, R. M., Martinsons, M. G., & Malaurent, J. (forthcoming). Improving action research by integrating methods. *Journal of the Association for Information Systems, 19*(6), 523–551.

Day, D. V. (2001). Leadership development: A review in context. *Leadership Quarterly, 11*(1), 581–613.

Denning, P. (2003). The great principles of computing. *Communications of the ACM, 46*(11), 15–20.

Denning, P. (2010, September–October). The great principles of computing. *American Scientist, 98*, 369–372.

Earl, M. J. (1989). *Management strategies for information technology*. Hoboken, NJ: Prentice-Hall.

Edwards, B. A. (2000). Chief executive officer behaviour: The catalyst for strategic alignment. *International Journal of Value-Based Management, 13*(1), 47–54.

Fehr, R., Fulmer, A., Awtrey, E., & Miller, J. A. (2017). The grateful workplace: A multi-level model of gratitude in organizations. *Academy of Management Review, 42*(2), 361–381. doi:10.5465/amr.2014.0374

Gable, G. G. (2020). Viewpoint: Information systems research strategy. *Journal of Strategic Information Systems, 29*(2), 1–19. doi:10.1016/j.jsis.2020.101620

Haimes, Y. Y. (2012). Modelling complex systems-of-systems with phantom systems models. *Systems Engineering, 15*(3), 333–346.

Henderson, J. C., & Venkatraman, H. (1993). Strategic alignment: Leveraging information technology for transforming organizations. *IBM Systems Journal, 32*(1), 472–484. doi:10.1147/sj.382.0472

Henderson, J. C., & Venkatraman, H. (1999). Strategic alignment: Leveraging information technology for transforming organizations. *IBM Systems Journal, 38*(2.3), 472–484. doi:10.1147/sj.1999.5387096

Hirschheim, R., & Klein, H. K. (2012). A glorious and not-so-short history of the information systems field. *Journal of the Association for Information Systems, 13*(4), 188–235. Retrieved from https://pdfs.semanticscholar.org/2e37/705bf83086f376a87f21fe2703766fe7f9cb.pdf

Hope, B., & Reinelt, C. (2010). Social network analysis and the evaluation of leadership networks. *The Leadership Quarterly, 21*, 600–619.

Hu, Q., & Huang, C. D. (2006). Using the balanced scorecard to achieve sustained IT-business alignment: A case study. *Communications of the Association for Information Systems, 17*(1), 181–204.

Jacelon, C. S., Donoghue, L. C., & Breslin, E. (2010). Scholarship in residence: An innovative application of the scholarship of engagement. *Professional Nursing, 26*(1), 61–66.

Johnson, A. M., & Lederer, A. L. (2010). CEO/CIO mutual understanding, strategic alignment, and the contribution of IS to the organization. *Information & Management, 47*(3), 138–149. doi:10.1016/j.im.2010.01.002

Kappelman, L., Johnson, V. L., McLean, E., Torres, R., Snyder, M., Kim, K., ... Guerra, K. (2020). The 2019 SIM IT issues and trends study. *MIS Quarterly Executive, 19*(1), 69–104.

Kappelman, L., McLean, E., Johnson, V. L., Torres, R., Nguyen, Q., Maurer, C., & Snyder, M. (2017). The 2016 SIM IT issues and trends study. *MIS Quarterly Executive, 16*(1), 47–80.

Kepes, S., Bennett, A. A., & McDaniel, M. A. (2014). Evidence-based management and the trustworthiness of our cumulative scientific knowledge: Implications for teaching, research, and practice. *The Academy of Management Learning and Education, 13*(3), 446–466. doi:10.5465/amle.2013.0193

Krotov, V. (2015). Bridging the CIO-CEO gap: It takes two to tango. *Business Horizons, 58*(3), 275–283. doi:10.1016/j.bushor.2015.01.001

Lee, H., & Bonk, C. H. (2014). Collaborative learning in the workplace: Practical issues and concerns. *International Journal of Advanced Corporate Learning, 7*(2), 10–17.

Luftman, J., & Brier, T. (1999). Achieving and sustaining business-IT alignment. *California Management Review*, *42*(1), 109–122.

Luftman, J., & Derksen, B. (2012, December). Key issues for IT executives 2012: Doing more with less. *MIS Quarterly*, *11*(4), 207–218.

Luftman, J., & McLean, E. R. (2004, June). Key issues for IT executives. *MIS Quarterly*, *3*(2), 89–104.

Lyytinen, K., & Hirschheim, R. (1987). Information systems failures - a survey and classification of the empirical literature. *Oxford Surveys in Information Technology*, *4*, 257–309.

Matzler, K., Füller, J., Hutter, K., Hautz, J., & Stieger, D. (2016). Crowdsourcing strategy: How openness changes strategy work. *Problems and Perspectives in Management*, *14*(3–2), 450–460. doi:10.21511/ppm.14(3-2).2016.01

McDonagh, J. (2004). *Modernising service delivery: A blueprint for development and change*. Dublin: Department of Social Protection.

McDonagh, J. (2006). *Modernising health service organizations: Learning from the PPARS Saga*. Dublin: Health Service Executive.

McDonagh, J. (2008). Working across boundaries. Presentation to the International Federation of Information Processing, International Professional Practice Programme [IFIP, IP3], Dublin, Ireland, 10 April.

McDonagh, J. (2009). *Embracing the challenge of transformational change: A blueprint for ICT-enabled reform*. Report prepared for the Northern Ireland Civil Service, Department of Finance and Personnel, 1–28, September.

McDonagh, J. (2010). *Maximizing the business value of ICT resources and capabilities: A blueprint for reform*. Report prepared for the United Nations System, Chief Executives Board for Co-ordination, High-level Committee on Management, 1–38, August.

McDonagh, J. (2015a). Why change programmes don't produce change: The case of IT-enabled change in public service organizations. In S. Gao & L.Rusu (Eds.), *Modern techniques for successful IT project management* (pp. 285–306). Hershey, PA: IGI Global.

McDonagh, J. (2015b). *From intention to action: The role of senior managers as agents of development and change in government organizations*. Presentation to Environmental Protection Agency, Senior Management Network, Conference on Corporate Strategy Development, Wexford, Ireland, 15 November.

McDonagh, J., Burke, L., & O'Leary, G. (2018). Tracing the evolution and development of senior management networks in government organizations: The case of the environmental protection agency. *Administration*, *66*(4), 27–48.

McDonagh, J., & Coghlan, D. (1999). Can OD help solve the IT dilemma? OD in IT-related change. *Organization Development Journal*, *17*(4), 41–48.

Merali, Y., Papadopoulos, T., & Nadkarni, T. (2012). Information systems strategy: Past, present, and future?. *Journal of Strategic Information Systems*, *21*, 125–153.

Moon, Y. J., Choi, M., & Armstrong, D. J. (2018). The impact of relational leadership and social alignment on information security system effectiveness in Korean governmental organizations. *International Journal of Information Management*, *40*(December 2017), 54–66. doi:10.1016/j.ijinfomgt.2018.01.001

Morgan, G., & Knights, D. (1991). Gendering jobs: Corporate strategy, managerial control and dynamics of job segregation. *Work, Employment & Society*, *5*(2), 181–200. doi:10.1177/0950017091005002003

National Audit Office. (2013). *Over-optimism in government projects*. Report by National Audit Office, London, December.

Parke, B., Stevenson, L., & Rowe, M. (2015). Scholar-in-residence: An organizational capacity-building model to move evidence to action. *Nursing Leadership*, *28*(2), 10–22.

Pasmore, W., Winby, S., Mohrman, S. A., & Vanasse, R. (2019). Reflections: Sociotechnical systems design and organization change. *Journal of Change Management*, *19*(2), 67–85.

Preston, D. S., & Karahanna, E. (2005). The development of a shared CIO/executive management understanding and its impact on information systems strategic alignment. *Information Systems Control Journal*, *2*, 19–26.

Preston, D. S., & Karahanna, E. (2009). Antecedents of IS strategic alignment: A nomological network. *Information Systems Research*, *20*(2), 159–179. doi:10.1287/isre.1070.0159

Rahimi, F., Møller, C., & Hvam, L. (2016). Business process management and IT management: The missing integration. *International Journal of Information Management, 36*(1), 142–154. doi: 10.1016/j.ijinfomgt.2015.10.004

Reich, B. H., & Benbasat, I. (1996). Measuring the linkage between business and information technology objectives. *MIS Quarterly, 20*(1), 55. doi:10.2307/249542

Reich, B. H., & Kaarst-Brown, M. L. (2003). Creating social and intellectual capital through IT career transitions. *Journal of Strategic Information Systems, 12*(2), 91–109. doi:10.1016/S0963-8687(03)00017-9

Rosenbloom, P. (2004, November). A new framework for computer science and engineering. *IEEE Computer, 37*, 31–36.

Sage, D., Dainty, A., & Brookes, N. (2014). A critical argument in favor of theoretical pluralism: Project failure and the many and varied limitations of project management. *International Journal of Project Management, 32*(4), 544–555. doi:10.1016/j.ijproman.2013.08.005

Schein, E. H. (1991). *Legitimating clinical research in the study of organizational culture.* Working Paper, WP#3288-91-BPS. Sloan School of Management, Massachusetts Institute of Technology, Cambridge, MA.

Schein, E. H. (1992). The role of the CEO in the management of change: The case of information technology. In T. A. Kochan & M. Unseen (Eds.), *Transforming organizations* (pp. 80–96). New York, NY: Oxford University Press.

Schein, E. H. (1995). Process consultation, action research and clinical inquiry: Are they the same? *Journal of Managerial Psychology, 10*(6), 14–19.

Schein, E. H. (1996). The three cultures of management: The key to organizational learning. *Sloan Management Review, 38*(1), 9–20. Fall.

Schein, E. H. (2013). Humble inquiry. *Reflections, 13*(2), 1–9.

Schlosser, F., Beimborn, D., Weitzel, T., & Wagner, H. T. (2015). Achieving social alignment between business and IT - an empirical evaluation of the efficacy of IT governance mechanisms. *Journal of Information Technology, 30*(2), 119–135. doi:10.1057/jit.2015.2

Scott-Morton, M. S., & Rockart, J. F. (1984). Implications of changes in information technology for corporate strategy. *Informs: Journal of Applied Analytics, 14*(1), 84–95. doi:10.1287/inte.14.1.84

Shani, A. B. (Rami), & Coghlan, D. (2021). *Collaborative inquiry for organization development and change.* Cheltenham: Edward Elgar Publishing.

Shao, Z. (2019). Interaction effect of strategic leadership behaviors and organizational culture on IS-business strategic alignment and enterprise systems assimilation. *International Journal of Information Management, 44*(13), 96–108. doi:10.1016/j.ijinfomgt.2018.09.010

Sidorova, A., Evangelopoulos, N., Valacich, S., & Ramakrishnan, T. (2008). Uncovering the intellectual core of the information systems discipline. *MIS Quarterly, 32*(3), 467–482.

Stadler, C., Hautz, J., & von den Eichen, S. F. (2020). Open strategy: The inclusion of crowds in making strategies. *NIM Market Intelligence Review, 12*(1), 36–41. doi:10.2478/nimmir-2020-0006

Street, C., Gallupe, B., & Baker, J. (2018). The influence of entrepreneurial action on strategic alignment in new ventures: Searching for the genesis of alignment. *Journal of Strategic Information Systems, 27*, 59–81.

Taylor, H., Dillon, S., & van Wingen, M. (2010). Focus and diversity in information systems research: Meeting the dual demands of a healthy applied discipline. *MIS Quarterly, 34*(4), 647–667.

Teubner, R. A., & Stockhinger, J. (2020). Literature review: Understanding IS strategy in a digital age. *Journal of Strategic Information Systems, 29*(4), 1–28.

Tomeski, E., & Lazarus, H. (1975). *People-oriented computer systems: The computer in crisis.* New York, NY: Van Nostrand Reinhold.

Van Grembergen, W. (2004). *Strategies for information technology governance.* Hershey, PA: Idea Group Publishing.

Van de Ven, A. H. (2007). *Engaged scholarship.* New York, NY: Oxford University Press.

Van de Ven, A. H., & Johnson, P. E. (2006). Knowledge for theory and practice. *Academy of Management Review, 31*(4), 802–821.

Vial, G. (2019). Understanding digital transformation: A review and a research agenda. *Journal of Strategic Information Systems, 28*, 118–144. doi:10.1016/j.jsis.2019.01.003

Wasylyshyn, K. M., & Masterpasqua, F. (2018). Developing self-compassion in leadership development coaching: A practice model and case study analysis. *International Coaching Psychology Review, 13*(1), 21–34. Spring.

Williams, J., Torres, H., & Carte, T. (2018). A review of the IS strategic alignment literature: A replication study. In *Proceedings of the 24th Americas conference on information systems.* Retrieved from https://aisel.aisnet.org/amcis2018/Replication/Presentations/3/

Winby, S., & Mohrman, S. A. (2018). Digital sociotechnical system design. *Journal of Applied Behavioral Science, 54*(4), 399–423.

Yeow, A., Soh, C., & Hansen, R. (2018). Aligning with new digital strategy: A dynamic capabilities approach. *Journal of Strategic Information Systems, 27*, 43–58.

REFLECTIONS: CHANGE MANAGEMENT IS NOT ORGANIZATION DEVELOPMENT

W. Warner Burke

ABSTRACT

The purpose of this paper is twofold. First, Part One is to make a comparison of organization development (OD) and change management (CM) across eight concepts that are relevant to both OD and CM. The concepts or characteristics are (1) guiding philosophy, (2) value system, (3) theory, (4) primary skill, (5) intervention mode, (6) change model, (7) change activities, and (8) sustainment of change. OD stresses development of people and change regarding the organization, whereas CM emphasizes facilitation and expanding their business with the client organization. A concluding statement for the comparison of OD and CM is that OD has a rich underpinning of theory *and a clear set of* values *that provide guidelines for the work with clients and CM has neither. Thus, CM is a misnomer. Part Two concerns the longer term and includes some consequences for OD from the pandemic of 2020–2021, such as the virtual workplace and leadership. The article concludes with some things to remember, suggesting the importance of group size, large group interventions, and loosely coupled systems.*

Keywords: Organization development; change management; OD values; leadership; teams; large groups; loosely coupled systems

Early in 1976, the movie *Network*, starring Albert Finch along with a number of Hollywood luminaries – Faye Dunaway, William Holden, and Robert Duval – hit the big screen. Finch plays the role of a TV newscaster who has burned out and is fed up with reading on the air news that isn't. To describe much of what Finch airs, he uses the word "fake," a prescient term for sure. With a

Research in Organizational Change and Development, Volume 29, 261–274
Copyright © 2022 Emerald Publishing Limited
ISSN: 0897-3016/doi:10.1108/S0897-301620210000029011

combination of anger and despair, he yells on the air at the top of his lungs, "I am mad as hell and I'm not going to take it anymore!" He then admonishes his audience at home to go to their nearest window, open it, and scream as loudly as possible, "I am mad as hell and I'm not going to take it anymore!" And they do just that.

Although I have not quite reached the stage of yelling this famous line from *Network* and asking readers of this article to go to their windows, I am definitely irked these days about the status of organization development (OD) vis-a-vis change management (CM). Anger can be an appropriate motive for declaring myself as long as I maintain my sanity and keep my wits about me unlike the newscaster in the movie. You can be the judge.

In a number of ways, CM is a disassociation from OD and appears to be more acceptable. The big consulting firms, Accenture, Ernst and Young, Korn Ferry, KPMG, McKinsey, PriceWaterhouseCoopers, and others, prefer CM as the label for what they provide for their clients rather than OD.

It may be that this dissociation from OD is due in part to the fact that many believe the field is out of date. After all, OD is 60 years old; maybe not retirement age just yet but close. OD's founders, the first generation, are all dead – Lewin, of course, Marrow, Beckhard, Bennis, McGregor, Shepard, Blake and Mouton, Argyris, Levinson, Ackoff, and Shel Davis, to name most of them – and therefore OD is past its prime. Without these influential contributors that started and crafted the field, one might argue that their replacements have not emerged. In fact, speaking for myself, I am on record for claiming that (Burke, 2018) there has been no new social technology within OD since appreciative inquiry (Cooperrider & Srivastva, 1987).

I have been challenged regarding this claim by Kim Cameron (2020). He argued that positive psychology particularly when applied to OD appropriately represents new social technology for the field. He makes a good case, I must say.

Like myself, Mike Beer wrote an early text for the field (Beer, 1980), but in the years since developed his own scheme for changing organizations referred to as *Strategic Fitness Process* (SFP). In short, SFP provides

> …a way for senior teams to receive feedback from lower levels about leadership, management, and organizational barriers to effective implementation of the strategy and required their development of action plans for change. (Beer, 2020, p. 510)

Beer also links his approach to Argyris's work on action science (Argyris, Putnam, & Smith, 1985). New applications of linking knowledge to action and vice versa within the broader context of action science, Beer might argue, represents new technology since the advent of appreciative inquiry. If so, no argument from me.

To my dismay, however, is the treatment of OD by Jick and Sturtevant (2017). They classify OD as a subcategory of CM and therefore have driven me back to the window to yell the *Network* charge. In other words, CM has taken over. And I said as much at the outset of this article. The Jick and Sturtevant paper takes stock of CM over the past 30 years. Their conclusion is that CM needs a "reboot" – a transformation. I agree. After all successful organization change remains no more than 30%. Where I disagree is the "reclassification" of OD as a subfield. If it were not for the invention of OD in the late 1950s, there would be no field of CM today.

So, CM has replaced OD particularly in large consulting firms where no one even whispers "OD." But before we draw such a conclusion, let us make a deeper comparison. My intent is, first, to explore this difference in Part One of this article. Then in Part Two, we will explore where we in the field of OD go from here.

PART ONE: COMPARING CHANGE MANAGEMENT AND ORGANIZATION DEVELOPMENT

For the basis of our comparison, I have selected eight components or aspects of organization change that are relevant for both CM and OD. The criteria for the choices of these eight organization change components are twofold. The initial three change components – guiding philosophy, value system, and theory – represent the larger picture, the mission, principles, beliefs, and the science to be applied which provide the foundation for a given discipline or field. The remaining five change components represent the nature of the actions to be taken. These actions are therefore grounded in a philosophy, a set of values, science, and theory that link consistently to actions that lead to organization change. See Table 1 for a summary of the overall comparisons.

We will now proceed with a broader and deeper explanation of each of the eight components.

Guiding Philosophy

Being perceived as practical, down-to-earth, and smart is uppermost for CM consultants. They hold beliefs that emphasize the importance of getting a job done efficiently, solving problems promptly, correcting mistakes immediately if not before they arise, and anticipating what a client needs now and in the short-range future. In general, CM consultants are managers while their clients are leaders or at least the objective is for clients to become more leader-like and leave the daily humdrum of management for the consultants. The primary objective for CM consultants is to make work life easier for their clients, that is, to give them more time to think, to be visionary regarding the future.

OD consultants seek to understand the client organization's belief system, their mission, its culture, i.e., the primary norms that guide organizational behavior, and, in short, the client organization's purpose, its reason for being. Once this understanding becomes clear, the OD consultant provides feedback to the client organization accordingly. It's as if the OD consultant is holding a mirror for the client to look into. This initial process is then followed by a plan for change to include both (1) what needs reinforcing; for example, what accounts for the strengths of the organization that can be reinforced and highlighted more, and (2) what needs to be fundamentally changed. The primary objectives for the

Table 1. A Comparison of Change Management (CM) and Organization
Development (OD).

Organization Change Component	Change Management	Organization Development
Guiding philosophy	Guided by pragmatism; provide more time for client managers to be leaders; save time for client managers to be less operational and more strategic	The primary role for the OD consultant is to be a diagnostician; to help the client organization to understand itself more thoroughly by "holding up a mirror," to focus both on strengths and limitations, and to maximize agile learning
Value system	Guided by a need to expand the client contract and grow the CM business	Guided by a set of values that emphasize social justice participation, openness, truth to power, etc.
Theory	Atheoretical	Guided by open system theory, Lewin's formula and three-step model, gestalt psychology, theory Y, group relations, and social psychology
Primary skill	Facilitation of interpersonal relations and group dynamics	System thinking and approach
Intervention mode	Consultative team who work alongside client employees as an extra pair of hands	Consultative individuals and teams deployed according to expertise in areas such as change leadership, power confrontation, strategy, culture, organization design, and reward systems
Change model	Guided by previously made decisions to change by client executives; CM consultants implement their decisions by providing facilitation	Guided by evidence-based model for implementing planned change based on a vision for the future
Change activities	Guided by an array of exercises and interventions that facilitate discussion and a sense of involvement	Guided by a framework or model of organization change and performance that is research – theory – and evidence-based for changing the total system in fundamental ways, e.g., organization culture
Sustainment of change	Expand the work of CM facilitators to as many functions as possible so that billable hours continue to increase	Continuously gather data that provide information and knowledge about context so that implementation of the change steps is not unduly resisted

OD consultant are to gather data on a regular basis according to (1) and (2)
above and serve as a diagnostician applying the metaphor of a mirror not a fixer
of problems, which is the role of managers in the client organization. In summary, the descriptions are guidelines for the remaining seven comparisons.

Value System

Values are based on what one believes are important and justifiable. CM consultants are guided in their beliefs of building and expanding the business of their consulting firm. Growth of their work with the client is the ultimate objective. Growth is good for the client organization and for the consulting firm as well as for the larger societal economy. In short, and in any case, the consulting firm's value system is the dominant one, not the client's value system. CM consultants do not follow a discipline's set of values. Instead, their mantra comes from their employers' value system.

For OD consultants, the key term is *development* – achieving a new stage in a changing situation. Change is a constant, and thus the goal is to *focus* on the change. This focus is guided by a set of beliefs that include and emphasize social justice, participation in decision-making, being open, honest and speaking truth to power, creating and maintaining psychological safety for clients, and being goal-oriented. A significant goal for OD consultants is to strengthen these beliefs and values in the client organization with a particular emphasis on integrating them into its culture. And, finally, an OD consultant's work is to provide support in the client organization for employees to have *choice* regarding an absence of arbitrary decision-making by management, how to conduct their work, and having career options.

In a nutshell, then, CM consultants work for their consulting firm, whereas OD consultants work for their client organization which may be their employer, thus as an internal consultant or as an external consultant.

Theory

It comes as quite a challenge to find any theory that undergirds the work of CM consultants. Since most of their work is likely to be facilitating group meetings and providing feedback from some survey, we might argue that group dynamics and process consultation provide a skill base that comes from theory. Group relations concepts from Travistock are based on theory from Bion and process consultation from the work of national training laboratories (NTL)-trained consultants, in particular the writings of Ed Schein. And survey feedback is a method, not a theory. Frankly regarding these statements, I have just written, I wonder if most CM consultants would know what I am talking about.

OD consultants have an abundance of theory to bolster their work. There are three mainstreams: open system theory, the work of Kurt Lewin, and motivation theory emanating primarily from Maslow's contributions. Open system theory comes from cell biology and is applied via the well-known framework of input–throughput–output with a feedback loop that reconnects output with input. OD consultants typically begin with this mode of understanding any organization as an open system beginning with its external environment (input), which precipitates and guides the change (throughput) and in turn determines the organization's performance (output) and thus via feedback modifies the next round of input, etc. Lewin is credited with spawning the field of social psychology, but earlier before leaving Germany, he began with a hefty dose of Gestalt psychology (looking for patterns of human behavior) and applied physics to undergird his subsequent theoretical thinking regarding a "field of forces" that drive and simultaneously restrain behavior. Also, Lewin's famous formula explaining behavior as a function of the interaction of personality (or the person) and that person's view of his or her environment, Bf(P,E), is also based on open system theory. Well-known, of course, is Lewin's three-phase theory of unfreeze–change–refreeze which has stood the test of time. For an update on these significant contributions from Lewin, see the articles by Burnes (2004, 2020). Finally concerning the third mainstream, McGregor's Theory Y versus Theory X was heavily influenced by Maslow's hierarchy of needs and related motivation theory, which in turn set the stage for deeper understandings of work motivation and job design and enrichment. We in the world of OD owe a great debt to the contributions of Wilford Bion, Kurt Lewin, and Abraham Maslow.

Primary Skill

The primary skill for CM consultants is facilitation. Whatever the client decides or acquires from the consulting firm, say, a leadership survey, the CM consultant provides some form of facilitation to make the acquisition work. Meetings in organizations happen all the time. Most organizational members, especially managers, hate these gatherings and typically find them to be a waste of time. If the CM consultant can help with meetings in terms of keeping group members focused on the task, monitor time, and help to resolve differences, then the client is likely to be pleased. Sometimes even the CM consultant conducts certain meetings on behalf of a client manager. More often, however, the CM consultant provides coaching to help the managers to lead their own meetings. In any case, many CM consultants are becoming certified in coaching, a skill that clients these days seem to want. With the primary skill being facilitation, little change on the part of the client is needed; thus learning is not required, and the client becomes more and more dependent on the CM consultant. The work is not about facilitating organization change, rather, the CM consulting process concerns dealing with day-to-day necessities that the client does not want to do or simply has little to no facilitative skills.

The primary skill of the OD consultant is change leadership based on system thinking and clear goals for change. Operationally, this means being highly adept at diagnosis, particularly with respect to the client organization's culture. A related skill is collaboration, that is, establishing effective working relationships with key clients, so they can learn and implement decisions that have been jointly derived. I could list a number of more specific skills that an OD consultant needs to have, such as process consultation, coaching, listening, participation, knowing how to lead, how to follow, and when to deploy each role, to name a few additional key skill sets. Perhaps an appropriate way to summarize such a list and consolidate the many versions of OD skills is to think of the OD consultant as a teacher or an educator, both in the formal sense and via role modeling. An overriding goal of OD work is to leave the client with more skills than when the work began. This means following a value of "giving away" what we know and can be transferred to others.

Intervention Mode

Essentially, the intervention mode of CM consultants is to work alongside client managers of the organization and provide an extra pair of hands for the work of the organization. The benefit here is the consulting firm charges a healthy fee for this help and the client organization gains by not having to hire and train a larger-than-necessary workforce. I have personally witnessed this arrangement by McKinsey with a highly professional client in the United Kingdom. McKinsey consultants were everywhere and clearly running the organization, more than just an extra pair of hands. To be fair, McKinsey was trying to improve management, but the client organization's managers, albeit not highly competent, saw the consultants as "messing" with their culture and that was forbidden. The organization's managers were indeed skillful, just not at management; their skill was being deft at resistance. The consultation therefore was not really about change, instead the work concerned keeping the organization as it had always been. An additional mode of intervention by CM consultants is the use of questionnaires to generate data about such processes as leadership, teamwork, learning agility, and the like to improve certain organizational behaviors (and to charge the client accordingly) and perhaps provide coaching regarding feedback from the behavioral instruments for individual managers, which can lead to additional needs for management development, i.e., more business for the CM consultants. These interventions may be helpful for individuals in the client organization but rarely, if ever, contribute to organization change.

If we follow Lewin to the "letter of his law" in OD consultation, then we are involved in two primary modes of intervention – his three-step model of change (unfreeze, movement, and refreeze) and action research. Assuming that a system-wide change goal has been identified, e.g., implementing a merger or changing to a more diverse workforce, then at the outset of such a change effort, the process is largely diagnostic applying field theory to identify forces that are likely to drive the change and those forces that are likely to block or restrain change. Working on the restraining side of this change ledger and finding ways to unfreeze the system, the OD consultant would then implement an intervention to attempt this early step of change, for example, an off-site meeting of key executives to decide what they need to do individually and collectively to lessen certain restraints (read resistance). At the conclusion of the executive meeting (an intervention), evaluative data would be collected to determine not so much how well the meeting went but what should be the next steps in the unfreezing process. Based on these data (research), a subsequent step would be planned and immediately implemented (action). This approach would then be followed as the system moves into the change mode (step 2). Lewin was cautious about system change taking a directional and well-contained step toward the change goal, collect data again, and then implement this interactive mode of action and evaluative data collection. For an elaboration of this all-too-brief explanation of the OD mode of intervention, see the article by Burnes (2020).

Change Model

In a nutshell, the change model for CM consultants is to facilitate the decisions that have already been made by senior management. In other words, the client organization's executives usually starting with the CEO have at sometimes in the recent past decided that certain changes needed to be made in the organization; for example, the current structure does not seem to be working well and needs to be changed, or there is a need to begin the process of changing a particular operation from people conducting the manufacturing to a robotic system of producing certain products. The executives are fully aware of the fact that this change will lead to a reduction of certain employees and create controversy in the existing operation as well as anxiety throughout the larger organization. These executives realize they will need help. Besides, they do not want to have to deal directly with the employees involved. They decide to hire a CM consulting firm to deal with it all, i.e., facilitate and implement a change that has already been decided. The job for the CM consultants is simply to facilitate, not collaborate or participate in any way regarding the change decisions; "just make it happen" is the charge.

In the OD world, consultants are involved from the beginning, otherwise there will be no agreement to work together, no contact. As of this writing, the organization change failure rate remains around 70%. To be in the 30% that succeeds requires (1) substantive knowledge about how system-wide change works and (2) an array of sophisticated consulting skills to implement the highly complex process. Over the years many OD consultants broadly following Lewin's three-step model have created their own more detailed model that typically involves at least four steps and often more. Kotter (1996), for example, has an eight-step model. Examples of other models include Beer (Beer, Eisenstat, & Spector, 1990) with 6 steps and Kanter with 10 steps (Kanter, Stein, & Jick, 1992). Stouten, Rousseau, and DeCremer (2018) have reviewed these and several additional models to see if they were supported by research evidence, that is, do they work and help practitioners to be within the success rate 30%? These scholars found mixed results throughout their reviews and subsequently selected only the steps of leading change that could be supported with evidence. They concluded that 10 steps if followed in order would likely help sufficiently to bring about organization change successfully. The steps are listed as follows:

(1) Get facts regarding the nature of the problem(s) – Diagnosis Step 1
(2) Assess and address the organization's readiness for change – Diagnosis Step 2
(3) Implement evidence-based change interventions
(4) Develop effective change leadership throughout the organization
(5) Develop and communicate a compelling change vision
(6) Work with social networks and tap their influence

(7) Use enabling practices to support implementation
(8) Promote microprocesses and experimentation
(9) Assess change progress and outcomes over time
(10) Institutionalize the change to sustain its effectiveness

For OD consultants, then, these are revised steps that are consistent with Lewin's thinking and are evidence-based and, therefore when followed, are likely to increase our success rate.

Change Activities

CM consultants have a large array of activities, for example, World Café, and other large group interventions that help to facilitate interaction, involvement, and wide-ranging discussion. In fact, experienced OD consultants have produced such materials; see the following for examples: Beckhard's (1967) confrontation meeting, Bunker and Alban (1997) on large group interventions, Cooperrider (2012) on the latest regarding appreciative inquiry, Delbecq, Van de Ven, and Gustafson (1975) on small group decision-making, Levinson (1972) on organizational diagnosis, Schein (2013) on interviewing, and Weisbord (1978) on using his six-box model. The expectation that the client organization has of the CM consultant is to keep their employees busy via training and experiential learning activities. The point is that CM consultant activities may help with individual learning, but for what purpose? The answer to this question is rarely clear and, in any case, does not address organization change.

For OD consultants, change activities are defined according to the 10-step model by Stouten and his colleagues. These activities emphasize diagnosis, readiness assessments, visioning, network analysis, experimentation, and evaluative data collection. Also providing an overall model that emphasizes both content and process can be helpful. Naturally, I recommend the Burke–Litwin model (Burke & Litwin, 1992). For a recent case of successful organization change deploying the model, see Coruzzi (2020).

Sustainment of Change

This final comparison is comparatively brief. The objective for CM consultants is simple and clear – expand the business for the consulting firm as much as possible. The sustainment objective does not concern organization change for the client. Rather, success for the CM consultant is to sell more business.

For the OD consultant, sustainment is twofold. First, when the change does not proceed as planned, which is most of the time, the consultant moves as fast as possible to correct the problem and takes the necessary steps to get the change process back on track. Second is to frequently assess how the overall change is going, especially monitoring the ever-changing external environment, and make modifications as required continuing to apply the action research process. And finally celebrate successes along the way, especially small wins.

In conclusion for Part One, fundamentally the difference between CM consulting and OD is that OD has a rich underpinning of *theory* and a clear set of *values* that provide guidelines for the work and CM has neither. Moreover, the title of "change management" is a misnomer.

PART TWO: WHERE DO WE GO FROM HERE?

Pandemic of 2020–2021

The second part of this article expresses some thoughts about the future particularly for OD consultants to consider. *First* to be addressed are some consequences of the current coronavirus pandemic for us in the field of OD. At the outset, we should note that the *Journal of Applied Behavioral Science* has devoted a special section of the September 2020 issue to a call for research on the consequences of COVID-19 (Schwarz & Stensaker, 2020) and to a series of essays and dialogues on the subject to stimulate thought and scholarly action. And, *second* are simply some things to remember going forward specifically in the context of what needs to be added to our professional practices.

With respect to the present, as of this writing, we are heavily involved in the vaccination process worldwide. A year or two from now we will begin to learn about the short-term versus long-term effects of this pandemic on human behavior. Our interest as OD consultants is in behavior that is addressed with research by organizational psychologists and more specifically in the workplace. With respect to the near-term behavior change that is short-lived compared with behavior change that has a longer term impact, the current mandate of maintaining 6 feet apart from one another, the so-called social distance rule, will be short-lived. The May-June 2020 demonstration in cities worldwide addressing "Black Lives Matter" is a good example of short-lived. Moreover, we humans are social creatures. Pretty soon, we'll be back together again.

Longer term effects of the current pandemic that have an impact on OD consultants, in particular, and organizational psychologists more generally concern leadership. It seems now and will for some time to come that followers especially in a time of crisis causing fear and great anxiety want leaders to tell them the truth regardless of how bad the news may be. President Joe Biden has been admired for his openness and honesty. Practically every day he has held at least a brief news conference loaded with data about the status of the COVID-19 pandemic, always telling us the bare facts regarding the death rate and number of hospitalizations of people with the illness, and of course, he adds a few words about the economy albeit dismal at times. Even though these data, especially regarding the pandemic, are not exactly heartwarming, people want to know. Time and again, I have heard people express their deep appreciation for President Biden's reports. "He tells us the truth," they say. My data are not scientific. I predict nevertheless that this desire for the truth will last if not increase. Our world becomes daily and exponentially more complex. We want more factual information; otherwise, conspiracy theories will abound. The realization that so few leaders are telling us the truth about the pandemic in particular, combined with the former President of the United States being a chronic and consummate liar, in general, tells me that followers' need for facts and honesty has never been greater and telling the truth openly reigns supreme as a quality of exceptional leadership. Yes, it is incumbent on us OD consultants to encourage followers to "speak truth to power," yet it is just as important for leaders to speak the truth to followers. We therefore must also help leaders to craft their pronouncements in a factual and truthful manner.

Even though the pandemic brought about a lockdown of many businesses, with some going out of business never to return, and keeping most of us indoors and away from one another, there is one aspect of our lives that has grown in terms of impact – the Internet. The power of the Internet looms even larger than ever. I am, for example, feeling more and more dependent on Zoom, Skype, FaceTime, and the like. In other words, operating virtually is becoming a way of life. What this means for the practice of OD is that in many ways and situations we will not have the data we have become accustomed to – nonverbal behavior. As a consultant I rely, of course, on what people say, but I pay even more attention to what they do not say and what they convey with their eyes, their body movements, and, in general, how natural and comfortable they come across as they interact with others. Let me be clear: I think people as a rule speak the truth, and I am not a conspiracy theorist, but what they are simply unwilling to talk about speaks volumes. With Zoom, therefore, I am limited considerably more than when I am face-to-face. Data are missing. Not that I am expert at "reading minds," but when physically together I know better than when virtual what follow-up questions to ask. For OD practice to substitute for these limitations, we may need to use quick surveys with these "audience response devises," yes-no answers or even a five-point Likert scale. We may also need to rely more on breakout sessions rather than remaining in the total group for the entire meeting.

As a consequence of the pandemic of 2020–2021, I, like others, have drawn a sharper distinction as to what is essential and what is not that essential. A remarkable "tradition" quickly emerged in New York City. At 7 p.m. sharp, *every day*, people raised their apartment windows, rain or shine, and applauded, banged a spoon on a pan, and otherwise made noise of appreciation and thanks to those essential workers dealing with the pandemic and making self-sacrifices – doctors, nurses, ambulance drivers and emergency medical professionals, firemen, the police, subway operators and cleaners, bus drivers, sanitation workers, and the list goes on. This act of appreciative noise making reached the pinnacle of recognition by an artist's rendition on the cover of the April 27, 2020 issue of the *New Yorker* magazine. As we conduct our work in OD, it is important and useful for us to think about what we actually do and accomplish with our client organizations in terms of just what is essential and what is not.

And finally, in thinking about what is important, we may be considering also our social needs more than ever before. For example, I am a hugging person. I like to hug people especially when I have not seen the person in a long time. With this pandemic, I have missed hugging. And I don't think I realized how important this simple act of showing friendship and affection is to me.

Things to Remember

In OD, we conduct our practice from time to time with an individual client when interviewing, coaching, and providing feedback to a manager or executive, but just as often if not more so, we work with groups, small and large. These group activities are extremely important for here is where we have the most impact regarding organization change. In one way or the other, we are dealing with norms, values, and a cumulative culture, the nexus organizationally of change. Let us therefore review just a couple of things to remember about group dynamics: virtual groups and group size.

In my opinion, the word team is used too loosely. Sometimes nothing more than a "gathering" of people is referred to as a team. Moreover, what is expected from a gathering of people is rarely crystal clear. Even more loosely we refer to virtual groups and gatherings as teams. To clarify, let us consider a virtual network compared with a face-to-face group that may or may not be a team.

A team is a group of individuals who have a common *goal* or set of goals. The goal is the same for everyone. Second, a team consists of individuals who fill a variety of *roles* with each individual contributing something relatively unique toward accomplishment of the goal and who has responsibility and authority for what. Third, a team has an acceptable set of behavioral ways of working together, that is, agreed-upon *processes* and procedures for how work gets done interactively, for example, how decisions get made. Finally, a team makes sure that their *interpersonal* relationships help rather than hinder goal accomplishment such as dealing with differences and conflict readily and effectively rather than allowing resentments to fester. These four – goals, roles, processes, and interpersonal relationships – establish key criteria for teams and teamwork. This so-called goals, roles, processes/procedures and interpersonal relationships (GRPI) model was created quite some time ago by Beckhard (1972) and established the way for how to approach team building.

An assemblage coming together virtually for a meeting may be a team but more often than not is a gathering or at best a group trying to get work done but more individually than together interpersonally. In fact, the assemblage may be more like a network than a group, much less a team. The point is that the GRPI model is probably not appropriate for helping this assemblage. Regardless of what the label may be, it is not a team, rather it is a loosely coupled system. Instead of GRPI we would need to consider a social network analysis, see the article by Ogle, Tenkasi, and Brock (2020) for recent research on the interaction between network analysis and OD, and possibly other interventions more suitable for loosely coupled systems – see Burke (2014).

Virtual meetings and groups are here to stay. Calling these gatherings teams is confusing and not appropriate; however, virtual groups have advantages: they save time and expense, and they can be more efficient than face-to-face meetings. There are disadvantages, of course, such as (1) losing the potential for collaboration and consequent creativity from highly intensive exchanges, (2) psychological safety becomes a stronger issue and complication to deal with, and (3) not having adequate access to nonverbal behavior. In any case, our traditional team building tools are not likely to be useful for virtual "teams." We need to become more adept at using "loose" measuring tools such as social network analysis, organizational network analysis, and audience response devises to gather scattered data rapidly.

Allow me to close with a word about the importance of group size. Let us begin with a note about context. Consider the question of how many people we human beings can keep up with at any given time. By keep up with, I mean passing someone in the hallway of your building and recognizing the person as one who works in another department and you speak to this individual and remember that she is in accounting. So, she is an acquaintance, not a close friend. On this scale of acquaintance to close friend, how many people can you keep up with? A good rule of thumb is the "magic number of 150." According to Dunbar's (1992) research studying *social channel capacity*, the exact number is 147.8. We are close enough with the easy number of 150 to remember. Thus, consulting with a network, the maximum size should probably be no more than 150. Some organization experts swear by this number, that is, never allowing any organizational unit to be larger than 150.

Now to my closing point, we OD professionals need to stay knowledgeable and adept at large group interventions (Bunker & Alban, 1997). These interventions (1) gain involvement, (2) give us valuable data almost immediately, (3) are amenable to Lewin's formula (see Burnes, 2020) of action research, that is, finding mistakes and taking corrective steps quickly, and (4) help us to work with loosely coupled systems effectively.

So there! I have dealt with my anger and I feel better already. It is therefore thanks to you that I have been able to deal with my feelings in a reasonably focused manner. Thank you. And I hope to see you some day soon other than virtual. Expect a hug.

REFERENCES

Argyris, C., Putnam, R., & Smith, D. M. (1985). *Action science: Concept, methods, and skills for research and intervention.* San Francisco, CA: Josessy-Bass.

Beckhard, R. (1967). The confrontation meeting. *Harvard Business Review, 45*(2), 149–155.

Beckhard, R. (1972). Team-building efforts. *Journal of Contemporary Business, 1*, 23–32.

Beer, M. (1980). *Organization change and development: A systems view.* Glenview, IL: Scott Foresman.

Beer, M. (2020). Making a difference: Developing actionable knowledge for practice and theory. *The Journal of Applied Behavioral Science, 56*, 506–520.

Beer, M., Eisenstat, R. A., & Spector, B. (1990). *The critical path of corporate renewal.* Boston, MA: Harvard Business School Press.

Bunker, B. B., & Alban, B. T. (1997). *Large group interventions: Engaging the whole system for rapid change.* San Francisco, CA: Jossey-Bass.

Burke, W. W. (2014). Changing loosely coupled systems. *The Journal of Applied Behavioral Science, 50*, 423–444.

Burke, W. W. (2018). The rise and fall of the growth of organization development: What now? *Consulting Psychology Journal: Practice and Research, 70*, 186–206.

Burke, W. W., & Litwin, G. H. (1992). A causal model of organization performance and change. *Journal of Management, 18*, 523–545.

Burnes, B. (2004). Kurt Lewin and the planned approach to change: A re-appraisal. *Journal of Management Studies, 41*, 972–1002.

Burnes, B. (2020). The origins of Lewin's three-step model of change. *The Journal of Applied Behavioral Science, 56*, 32–59.

Cameron, K. (2020). Responses to the problem of OD stagnation: A tribute to Warner Burke. *The Journal of Applied Behavioral Science, 56*, 462–481.

Cooperrider, D. L. (2012). The concentration effect of strengths: How the whole system "AI" summit brings out the best in human enterprise. *Organizational Dynamics, 41*(2), 106–117.

Cooperrider, D. L., & Srivastva, S. (1987). Appreciative inquiry in organizational life. In W. A. Pasmore & R. W. Woodman (Eds.), *Research in organizational change and development* (Vol. 1). Greenwich, CT: JAI Press.

Coruzzi, C. A. (2020). Leading change with intelligence: The power of diagnosis in creating organizational renewal. *The Journal of Applied Behavioral Science, 56*, 420–436.

Delbecq, A. L., Van de Ven, A. H., & Gustafson, D. H. (1975). *Group techniques for program planning: A guide to nominal group and Delphi: Processes.* Glenview, IL: Scott Foresman.

Dunbar, R. I. M. (1992). Neocortex size as a constraint on group size in primates. *Journal of Human Evolution, 20*, 469–493.

Jick, T. D., & Sturtevant, K. D. M. (2017). Taking stock of 30 years of change management: Is it time for a reboot?. In A. B. Shani & D. A. Noumair (Eds.), *Research in organizational change and development* (Vol. 25, pp. 33–79). Bingley: Emerald Publishing Limited.

Kanter, R. M., Stein, B. A., & Jick, T. D. (1992). *The challenge of organizational change.* New York, NY: Free Press.

Kotter, J. P. (1996). *Leading change.* Boston, MA: Harvard Business School Press.

Levinson, H. (1972). *Organizational diagnosis.* Cambridge, MA: Harvard University Press.

Olge, D. L., Tenkasi, R., & Brock, W. B. (2020). The social media presence of organization development: A social network analysis using big data. In D. A. Noumair & A. B. Shani (Eds.), *Research in organizational change and development* (Vol. 28, pp. 1–41). Bingley: Emerald Publishing Limited.

Schein, E. H. (2013). *Humble inquiry: The gentle art of asking instead of telling.* San Francisco, CA: Berrett-Koehler.

Schwarz, G. M., & Stensaker, I. (2020). Researching a pandemic: Letting Covid-19 drive our research. *The Journal of Applied Behavioral Science, 56*, 261–265.

Stouten, J., Rousseau, D. M., & DeCremer, D. (2018). Successful organizational change. *The Academy of Management Annals, 12*(2), 752–788.

Weisbord, M. R. (1978). *Organizational diagnosis: A workbook of theory and practice.* Reading, MA: Addison-Wesley.